Interventions for Children With or At Risk for Emotional and Behavioral Disorders

Kathleen L. Lane
Peabody College of Vanderbilt University

Frank M. Gresham
University of California, Riverside

Tam E. O'Shaughnessy
Georgia State University

Allyn and Bacon
Boston ▪ London ▪ Toronto ▪ Sydney ▪ Tokyo ▪ Singapore

Executive Editor: *Virginia Lanigan*
Editorial Assistant: *Erin Liedel*
Executive Marketing Manager: *Amy Cronin*
Editorial-Production Service: *Matrix Productions Inc.*
Composition and Prepress Buyer: *Linda Cox*
Manufacturing Buyer: *Julie NcNeill*
Cover Administrator: *Kristina Mose-Libon*
Electronic Composition: *Omegatype Typography, Inc.*

Between the time Website information is gathered and then published, it is not unusual for some sites to have closed. Also, the transcription of URLs can result in unintended typographical errors. The publisher would appreciate notification where these occur so that they may be corrected in subsequent editions.

Library of Congress Cataloging-in-Publication Data

Lane, Kathleen L.
    Interventions for children with or at risk for emotional and behavioral disorders/ Kathleen L. Lane, Frank M. Gresham, Tam E. O'Shaughnessy.
        p. cm.
    Includes bibliographical references and index.
    ISBN 0-205-32182-8
        1. Mentally ill children—Education. 2. Behavior disorders in children. I. Gresham, Frank M. II. O'Shaughnessy, Tam E. III. Title.

LC4165 .L36 2001
371.94—dc21

                                                                                    2001046367

Printed in the United States of America
10 9 8 7 6 5 4 3 2 1   06 05 04 03 02 01

This book is dedicated to

Craig, my rock; Nathan, my gift; and Katie Scarlett,
my joyous surprise, for giving me the confidence and the time;
Diet soda and dark chocolate, without which
this book would not have happened

K. L. L.

Laura, Matt, and Luke

F. M. G.

To my parents,
Richard and Julia O'Shaughnessy,
For everything.

T. E. O.

CONTENTS

6 Reading and Students with E/BD: What Do We Know and Recommend? 87

Candace S. Bos, Maggie Coleman, and Sharon Vaughn

7 Teaching Writing to Students with Behavior Disorders: Metaphor and Medium 104

Gerald Tindal and Lindy Crawford

8   Mathematics: Screening, Assessment, and Intervention   125

George H. Noell and Kristin A. Gansle

9   Homework and Students with Emotional and Behavioral Disabilities   144

Edward J. Sabornie

10 Designing Classroom Organization and Structure   159

Geoff Colvin

PART THREE   Managing Challenging Behaviors   175

11 Developmental Prevention of At-Risk Outcomes for Vulnerable Antisocial Children and Youth   177

Hill M. Walker and Herbert H. Severson

———

PREFACE

Upon reviewing the existing texts aimed at intervening and educating children with behavior disorders, it was surprising to see that the majority of the texts available did not present a balanced framework for exploring the relationship between academic underachievement and behavior problems. Instead, the majority of the texts focused almost exclusively on social-behavioral issues related to the education of children with or at risk for behavior disorders; in fact, some texts included only one chapter on academic issues. It seemed odd that so little space was devoted to meeting these children's academic needs given that—by definition—many of these youngsters experience academic underachievement.

This experience prompted the desire to design a textbook that would provide the field with a comprehensive, research-based text that presents best-practices information on how to best educate and intervene with students who have or are at risk for emotional and behavioral disorders. Specifically, whereas most texts intended for this population of students were aimed primarily at managing challenging behaviors, we wanted to develop a text that would (a) provide needed information on how to instruct these students in academic and social-behavioral domains and (b) illustrate the relationship between academic underachievement and problem behaviors.

In brief, this book is designed for general and special educators, school psychologists, and school counselors who will serve children with or at risk for behavior disorders. The overarching objective is to provide research-based best practices on how to identify, assess, educate, and intervene with these children to better meet their educational and social-behavioral needs. To this end, the text is organized into five parts.

Part One contains three chapters devoted to exploring the relationship between academic underachievement and problem behavior with a particular emphasis on early detection and assessment. Part Two presents seven chapters addressing academic behaviors and instructional issues. Topics include instructional issues in specific content areas (e.g., reading, written expression, and mathematics) as well as more general instructional issues such as lesson design and delivery (Chapter 4 by Howell and Kelley), homework (Chapter 9 by Sabornie), and classroom structure (Chapter 10 by Colvin). Part Three focuses on managing challenging behaviors. In this section, topics include antisocial behavior (Chapter 11 by Walker and Severson), the co-occurrence of conduct problems and hyperactivity-impulsivity-attention problems (Chapter 13 by Gresham, Lane, and Lambros), internalizing behaviors (Chapter 14 by Morris, Shah, and Morris), and social skills (Chapter 15 by Gresham). Part Four consists of three chapters devoted to providing an integrated approach to services. Specific topics include parent–school collaboration (Chapter 16 by Webster-Stratton and Reid), the role of paraprofessionals (Chapter 17 by Doyle), and transition issues (Chapter 18 by Clark and colleagues). The final section contains one chapter devoted to exploring future directions for the field of behavior disorders (Chapter 19 by Lane, Gresham, and O'Shaughnessy).

We are honored to have the contributions of so many leaders in the field of behavior disorders. Furthermore, we are most appreciative of not only the time and expertise provided but also the graciousness with which the contributors participated despite the hectic demands of their daily schedules. In addition, we appreciate the valuable input of the following manuscript reviewers: Beverley H. Johns, Program Supervisor, Garrison School; Oma Gail Simmons, Frostburg State University; and Donna E. Wadsworth, University of Louisiana at Lafayette. It is our hope that this text will fulfill the intended purpose of providing a tool to better serve children with or at risk for emotional and behavioral disorders.

K. L. L.
F. M. G.
T. E. O.

ABOUT THE AUTHORS

Kathleen Lynne Lane, Ph.D.

Dr. Kathleen Lane is an Assistant Professor in the Department of Special Education at Peabody College of Vanderbilt University. She earned her master's degree and doctorate in education from the University of California, Riverside. Prior to entering academia, Dr. Lane served as a classroom teacher of general and special education students for five years and provided consultation, intervention, and staff development services to five school districts in Southern California for two years in her role as a Program Specialist. Dr. Lane's research interests focus on investigating the relationship between academic underachievement and externalizing behaviors with children with or at risk for emotional and behavioral disorders (E/BD). She has designed and implemented several school-based interventions examining the impact of improved early literacy skills on academic and socio-behavioral outcomes for young children at risk for E/BD. Dr. Lane also serves on the editorial board for the *Journal of Emotional and Behavioral Disorders.*

Frank M. Gresham, Ph.D.

Dr. Frank M. Gresham is Distinguished Professor and Director of the School Psychology Program at the University of California, Riverside. He is a Fellow of the American Association for the Advancement of Science and is a Fellow of the American Psychological Association (APA) and holds Fellow status in three APA divisions (Evaluation, Measurement, and Statistics; School Psychology; and Mental Retardation/Development Disabilities). He is a member of the Society for the Study of School Psychology and was a recipient of the Lightner Witmer Award for outstanding research contributions in school psychology. Dr. Gresham's research interests include assessment and classification practices in learning disabilities, social skills assessment and training, emotional/behavioral disorders, and behavioral consultation in school settings. He serves on various editorial boards in special education and school psychology including: *Journal of Learning Disabilities, Journal of Special Education, Exceptionality, Journal of School Psychology,* and *Canadian Journal of School Psychology.*

Tam E. O'Shaughnessy, Ph.D.

Dr. Tam E. O'Shaughnessy is Assistant Professor of School Psychology at Georgia State University. Her work in designing and evaluating interventions for students placed at risk for reading difficulties and disabilities has resulted in a number of awards, grants, and publications. Dr. O'Shaughnessy is principal investigator of

Project Early Literacy–School Engagement, a U.S. Department of Education funded longitudinal study of school engagement and early literacy acquisition in K–2nd grade children. Dr. O'Shaughnessy holds a master's degree in biology and a doctorate in education from the University of California, Riverside. In addition to her work in literacy, she is an award-winning coauthor of four children's science books.

PART ONE

Relationship between Academic Underachievement and Problem Behavior

1

Students With or At Risk for Learning and Emotional-Behavioral Difficulties

An Integrated System of Prevention and Intervention

TAM E. O'SHAUGHNESSY
Georgia State University

KATHLEEN L. LANE
Peabody College of Vanderbilt University

FRANK M. GRESHAM AND MARGARET E. BEEBE-FRANKENBERGER
University of California, Riverside

Introduction

To be successful in school, it is essential for children to develop academic and social competence. Unfortunately, many children fail to form satisfactory interpersonal relationships with their teachers and classmates and to acquire academic skills commensurate with those of their peers. This places them at serious risk for a variety of negative outcomes including school failure, peer rejection, absence of close friendships, substance abuse, and school dropout (Hinshaw, 1992; Parker & Asher, 1987; Walker, Colvin, & Ramsey, 1995).

The majority of children who are vulnerable to school failure are referred by their teachers or parents because of chronic achievement and/or behavioral problems. In particular, children are most often referred when they have persistent reading difficulties, disruptive or aggressive behavior problems, or both (Gerber

3

& Semmel, 1984; Lloyd, Kauffman, Landrum, & Roe, 1991). When a child is referred to a prereferral intervention team or similar school team, this development is a signal that the teacher has reached the limit of his or her tolerance with respect to individual differences. No longer is the teacher optimistic about his or her ability to manage the child's maladaptive behavior or to provide effective instruction within the context of the larger group (Gerber & Semmel, 1984).

Once a referral is made, schools typically engage in a process of determining whether the general education classroom can be modified sufficiently to accommodate a child's difficulties. This process of prereferral intervention is designed to provide a forum for general education teachers to plan and implement interventions for students who are experiencing difficulties in the general education setting. Unfortunately, the nature of modifications is frequently insufficient, and the outcomes of interventions are often evaluated unsystematically (Flugum & Reschly, 1994; Fuchs & Fuchs, 1992). For example, behaviors that are targeted for intervention often lack habilitative validity (Hawkins, 1991). That is, instead of focusing on behaviors that will have a lasting impact on a child's educational experience (e.g., improving reading skills, teaching replacement behaviors), too often behaviors are selected that are aimed primarily at creating a more peaceful classroom environment (e.g., reducing out-of-seat behaviors or noncompliance). Although these behaviors may be socially valid from a teacher's perspective, they may not represent behaviors that will have a broad and lasting effect (Lane, Beebe-Frankenberger, Lambros, & Pierson, 2001).

In addition, many teachers report they lack the knowledge, skills, and resources necessary to accommodate children with diverse learning needs effectively (Schumm & Vaughn, 1995). This is a serious concern because today's classrooms are increasingly more diverse (Baker, Simmons, & Kame'enui, 1995). It is not unusual in some schools for elementary schoolteachers to be responsible for a class of 24 or more children who possess a wide range of academic skills; who speak little or no English; and who have, or are at risk for, learning disabilities, mild mental retardation, emotional disturbance, or attention difficulties (Baker et al., 1995). Compounding matters, it is estimated that 20% to 40% of school-age children are at risk for school failure (U.S. Department of Education, 1999b). Thus, it is not surprising that many teachers feel overwhelmed and ill equipped to deal with the many academic and behavior problems presented to them each day (Schumm & Vaughn, 1995). In turn, it is not surprising that many children who receive school-based interventions show little noticeable improvement (Reid, 1993).

Once a school decides that modifications to regular education have been unsuccessful, students are evaluated to determine whether they are eligible for special education and, if found eligible, to decide what services they will receive and in what setting services will be delivered (i.e., general education, resource room, special day class). The vast majority of students (i.e., 70%) qualify for special education under one of the mild disabilities categories that includes students with learning disabilities, emotional and behavioral disorders, and mild mental retardation (U.S. Department of Education, 1999a). However, most children with learning or behavioral problems are not identified until they are about 8 or 9 years old (e.g., Duncan, Forness, & Hartsough, 1995; Francis, Shaywitz, Steubing, Shaywitz, & Fletcher, 1996; Kazdin, 1987). Moreover, because many schools have adopted a policy of inclusion, a large percentage of students with mild disabilities are served in general education classrooms (Council for Exceptional Children, 1994; Tomlinson, Callahan, Tomchin, Eiss, Imbeau, & Landrum, 1997), which often provide too little support to meet their needs (Fuchs, Fuchs, Hamlett, Phillips, & Karns, 1995; Scruggs & Mastropieri, 1996).

Unfortunately, these practices often translate into missed opportunities for preventive intervention because the longer children go without identification and intervention, the more difficult it is to intervene successfully. That is, children with learning and/or behavioral problems tend to become less responsive to intervention as they grow older and their difficulties increase in scope and severity (Bullis & Walker, 1994; Francis et al., 1991). For example, providing a child with reading intervention after he or she has failed in reading for 2 to 3 years may not be effective for any number of reasons. The child's initial problem of underdeveloped phonemic awareness in kindergarten may have extended into word recognition, reading fluency, and reading comprehension by second or third grade. Furthermore, by this time the child is likely to have developed low motivation, poor self-concept, and/or disruptive behavior problems. Similarly, providing a child with social skills training after he or she has displayed antisocial behaviors for several years may not be very effective. In this case, the child's initial problem of being uncooperative with teachers and peers may have escalated into aggression, low achievement, and teacher and peer rejection. Any or all of these secondary problems can interfere with a child's progress during intervention.

Paradoxically, the early signs of learning difficulties (e.g., Torgesen & Wagner, 1998) and behavior problems (e.g., Hinshaw, Han, Erhardt, & Huber, 1992) are evident even during the preschool years. For example, early language difficulties (Torgesen & Wagner, 1998) and oppositional and hyperactive behavior problems (Walker et al., 1995) can be identified when children are very young. Without early detection, these relatively mild problems during infancy can develop into more severe difficulties (e.g., reading problems and antisocial behavior patterns) during childhood. Moreover, a compelling body of evidence indicates that most children at risk for learning (O'Shaughnessy & Swanson, 2000; Vellutino et al., 1996) and behavior (Dodge, 1993; Reid, 1993) problems are responsive to early, informed intervention. Thus, early identification and intervention are not only possible but essential.

In summary, many schools do not take advantage of current knowledge about early identification and prevention/intervention strategies for children with learning difficulties and/or emotional or behavioral problems. Too many schools have a policy of waiting for teachers to refer children who are having academic and/or behavioral difficulties *after* problems appear rather than identifying children who are at risk *before* problems occur (also see Forness, Kavale, MacMillan, Asarnow, & Duncan, 1996; Lane, 1999; Torgesen & Wagner, 1998). Because of the progressive nature of many learning and social/emotional difficulties, it is essential that more schools adopt proactive practices. Furthermore, a great deal is known about how children's learning and behavioral problems develop and how to intervene effectively. Thus, the present challenge lies in finding effective and practical ways to incorporate current knowledge into school practices (O'Shaughnessy & Gresham, in press). The importance of meeting this challenge is underscored by (a) the high percentage of students who have, or are at risk for, learning and emotional or behavioral problems; (b) the bleak long-term outcomes for students who do not master basic academic skills and develop adaptive behaviors, and (c) the lack of clearly defined guidelines for assessing learning and behavior problems; linking assessment data to interventions, and monitoring student progress.

Figure 1.1 shows the developmental progression of reading difficulties and/or disruptive or aggressive behaviors without (upper panel) and with (lower

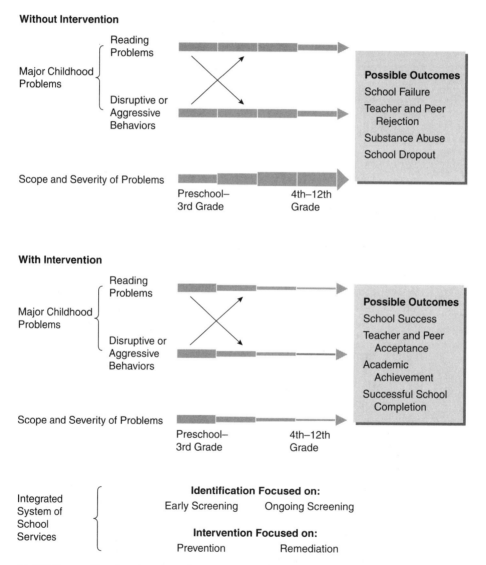

FIGURE 1.1   The developmental progression of reading difficulties and externalizing (disruptive or aggressive) emotional/behavior problems without and with early identification and informed intervention.

panel) early identification and informed intervention. It also shows that some children may possess *both* reading and externalizing behavior problems (crossed arrows). The upper panel depicts both of these major childhood problems as broad bands representing large numbers of children. Without early identification and intervention, relatively few children are able to overcome their difficulties, and many children's problems increase in scope and severity over time. Some of the possible negative outcomes associated with reading failure and/or disruptive or aggressive behavior problems include school failure, teacher and peer rejection, substance abuse, and school dropout. The lower panel in Figure 1.1 shows that with early identification and informed intervention, far fewer children continue to display learning and/or behavioral difficulties in later grades. Some of the possible positive outcomes associated with early intervention include academic achievement, school success, teacher and peer acceptance, and high school graduation.

The purpose of this chapter is to outline an integrated system of early identification and prevention/intervention. This chapter focuses primarily on young children's reading difficulties and externalizing (i.e., disruptive or aggressive) behavior problems because these are major causes of concern in most elementary schools.

An Integrated System of Early Identification and Prevention/Intervention

The fundamental premise of this chapter is that schools (i.e., administrators, teachers, prereferral intervention teams, school psychologists, counselors, and speech and language therapists) can better serve children with learning difficulties and emotional or behavior problems if they (a) possess knowledge of current identification and prevention/intervention strategies and (b) apply this knowledge in a systematic way. In addition, children's learning difficulties and social/emotional problems are too often considered separately when in reality they develop concurrently and interact in ways that either promote or hinder school success. An incomplete understanding of a child's difficulties can lead to misidentification and, more important, a mismatch between intervention (prereferral intervention or individual education plan [IEP] goals) and a child's problems (Kavale & Forness, 1998; Torgesen & Wagner, 1998). Thus, each child is best viewed from a developmental perspective. That is, each child will vary in the scope and severity of her or his academic and behavioral difficulties across both continua (MacMillan, 1998). Moreover, even children with the same problems at about the same level of severity may vary widely in motivation, family support, and compensating strengths. All of these factors must be considered.

Early Identification

The importance of early identification is clear. Research has shown that most children who have not learned to read by the third grade continue to have reading problems in high school and adulthood (Bruck, 1992). Moreover, the longer children experience reading failure, the more likely other problems will arise. It is not uncommon for children with reading difficulties to have co-occurring behavioral problems including higher levels of aggression, depression, and school dropout, as well as lower levels of motivation, social skills, and self-concept (Bryan, 1991; Gresham, 1986; Hinshaw, 1992; Kavale & Forness, 1998). Similarly, most children who have not developed prosocial behaviors by about third grade continue to display some degree of antisocial behavior throughout their lives (Bullis & Walker, 1994; Kazdin, 1987). In this case, too, the longer children go without informed intervention, the more likely secondary problems will develop. It is not unusual for children with antisocial behavior patterns to also experience reading difficulties, depression, and anxiety (e.g., Hinshaw, 1992) (see Chapter 14 by Morris, Shah, & Morris in this text).

Based on current knowledge, it is recommended that proactive screening of young children at risk for learning and/or emotional or behavioral problems take place in preschool and kindergarten, and in later grades to assure ongoing identification of high-risk students. A number of norm-referenced and criterion-referenced assessment tools can be used to identify young children who would benefit from intervention. The following are several assessment instruments that are research based, easy to use, and diagnostic of behavioral problems and reading and reading-related skills. Although some of these assessment tools and approaches have been available for several years, they do not appear to be widely used by many schools.

Behavioral Assessment.   Early identification of children who are at risk for emotional or behavioral difficulties is the key to prevention. Research indicates that children with emotional or behavioral problems can be identified as early as 3 years of age (e.g., Kazdin, 1987). Unfortunately, preschool early screening programs are rare. Consequently, too many children arrive in kindergarten unable to interact in a positive way with their peers and teachers and unable to direct their attention toward learning. This immediately places them at risk for peer rejection and academic failure (Bullis & Walker, 1994). The following assessment instruments and approaches can be used to identify young children who are at risk for emotional, behavioral, and academic difficulties.

The School Archival Records Search (SARS; Walker, Block-Pedego, Todis, & Severson, 1991) provides a way to quantify a child's cumulative file systematically based on 11 variables frequently found in school records. This procedure provides valuable information about a child's current status and educational and behavioral histories. SARS information includes (a) the number of different schools attended, (b) attendance records, (c) academic achievement test scores, (d) grade retentions, (e) academic and behavioral referrals, (f) outcomes of referrals, (g) special services received, and (h) disciplinary contacts, among others. Many of these variables are important risk indicators. For example, poor attendance in elementary school is highly predictive of later school dropout (Nichols & Nichols, 1990).

The *Early Screening Project* (ESP; Walker, Severson, & Feil, 1994) and *Systematic Screening for Behavioral Disorders* (SSBD; Walker & Severson, 1990) are assessment instruments designed for schoolwide screening of students who are at risk for either externalizing (e.g., disruptive or aggressive behaviors) or internalizing (depression, anxiety, social avoidance) behavior problems. The ESP is designed to identify high-risk children in preschool and kindergarten; the SSBD is designed to identify high-risk children in grades 1 through 6. Both the ESP and SSBD involve three sequential stages of assessment. In the first stage, the general education teacher nominates and ranks children whose behaviors match the characteristics of externalizing or internalizing behavior patterns. In stage 2, the three highest-ranked children in each category are rated by their teachers on the Critical Events Index (i.e., lies, steals, vomits after eating) and on a checklist of both adaptive (i.e., follows established classroom rules) and maladaptive (i.e., pouts or sulks) behaviors called the Combined Frequency Index. In stage 3, children who exceed normative criteria on teacher ratings in stage 2 are directly observed in both structured and unstructured settings. The focus of observations in a structured setting is on children's responsiveness to teacher directives and in an unstructured setting is on children's interactions with their peers (Walker et al., 1995). At stage 3, parents or guardians also rate their child's behavior, providing important information about a child's behavior at home (see Chapter 11 by Walker & Severson in this text).

The *Social Skills Rating System* (SSRS; Gresham & Elliott, 1990) provides a comprehensive, norm-referenced assessment of students' social behaviors that may affect teacher–student relations, peer acceptance, and academic performance. It can be used with preschool, elementary, and high school students. The SSRS is designed to quantify the perceived frequency and importance of behaviors that influence the development of social competence and adaptive functioning at school and at home. It also includes an assessment of perceived problem behaviors (externalizing, internalizing, and hyperactivity) and academic competence. The SSRS is an effective instrument for identifying children at risk for developing social behavior problems and learning difficulties; for categorizing behavior difficulties as skill, performance, or fluency deficiencies; and for planning interventions. With each of the measures cited here (i.e., SARS, ESP, SSBD, and SSRS), both risk and resilience factors can be obtained and used to plan interventions.

Finally, *functional assessment* "refers to the full range of strategies used to identify the antecedents and consequences that control problem behavior" (Horner, 1994, p. 401). The underlying assumption of functional assessment is that all behavior is purposeful (Iwata, Dorsey, Slifer, Bauman, & Richman, 1982). Thus, the goal is to understand the purpose or function of a child's behavior and then to use this information to develop an intervention. To identify the function of behavior, information is gathered from multiple sources using both qualitative (e.g., review of records, behavior rating scales, direct observation) and quantitative procedures (e.g., functional analysis). In school, the most common purposes of children's misbehavior are to escape from task demands or to get attention from teachers or peers (Lane, Umbreit, & Beebe-Frankenberger, 1999). Once the function of a child's behavior is identified, appropriate interventions can be designed and implemented to teach and/or reinforce adaptive replacement behaviors.

Functional assessment can also be used to determine whether a child's difficulties are skill, performance, or fluency related. The specific nature of a child's maladaptive behavior or low academic performance is important because it affects intervention. *Skill deficits* refer to behaviors or skills that are not yet part of a child's repertoire. For example, a child may not have had sufficient opportunity to learn word identification strategies or positive social skills. In these cases, intervention should focus on teaching these skills, because no amount of incentive can motivate children to do something they don't know how to do. *Performance deficits* refer to behaviors or skills that a child possesses but does not perform on a regular basis. For example, a child may know how to say "thank you" and raise a hand before speaking in class but seldom does so. Interventions to address performance deficits often include positive reinforcement programs (e.g., home–school notes) to increase the probability of the behavior or skill being practiced. Sometimes, an emotional or behavioral problem (e.g., low motivation or inattention) interferes with the performance of a learned skill. In this case, intervention should include strategies to reduce the interfering problem behavior, as well as increase the likelihood of the desired behavior or academic skill being performed. Finally, *fluency deficits* refer to behaviors or skills that have been learned but are not yet automatic. For example, a child may possess knowledge of letter–sound correspondences and a large sight word vocabulary yet read connected text very slowly. In this case, intervention would involve extensive practice reading connected text to help the child develop more fluent reading skills.

Reading Assessment.   Early identification of, and subsequent intervention with, children who are at risk for reading difficulties is critical to preventing reading problems. Fortunately, a great deal is known about how reading skills develop and why some children struggle to learn to read. Extensive research conducted over the past two decades indicates that most children's reading problems arise from difficulties processing the phonological features of language (e.g., Torgesen & Wagner, 1998). Specifically, it appears that the most common cause of reading problems lies in phonological processing deficits that interfere with the development of phonological awareness, letter–sound mapping, name retrieval, and verbal memory (Torgesen & Wagner, 1998). What is more, this has been found to be true for children who are poor readers whether or not they have an identifiable learning disability (e.g., Stanovich & Siegel, 1994). Thus, most children at risk for reading problems can be identified when they are very young using assessment procedures that measure these skills.

The *Comprehensive Test of Phonological Processes* (CTOPP; Wagner, Torgesen, & Rashotte, 1999) evaluates each of the phonological skill areas. The CTOPP contains multiple subtests to assess phonological awareness skills (analysis and synthesis), verbal memory, and rapid-naming skill. Normative criteria are provided for kindergarten and first grade (level 1) and for second grade through early adulthood (level 2). Below-average performance on one or more of these measures is a strong indicator of future reading problems and the need for intervention.

Dynamic Indicators of Basic Early Literacy Skills (DIBELS; Kaminski & Good, 1996) was recently developed to provide a measure of fluency on several key indicators of early literacy skills (i.e., phonological awareness, knowledge of letter names, and word attack skills). DIBELS can be used with children in preschool through second grade. This assessment tool has adequate psychometric properties, especially for young children who are poor readers, and it can be administered easily, repeatedly, and frequently using 1-minute timed probes. Thus, it can be used to screen students at risk, monitor individual student progress, and evaluate the effectiveness of intervention. Currently, DIBELS contains four subtests (i.e., Phoneme Segmentation Fluency, Letter-Naming Fluency, Nonsense Word Fluency, and Onset Recognition Fluency), with 20 alternative forms for each subtest.

Curriculum-Based Measurement (CBM) is a standardized approach to measuring academic achievement using a school's curriculum (Fuchs & Fuchs, 1992) or assessment materials closely related to a school's curriculum (Fuchs & Deno, 1994). Some of the uses of CBM include screening students who are at risk for learning problems (e.g., reading, spelling, mathematics), monitoring individual student progress, and evaluating intervention effectiveness (Fuchs, Deno, & Mirkin, 1984). In reading, CBM is used to evaluate a student's oral reading fluency (i.e., oral and accuracy using 1-minute timed probes). For average readers, this usually begins in the middle of first grade, after formal reading instruction has begun. Typically, a student reads a passage that has been taken from the class's basal reader. Oral reading fluency is a sensitive measure of growth in reading skills and is highly correlated with reading comprehension, the ultimate purpose of reading (Shinn, 1989). In addition to being curriculum referenced, CBM is also a norm- and individually referenced assessment method (Knutson & Shinn, 1991). When using CBM, local norms are gathered to provide a relevant set of norm-referenced criteria. Using local norms, a child's reading rate and accuracy can be compared to those of same-grade or across-grade peers. Similarly, CBM is individually referenced because an individual student's growth in reading skills can be measured repeatedly over time and graphed to evaluate her or his level and rate of progress. Similar to DIBELS, CBM measures are brief and easy to administer. This enables data to be collected repeatedly over time with one student or all at one time with a large number of students.

Alternative assessment procedures, like those described here, are important because they go beyond traditional assessment methods. That is, these approaches are diagnostic of a child's strengths and weaknesses, sensitive to a child's progress, and inform instruction. With approaches like these, assessment information can be directly linked to intervention, and individual student progress can be monitored regularly. These features enable teachers to modify instruction to match a child's current instructional level. They also allow teachers to use a child's responsiveness to intervention as a means of modifying the focus and intensity of intervention (Fuchs & Fuchs, 1998; Vellutino, Scanlon, & Tanzman, 1998).

Prevention and Intervention

As discussed earlier, children who are at risk for reading difficulties and emotional or behavioral problems tend to be more responsive to intervention from preschool to about third grade. Needless to say, beyond this point intervention is still critically important and likely to have a positive impact. However, it is often more difficult to intervene as children grow older because their learning and/or behavioral problems tend to become more pervasive. Thus, it is critically important that intervention increase in focus, intensity, and comprehensiveness based on the scope and severity of a child's difficulties. In turn, this means that intervention must be responsive to the unique needs of individual children.

How can current knowledge be incorporated into school-based intervention practices? An effective approach is to establish an integrated system of early identification and prevention/intervention, with three progressive levels of intervention: primary, secondary, and tertiary (Caplan, 1964; Forness et al., 1996). These intervention levels share a comprehensive approach to dealing with academic and behavior problems in that they (a) emphasize teaching appropriate behaviors and basic skills rather than punishing unwanted behavior and waiting for academic skills to emerge, (b) match the level of intervention resources to the level of academic or behavior challenge presented by students, and (c) integrate multiple systems to intervene with the full range of academic and behavior challenges (Consortium on the School-Based Promotion of Social Competence, 1994).

At the first level, low intensity, primary intervention is aimed at preventing learning and behavioral problems. This level of intervention is received by all children and includes activities such as schoolwide "balanced" reading instruction, social skills training, and conflict resolution curricula. Work by Colvin et al., (1993) and others suggests that of the total student body in an elementary or middle school, about 80% will respond favorably to a primary prevention program.

At the second level, more intensive, secondary interventions are provided to children identified as being at risk for learning and/or behavioral problems. Secondary interventions are provided to children who are less responsive to primary intervention than their peers. These are more focused and intensive interventions and involve fewer children. Examples of secondary interventions include small-group instruction in social problem solving skills, anger management training, and word identification strategy training. Research suggests that approximately 10% to 15% of students will require these more intensive, secondary intervention services (e.g., Gresham, Sugai, Horner, Quinn, & McInerney, 1998).

Finally, tertiary interventions are highly intensive, individualized interventions for children with severe difficulties and entail special education placement if appropriate. Examples of tertiary intervention include individualized reading tutoring, self-monitoring instruction, and study skills training. In addition, although schools provide an important setting for intervening with children who have behavioral and/or learning problems, frequently children need intervention that extends to the home (Adams, 1990; Walker et al., 1995). Interventions that involve parents/guardians facilitate the development of academic and prosocial skills in the home. Moreover, home–school collaborations can build important connections among children, families, teachers, and other school personnel (Christenson, Sinclair, Evelo, & Thurlow, 1995). Current evidence indicates that about 1% to 7% of students will display chronic patterns of disruptive or destructive behaviors and/or learning difficulties, almost invariably in reading (Hinshaw, 1992; Kame'enui & Darch, 1995).

At each level of intervention, it is critical to monitor treatment integrity, individual student progress, and social validity. Evaluating treatment integrity ensures that an intervention is implemented as it was planned (Gresham, 1989) and is a powerful means of providing feedback to teachers. Monitoring individual student progress enables teachers to modify the focus and intensity of intervention based on each child's individual needs and progress. Finally, assessing social validity assures that intervention goals are significant, intervention procedures are acceptable, and intervention outcomes are important (Wolf, 1968). Because these factors directly impact the likelihood of teachers implementing high-quality intervention and students actively engaging in learning activities, it is important to assess social validity from both teacher and student perspectives (Lane et al., 1999).

Finally, a rich literature has established many of the critical components of effective teaching that apply to all students whether or not they are at risk of school failure (e.g., Algozzine & Ysseldyke, 1992; Rosenshine, 1983). Figure 1.2 shows the major components of effective intervention. Some of the most important elements include establishing high expectations, managing behavior problems effectively, ensuring that students are actively engaged in learning and actively responding, providing students with successful experiences that foster motivation, and including strategies to promote maintenance and generalization of skills. In addition, effective teaching includes coordinating intervention with the general education curriculum so that learning activities are consistent and reinforced throughout the school day.

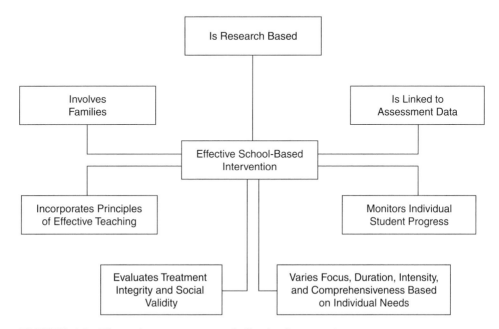

FIGURE 1.2   The major components of effective intervention.

Summary

This chapter outlined an integrated system of early identification and prevention/intervention for children who are vulnerable to school failure. Box 1.1 provides recommendations for adopting this system. Its essential features include (a) a schoolwide system of early screening and ongoing identification of at-risk students and (b) a schoolwide system of progressive intervention for students with, or at risk for, learning and emotional/behavioral difficulties.

As discussed in this chapter, several major conclusions can be drawn from current knowledge about these major problems of childhood. First, children at risk for developing learning and emotional/behavioral difficulties need to be identified early, before their problems become too deeply entrenched and secondary problems arise. Research strongly indicates that the optimal time for preventing most learning and behavioral difficulties is from preschool to about third grade.

Second, the assessment information gathered during the identification process needs to be relevant and useful. By using assessment tools that diagnose a child's strengths and weaknesses, assessment information can be used to plan intervention. Assessment tools also need to be sensitive enough to measure a child's

---

BOX **1.1**

Recommendations

1. Establish an integrated system of proactive practices that includes:
   - A schoolwide system of early screening.
   - The optimal time for preventing learning and/or emotional/behavioral difficulties is from preschool to about third grade.
   - A schoolwide system of ongoing identification.
   - A schoolwide system of sequential interventions. Primary, secondary, and tertiary intervention levels progressively increase in focus, duration, intensity, and comprehensiveness.
2. Employ research-based assessment instruments and procedures that are:
   - Diagnostic of strengths and weaknesses.
   - Sensitive to student growth.
3. Implement research-based interventions that:
   - Vary in focus, duration, intensity, and comprehensiveness based on individual needs.
   - Are linked to preintervention baseline data and ongoing progress monitoring.
   - Involve families.
4. View each student from a developmental perspective.
   - Each student will vary in the scope and severity of her or his difficulties across many variables, including social, emotional, academic, and linguistic.
   - Each student will also vary in compensating strengths, including motivation and family and community support.
5. Provide extensive professional development in:
   - Current knowledge of learning and emotional/behavioral difficulties.
   - Current knowledge of early identification and prevention/intervention strategies.

growth during intervention. These data can be used to monitor student progress and determine whether an intervention needs to be modified (e.g., intensity, duration, comprehensiveness).

Third, each child needs to be viewed from a developmental perspective. Each child will vary in the scope and severity of his or her difficulties across many variables (e.g., academic, social, emotional, motivation, family). An effective intervention system accommodates the unique needs of individual children, matching intervention to each child's current developmental level. This can be accomplished by establishing an integrated system of progressively more intensive intervention levels (i.e., primary, secondary, and tertiary interventions). The purpose of primary intervention is to ensure that all students possess the fundamental skills to be successful in school. The goal of secondary intervention is to give at-risk students the more intensive instruction and support they need to catch up to their peers.

Finally, the aim of tertiary intervention is to assist children with severe learning and behavioral difficulties by providing them with highly intensive and individualized intervention. In addition, although early intervention is critically important, it may not always be enough to address the many needs of some children (Lane, 1999; O'Shaughnessy & Gresham, in press; Walker et al., 1995). For these children, continued and comprehensive support over several years may be needed to help them overcome or minimize their problems.

Research clearly indicates that the process of developing adaptive behaviors and the precursors of academic skills begins very early in a child's life. While most children arrive at school with the motivation to learn and the necessary academic, linguistic, cognitive, and behavioral skills to succeed, many other children do not. This immediately places them at risk for school failure (e.g., Bullis & Walker, 1994; Hart & Risley, 1995). Although schools cannot be expected to solve all of the problems facing these children, schools can provide an important context for intervention (Walker et al., 1995).

REFERENCES

Adams, M. J. (1990). *Beginning to read: Thinking and learning about print.* Cambridge, MA: MIT Press.

Algozzine, R., & Ysseldyke, J. (1992). *Strategies and tactics for effective instruction.* Longmont, CO: Sopris West.

Baker, S. K., Simmons, D. C., & Kame'enui, E. J. (1995). *Characteristics of students with diverse learning and curricular needs.* Eugene: Center to Improve the Tools of Educators, University of Oregon.

Bruck, M. (1992). Persistence of dyslexics' phonological awareness deficits. *Developmental Psychology, 28,* 874–886.

Bryan, T. (1991). Social problems in learning disabilities. In B. L. Wong, (Ed.), *Learning about learning disabilities* (pp. 195–226). New York: Academic Press.

Bullis, M., & Walker, H. M. (1994). *Comprehensive school-based systems for troubled youth.* Eugene: Center on Human Development, University of Oregon.

Caplan, G. (1964). *Principles of preventive psychology.* New York: Basic Books.

Christenson, S. L., Sinclair, M., Evelo, D., & Thurlow, M. (1995). *Tip the balance: Practices and policies that influence school engagement for youth at high risk for dropping out.* Minneapolis: College of Education and Human Development, Institute on Community Integration, University of Minnesota. (ERIC Document Reproduction Service No. ED 398 673)

Colvin, G., Sugai, G., & Kame'enui, E. (1993). *Proactive school-wide discipline: Implementation manual.* Eugene: Project PREPARE, Behavioral Research and Teaching, College of Education, University of Oregon.

Consortium on School-Based Promotion of Social Competence. (1994). Social competence. In R. Haggerty, L. Sherrod, N. Garmezy, & M. Rutter (Eds.), *Stress, risk, and resilience in children and adolescents.* New York: Cambridge University Press.

Council for Exceptional Children. (1994). Statistics profile of special education in the United States, 1994. *Teaching Exceptional Children, 26,* Supplement.

Dodge, K. (1993). The future of research on conduct disorder. *Development and Psychopathology, 5,* 311–320.

Duncan, B., Forness, S. R., & Hartsough, C. (1995). Students identified as seriously emotionally disturbed in day treatment: Cognitive, psychiatric, and special education characteristics. *Behavioral Disorders, 20,* 238–252.

Flugum, K. R., & Reschly, D. J. (1994). Prereferral interventions: Quality indices and outcomes. *Journal of School Psychology, 32,* 1–14.

Forness, S. R., Kavale, K. A., MacMillan, D. L., Asarnow, J. R., & Duncan, B. B. (1996). Early detection and prevention of emotional or behavioral disorders: Developmental aspects of systems of care. *Behavioral Disorders, 21,* 226–240.

Francis, D. J., Shaywitz, S. E., Stuebing, K. K., Shaywitz, B. A., & Fletcher, J. M. (1991). Analysis of change: Modeling individual growth. *Journal of Consulting and Clinical Psychology, 59,* 27–37.

Fuchs, L. S., & Deno, S. L.(1994). Must instructionally useful performance assessment be based in the curriculum? *Exceptional Children, 61,* 15–24.

Fuchs, L. S., Deno, S. L., & Mirkin, P. K. (1984). Effects of frequent curriculum-based measurement and evaluation on pedagogy, student achievement, and student awareness of learning. *American Educational Research Journal, 21,* 449–460.

Fuchs, L. S., & Fuchs, D. (1992). Identifying a measure for monitoring student reading progress. *School Psychology Review, 21,* 45–52.

Fuchs, L. S., & Fuchs, D. (1998). Treatment validity: A unifying concept for reconceptualizing the identification of learning disabilities. *Learning Disabilities Research & Practice, 13,* 204–219.

Fuchs, L. S., Fuchs, D., Hamlett, C. L., Phillips, N. B., & Karns, K. (1995). General educators' specialized adaptation for students with learning disabilities. *Exceptional Children, 61,* 440–459.

Gerber, M. M., & Semmel, M. I. (1984). Teacher as imperfect test: Reconceptualizing the referral process. *Educational Psychologist, 19,* 137–148.

Gresham, F. M. (1986). Conceptual issues in the assessment of social competence in children. In P. Strain, M. Guralink, & H. Walker (Eds.), *Children's social behavior: Development, assessment, and modification* (pp. 143–186). New York: Academic Press.

Gresham, F. M. (1989). Assessment of treatment integrity in school consultation and prereferral intervention. *School Psychology Review, 18,* 37–50.

Gresham, F. M., & Elliott, S. N. (1990). *Social Skills Rating System.* Circle Pines, MN: American Guidance Service.

Gresham, F. M., Sugai, G., Horner, R., Quinn, M., & McInerney, M. (1998). *Classroom and schoolwide practices that support students' social competence: A synthesis of research.* Washington, DC: Office of Special Education Programs.

Hart, B., & Risley, T. R. (1995). *Meaningful differences in the everyday experience of young American children.* Baltimore, MD: Brookes.

Hawkins, R. (1991). Is social validity what we are interested in? Argument for a functional approach. *Journal of Applied Behavior Analysis, 24,* 205–213.

Hinshaw, S. (1992). Externalizing behavior problems and academic underachievement in childhood and adolescence: Causal relationships and underlying mechanisms. *Psychological Bulletin, 111,* 127–155.

Hinshaw, S., Han, S., Erhardt, D., & Huber, A. (1992). Internalizing and externalizing behavior problems in preschool children: Correspondence among parent and teacher ratings and behavior observations. *Journal of Clinical Child Psychology, 21,* 143–150.

Horner, R. H. (1994). Functional assessment: Contributions and future directions. *Journal of Applied Behavior Analysis, 27,* 401–404.

Iwata, B. A., Dorsey, M. F., Slifer, K. J., Bauman, K. E., & Richman, G. S. (1982). Toward a functional analysis of self-injury. *Analysis and Intervention in Developmental Disabilities, 2,* 3–20.

Kame'enui, E., & Darch, D. (1995). *Instructional classroom management: A proactive approach to behavior management.* White Plains, NY: Longman.

Kaminski, R. A., & Good, R. H. (1996). Toward a technology for assessing basic early literacy skills. *School Psychology Review, 25,* 215–227.

Kavale, K. A., & Forness, S. R. (1998). Covariance in learning disability and behavior disorder: An examination of classification and placement issues. In T. E. Scruggs & M. A. Mastropieri (Eds.), *Advances in learning and behavioral disabilities* (pp. 1–42). Greenwich, CT: JAI.

Kazdin, A. (1987). Treatment of antisocial behavior in children: Current status and future directions. *Psychological Bulletin, 102,* 187–203.

Knutson, N., & Shinn, M. R. (1991). Curriculum-based measurement: Conceptual underpinnings and integration in problem-solving assessment. *Journal of School Psychology, 29,* 317–393.

Lane, K. L. (1999). Young students at-risk for antisocial behavior: The utility of academic and social skills interventions. *Journal of Emotional and Behavioral Disorders, 7*(4), 211–223.

Lane, K. L., Beebe-Frankenberger, M., Lambros, K. L., & Pierson, M. E. (2001). Designing effective interventions for children at-risk for antisocial behavior: An integrated model of components necessary for making valid inferences. *Psychology in the Schools 38*(4), 365–379.

Lane, K. L., Umbreit, J., & Beebe-Frankenberger, M. (1999). Functional assessment research on students with or at risk for EBD: 1990 to the present. *Journal of Positive Behavior Interventions, 2,* 101–111.

Lloyd, J. W., Kauffman, J. M., Landrum, T. J., & Roe, D. L. (1991). Why do teachers refer pupils for special education? An analysis of referral records. *Exceptionality, 2,* 115–126.

MacMillan, D. L. (1998). Unpackaging special education categorical variables in the study and teaching of children with conduct problems. *Education and Treatment of Children, 1,* 234–245.

Nichols, C. E., & Nichols, R. E. (1990). *Dropout predication and prevention.* Brandon, VT: Clinical Psychology.

O'Shaughnessy, T. E., & Gresham, F. M. (in press). The efficacy of paraeducator-led, small group reading intervention for 2nd grade at-risk readers. *School Psychology Review.*

O'Shaughnessy, T. E., & Swanson, H. L. (2000). A comparison of two reading interventions for children with reading disabilities. *Journal of Learning Disabilities, 33*(3), 257–277.

Parker, J., & Asher, S. (1987). Peer relations and later personal adjustment: Are low accepted children at risk? *Psychological Bulletin, 102,* 357–389.

Reid, J. (1993). Prevention of conduct disorder before and after school entry: Relating interventions to developmental findings. *Development and Psychopathology, 5,* 243–262.

Rosenshine, B. V. (1983). Teaching functions in instructional programs. *Elementary School Journal, 83,* 335–352.

Schumm, J. S., & Vaughn, S. (1995). Getting ready for inclusion: Is the stage set? *Learning Disabilities Research & Practice, 10,* 169–179.

Scruggs, T. E., & Mastropieri, M. A. (1996). Teacher perception of mainstreaming/inclusion, 1958–1995: A research synthesis. *Exceptional Children, 63,* 59–74.

Shinn, M. R. (1989). *Curriculum-based measurement: Assessing special children.* New York: Guilford.

Stanovich, K. E., & Siegel, L. S. (1994). Phenotypic performance profile of children with reading disabilities: A regression-based test of the phonological-core-variable-difference model. *Journal of Educational Psychology, 86,* 24–53.

Tomlinson, C. A., Callahan, C. M., Tomchin, D. M., Eiss, N., Imbeau, M., & Landrum, M. (1997). Becoming architects of communities of learning: Addressing academic diversity in contemporary classrooms. *Exceptional Children, 63,* 269–282.

Torgesen, J. K., & Wagner, R. K. (1998). Alternative diagnostic approaches for specific developmental reading disabilities. *Learning Disabilities Research & Practice, 13,* 220–232.

U.S. Department of Education. (1999a). *Office of Educational Research and Improvement Request for Proposals.* Washington, DC: Author.

U.S. Department of Education. (1999b). *Twenty-first annual report to Congress on the implementation of the Individuals with Disabilities Education Act.* Washington, DC: Author.

Vellutino, F. R., Scanlon, D. M., Sipay, E. R., Small, S. G., Pratt, A., Chen, R., & Denckla, M. B. (1996). Cognitive profiles of difficult-to-remediate and readily remediated poor readers: Early intervention as a vehicle for distinguishing between cognitive and experiential deficits as basic causes of specific reading disability. *Journal of Educational Psychology, 88,* 601–638.

Vellutino, F. R., Scanlon, D. M., Tanzman, M. S. (1998). The case for early intervention in diagnosing specific reading disability. *Journal of School Psychology, 36*(4), 367–397.

Wagner, R. K., Torgesen, J. K., & Rashotte, C. A. (1999). *Comprehensive Test of Phonological Processes.* Austin, TX: Pro-Ed.

Walker, H. M., Block-Pedego, A., Todis, B., & Severson, H. (1991). *School Archival Record Search.* Longmont, CO: Sopris West.

Walker, H. M., Colvin, G., & Ramsey, E. (1995). *Antisocial behavior in school: Strategies and best practices.* Pacific Grove, CA: Brooks/Cole.

Walker, H. M., & Severson, H. H. (1990). *Systematic Screening for Behavior Disorders (SSBD): User's guide and technical manual.* Longmont, CO: Sopris West.

Walker, H. M., Severson, H. H., & Feil, E. G. (1994). *The Early Screening Project: A proven child-find process.* Longmont, CO: Sopris West.

Wolf, M. M. (1968). Social validity: The case for subjective measurement or how applied behavior analysis is finding its heart. *Journal of Applied Behavior Analysis, 11,* 203–214.

2

Proactive Approaches for Identifying and Treating Children At Risk for Academic Failure

EDWARD J. DALY III
Western Michigan University

GARY J. DUHON
Louisiana State University

JOSEPH C. WITT
Louisiana State University

Introduction

We judge it highly unlikely that starting this chapter with a recent statistic about the frequency of academic performance problems will further convince the reader of the importance of this topic. True, the statistic may provide you some comfort in knowing that other professionals are in a similar situation ("Misery loves company"). However, because decisions are made about *the* child, irrespective of whether the child is grouped or not, we will boldly pursue another tactic of introducing the chapter by looking at the individual child described as "at risk."

One might ask how this child comes to be identified as "at risk" in the first place. In the case of potential academic failure, "at riskness" is attributed to a child when someone notices that he or she persistently does not give the correct answer "on demand." A series of events occurs—something like the following: The teacher tells the class to take out their math workbooks and finish the problems on page 73. The student who is our "at-risk" candidate either fails to do all of the problems or does many of them wrong. The teacher is dissatisfied with the results and may recall similar such events (e.g., the child has never finished the math work correctly and didn't finish his science work correctly, either). If there are inappropriate behaviors (e.g., acting up in class) that correlate with poor work completion, the teacher is likely to take notice even sooner (see chapter 1 by O'Shaughnessy, Lane, Gresham, & Beebe-Frankenberger). A referral may ensue if the teacher is percep-tive and genuinely concerned about how well the student is learning. The referral is a plea of sorts that may be motivated by a desire to find out either what is wrong with the child or how someone can actually help the child learn better.

To understand what went wrong for this child, let's contrast this child's situ-ation with that of another child in the class who *is not* or *will not* be referred. This student completes all of the problems on page 73 correctly and turns them in on time. The teacher infers that the child is "learning" or "knows the material" because the request to do work led to a series of behaviors that produced the product the teacher wanted: correct answers in the workbook done in a timely fashion. If one inspects the situation more closely, one discovers that the skill they are working on in the classroom (e.g., triple-digit addition with regrouping) is a complex behavior that is made up of combinations of smaller slices of behavior (i.e., component skills, such as adding the numbers in the ones column, carrying part of the answer to the tens column, etc.).

To explain this phenomenon, Lindsley (1996) has hypothesized that students demonstrate that they have "learned" the skill when these component behaviors are coordinated in a sequence that produces a fluent response. The teacher infers learning when the math problem occasions a correct response on the part of the student; put differently, student responding comes under the control of the math problem (Vargas, 1984). Within this conceptualization, the math problem occasions a student behavior (adding in the ones column), which occasions another behavior (e.g., writing the response), which occasions yet another behavior (carrying) until the problem is finished. The teacher is primarily concerned with how well the stu-dent performs the combination behaviors all together at once and "on demand." Lindsley's (1996) perspective is useful because it points out how teacher and stu-dent behaviors can be viewed as interlocking links in a continuous chain. When a rupture occurs in this continuous chain, teacher and student behaviors are no longer functionally related in ways that allow the student to get right answers (Greer & McDonough, 1999). The teacher becomes concerned and may actually refer the child. Professionals come to view the child as at risk because they are aware of the future consequences for the child of not learning to read, do math, and perform other skills (See, e.g., Greenwood, Hart, Walker, & Risley, 1994).

Though practitioners in some settings (e.g., a large urban school district) may be dealing with high numbers of children deemed at risk for academic failure, treatment methods should lead to constructive solutions for as many individual children as possible. This does not mean that an individualized intervention is nec-essary in every case; individualized interventions probably will only be feasible in a smaller number of cases, if at all. However, solutions are necessary for each and every child if they are to receive an equal educational opportunity. The teacher faces a similar situation. He or she is responsible for teaching *every* child, regard-less of whether instruction is carried out with groups of children or not. In our example, if several children did not complete the assignment, the reasons might differ for each child. What is the same for all of the children at risk for failure is that teacher and student behaviors are no longer functionally related in productive ways.

Practitioners need methods that allow schools to meet the needs of all these children. Tradition has led them to focus on diagnosing what's wrong with the learner. This strategy is largely counterproductive. No amount of additional effort on the part of the teacher will correct the situation if those efforts do not reestablish appropriate functional links between teacher and student behavior. Englemann, Granzin, and Severson (1979) articulately express the essence of this approach when they say, "The only valid way to draw conclusions about deficiencies involves first determining the degree to which the learner's performance is controlled by instruction" (p. 362). Therefore, although the child serves as the unit of analysis for assessing outcomes, it is the learning situation (child in a classroom within a curriculum with a relationship to a particular teacher who follows a particular pattern of procedures for teaching) that should be the focus of analysis in any models that attempt to identify, prevent, and intervene with academic performance problems. In this chapter, we will pursue this topic by focusing on methods that may potentially lead to better learning environments for all children at risk for academic failure. In the development of the model described in this chapter, every effort was made to balance efficiency with a reasonable degree of certainty about what should be done next to help the learner. This is not to say that intervention using this model is easy to do. But, in the words of one astute practitioner, "Would you expect anything less for *your child?*"

A System of Early Identification and Prevention/Intervention for Academic Failure

This chapter will describe a multistep model for the identification, prevention, and intervention for academic failure. Because of problems intrinsic to traditional approaches to screening, we view it as more fruitful to determine first whether there are a large number of students who are at risk as an alternative to trying to identify particular students who are at risk. If a high number of students are at risk, the first step should be to implement one or more empirically validated models of instructional design at a systems level (i.e., at the school level or even at the district level). For reasons we will explore later, practitioner time is better spent in systems-level consultation in these circumstances. For those students who continue to have academic performance problems in these settings or in settings without a high incidence of students with academic performance problems, the next step is to use continuous measurement (e.g., formative evaluation) to improve instructional decision making. If some students' academic skills are still not improving, then practitioners should pursue specific forms of intervention assistance.

We will describe the rationale and general strategies for each step. Because other chapters in this text describe effective teaching methods (see chapter 4 by Howell & Kelley) and Direct Instruction (see chapter 5 by Edwards & Kame'enui), the primary focus of this chapter will be on the last step: what to do when additional intervention assistance is needed for academic performance. We will describe a model that has been extensively field-tested and is grounded in empirically validated practices (Witt, Daly, & Noell, 2000).

Early Identification

The first chapter of this book clearly and appropriately outlines the importance of early identification for academic and behavior problems. Traditionally, as a first step in identifying students at risk for problems, professionals have used screening practices. Quick and efficient methods are believed to provide initial information about who needs help. A common example of this approach is kindergarten language screenings. Even authoritative sources like a committee formed by the National Academic of Sciences are advocating wide-scale screenings on early literacy skills (Snow, Burns, & Griffin, 1998). One or more psychological or educational measures are administered to a large number of students to sort out who is at risk and who is apparently not at risk. A conscientious examiner carefully scrutinizes a test's manual for reliability and validity data and uses only measures that correlate highly with themselves under differing conditions (e.g., across time, across items, etc.) and with other measures of the same variables. Because it's "just a screening," however, school districts are usually willing to accept measures with less than stellar psychometric credentials.

Unfortunately, however honorable the psychologist's intentions are in selecting high-quality measures, his or her efforts may be misguided. From the point of view of the child at risk for academic failure, the psychometric properties of the *decisions* are what is crucial (Barnett, Lentz, & Macmann, 2000). A measure with acceptable reliability and validity coefficients may still lead the psychologist down the wrong path in attempts to help the child. The practice of screening to sort students, for example, leads to high error rates for reasons independent of the psychometric properties of the measures themselves. More than 40 years ago, Meehl and Rosen (1955) demonstrated that unless actuarial data (base rates) are considered, the use of psychological tests *decreases* the accuracy of prediction in most situations. This limitation to screening has still not been successfully resolved (Adelman, 1982; Barnett, Macmann, & Carey, 1992; Dawes, 1995). Furthermore, when agreements and disagreements across screening measures have been examined, higher rates of disagreements than agreements have been found (Hall & Barnett, 1991). A more appropriate focus for the practitioner is to strive to establish the reliability of any and all educational *decisions* (Barnett et al., 2000).

Although the approach to be described in this chapter relies primarily on direct measures of behavior (vs. inferred constructs on norm-referenced tests; Shapiro, 1996), these measures do not themselves overcome the intrinsic limitations of screening practices. Practitioners should beware of potential decision errors when they do large-scale screenings of students using, for example, curriculum-based measurement. The results *may* improve social validity and treatment validity when they prompt educators to improve deficits in valued and valuable skills that increase the chances of later academic and social success. The results *may* improve decision reliability when they prompt educators to determine whether the initial findings were reliable, as one would do in gathering additional data to establish a baseline of performance. Screening is still risky, however. If the child is not identified as at risk through the screening (a false negative), professionals are less likely to follow up to see how the child is doing in the classroom.

We propose that early identification should focus not on sorting students into different categories but rather on (a) identifying the base rate for academic performance problems across the student body in the local setting to decide the breadth of intervention plans and (b) examining the adequacy of the instructional practices for meeting students' needs at a level that is appropriate for the number of students who need intervention. Practitioners can accomplish the former task by referring to currently existing databases for *groups of students* on measures of academic performance (e.g., group administered, norm-referenced achievement tests) or on measures of variables that correlate with academic success or failure (e.g., socioeconomic status). Practitioners may accomplish the latter task by helping teachers to realign instructional practices with empirically validated models of instructional design.

Improving Learning by Improving the Instruction.   Several other chapters in this book deal specifically with characteristics and implementation of empirically valid instructional design models (i.e., models of effective teaching and direct instruction). For practitioners facing high base rates of children at risk for academic failure, there is no way they can hope to develop specific interventions for all of the children. A more time-efficient strategy is to work at a systems level to bring about widespread adoption of effective models of instructional design that will be implemented with all students. Because there is a high base rate for the problem in this case, it seems reasonable to assume that all students will benefit from improved teaching methods. This approach is more time-efficient because the practitioner spends less time trying to identify particular children through mass screenings (where there will be high error rates) and more time improving the overall quality of instruction in the school or district. Direct Instruction is by far the best model of instructional design for students at risk for academic failure (Edwards & Kame'enui, this text; Gersten, Woodward, & Darch, 1986; Watkins, 1998).

Improving Learning by Improving the Measurement of Learning.   When teachers measure learning carefully for instructional decision-making purposes, large achievement gains generally result. For instance, measuring and plotting academic responding is the core of Precision Teaching, a model that has been successfully applied in industry and sports as well as in education (Binder, 1996; Johnston & Layng, 1992, 1994; Lindsley, 1990). Another measurement model that has been shown to produce large achievement gains is formative evaluation. *Formative evaluation* refers to continuous progress monitoring on global indicators of basic academic skills using measures that are sensitive to instructional changes (Deno, 1986). In a meta-analysis, Fuchs and Fuchs (1986) found an average effect size of 0.70 for the use of formative evaluation by teachers and an average effect size of 1.21 when continuous progress monitoring was coupled with behavior modification strategies. In an investigation of effects on teachers, Fuchs, Fuchs, and Stecker (1989) found that when teachers used curriculum-based measurement data for instructional decision making, teachers had more specific, acceptable goals, felt less optimistic about goal attainment, relied more on objective sources of data for decision making, and made more frequent instructional modifications. Measurement models like these can actually improve achievement. The practitioner who is faced with too many students at risk for failure can help teachers set up monitoring systems and guide them in the use of objective data sources for instructional decision-making purposes as a locus of intervention.

Tools for Specific Intervention Assistance.   When individual intervention assistance is necessary, the practitioner must gather additional types of information for intervention purposes. Specifically, interviews, observations, curriculum-based measurement data, and permanent products will provide valuable information when they are integrated into a coherent, effective, and efficient model for designing interventions. The actual model and use of the tools are described in the next section.

To be useful for designing interventions, interviews should provide information about what the teacher expects the student to do, prerequisite skills that are necessary for the student to be successful, and how the teacher perceives the student as functioning (i.e., what the student actually does). Because interviews are inadequate as a sole source of data for intervention planning (Lentz & Wehmann, 1995), they should guide classroom observations and other assessment activities. To this end, interviews should give information about classroom activities an observer will see during the most problematic times, curriculum materials, and the types of instructional activities the teacher is relying on to teach the referred child. The Instructional Environment System–II (Ysseldyke & Christenson, 1993) contains thorough teacher interview questions that are linked to empirically validated dimensions of instructional planning and delivery. The information is integrated into ratings of the instructional environment. Those ratings can then be used for planning interventions. Shapiro's (1996) text on direct assessment contains interviews for academic performance problems. The interview format has lots of questions relating to how instruction is planned and organized. The interview formats that we have developed (Witt et al., 2000) are designed to be brief and provide both topographical (i.e., what instructional activities will look like during observation periods) and functional (i.e., what motivating and instructional variables are present or not present) information about the instructional environment. This information leads the evaluator to investigate specific forms of academic performance.

Direct observations of the student in the classroom are useful for assessing student behavior and instructional and classroom factors that may be affecting the student's performance. Because schools are supposed to educate children, academic responding should be the focus of observations and assessments of student performance (Daly & Murdoch, 2000). Several observation formats directly target academic engagement. The Ecobehavioral Assessment Systems Software (Greenwood, Carta, Kamps, & Delquadri, 1995) is a computer-based observational format that allows the evaluator to quantify students' academic engagement and concurrent classroom events (e.g., instructional structure). The observation format described by Shapiro (1996), the Behavioral Observation of Students in Schools (BOSS), also quantifies academic engagement and concurrent classroom conditions (e.g., teacher-directed instruction, peer behavior). Although these observation systems focus on academic responding, however, they rely primarily on time sampling data. Time sampling data do not allow the observer to identify which forms of academic responding were observed, and they are not as sensitive as rate measures of behavior. Finally, these observational systems are not tied to a conceptual model for academic intervention. The academic observation format developed for the intervention model described in this chapter is linked to functional questions that should guide the observation of student, teacher, and peer behavior. The observer is seeking answers to specific questions on factors that have been shown to affect student performance (Daly, Witt, Martens, & Dool, 1997).

The other tools necessary for intervention design are curriculum-based measures (Shinn, 1989) and permanent products. Curriculum-based measures provide high-quality information about students' proficiency with basic academic skills (oral reading, writing, math computation, and spelling), the necessary prerequisites for more complicated skills (e.g., math word problems, comprehending content area texts, etc.). Permanent products are student work products such as the completed copy of page 73 of the math workbook in the example at the beginning of the chapter. Permanent products are an easy-to-obtain and efficient source of information because teachers usually require them of students. They also can be easily modified to provide the rate of responding data, which is very desirable (Witt et al., 2000). For example, if a child's problem is that she is not writing sufficiently, journal entry time can be standardized to be the same amount each day (e.g., 20 minutes), and student entries can be quantified as number of correctly spelled words, total number of words, number of letters written, or some other feature of writing. Permanent product information is especially important as an alternate source of information if the student is found *not* to have a problem with the basic skills assessed with curriculum-based measures. Furthermore, if the target of intervention outcomes is permanent products, an independent observer is not necessary for continuous progress-monitoring purposes.

Prevention and Intervention

The remainder of this chapter will describe a functional assessment model for academic performance problems (Witt et al., 2000). The first step, Problem Validation, is conducted to determine how severe the problem is and what type of problem it is. Interview information, classroom observations, and student, classwide, and individual probes of basic academic skills are gathered during this part of the process. Included in the individual probes as a part of the problem validation phase is an assessment to determine whether it is a "can't do" or "won't do" problem. The whole process can be conducted in less than 2 hours. If the problem is validated but the strong intervention strategies did not lead to a successful resolution of the problem, a more comprehensive assessment is done as a part of the model.

An overview of how to conduct more comprehensive functional assessments of academic problems is described.

Problem Validation.   In attempting to design and implement treatments for at-risk students, it must first be determined where along the continuous chain of teacher and student behaviors the rupture exists. Does the rupture lie with teacher behaviors (which would affect the entire class) or with individual student behavior? If with student behaviors, what is the depth of the problem? Is there a lack of skill on the part of the student, or is motivation the primary reason for substandard performance? Problem validation procedures are screening devices that attempt to identify these ruptures by answering several questions (see Box 2.1). These questions focus on determining where problems lie and whether they warrant further

---

B O X **2.1**

Problem Validation: Questions Answered and Expected Results

Is There a Problem?
Does the referred child stick out like a sore thumb? If it is a problem limited to the child who was referred, does he or she rank at or near the bottom of the class? If not, this is a good indication that this may not be a child with a potential disability. Don't waste time with testing designed for *classification.*

What Type of Problem Is It?
Individual child problem. If only one child in the class has a problem, then is it a:

> **Skill deficit?** Child can't do work and needs instruction.

> **Performance deficit?** Child can do work but needs motivation.

Classwide problem. Other children in the class are also having problems, and it may be better to address them as a group instead of an individual referral of one after another.

What Can Be Done *Quickly* about the Problem?
Intervention is linked to can't do and won't do. A short-term intervention is put into place with the teacher, and the results are monitored for at least 5 days.

What Results Can Be Expected from Problem Validation?
> *Faster services.* The can't do/won't do intervention is put in place the first day.

> *Decrease in referrals.* The accuracy of referrals is increased.

> *Increase in equity and fairness of referrals.* Overreferral of any one ethnic group is less likely if referral is based on bias or lack of tolerance.

> *Improved school achievement.* Since groups of low-achieving students can be quickly targeted, they can be assisted more effectively and efficiently.

consideration, whether the problem is specific to the child or common to the class, and whether the problem can be improved quickly through brief intervention (Witt et al., 2000). This problem validation process consists of three phases that assess performance, analyze the information obtained, and use this analysis to identify an effective treatment for problem areas. These three phases are, respectively, academic assessment, problem identification, and treatment development.

The first step in problem validation is to complete an academic assessment. This assessment consists of a teacher interview, classwide probes, and an individual child assessment. The teacher interview is designed to identify the reason for the referral, identify curriculum materials used to complete the academic assessment, and familiarize the teacher with the process to be undertaken.

Classwide probes are then administered to assess the academic performance of the target student and compare that to peer performance. Curriculum-based grade-level probes in math, reading, and writing are administered to the entire class in order to determine the target student's specific level of performance. Completed in the regular classroom setting, these probes are consistent with typical teacher-directed routines. The math probe is a 2-minute exercise constructed from the recently completed math curriculum and scored for digits correct. The writing probe consists of a 3-minute free-writing task completed from a teacher-derived story starter and scored for words written correctly. Reading assessment involves identifying grade-level reading passages from the current reading text and administering a 1-minute reading probe to the target student and two peers identified by the teacher as having similar reading skills. The reading probes are scored for words read correctly and are only administered to three students due to the amount of time and resources needed to conduct 1-minute probes on an entire classroom. Upon completion of the classwide probes, they are scored appropriately, and all scores are placed in rank order.

The final step in the academic assessment is an individual assessment. This phase of problem validation is conducted to determine whether the use of incentives for improved performance has a positive effect on student performance when compared to the student's classwide assessment scores. In this phase, the target student is asked to complete a similar version of each academic probe completed during the classwide assessment. Through the use of performance goals identical to that of the classwide assessment scores, the student will be rewarded if this performance goal is exceeded during the individual assessment. The probes are administered and scored in the same manner as in the classwide assessment and are also compared to the scores from the classwide assessment. Finally, the individual assessment scores are placed in the rank order for analysis during the problem identification phase.

The problem is identified based on a multistep process that attempts to answer several questions. The first question to be answered attempts to determine whether the problems warrant further consideration and, if so, in what area or areas do these problems exist. This can be accomplished by comparing the target student's scores from the academic assessment to two reference groups: peers within the same class and national standards. Because the data obtained through this assessment are similar to standard curriculum-based probes, the results can be compared to "normative" standards for such probes by noting, for example, whether the child's performance is in the frustrational range, instructional range, or mastery range for a particular grade level. A problem may warrant further consideration if the target student's performance, when compared to national standards, would be considered "at risk." However, if other children in the classroom are also at risk, then this may suggest looking more closely at classroom or even schoolwide instructional variables. This possibility is addressed next.

The second question focuses on determining whether the problem is specific to the student referred or whether poor academic performance is a classwide problem. For each subject area previously identified as a problem for the referred student, the rank order should be reviewed. If the target student's rank from the academic assessment is above the 1st quartile for any subject determined to be a problem, and other members of the class are "at risk" based on national standards, then that academic subject area might be better approached as a classwide problem. The rationale behind this decision is simply that if more than one-quarter of the class performs in an "at-risk" range by national standards, then some type of academic problem exists with a large enough proportion of the class to warrant a group approach in designing an intervention rather than several individual interventions.

In the typical case, an individual child with an academic problem will be identified. Two possible reasons account for a student not performing adequately in a subject area. These reasons focus on either a lack of ability to perform the task at hand or a lack of motivation. Often these are referred to, respectively, as *skill deficits* and *performance deficits*. These deficits can be identified by comparing the student's performance from the academic assessment to that of the individual assessment. Because incentives are used in the individual assessment, if performance in the individual assessment is considerably higher than that of the academic assessment, a performance deficit is present. A student is considered to have a marked jump in performance between the two occasions when the score from the individual assessment increases to such an extent that it would not be considered a problem if compared to normative standards. If there is no difference or just a minor difference in performance in the two settings, a skill deficit is presumed to be present.

In developing treatments for performance or skill deficits, a general model should be followed. Performance deficits indicate that the ability to perform the task is present, but motivation is lacking. Treatments for performance deficits should focus on increasing motivation to engage in the task through rewards or incentives. Skill deficits, on the other hand, refer to a situation in which a skill or part of a skill is missing from the student's repertoire. In this case the skill or component skill must be taught to the student. Specific intervention strategies can be found in Witt et al. (2000).

Next Steps When the Problem Is Not Resolved.   This phase of the assessment and intervention process is necessary when the intervention developed as a result of problem validation is either not effective or effective but too difficult to be carried out with the resources that are available. The purpose of this phase of assessment is to generate information that should lead to solutions tailored to the needs and circumstances of the referred student.

There are two parts to this step of the intervention process: direct observations and brief tests of treatments. The observation format outlined in Witt et al. (2000) is tied to explicit questions about how well instruction is being delivered to the referred child. If you would like more direct information about the potential effects of an intervention, you can briefly test various treatment strategies. To do so, it is necessary to set up several conditions and administer them to the child. The first test condition is generally a "baseline" or control condition in which student responding is measured but no assistance or intervention is provided. Subsequent test conditions include intervention components. The effects of each condition are compared with baseline and prior test conditions.

To carry out this type of analysis, it is necessary to (a) select intervention components to be tested, (b) structure the conditions in a way that allows one to draw conclusions about the effectiveness of potential treatment components based on the results of the test conditions (evaluation design), and (c) reliably measure results. The first step of selecting intervention components is easier if they are tied to a conceptual model. For example, the conceptual model we have described elsewhere (Daly et al., 1997) has been used as a rationale for how treatments have been chosen in several investigations (Daly, Martens, Dool, & Hintze, 1998; Daly, Martens, Hamler, Dool, & Eckert, 1999). A format for prioritizing intervention components and how to structure the conditions is described in Witt et al. (2000). Some examples include rewards, choice, modeling, practice, and performance feedback. These analyses borrow single-case experimental design elements to allow the evaluator to arrive at conclusions regarding treatment effectiveness (Martens, Eckert, Bradley, & Ardoin, 1999). Finally, because many referred children have deficits in basic academic skills, curriculum-based measures have proven useful for gathering assessment data, although carefully standardized work products can be used as well.

Case Example Demonstrating the Use of Brief Analyses for Generating an Intervention

Fred was a fifth-grade student referred for reading difficulties. The results of a brief experimental analysis of treatment components for Fred are reported in detail in Daly et al. (1998), they will be summarized here. In addition, progress-monitoring data were collected while an intervention was administered regularly to Fred. The procedures and outcomes will also be described to illustrate the process of linking brief functional analyses to treatment selection and formative evaluation. Fred's reading fluency was monitored in the fifth-grade basal reader in which he was being instructed. For each assessment, three randomly chosen passages were administered. The median number of correctly read words (CRW) and errors per minute were calculated. Baseline data are displayed in Figure 2.1. Fred was reading at a median rate of 49 CRW/minute with 7 errors. The trend was stable and nonincreasing. There was, however, a lot of variability in the data (range, 33 CRW/minute to 64 CRW/minute).

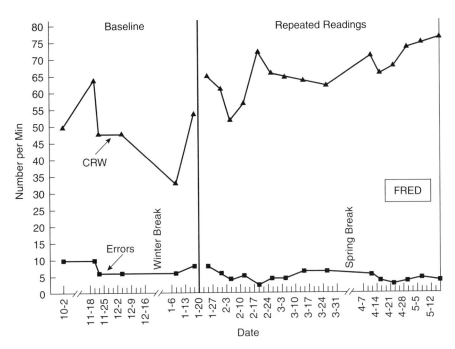

FIGURE 2.1   Number of correctly read words per minute for Fred

A brief functional analysis was conducted while baseline data were collected. A visual display of the results appears in Daly et al. (1998). Five test conditions were administered, and a minireversal was conducted to replicate the results. The minireversal consisted of a return to baseline and a readministration of the selected intervention. Different stories were used for each condition in a reading series that was different from that used for classroom instruction and progress monitoring. Outcomes were measured in both instructional and generalization passages immediately following administration of the condition. The test conditions consisted of baseline (B), contingent reward (CR), repeated readings (RR), listening passage preview plus phrase drill (LPP/PD), and listening passage preview plus phrase drill and repeated readings (LPP/PD/RR). B was an assessment-only condition. In RR, Fred read the instructional passages aloud four times. In the CR condition, Fred could earn a reward for reading the *generalization* passage at a criterion rate of 100 CRW/minute. No further assistance was provided. In the LPP/PD condition, the examiner first read the passage to Fred. Fred then read the passage once while the examiner marked errors on the examiner copy of the story. Next, the examiner read the error words to Fred and had Fred repeatedly read all phrases containing error words three times. The LPP/PD/RR condition was similar to the LPP/PD condition with the exception that Fred read the passage aloud four times after the LPP procedure and before the error correction procedure.

In the baseline condition, Fred read 42 CRW/minute in the instructional passage and 50 CRW/minute in the generalization passage. His performance improved only slightly in the CR condition. He read 35 CRW/minute in the instructional passage and 61 CRW/minute in the generalization passage. Fred's performance improved more dramatically in the RR condition. He read 93 CRW/minute in the instructional passage and 86 CRW/minute in the generalization passage. The improvement in the generalization passage is noteworthy because the treatment was *not* applied in this passage. The following treatment conditions did not improve his performance beyond the effects obtained by the RR condition. Indeed, his performance dropped in the following condition—LPP/PD. He read 73 CRW/minute in the instructional passage and 56 CRW/minute in the generalization passage. Interestingly, this condition provided fewer opportunities to respond than the RR condition. Fred read the passage fewer times. Fred's performance improved again in the LPP/PD/RR condition. He read 97 CRW/minute in the instructional passage and 75 CRW/minute in the generalization passage.

Because the addition of LPP/PD to the RR condition did not lead to an incremental improvement in Fred's performance, RR was chosen as the easiest intervention (i.e., requiring the least amount of adult supervision) that produced the greatest improvement in his performance. The minireversal replicated the results of prior conditions. Fred's performance in the baseline condition was 32 CRW/minute in the instructional passage and 36 CRW/minute in the generalization passage. His performance in the RR condition during the minireversal was 59 CRW/minute in the instructional passage and 66 CRW/min in the generalization passages. Effects were not of the magnitude of the prior administration of this condition. However, his performance in the generalization passage was higher than any prior condition that did *not* contain an RR component.

The results of the brief analysis suggested that RR was a promising instructional intervention for improving Fred's reading fluency. An instructional aide was trained in the administration of RR and conducted reading sessions at least twice a week with Fred for half-hour periods while Fred's reading fluency was monitored continuously by the consultant. The results are displayed in Figure 2.1. There is a steady increasing trend in Fred's performance over a 4-month period. Very few of the data points fall below the highest baseline data point. By the end of the intervention period, Fred was reading at a rate greater than 70 CRW/minute. All three of the last data points are above 70 CRW/minute (73, 74, and 76 CRW/minute). His error rate had dropped to four or fewer errors per min. Peer normative data had been gathered in the spring in the school that Fred attended. The results of the peer norms indicated that the average student in fifth grade was reading at a rate of 78 CRW/minute in fifth-grade materials with four errors. Fred's reading fluency in fifth-grade materials was at a level commensurate with that of his average peers.

This case illustrates one way in which an academic intervention can be empirically derived and how outcomes can be monitored across time. In Fred's case, a rather simple instructional strategy was indicated by the brief analysis. Because an experimental design that permitted experimental control (e.g., a multiple baseline design across students) was not used, one cannot conclude that the outcomes are attributable to the intervention only. Nevertheless, the A/B design used for monitoring outcomes across time is more suitable to practitioners for demonstrating accountability.

Summary

The key to increasing achievement for students at risk for academic failure is improving the decision making of educators responsible for these children. Educators must reevaluate the utility of common assessment practices and adopt models that can be shown to meet students' needs at both the group and the individual levels. The first step is to identify the appropriate breadth of intervention efforts. When educators practice in settings with large numbers of students who are at risk for academic failure, systems-level adoption of effective instructional models and student monitoring are the best first step. While avoiding problems with error-prone assessment practices, these actions will alleviate many academic difficulties and unnecessary referrals for special education.

When educators practice in settings with low numbers of students who are at risk, or when the systems-level intervention(s) are not working, more careful analysis and child-specific forms of intervention assistance are necessary. This chapter briefly outlined a model for this level of prevention and intervention. The model draws on current assessment and evaluation methods and is designed to narrow intervention efforts quickly and efficiently with follow-up procedures for when further problem solving is required. In many cases, a functional intervention plan (i.e., one based on probable reasons for academic deficits) can be put in place within hours of the beginning of the assessment process. In some cases, it may take more time. The prior assessment information, however, is useful for individualizing the intervention procedures.

REFERENCES

Adelman, H. S. (1982). Identifying learning problems at an early age: A critical appraisal. *Journal of Clinical Child Psychology, 11*, 255–261.

Barnett, D. W., Lentz, F. E., Jr., & Macmann, G. (2000). Psychometric qualities of professional practice. In E. S. Shapiro & T. R. Kratochwill (Eds.), *Behavioral Assessment in Schools: Theory, Research, and Clinical Foundations* (2nd ed., pp. 355–386). New York: Guilford.

Barnett, D. W., Macmann, G. M., & Carey, K. T. (1992). Early intervention and the assessment of developmental skills: Challenges and directions. *Topics in Early Childhood Special Education, 12*, 21–43.

Binder, C. (1996). Behavioral fluency: Evolution of a new paradigm. *The Behavior Analyst, 19*, 163–197.

Daly, E. J., III, Martens, B. K., Dool, E. J., & Hintze, J. M. (1998). Using brief functional analysis to select interventions for oral reading. *Journal of Behavioral Education, 8*, 203–218.

Daly, E. J., III, Martens, B. K., Hamler, K. R., Dool, E. J., & Eckert, T. L. (1999). A brief experimental analysis for identifying instructional components needed to improve oral reading fluency. *Journal of Applied Behavior Analysis, 32*, 83–94.

Daly, E. J., III, & Murdoch, A. (2000). Direct observation in the assessment of academic skills problems. In E. S. Shapiro & T. R. Kratochwill (Eds.), *Behavioral assessment in schools: Theory, research, and clinical foundations* (2nd ed., pp. 46–77). New York: Guilford.

Daly, E. J., III, Witt, J. C., Martens, B. K., & Dool, E. J. (1997). A model for conducting a functional analysis of academic performance problems. *School Psychology Review, 26*, 554–574.

Dawes, R. M. (1995). Standards of practice. In S. C. Hayes, V. M. Follette, R. M. Dawes, & K. E. Grady (Eds.), *Scientific Standards of Psychological Practice: Issues and Recommendations* (pp. 49–66). Reno, NV: Context.

Deno, S. L. (1986). Formative evaluation of individual student programs: A new role for school psychologists. *School Psychology Review, 15*, 358–374.

Englemann, S., Granzin, A., & Severson, H. (1979). Diagnosing instruction. *Journal of Special Education, 13*, 355–363.

Fuchs, L. S., & Fuchs, D. (1986). Curriculum-based assessment of progress toward long-term and short-term goals. *Journal of Special Education, 20,* 69–82.

Fuchs, L. S., Fuchs, D., & Stecker, P. M. (1989). Effects of curriculum-based measurement on teachers' instructional planning. *Journal of Learning Disabilities, 22,* 51–59.

Gersten, R., Woodward, J., & Darch, C. (1986). Direct-instruction: A research-based approach to curriculum design and teaching. *Exceptional Children, 53,* 17–31.

Greenwood, C. R., Carta, J. J., Kamps, D. M., & Delquadri, J. (1995). *Ecobehavioral assessment systems software: Technical manual and software.* Kansas City: Juniper Gardens Children's Project, University of Kansas.

Greenwood, C. R., Hart, B., Walker, D., & Risley, T. (1994). The opportunity to respond and academic performance revisited: A behavioral theory of developmental retardation and its prevention. In R. Gardner III, D. M. Sainato, J. O. Cooper, T. E. Heron, W. L. Heward, J. W. Eshleman, & T. A. Grossi (Eds.), *Behavior Analysis in Education: Focus on Measurably Superior Instruction* (pp. 213–224). Pacific Grove, CA: Brooks/Cole.

Greer, R. D., & McDonough, S. H. (1999). Is the learn unit a fundamental measure of pedagogy? *The Behavior Analyst, 22,* 5–16.

Hall, J. D., & Barnett, D. W. (1991). Classification of risk status in preschool screening: A comparison of alternative measures. *Journal of Psychoeducational Assessment, 9,* 152–159.

Johnson, K. R., & Layng, T. V. J. (1992). Breaking the structuralist barrier: Literacy and numeracy with fluency. *American Psychologist, 47,* 1475–1490.

Johnson, K. R., & Layng, T. V. J. (1994). The Morningside model of generative instruction. In R. Gardner III, D. M. Sainato, J. O. Cooper, T. E. Heron, W. L. Heward, J. W. Eshleman, & T. A. Grossi (Eds.), *Behavior Analysis in Education: Focus on Measurably Superior Intruction* (pp. 173–198). Pacific Grove, CA: Brooks/Cole.

Lentz, F. E., Jr., & Wehmann, B. A. (1995). Interviewing. In A. Thomas & J. Grimes (Eds.), *Best Practices in School Psychology III* (pp. 637–650). Washington, DC: National Association of School Psychologists.

Lindsley, O. R. (1990). Precision teaching: By teachers for children. *Teaching Exceptional Children, 22,* 10–15.

Lindsley, O. R. (1996). Is fluency free-operant response-response chaining? *The Behavior Analyst, 19,* 211–224.

Martens, B. K., Eckert, T. L., Bradley, T. A., & Ardoin, S. P. (1999). Identifying effective treatments from a brief experimental analysis: Using single-case design elements to aid decision making. *School Psychology Quarterly, 14*(2), 163–181.

Meehl, P., & Rosen, A. (1955). Antecedent probability and the efficiency of psychometric signs, patterns, and cutting scores. *Psychological Bulletin, 52,* 194–216.

Shapiro, E. S. (1996). *Academic Skills Problems: Direct Assessment and Intervention* (2nd ed.). New York: Guilford.

Shinn, M. R. (1989). *Curriculum-Based Measurement: Assessing Special Children.* New York: Guilford.

Snow, C., Burns, S., & Griffin, P. (1998). *Preventing Reading Difficulties in Young Children.* Washington, DC: National Research Council.

Vargas, J. S. (1984). What are your exercises teaching? An analysis of stimulus control in instructional materials. In W. L. Heward, T. E. Heron, D. S. Hill, & J. Trap-Porter (Eds.), *Focus on Behavior Analysis in Education* (pp. 126–141). Columbus, OH: Merrill.

Watkins, C. (1998). Results of district-wide implementation of direct instruction in an urban school district. In C. Donley (Chair), *Effective Educational Strategies in America's Schools.* Symposium presented at the annual international convention of the Association for Behavior Analysis, Orlando, FL.

Witt, J. C., Daly, E. J., III, & Noell, G. H. (2000). *Functional Assessments: A Step-by-Step Guide to Solving Academic and Behavior Problems.* Longmont, CO: Sopris West.

Ysseldyke, J., & Christenson, S. (1993). *The Instructional Environment System–II.* Longmont, CO: Sopris West.

Author Note

The authors wish to thank Sandra Chafouleas and James Carr for their helpful comments on an earlier version of the manuscript. They also would like to thank Eric J. Dool for contributing the results of this case study to the chapter and his assistance with the preparation of Figure 2.1.

3

Proactive Approaches for Identifying Children At Risk for Sociobehavioral Problems

HERBERT H. SEVERSON
Oregon Research Institute
Eugene, Oregon

HILL M. WALKER
University of Oregon

Introduction

The importance of screening to accomplish early detection is well established in the medical literature, which has persistently called for sensitive, accurate screening tests leading to early treatment. According to the American Cancer Society (ACS), screening and early detection of cancers saves untold lives annually in the United States (ACS, 1999). Medical experts believe a reservoir of undetected disease could be eliminated through aggressive screening and intervention (Kaplan, 2000). In much the same model, mental health screening can reduce the need for intensive treatment and improve prognosis.

Many assume that disease is binary; that is, you either have it or you do not. However, most diseases involve linear or developmental processes and likely have begun long before they are diagnosed. For example, young adults who suffer from cardiovascular disease have fatty streaks in their coronary arteries at an early age, which indicates the onset of coronary disease (Strong, Greene, Hoppe, Johnston, & Olesen, 1999). Similarly, screening and early detection can help save the lives of young people who are at high risk for developing serious behavioral and emotional disorders that will decrease their quality of life. This diagnostic pathway of early screening, which leads to early intervention, can have a significant impact on increasing the likely success of the individual in dealing with the demands of peer, parental, school, and community contexts.

It is increasingly clear that sociobehavioral factors are evident in the lives of young children that are highly predictive of continued school and social adjustment problems, and subsequent serious emotional and behavioral problems. Ironically, although we know more and more about the factors that are predictive of later serious emotional and behavioral problems, and although we increasingly can provide accurate measurement of these factors at earlier ages, the number of children screened, identified, and intervened with at early ages remains relatively static. It is indeed ironic that teachers consistently rank children with severe behavior disorders (BDs) as one of their highest service priorities, but prevalence studies indicate a serious underserving of this population of students (Bullis & Walker, 1994). There are a number of likely reasons for this consistent underidentification of behavior-disordered children. These include the stigmatizing nature of the Seriously Emotionally Disturbed (SED) label, problems with the federal definition of SED, and the resulting subjectivity involved in certifying whether someone meets its eligibility criteria, concerns about the costs of specialized services that might be required of students who are identified as SED, and administrative concerns involved in overidentification without being able to provide adequate services for these children. Kauffman (1999) has provided an insightful analysis of how the field of education actually "prevents prevention" of serious behavioral and emotional disorders of at-risk children through well-meaning efforts to "protect" them from such factors as labeling and stigmatization.

The past 25 years has experienced a sustained and productive surge of research on conduct disorder and antisocial behavior problems (see Loeber & Farrington, 1998; Patterson, Reid, & Dishion, 1992). It is probably fair to say that we now know more about this cluster of problems and disorders than any other set of behavioral problems affecting youngsters (Reid, 1993). An increasing number of longitudinal studies have identified sets of powerful antecedents that are predictive of later serious conduct problems. These antecedents are related in a life course trajectory to conduct disorders, and their presence is often clearly evident well before school entry.

Children and adolescents who demonstrate aggressive and noncompliant patterns of behavior are at high risk for developing persisting psychiatric, academic, and social impairments (Graham, Rutter, & George, 1973; Reid, 1993; Robins, 1978). The most common reason young children are referred for services is for the display of behaviors that are symptomatic of conduct disorders. A failure or inability to comply with school rules is often cited as the leading cause for at-risk children and youth falling behind their age groups in school and facing rejection by their peers in school settings (Walker, Colvin, & Ramsey, 1995).

Most current systems for identifying and serving SED children are primarily reactive in nature. That is, the process waits for children to be referred after their problems arise rather than being "proactive" in seeking out potential problems prior to their becoming severe in nature. The purposes of this chapter are to provide an overview of early screening and identification procedures that are proactive in nature and to describe a means for the early detection and prevention of the continued escalation of these problem behaviors. Early detection implies that a problem will be recognized before it becomes a matter for referral. This is particularly critical since it is estimated that only 20% of children who need services for emotional disorders actually receive them (Institute of Medicine [IOM], 1994; Offord, 1987). Furthermore, Duncan, Forness, and Hartsough (1995) report that, in general, five or more years pass between the early display of problematic behaviors and recognition by the school system that services are needed. That is, while many children exhibit high-risk behaviors of an emotional and social nature at age 6, the median age for these children to receive services is typically 11 or 12. Duncan and colleagues conclude that the continued emphasis on treatment and remediation over prevention and early intervention demonstrates a lack of appreciation regarding the progressive nature of many social and emotional problems.

Early Identification

Children who have not learned to achieve their social goals other than via coercive behavioral strategies by about the third grade are likely to continue displaying some degree of antisocial behavior throughout their lives (Bullis & Walker, 1994; Kazdin, 1987; Loeber & Farrington, 1998). The longer such children go without access to effective intervention(s), the more likely it is these problems will escalate in intensity and develop into more serious problems. It is not unusual for children who display early antisocial behavior patterns also to subsequently experience reading difficulties, depression, anxiety, and other adjustment problems (e.g., Hinshaw, 1992). It is highly recommended that the proactive screening of young children at risk for emotional and behavioral problems take place in preschool, kindergarten, or early elementary grades to assure ongoing identification of high-risk students needing access to intervention services and support.

Research indicates that children with emotional and behavioral problems can be identified as early as 3 years of age (e.g., Kazdin, 1987; Patterson et al., 1992). Unfortunately, early screening programs for behavioral and emotional difficulties are very rare. Consequently, too many children arrive in school unable to interact in a positive way with either their peers or teachers and to cope with the necessary demands of schooling.

Students arriving in school have to make two major adjustments: (a) responding to the expectations of peers, learning how to make friends and get along with others in a new setting, and (b) adjusting to the expectations and demands of teachers. Failure in either of these adjustment areas can lead to school failure, peer rejection, and/or development of problematic behavior patterns (Walker, Colvin, et al., 1995). These outcomes, in turn, are predictive of serious problems such as school dropout and later delinquency (Loeber & Farrington, 1998). Instruments and procedures to be described herein can be used to identify young children who are at risk for these emotional, behavioral, and academic difficulties.

The regular classroom teacher still represents the primary link between students who exhibit problematic behavior and their access to appropriate, school-based services (see chapter 1 by O'Shaughnessy, Lane, Gresham, & Beebe-Frankenberger). Teachers are an underutilized resource with the potential to assist appropriately in the evaluation and referral of at-risk students for specialized services. Analysis of existing school practices indicate that students whose behavior problems are externalizing in nature (i.e., exhibiting noncompliant, aggressive, or disruptive behavior and/or teacher defiance) have the highest probability of referral (Grosenick, 1981; Noel, 1982). Students with internalizing problems (depression, social isolation, avoidance, and school phobia) are rarely referred by teachers for their behavioral problems even though such students are at risk for serious long-term development of social and emotional problems (Horne & Packard, 1985; Parker & Asher, 1987; Robins, 1966). Evidence also indicates that externalizing students with moderate to severe degrees of adjustment impairment are also infrequently referred by their teachers (Walker et al., 1988). Unfortunately, students at risk for serious behavior problems, of both an externalizing and internalizing nature, will continue to be substantially underidentified and underserved as long as we rely *only* on idiosyncratic teacher referrals alone to initiate the referral process.

Alternatives have been proposed that would institute universal, systematic screening of all students in elementary school settings with respect to both internalizing and externalizing forms of problematic behavior. Screening systems exist that can accomplish this task with relative precision at both the preschool and elementary levels (Walker & Severson, 1990; Walker, Severson, & Feil, 1995). However, as noted, such systems are conspicuous by their absence within current school-based service delivery practices. Some authors have suggested that teacher judgments of child behavior and performance can provide the strongest empirical database for making screening decisions for behavior disorders (Gerber & Semmel, 1984; Greenwood, Walker, Todd, & Hops, 1979; Gresham, 1986). Gerber and Semmel (1984) argue, for example, that the classroom teacher is the best, most knowledgeable, and most accurate judge of whether a pupil can benefit from instruction in the regular classroom. In a notably radical departure from common practice, they suggest that traditional psychometric procedures should be validated against teacher judgment. Forness and Kavale (1996) similarly have advocated for a more instrumental role of the classroom teacher in the screening and identification of school-age, behavior-disordered children and youth.

Walker and Severson (1990) have provided a systematic method for using teacher judgment in a multiple-gating system to provide for the screening of all students for behavior disorders in the elementary grades. When teacher judgments are structured and solicited in the right context, they can be highly accurate and extremely useful. Jackson, Reed, Patterson, Schaughency, and Ray (1990) found that classroom teachers, when using a structured teacher rating form, were more accurate compared to both mothers' and fathers' Child Behavior Checklist (CBCL) externalizing scores in predicting a boy's arrest frequencies in early adolescence. In an important recently reported study, Loeber and his colleagues found that teacher appraisals of child behavior were more accurate than those of either parents or peers (Loeber, Green, Lahey, Frick, & McBurnett, 2000).

We believe that a careful structuring of regular teacher's appraisal of *all* students in a classroom setting via teacher nomination and rank-ordering procedures, referenced to objective behavioral criteria that define at-risk status, can yield significant improvements in naturally occurring teacher referral practices. These improvements can be achieved through the adoption of more objective definitional criteria for school behavior disorders via a structured, multiple-gating process for initial screening and assessment of behaviorally at-risk students. The use of multiple-gating procedures can substantially improve both the precision and cost-effectiveness of screening processes (see Loeber, Dishion, & Patterson, 1984; Walker, Hops, & Greenwood, 1984; Walker & Severson, 1990).

Students who experience externalizing behavior problems early in their school careers are at serious risk for a host of long-term adjustment problems, including school dropout, delinquency, and adjustment disorders in adulthood (Kazdin, 1987; Loeber & Farrington, 1998). Pupils with internalizing behavior problems early in their school careers are similarly at serious risk for school and peer adjustment problems, which include academic underachievement and peer neglect or rejection (Hops, Finch, & McConnell, 1985). Horne and Packard (1985) found that early learning problems during the elementary school years were best predicted by attention distractibility, internalizing behavior problems, and language variables (Horne & Packard, 1985).

Externalizing symptoms are regarded by many as the single best predictor of risk status for future conduct disorder and antisocial behavior (Loeber, 1991; Lynam, 1996; Moffitt, 1993; Patterson, 1993; Yoshikawa, 1994). It has been suggested that even in nonclinic populations of children as young as 4 and 5 years, 50% or more of those with troublesome, externalizing symptoms will later develop persistent conduct problems (Campbell, 1995; Coie, 1996; Reid, 1993; Reid & Patterson, 1991). Since externalizing behavior problems in childhood are associated with increased risk for multiple, serious negative health and psychosocial outcomes in adolescence and adulthood (Bennett, Lipman, Brown, Racine, Boyle, & Offord 1999), and given the increasing evidence for the effectiveness of preventive interventions (Kazdin, 1987; Offord, 1987), there is a strong need for accurate, cost-effective methods of identifying children at an early age who meet this high-risk profile.

Using targeted interventions that focus on high-risk children and youth is an approach to early intervention that offers substantial advantages (IOM, 1994; Tolan, Gucera, & Kendall, 1995). Targeted interventions, for example, have the potential to increase coverage and population impact. When compared to universal programs, this approach is more efficient because only children in need receive the intervention. However, the success of targeted interventions depends heavily on having an accurate method of identifying children exhibiting high-risk behaviors. When such children are correctly classified, the impact of the intervention is enhanced. False-negative classification errors deny children the opportunity to receive the intervention that may benefit them. False-positive errors result in wasted resources, expose children to unnecessary programs, and risk the negative effects of labeling (McConaughy, 1993).

Specificity and Accuracy in Screening Instruments

When considering the use of a screening instrument or approach, it is important to address the concepts of specificity and accuracy. Essentially, the issue is whether the level of predictive accuracy is sufficiently high to justify use of the screening measures involved (Bennett et al., 1999). Table 3.1 shows the five key dimensions that are relevant to assessing predictive accuracy. *Sensitivity* is the proportion of individuals with the outcome (e.g., conduct problems) in whom the risk indicator (e.g., externalizing behavior symptoms) was present and equals a/a + c. *Specificity* is the proportion of individuals without the outcome in whom the risk indicator was not present and equals d/b + d. *Positive predictive value* (PPV) is the proportion of those classified as high risk who develop the outcome and equals a/a + b. *Negative predictive value* is the proportion of those classified as low risk who do not develop the outcome and equals d/c + d. The *prevalence* of the outcome being predicted equals a + c/a + b + c + d and provides the "prior probability" of outcome before a risk assessment method is applied. The overall *accuracy* of a risk assessment method is the proportion of individuals correctly classified and equals *a + d/a + b + c + d.*

Some authors have cautioned against the use of a categorical approach to classify children that is dependent on a single risk status measure (Bennett et al., 1999). While high- and low-risk groups can be defined using a single criterion, the use of multiple measures in decision making is highly recommended.

Bennett et al. (1999) systematically reviewed 13 studies that provided the necessary data to assess sensitivity and specificity and concluded that PPV was less than 50% under low prevalence conditions. They argued that dependence on a sin-

TABLE 3.1   Predictive Accuracy, Sensitivity Specificity, and Predictive Value Using Risk Indicators to Predict Outcomes

		Outcome	
		Present	Absent
Risk indicator	Present	a	b
	Absent	c	c

Sensitivity = a/a + c; specificty = d/b + d; positive predictive value = a/a + b; negative predictive value = d/c + d; prevalence = a + c/a + b + c + d; accuracy = a + d/a + b + c + d.

Source: Figure 1 (p. 471) on predictive accuracy, sensitivity, specificity, and predictive value using risk indicators to collect predicted outcomes from Bennett, Lippman, Brown, Racine, Boyle, & Offort (1999). Predicting conduct problems: Can high-risk children be identified in kindergarten and grade 1? *Journal of Consulting and Clinical Psychology, 1999, 67,* 470–480. Copyright © 1999 by the American Psychological Association. Reprinted with permission.

gle criterion, such as a measure of externalizing behaviors, resulted in low PPV and that multiple measures could significantly enhance the accuracy of the screening process. They suggest combining child and familial risk factors to increase the sensitivity and PPV of screening measures. For example, a relatively simple prediction rule—composed of teacher-identified oppositional defiant disorder (ODD) and attention deficit/hyperactivity disorder (ADHD) symptoms, gender, and family income—would require only a minimal input from parents and yet provide levels of sensitivity and PPV close to the criterion of 50% for outcomes 30 months later. While additional predictive accuracy can be achieved by collecting other data (e.g., parental depression), the cost of collecting this information may exceed its potential benefit.

Bennett et al. (1999) evaluated the accuracy of using a logistic regression approach of predicting conduct problems 30 months later in a nonclinic population of kindergarten children. They concluded that stability of externalizing behavior disorders did exist, but significant levels of misclassification could occur when "externalizing behavior disorder" was used to designate high-risk status under low-prevalence conditions in normal populations. They cite Loeber's multiple-gating model as an excellent way to improve sensitivity and specificity when compared to the use of teacher reports only (see Loeber et al., 1984).

Alternative approaches may provide a more valid approach and offer partial solutions to the problems described here. Multiple gating has proven to be an effective procedure for increasing the predictive accuracy of identifying children and youth at high risk for subsequent serious behavior disorders. Loeber and colleagues (1984) describe the use of a three-gate system in which the presence of externalizing symptoms at gate 1, based on teacher reports, and parent reports for screening gate 2 applied only to a subgroup of children who met gate 1 criteria of externalizing symptoms. A subsequent third gate further increased the predictive accuracy of identifying high-risk children who subsequently demonstrated delinquency risk in follow-up.

Multiple gating is a procedure that contains a series of progressively more extensive and precise assessments (i.e., gates) that (a) provide for the sequential assessment and cross-validation of multimethod forms of child assessment and (b) establish a decision-making structure for using information produced from different assessment sources. It appears that there is now a climate for adoption of such a model, given the widespread dissatisfaction with current BD assessment practices.

Description of the SSBD

The Systematic Screening for Behavior Disorders, or SSBD (Walker & Severson, 1990), constitutes a three-stage multiple-gating process that provides for cost-effective mass screening of all pupils enrolled in regular classroom setting in terms of their at-risk status for behavior disorders. The SSBD assesses students on two primary dimensions: externalizing and internalizing behavior disorders (Achenbach & Edelbrock, 1978; Ross, 1980). These two behavioral dimensions encompass a broad range of school behavior disorders that occur in the elementary age range. Achenbach and Edelbrock (1978), Ross (1980), Gresham (1985), and others have argued for the adoption of this two-group classification system to govern school-based assessment practices for the BD population. The SSBD links reliable definitional criteria, screening and assessment procedures, and normatively based eligibility decision making into one self-contained system. This procedure relies extensively on structured teacher judgment of the behavioral characteristics of students at the first two assessment stages. Independent observation of students' behavioral functioning within instructional and free-play settings provides an independent confirmation of teacher judgment in the third assessment SSBD stage or gate.

The SSBD contains three interrelated stages for screening that are graphically illustrated in Figure 3.1. As shown, efficient and low-cost screening procedures are implemented to identify students who may be at risk for either externalizing or internalizing behavior problems. The SSBD relies on multiple gating as a procedure to ensure the accuracy of its assessment processes. The primary advantage of a multiple-gating system is that, at the first assessment level, all children in the classroom are evaluated; as the process gets more specific and expensive in terms of time and effort in subsequent screening stages, fewer children are involved in the assessments. For example, while all students are considered in the nomination and rank-ordering procedures in screening Stage 1, only six children (three externalizing and three internalizing) are evaluated in SSBD Stage 2. Additionally, further criteria must be met to pass on to Stage 3, in which direct observation by an independent observer is used to confirm teacher judgment.

The SSBD is patterned after models developed and validated by Greenwood et al. (1979) for the preschool screening of children at risk for social withdrawal and Loeber et al. (1984) for the screening of pupils at risk for later adoption of a delinquent lifestyle. The SSBD provides all students with an equal chance to be screened and identified for both externalizing and internalizing behavior disorders (Walker et al., 1988). The first gate involves teachers' systematic evaluation of pupils in their classroom via nomination and rank ordering according to how closely their *characteristic* behavior patterns correspond respectively to externalizing and internalizing behavioral profiles. The three highest-ranked students from each behavioral dimension are then assessed using Stage 2 instruments. The Stage 2 measures include a critical events index and a frequency index that assesses both adaptive and maladaptive behaviors. These rating measures are completed by the teacher, and the results provide specific information on the content of pupils' behavior patterns.

Although Stage 2 assessments are more expensive in terms of the teacher's time, they are now conducted on only a small subset of the total students screened in Stage 1 (i.e., a total of six—three externalizing and three internalizing). Teachers rate each pupil's status on behavioral descriptors of externalizing and internalizing behavioral dimensions. Normative criteria and cutoff points on Stage 2 instruments are used to determine whether any of the rated students qualify for further observational assessments during screening Stage 3. Their observed behavior is compared to both generic and locally referenced normative standards defined by observation data recorded on a national sample of same-sex and grade-level peers.

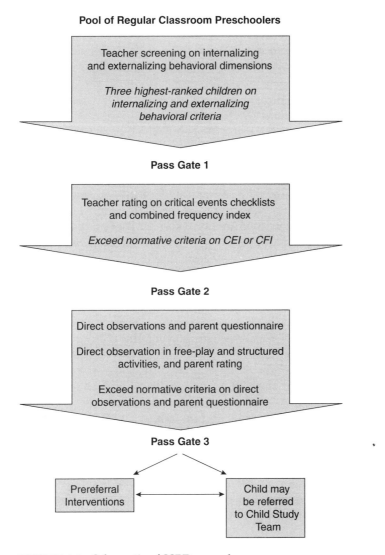

FIGURE 3.1 Schematic of SSBD procedure

Source: Walker and Severson (1990) *Systematic screening for behavior disorders (SSBD); User's guide and technical manual.* Longmont, CO: Sopris West.

In Stage 3, a school professional other than the teacher (e.g., school psychologist, counselor, behavioral specialist, resource teacher) observes these students in the classroom and playground. Their academic engaged time (AET) during seatwork periods and the quality and quantity of their social behavior during free-play periods are coded using structured observational procedures. Pupils exceeding normative criteria at stage 3 can be referred to a multidisciplinary team (MDT) for further evaluation, certification, and access to supports and services intervention. SSBD procedures and instruments, through each of the three linked screening stages, provide a self-contained standardized procedure that can be of significant value to school personnel in meeting the needs of the school-based behavior-disordered population.

Research on the SSBD

The results of multiple field trials of the SSBD screening system to date are encouraging. An initial field trial reported on by Walker et al. (1988) was subsequently replicated across two field sites (see Walker, Severson, Nicholson, Kehle, Jenson, & Clark, 1994; Walker et al., 1990). These results are considered to be robust, and several authors have described the SSBD as a state-of-the-art instrument for screening young children in the elementary grades (Forness, Kavale, MacMillan, Asarnow, & Duncan, 1996; O'Shaughnessy, Lane, Gresham, & Beebe-Frankenberger, this text; Gresham, Lane, & Lambros, 2000). The psychometric characteristics of the instruments comprising SSBD screening stages 1, 2, and 3 appear to meet acceptable levels of reliability and validity. They are cost-effective and efficient in terms of the time required to administer them and are user-friendly. The instruments are also highly sensitive in discriminating externalizing, internalizing, certified SBD, and control students from each other. The results of three studies, described briefly here, reported empirical databases supporting the SSBD's technical adequacy (Walker et al., 1994).

An early trial test of the SSBD evaluated the test–retest reliability of teacher rankings of students on the SSBD's externalizing and internalizing behavioral dimensions. Results for 168 ranked students were as follows: (a) Overall, 77% were identically classified 1 month later, and (b) 69% of the top three ranked externalizers were consistently ranked in the top three at follow-up. For internalizers, 132 of 165, or 80%, were classified in the same group on both ranking occasions ($p < .001$). In assessing the stability of 18 teachers' rankings, Spearman rank order coefficients ranged from .38 to .98 for the externalizing dimension (average of .76), and internalizing correlations ranged from .45 to .94 (average = .74). Test–retest reliability estimates over a 1-month period for the Stage 2 measures were .88 for the Adaptive Behavior Scale and .83 for the Maladaptive Behavior Scale. Internal consistency was also high for Stage 2 measures, with coefficient alphas of .85 to .88 for the Adaptive Scale and .82 to .87 for the Maladaptive Scale (Walker et al., 1988).

Concurrent validity of Stage 2 measures was evaluated by correlating SSBD instrument scores with the Achenbach Child Behavior Checklist (CBCL). The adaptive scale correlated with the CBC externalizing scale on average at −.65; the Maladaptive Scale correlated at .81 and .77 with the CBC externalizing scale.

Observation codes included in Stage 3 observational measures have proven to be quite reliable and provide the only available observation code that has age and gender norms of classroom and playground behaviors. The AET and peer social behavior (PSB) codes were evaluated using interobserver agreement coefficients between the observer/calibrator and each study observer. The mean agreement level for 19 AET reliability checks was .96; the mean reliability of the PSB was .84.

A discriminant function analysis provided support for the efficiency of the SSBD in correctly classifying study subjects into externalizers, internalizers, or control groups, on the basis of SSBD Stage 2 and 3 measures. The results indicated that 89.5% of study subjects were correctly classified into their respective groups (Walker et al., 1988). The psychometric properties of the SSBD appear solid, and subsequent studies have focused on providing additional validation and normative data on which to base decisions for calibrating the sensitivity of the screening procedures.

Two field trials of the SSBD conducted in Oregon and Washington school districts were reported by Walker et al. (1990). Normative data were collected from 170 teachers in one Oregon district and 40 teachers in 17 schools located in Washington. While the specific outcomes of this study are beyond the scope of this chapter, one key outcome deserves mention. The authors developed a measure of school archival data kept on all elementary school students. This measure, the School Archival Records Search (SARS), provides a systematic collection method for compiling school records profiles that can be used as an additional data source to further confirm SSBD screening results. The SARS profiles of Externalizers, Internalizers, and Non-Ranked students vary significantly and provide further documentation of the continuing and serious problems that children at risk for either externalizing or internalizing behavior disorders experience in school (Walker et al., 1990). The SARS has since been standardized, and reports of its use and norms are available (Walker, Block-Pedego, Todis, & Severson, 1991). The SARS provides information on three general factors: Needs Assistance, Disruption, and Low Achievement. For specific guidelines on the use of the SARS, see Walker et al. (1991).

In addition to the Washington sample closely replicating the normative levels for SSBD instruments repeated from the Oregon sample, the sensitivity of the SSBD for identifying certified SED students has also been assessed (see Walker et al., 1990). The SSBD correctly identified 39 of 45 certified SED students with externalizing behavior problems who were assigned previously to the 40 regular classrooms where teachers completed SSBD measures. Similarly, all nine SED students with internalizing problems appeared among the top three highest-ranked internalizing students. These results speak well to the sensitivity of SSBD Stage 1 procedures in identifying students with known histories of behavioral adjustments in school.

In yet another replication study evaluating use of the SSBD, Walker et al. (1994) conducted screening procedures with 58 elementary teachers in three Utah schools. At Stage 1, 1,468 children in first through fifth grade were screened. At Stage 2, 475 students were selected for further screening, and at Stage 3, 225 students were identified to be observed. In addition to providing additional normative data on Stage 2 and 3 measures, the Walker et al. (1994) study provided teacher satisfaction and cost analysis data, which confirmed the ease of use and modest cost per student of the SSBD screening procedures. On average, the cost to complete the SSBD process was $175, which included time and effort estimates for observers and teachers plus materials cost. The cost savings, especially in professional time, when compared to traditional assessment referral procedures, can be a significant factor in favor of adopting the screening procedures.

Professionals in the field have cited the SSBD as a substantial advance in systematic and comprehensive screening for behavior problems of general education students in the elementary school range (see Forness et al., 1996; Kaufman, 1999; O'Shaughnessy et al., this text; Phillips, Nelson, & McLaughlin, 1993). The SSBD provides behaviorally referenced criteria and a common set of standards for teachers to use in evaluating a student's at-risk status and identifies children who are acting out and aggressive as well as those who are neglected and withdrawn. It removes much of the idiosyncratic subjective nature of the current referral process. This proactive approach to identifying at-risk students can provide an opportunity to intervene early, heading off an escalation of problematic behaviors that may later prove to be resistant to intervention.

Early Screening Project (ESP)

A downward extension of the SSBD, which uses the same multistage system as the SSBD, has been developed for use in preschool and day care settings (Walker, Severson, et al., 1995). This system, called the Early Screening Project, or ESP, was developed by Hill Walker, Herb Severson, and Ed Feil as a viable alternative for screening in preschool or day care settings with children 3 to 5 years of age. The advantage of both the SSBD and ESP is that they were designed for wide-scale, classroom-based screening and are characterized by considerable economy of effort. The ESP instruments have been evaluated and have exceptionally good reliability and validity (Feil, Severson, & Walker, 1998; Feil, Walker, & Severson, 1995).

The ESP has been evaluated with 2,853 children aged 3 to 6 years, enrolled in general and special education, across eight states between 1991 and 1994. Stage 1 ESP ranking procedures on internalizing and externalizing behavioral descriptions are almost identical to those of the SSBD. However, the teacher nominates only five children on each list before ranking them from those who closest match a behavioral description (rank 1) to those least matching it (rank 5). The ESP stage 2, which relies on teacher ratings, consists of five measures as follows: The *Critical Events Index* (CEI) is a 16-item teacher checklist of behavioral events having high intensity and salience but relatively low frequencies (i.e., fire setting, physical assault of another). Scores on the CEI range from 0 to 16 and reflect the total number of critical events exhibited by the child within the past 6 months. The *Adaptive Behavior Scale* is composed of eight items tapping the child's adaptive behavioral levels (i.e., "follows established classroom rules") and is scored on a 7-point Likert scale (i.e., "never" to "frequently"). A child scoring 21 or less is considered to be at high risk. The *Maladaptive Behavior Scale* includes nine items, such as "disturbs classroom activities." It is scored on a 7-point Likert scale, and scores of 26 or more are considered high risk. There are two additional ESP measures that are typically used for externalizers versus internalizers, respectively. The *Aggressive Behavior Scale*, for use with externalizers, is composed of nine items (e.g., "damages others' property"), and a score of 19 or more is deemed high risk. The *Social Interactive*

Scale, for use with internalizers, includes eight items (e.g., "verbally initiates with peers"), a total of 27 or less is considered high risk.

The interrater reliability coefficients for these ESP measures were generally in the .80 range or above. Scores on each of these measures (with the exception of the Social Interaction Scale) can be converted to T scores for ease of interpretation. Total scores are transformed to T scores ($M = 50$, SD $= 10$), where T scores of nearly two or more standard deviations above the mean ($T > 65$) indicate problem areas and risk status (Sattler, 1992).

ESP stage 3 behavioral observations use a modified Peer Social Behavior code. As recommended by Sinclair, Del'Homme, and Gonzalez (1993) and Eisert, Walker, Severson, and Block (1989), observations of academic engaged time under structured classroom conditions like those that have been used in the SSBD were omitted in the ESP. The Social Behavior observations were further modified to create ease of use while maintaining accuracy in identifying at-risk preschool children. The ESP observation procedures use a duration recording method with a stopwatch. There is a highly significant correlation of .96 ($p < .01$) between partial interval and duration recording ESP systems, showing that they provide generally equivalent information (Walker, Severson, et al., 1995).

The duration method of recording both antisocial and nonsocial forms of behavior allows the observer to track externalizing and internalizing behavior patterns using a single observational criterion. In addition, the observer is able to provide important qualitative notes about the nature or quality of the behavior being observed.

Stage 3 ESP assessment involves direct observations of a child's social behavior in the classroom and on the playground. The Social Behavior Observation provides a record of the quality, level, and distribution of a child's social behavior during free-play settings. Children are observed for 20 minutes, and the stopwatch runs when the child exhibits antisocial or nonsocial behavior and is turned off when the child displays prosocial behavior. This procedure is repeated throughout the recording observation period to record the total time the child is involved in either antisocial or nonsocial behavior.

Psychometric Studies of the ESP

The ESP reliability and validity data also show strong results. The interrater reliability coefficients of most ESP measures are at least .80, which meets Salvia and Ysseldyke's (1988) guidelines for a screening instrument. Good psychometric outcomes have been attained to date despite the difficulties inherent in the assessment of young children (Martin, 1986). Validity studies show consistently high relationships with criterion measures, including the Connors Teacher Ratings Scales (Conners, 1989), Preschool Behavior Questionnaire (Behar & Stringfield, 1974), and Child Behavior Checklist Teacher Report (Achenbach & Edelbrock, 1978). Correlations with these measures are highly significant, ranging from .34 to .87, with most above .70. Further, a discriminant analysis provided a measure of the accuracy of the ESP with both specificity and sensitivity coefficients. Results for the ESP show good sensitivity (62%) and excellent specificity (94%), leading to accurate assessments with a minimal risk of misidentifying a child who exhibits developmentally inappropriate behavior.

The ESP has been found to be user-friendly, and reports from staff users and reviewers have been positive regarding both its length and simplicity (Yoshikawa & Knitzer, 1997). Further assessments of the concordance of the ESP with other concurrent measures of preschool adjustment status indicate high correspondence between the ESP and these measures. For example, correlations comparing the ESP with the Child Behavior Checklist and the Social Skills Rating Scale (Achenbach, 1991; Gresham & Elliott, 1990) show good agreement between measures and moderate agreement across raters (parents and teachers). This overall relationship is stronger among externalizing subjects than among internalizers. Coefficients range from .91 to .83 among the ESP aggressive scale, CBCL, and SSRS externalizing teacher measures subscales and range from .53 to .44 between the ESP Adaptive and Social Interaction and CBCL internalizing subscale teacher measures.

Overall, the ESP appears to be a highly useful instrument for screening preschool children who are at risk for either externalizing or internalizing behavior disorders. Several published reports indicate that the ESP can be utilized as part of early intervention programs in which systematic screening for school adjustment problems occurs on a regular basis (Feil et al., 1998). Use of all or part of the ESP system in Head Start settings has been especially effective (Del'Homme, Sinclair, & Kasari, 1994; Sinclair, 1993; Sinclair et al., 1993). Information collected using the ESP measures at stages 2 and 3 can be used for several specific purposes, including (a) determination of eligibility for special services, (b) intervention planning, and (c) monitoring progress in evaluating the outcomes of intervention over time. The ESP procedure, however, should be used in conjunction with other additional quantitative and qualitative assessment information. Even when a child exceeds normative criteria on the ESP measures, the child's behavior could be due to a variety of factors, such as too high or too low activity levels, poor supervision and instruction, speech and language delays, parental divorce or stress, immaturity, and cognitive delays (Feil et al., 1998). The ESP provides a broad range of information, yet additional assessments, such as parent and teacher interviews and/or sociometric assessments, are highly recommended as well for students exceeding ESP criteria.

Longitudinal Follow-up on ESP Measures

One stringent test of a screening instrument is to evaluate longitudinally whether students identified as high risk, and not intervened with, do in fact exhibit problematic behaviors at follow-up. To test the predictive ability of the ESP, we collected ESP data on 63 children enrolled in Head Start classrooms in the 1992–1993 school year. The 63 children were 45% female and 55% male in four classrooms with a total of eight teachers. Most of the children (65%) were 5 years of age at the time of evaluation. We followed up with these students in the spring of 1997 to evaluate their behavior via a school records review using the SARS (Walker et al., 1991). The longitudinal results from the school records review show a very accurate screening system and impressive predictive validity (see the results of logistic regression analysis reported in Table 3.2).

TABLE 3.2 Stepwise Logistic Regression of Longitudinal Follow-up Data Head Start Year (Pre-K) ESP Measurement and Third-Grade School Records Review

Preschool Measure	Third-Grade Record Review Data						χ^2 Value
	N	Mean	SD	N	Mean	SD	
	Behavioral Referral Present			**Nonbehavioral Referral Present**			
Critical events	4	2.67	1.53	33	0.88	1.08	4.87*
Structure engagement observation	4	0.70	0.19	33	0.89	0.11	6.45*
	Negative Narrative Comment			**No Negative Narrative Comments Present**			
Adaptive behavior	19	22.21	4.21	18	29.72	5.89	13.49***
	Discipline Contacts			**No Discipline Contacts**			
Aggressive behavior	7	1.86	1.57	30	0.83	1.02	4.32*
	Grade Retention			**No Grade Retention**			
Total positive social engagement observed	5	0.44	0.18	32	0.70	0.20	6.40*
Aggressive behavior	5	26.80	11.65	32	25.15	9.16	4.61*
	Special Education			**Not Eligible for Special Education**			
Adaptive behavior	9	21.00	3.87	28	27.43	6.17	7.28**
Aggressive behavior	9	26.00	9.93	28	25.18	9.35	8.37**
	Out-of-Classroom Placement			**All Regular Classroom Placement**			
Positive social engagement observed	11	0.18	0.09	26	0.30	0.16	5.69*
Negative social engagement observed	11	0.03	0.03	26	0.01	0.01	6.04*
Structure engagement observed	11	0.82	0.14	26	0.90	0.11	3.99*

*$p < .05$; ** $p < .01$; *** $p < .001$.

TABLE 3.3   Number of Negative Comments in the Third-Grade School Records Review by Preschool Risk Status on ESP in Head Start

	Number of Negative Comments in School Record				
	0	1–5	6–9	10+	Total
Number of children who are nonrisk status	12	0	0	0	12
Number of children who are at-risk status	6	12	5	2	25

Another less stringent, but informative evaluation of the predictive ability of the ESP screening procedure can be seen in the number of negative narrative comments contained in the school records of the children at follow-up. As seen in Table 3.3, children identified as at risk at 5 years of age had many more negative comments in their cumulative folders at the 4-year follow-up.

The ESP procedure appears to have good predictive ability to identify students who exhibit problematic behavior in schools 4 years later. The ESP can be utilized as a part of a best practice for early intervention programs by screening for school adjustment problems at an early age.

Other Screening Systems

Two other screening systems have been advocated by professionals. One approach is to use a combination of teacher nominations and teacher or parent ratings on the aggression subscale of the Achenbach Child Behavior Checklist (CBCL) to screen and identify at-risk students (Achenbach, 1991). Teachers can be asked simply to nominate students in their class who may manifest the following profile of antisocial students (i.e., antisocial students consistently violate classroom and playground rules, display aggressive behavior toward others, sometimes damage or destroy property, take things without permission, and are often in a sullen and agitated emotional state).

Teachers can nominate up to five students unless unusual circumstances exist that would indicate a larger number of needed nominations. They are then asked to rate each nominated student on the aggression subscale of the CBCL. The teacher form of the Achenbach aggression subscale is essentially identical to the parent form. The CBCL has set the standard for psychometric excellence in the study of child psychopathology and adjustment problems. Our experience with the aggression subscale indicates that it is highly sensitive in discriminating antisocial from nonantisocial students. Sample items in this subscale include "defiant; talks back to staff," "gets in many fights," "cruelty, bullying, or meanness to others," and "explosive and unpredictable behavior." Use of this subscale is highly recommended for assessing the behavioral status of potentially antisocial students with externalizing behavior problems.

Students who score two or more standard deviations above the mean on the CBCL aggression subscale should be considered as seriously at risk for antisocial behavioral patterns. If parent ratings also show an elevated profile on the aggression subscale, then the child's at-risk status may be even greater. Students who are identified by this screening approach should be exposed to early interventions to deal with their specific adjustment problems.

A number of behavioral indicators early in a child's life are predictive of the development of conduct disorders. Drummond (1993) has ingeniously adapted these indicators into a universal, mass-screening procedure for use by elementary teachers in identifying at-risk students. He has extensively developed and researched a seven-item scale for this purpose called the Student Risk Screening Scale (SRSS). Drummond used the following five criteria to guide development of the SRSS:

1. *Brief.* A screening instrument should have no more than 10 items.
2. *Research based.* The items should be those that most powerfully discriminate and predict antisocial behavior patterns.
3. *Easily understood.* The format, scoring, and administration instructions should be clear.
4. *Valid.* The instrument should be accurate and valid for the screening and identification of at-risk students.
5. *Powerful.* The instrument should be efficient in identifying those students who are truly at risk and who would benefit from early intervention programs.

The SRSS has proven to be easy to use, highly effective, and technically sound. It has excellent validity and reliability and powerfully distinguishes non-at-risk students from those who show the early signs of antisocial behavior (Drummond, Eddy, & Reid, 1998a, 1998b). The seven items of the SRSS are (a) stealing; (b) lying, cheating, sneaking; (c) behavioral problems; (d) peer rejection; (e) low academic achievement; (f) negative attitude; and (g) aggressive behavior. Each of the seven items is scored on a 0-to-3 Likert scale, in which 0 equals "never," 1 is "occasionally," 2 equals "sometimes," and 3 equals "frequently." Total scores on the SRSS can range from 0 to 21.

Longitudinal studies of the SRSS indicate that the scores are predictive of poor academic and behavioral outcomes up to 10 years later. Additional studies have evaluated 18-month and 3-year follow-up outcomes (Drummond, Eddy, Reid, & Bank, 1994). The SRSS appears to be a reliable and valid measure that can be used in conjunction with preventive interventions. Additional evaluations of the SRSS indicate that its risk scores are strongly correlated with the scores from longer and more extensive screening instruments of child behavior problems (Drummond et al., 1994). SRSS summary scores were significantly correlated ($r = .79$; $p < .001$) with the aggressive behavior subscale of the teacher version of the CBC. The SRSS, as a universal screening instrument, has been used successfully during elementary and middle school years and can provide a quick, reliable teacher measure of child behavior.

Conclusion

This chapter has reviewed the rationale for using universal and proactive screening procedures in public schools to identify at-risk students exhibiting either internalizing or externalizing behavior problems. Clear evidence indicates that at-risk behaviors observed at an early age in the primary grades and even earlier, in preschools, are predictive of further escalation of school-related, adjustment problems, and these behavior patterns can result in more serious adjustment problems later on. Reliable, valid, and cost-effective screening procedures can be implemented in public schools to accurately identify students who are exhibiting problematic behaviors at an age at which the child may be more amenable to interventions to alter the life course of at-risk behavior patterns. Additionally, these screening procedures provide target behaviors on which to focus interventions and also provide a baseline for evaluating the effectiveness of these interventions.

If we as a society are serious about altering the escalation of serious social and emotional problems for adolescents, we must institute screening procedures at an early age to effectively target students who exhibit problematic behaviors. Ample research and evaluation of systematic screening procedures suggest that they can be administered and instituted as regular procedures for public schools. The prevention of violence, for example, can be viewed as a public health problem, and we must consider applying methods that have been used successfully in the past to reduce injuries and death from other causes, such as motor vehicle crashes and cigarette smoking. A similar public health approach to behavioral problems would indicate proactive screening for all children and the provision of appropriate services for students identified as exhibiting high-risk behaviors. It is critical that validated, cost-effective home and school interventions take place early in the school career of children. Public policy should include universal screening to provide early detection and access to early intervention, as we now have empirical evidence that we can increase prosocial behavior and reduce aggressive behavior problems effectively (Loeber & Farrington, 1998; Reid, 1993; Walker et al., 1996).

R E F E R E N C E S

Achenbach, T. M. (1991). *Manual for the Teacher's Report Form and 1991 Profile.* Burlington: University of Vermont.

Achenbach, T. M., & Edelbrock, C. S. (1978). The classification of child psychopathology: A review and analysis of empirical efforts. *Psychological Bulletin, 85*(6), 1275–1301.

American Cancer Society. (1999). *Cancer Facts and Figures—1999* [Brochure]. Atlanta, GA: Author.

Behar, L., & Stringfield, S. (1974). *Manual for the Preschool Behavior Questionnaire.* Durham, NC: Behar.

Bennett, K. J., Lipman, E. L., Brown, S., Racine, Y., Boyle, M. H., & Offord, D. R. (1999). Predict-ing conduct problems: Can high-risk children be identified in kindergarten and Grade 1? *Journal of Consulting and Clinical Psychology. August, 67*(4), 470–480.

Bullis, M., & Walker, H. M. (1994). *Comprehensive School-Based Systems for Troubled Youth.* Eugene: University of Oregon, Center of Human Development.

Campbell, S. (1995). Behavior problems in preschool children: A review of recent research. *Journal of Child Psychology and Psychiatry, 36,* 113–149.

Coie, J. (1996). Prevention of violence and antisocial behaviour. In R. D. Peters & R. J. McMahon (Eds.), *Preventing Childhood Disorders, Sub-*

stance Abuse, and Delinquency (pp. 1–18). Thousand Oaks, CA: Sage.

Conners, C. K. (1989). *Manual for the Conners' Rating Scales.* North Tonawanda, NY: Multi-Health Systems.

Del'Homme, M., Sinclair, E., & Kasari, C. (1994). Preschool children with behavioral problems: Observation in instructional and free play contexts. *Behavioral Disorders, 19,* 221–232.

Drummond, T. (1993). *The Student Risk Screening Scale (SRSS).* Grants Pass, OR: Josephine County Mental Health Program.

Drummond, T., Eddy, J. M., & Reid, J. B. (1998a). *Follow-Up Study #3; Risk Screening Scale: Prediction of Negative Outcomes by 10th Grade from 2nd Grade Screening.* Unpublished technical report. Eugene, OR: Oregon Social Learning Center.

Drummond, T., Eddy, J. M., & Reid, J. B. (1998b). *Follow-Up Study #4; Risk Screening Scale: Prediction of Negative Outcomes in Two Longitudinal Samples.* Unpublished technical report. Eugene, OR: Oregon Social Learning Center.

Drummond, T., Eddy, M., Reid, J. B., & Bank, L. (1994, November). *The Student Risk Screening Scale: A Brief Teacher Screening Instrument for Conduct Disorder.* Paper presented at the Fourth Annual Prevention Conference, Washington, DC.

Duncan, B., Forness S. R., & Hartsough, C. (1995). Students identified as seriously emotionally disturbed in day treatment: Cognitive, psychiatric, and special education characteristics. *Behavioral Disorders, 20,* 238–252.

Eisert, D.C., Walker, H. M., Severson, H. H., & Block, A. (1989). Patterns of social-behavioral competence in behavior disordered preschoolers. *Early Childhood Development & Care, 41,* 139–152.

Feil, E. G., Severson, H. H., & Walker, H. M. (1998). Screening for emotional and behavioral delays: The Early Screening Project. *Journal of Early Intervention, 21(3),* 252–266.

Feil, E. G., Walker, H. M., & Severson, H. H. (1995). The Early Screening Project for young children with behavior problems. *Journal of Emotional and Behavioral Disorders, 3*(4), 194–202.

Forness, S. R., & Kavale, K. A. (1996). Treating social skills deficits and learning disabilities: A meta-analysis. *Learning Disability Quarterly, 19,* 2–13.

Forness, S. R., Kavale, K. A., MacMillan, D. L., Asarnow, J. R., & Duncan, B. B. (1996). Early detection and prevention of emotional or behavioral disorders: Developmental aspects of systems of care. *Behavioral Disorders, 21,* 226–240.

Gerber, M. M., & Semmel, M. I. (1984). Teacher as imperfect test: Reconceptualizing the referral process. *Educational Psychologist, 19*(3), 137–148.

Graham, P., Rutter, M., & George, S. (1973). Temperamental characteristics as predictors of behavior disorders in children. *American Journal of Ortho-Psychiatry, 43*(3), 328–339.

Greenwood, C. R., Walker, H. M., Todd, N. M., & Hops, H. (1979). Preschool teachers' assessment and treatment of socially withdrawn preschool children. *Behavioral Assessment, 4,* 273–297.

Gresham, F. (1986). Conceptual issues in the assessment of social competence in children. In P. S. Strain, M. J. Guralnick, & H. M. Walker (Eds.), *Children's Social Behavior: Development, Assessment, and Modification* (pp. 143–179). New York: Academic Press.

Gresham, F. M. (1985). Behavior disorder assessment: Conceptual, definitional, and practical considerations. *School Psychology Review, 4,* 495–509.

Gresham, F. M. & Elliott, S. N. (1990). *Social Skills Rating System.* Circle Pines, MN: American Guidance Service.

Gresham, F., Lane, K. L., & Lambros, K. M. (2000). Comorbidity of conduct and attention deficit hyperactivity problems: Issues of conceptualization, identification and intervention with "fledging psychopaths." *Journal of Emotional and Behavioral Disorders, 8*(2), 83–93.

Grosenick, J. (1981). Public school and mental health services to severely behavior disordered students. *Behavior Disorders, 6,* 183–190.

Hinshaw, S. P. (1992). Externalizing behavior problems and academic underachievement in childhood and adolescence: Causal relationships and underlying mechanisms. *Psychological Bulletin, 32,* 677–693.

Hops, H., Finch, M., & McConnell, S. (1985). Social skills deficits. In P. Bornstein & A. Kazdin (Eds)., *Handbook of Clinical Behavior Therapy with Children* (pp. 543–598). Homewood, IL: Dorsey.

Horne, W., & Packard, T. (1985). Early identification of learning problems: A meta-analysis. *Journal of Educational Psychology, 77*(5), 597–607.

Institute of Medicine. (1994). *Reducing Risks for Mental Disorder: Frontiers for Preventive Intervention Research.* Washington, DC: National Academy Press.

Jackson, J. M., Reid, J. B., Patterson, G. R., Schaughency, E. A., & Ray, J. A. (1990, November). *Inter-rater Reliability and Validity of the Child*

Behavior Checklist: Their Relationship to Parent Gender, Family Structure, and Age of Child. Paper presented at the 24th annual convention of the Association for the Advancement of Behavior Therapy, San Francisco.

Kaplan, R. M. (2000). Two pathways to prevention. *American-Psychologist, 55*(4), 382–396.

Kaufman, J. M. (1999). How we prevent the prevention of emotional and behavioral disorders. *Exceptional Children, 65*(4), 448–468.

Kazdin, A. E. (1987). *Conduct Disorders in Childhood and Adolescence.* London: Sage.

Loeber, R. (1991). Antisocial behavior: More enduring than changeable? *Journal of the American Academy of Child and Adolescent Psychiatry, 30,* 393–397.

Loeber, R., Dishion, T. J., & Patterson, G. R. (1984). Multiple-gating: A multistage assessment procedure for identifying youths at risk for delinquency. *Journal of Research in Crime and Delinquency, 21,* 7–32.

Loeber, R., & Farrington, D. P. (Eds.). (1998). *Serious and Violent Juvenile Offenders: Risk Factors and Successful Interventions.* Thousand Oaks, CA: Sage.

Loeber, R., Green, S. M., Lahey, B. B., Frick, P. J., & McBurnett, K. (2000). Findings on disruptive behavior disorders from the first decade of the developmental trends study. *Clinical Child and Family Psychology Review, 3,* 37–59.

Lynam, D. R. (1996). Early identification of chronic offenders: Who is the fledging psychopath? *Psychological Bulletin, 120,* 209–234.

Martin, R. P. (1986). Assessment of the social and emotional functioning of preschool children. *School Psychology Review, 15,* 216–232.

McConaughy, S. H. (1993). Responses to commentaries on advances in empirically-based assessment. *School Psychology Review, 22,* 334–342.

Moffitt, T. E. (1993). Adolescence-limited and life-course-persistent antisocial behavior: A developmental taxonomy. *Psychological Review, 100,* 674–701.

Noel, M. (1982). Public school programs for the emotionally disturbed: An overview. In M. Noel & N. Haring (Eds.), *Progress of Change: Issues in Educating the Emotionally Disturbed* (Vol. 2, pp. 11–28). Seattle: University of Washington Press.

Offord, D. R. (1987). Prevention of behavioral and emotional disorders in children. *Journal of Child Psychology and Psychiatry, 28,* 9–19.

Parker, J., & Asher, S. (1987). Peer relations and later personal adjustment: Are low accepted children at risk? *Psychological Bulletin, 102,* 357–389.

Patterson, G. R. (1993). Orderly change in a stable world: The antisocial trait as a chimera. *Journal of Consulting and Clinical Psychology, 61,* 911–919.

Patterson, G. R., Reid, J. B., & Dishion, T. J. (1992). *Antisocial Boys.* Eugene, OR: Castalia.

Phillips, V., Nelson, C. M., & McLaughlin, J. F. (1993). Systems change and services for students with emotional/behavioral disabilities in Kentucky. *Journal of Emotional and Behavioral Disorders, 1,* 155–164.

Reid, J. B. (1993). Prevention of conduct disorder before and after school entry: Relating interventions to developmental findings. *Development and Psychopathology, 5,* 243–262.

Reid, J. B., & Patterson, G. R. (1991). Early prevention and intervention with conduct problems: A social interactional model for the integration of research and practice. In G. Stoner, M. R. Shinn, & H. M. Walker (Eds.), *Interventions for Achievement and Behavior Problems* (pp. 715–739). Silver Spring, MD: National Association of School Psychologists.

Robins, L. N. (1966). *Deviant Children Grown Up: A Sociological and Psychiatric Study of Sociopathic Personality.* Baltimore, MD: Williams & Wilkins.

Robins, L. N. (1978). Sturdy childhood predictors of adult antisocial behavior: Replications from longitudinal studies. *Psychological Medicine, 63,* 611–622.

Ross, A. (1980). *Psychological Disorders of Children: A Behavioral Approach to Theory, Research and Therapy* (2nd ed.). New York: McGraw-Hill.

Salvia, J., & Ysseldyke, J. E. (1988). *Assessment in Special and Remedial Education.* Boston: Houghton Mifflin.

Sattler, J. M. (1992). *Assessment of Children* (3rd ed.). San Diego, CA: Jerome Sattler, Publisher.

Sinclair, E. (1993). Early identification of preschoolers with special needs in Head Start. *Topics in Early Childhood Special Education, 13,* 12–18.

Sinclair, E., Del'Homme, M., & Gonzalez, M. (1993). Systematic screening for preschool behavioral disorders. *Behavioral Disorders, 18,* 177–188.

Strong, D. R., Greene, R. L., Hoppe, C., Johnston, T., & Olesen, N. (1999). Taxometric analysis of impression management and self-deception on the MMPI 2 in child custody litigants. *Journal of Personality Assessment, 73*(1), 1–18.

Tolan, P. H., Guerra, N. G., & Kendall, P. (1995). A developmental-ecological perspective on antisocial behavior in children and adolescents: Toward a unified risk and intervention framework. *Journal of Consulting and Clinical Psychology, 63,* 579–584.

Walker, H. M., Block-Pedego, A. E., Todis, B. J., & Severson, H. H. (1991). *School Archival Record Search (SARS).* Longmont, CO: Sopris West.

Walker, H. M., Colvin, G., & Ramsey, E. (1995). *Antisocial Behavior in School: Strategies and Best Practices.* Pacific Grove, CA: Brooks/Cole.

Walker, H. M., Hops, H. & Greenwood, C. R. (1984). The CORBEH research and development model: Programmatic issues and strategies. In S. Paine, G. T. Bellamy, & B. Wilcox (Eds.), *Human Services That Work* (pp. 57–78). Baltimore, MD: Brookes.

Walker, H. M., Horner, R. H., Sugai, G., Bullis, M., Sprague, J. R., Bricker, D., & Kaufman, M. J. (1996). Integrated approaches to preventing antisocial behavior patterns among school-age children and youth. *Journal of Emotional and Behavioral Disorders, 4,* 193–256.

Walker, H. M., & Severson, H. H. (1990). *Systematic Screening for Behavior Disorders: User's Guide and Administration Manual.* Longmont, CO: Sopris West.

Walker, H. M., Severson, H. H., & Feil, E. G. (1995). *Early Screening Project: A Proven Child-Find Process.* Longmont, CO: Sopris West.

Walker, H. M., Severson, H. H., Nicholson, F., Kehle, T., Jenson, W. R., & Clark, E. (1994). Replication of the Systematic Screening for Behavior Disorders (SSBD) procedure for the identification of at-risk children. *Journal of Emotional and Behavioral Disorders, 2*(2), 66–77.

Walker, H. M., Severson, H. H., Stiller, B., Williams, G. J., Haring, N., Shinn, M., & Todis, B. (1988). Systematic screening of pupils in the elementary age range at risk for behavior disorders: Development and trial testing of a multiple-gating model. *RASE: Remedial and Special Education, 9*(3), 8–20.

Walker, H. M., Severson, H. H., Todis, B. J., Block-Pedego, A. E., Williams, G. J., Haring, N. G., & Barckley, M. (1990). Systematic Screening for Behavior Disorders (SSBD): Further validation, replication, and normative data. *RASE: Remedial and Special Education, 11*(2), 32–46.

Yoshikawa, H. (1994). Prevention as cumulative protection: Effects of early family support and education on chronic delinquency and its risks. *Psychological Bulletin, 115,* 28–54.

Yoshikawa, H., & Knitzer, J. (1997). *Lessons from the Field: Head Start Mental Health Strategies to Meet Changing Needs.* New York: National Center for Children in Poverty.

PART TWO

Academic Behaviors and Instructional Issues

4 Curriculum Clarification, Lesson Design, and Delivery

KENNETH W. HOWELL AND
BRIDGET KELLEY
Western Washington University

Introduction

Susan Sanchez is a first-year teacher in a self-contained classroom designated for those students who exhibit severe behavioral and emotional problems. Susan's current caseload is 10 students, 2 girls and 8 boys ranging in age from 6 to 12 years old. All 10 students spend a portion of their day in general education settings, from general education classrooms for grade-level academics to the gym for PE instruction to computer technology instruction. The 10 students use various tools to self-monitor their behaviors in these general education settings. These students also receive remedial academic and social skill instruction. The students periodically use the special education setting as a time-out area when they need to be removed, either voluntarily or involuntarily, from the general education setting.

All of Susan's students exhibit some form of physical aggression toward other students and adults. The topography of the aggressive acts varies from choking to hitting to throwing objects at other students and adults. Seven students take medication associated with their behavior problems or other comorbid conditions. While all the students are involved in the use of classroom contingency management systems and communication labs led by the school counselor, none of these students receives specific instruction to teach alternatives to their aggressive behavior. Susan and the staff tend to react to the aggressive acts rather than instruct students in the use of prosocial behaviors.

One fall, Susan, together with the principal, decides that social skill instruction might help prevent the continuation of aggressive acts exhibited by these students. The principal agrees and promises to support the effort, but Susan is somewhat uncertain as to what the first step should be. After exploring the closets of the special education rooms, she finds several published social skills programs. However, she is somewhat hesitant to "just open a package" and begin using a basal program.

To improve social skills, it is necessary to design and deliver effective instruction. But design and delivery both need to be aligned with the curriculum. This chapter begins with a discussion of the general principles of curriculum development, as this is a prerequisite for planning *what to teach* and *how to teach*. Next, the authors will discuss instructional design. Along the way we should find some information that will help Susan and other teachers like her solve problems within the area of social skills.

Curriculum Clarification

Ysseldyke and Christenson (1996) describe effective lesson design as the process that ensures a match between the student's needs and instruction. They then go on to say that, during the process of instructional planning, student characteristics such as background knowledge must be matched with curriculum characteristics such as content and skill sequence. This description calls attention to one of the most fundamental principles of lesson design and delivery: all components of a lesson must be *aligned*. This is true whether one is teaching reading or whether one is teaching social skills.

At the design level, the basic principles and actions (e.g., alignment) of curriculum development for students with severe behavioral or emotional problems are no different from those for students without such problems. The only real difference resides in the tasks the students need to be taught. This point is not a simple opening statement. It speaks to a general constraint on the design of all instruction. That constraint is the *curriculum* or *what* students are taught. All instructional decisions are guided by the nature of the tasks being taught (Howell & Nolet, 2000).

The curriculum is a structured set of prespecified learning outcomes (Johnson, 1967). The prespecified nature of these outcomes means that clarification about the body of things the student might learn is usually made before the child arrives. Ideally, clarification decisions will be based on an empirical analysis of what must be learned if a student is going to meet a critical social expectation. This means that the objectives a student might be taught (on the basis of their alignment with student need) are derived from an analysis of skills needed to access social settings and interactions successfully.

The curriculum includes more than isolated skills. The dynamic principles of learning also impact the structure of curriculum (Marzano et al., 1988). When we say that a curriculum needs to be "structured," we are saying that the various elements of knowledge and behavior within it need to be arranged for the most efficient acquisition of skills (e.g., addition is taught before addition of fractions). The structure and sequence of learning outcomes can be packaged in ways that complement certain long-term expectations. For example, if a skill is to be used in settings other than the classroom, then specific generalization objectives must be included in the sequence.

Curriculum is often confused with specific prepackaged programs such as *Cool Kids* (Fister, Conrad, & Kemp, 1998), *Skillstreaming the Adolescent, Revised Edition* (Goldstein, 1997), and *Tough Kid Social Skills* (Sheridan, 1995). Many of these programs contain series of lesson objectives. However, like all instructional materials, they are not a fully developed curriculum because they only present a slice of what a socially competent person needs to know. And these slices may not be appropriate for everyone.

With the development of more published programs, lists of tasks are now becoming easier to find. For example, one can easily open the manual for any of the programs just mentioned to find a list of the behaviors addressed. However, lists from some popular programs are problematic because they only address one context—namely, classrooms. Classroom-specific behaviors include raising hand to ask permission to talk or staying in seat. While it is true, for example, that Susan's students fail to exhibit proficiency at such tasks, and thereby threaten their own learning, it is obvious that classroom-specific expectations do not represent all social contexts and would certainly be insufficient for a transition plan (Hasazi, Furney, & Destefano, 1999).

There is no clear boundary between classroom and social behavior. Still, one must understand that building compliance in the classroom is not the same as teaching the social skills needed for success in *and* outside the class. Many of the content lists found in published programs just do not contain the social behaviors necessary for the generalization leading to success outside the general or special education classroom (Sargent, 1998). So how can these lists be expanded to define a richer view of behavior?

Table of Specifications

Table 4.1 shows how a small sequence of social content can be transformed into a larger curriculum component (set of learning outcomes) by using a simple template to expand the content statements. In Table 4.1 the left vertical axis is the content axis (saying "No"; answering a complaint and entering a conversation). The content was selected because learning to say no appropriately is one alternative to the aggressive interactions currently occurring in Susan's class. To make a useful grid, the top axis of the template must be selected to complement the content. In this case, condition statements (with familiar peers; with strangers) have been imposed on the horizontal axis along with behavior statements (explain the steps; carry out the steps). The resulting grid is called a *table of specifications* (Bloom, Madaus, & Hastings, 1981). Once such a template is developed for a specific skill or set of skills, only minor adjustments will be needed in the future. The same table of specifications can be used year after year with minor renovation.

Table 4.1 shows a grid with numbered squares that represent potential objectives. For example, the ninth cell, corresponding to the ninth objective listed below the table, calls for the student to explain the steps of the strategy in the presence of

TABLE 4.1   Specifications and Objectives for Saying No: Behavior and Conditions

Content	With Familiar Peers		With Strangers	
	A: The Student Will Explain the Steps	B: The Student Will Carry Out Steps	C: The Student Will Explain Steps	D: The Student Will Carry Out Steps
For saying "no"	9	10	11	12
For answering a complaint	5	6	7	8
For entering a conversation	1	2	3	4

1. With familiar peers the student will explain the steps for entering a conversation: criterion 100%.
2. With familiar peers the student will carry out steps for entering a conversation: criterion to be determined by observing peers (same as peers).
3. With strangers the student will explain steps for entering a conversation: criterion 100%.
4. With strangers the student will carry out steps for entering a conversation: criterion to be determined by observing peers (same as peers).
5. With familiar peers the student will explain the steps for answering a complaint: criterion 100%.
6. With familiar peers the student will carry out steps for answering a complaint: criterion to be determined by observing peers (same as peers).
7. With strangers the student will explain steps for answering a complaint: criterion 100%.
8. With strangers the student will carry out steps for answering a complaint: criterion to be determined by observing peers (same as peers).
9. With familiar peers the student will explain the steps for saying no: criterion 100%.
10. With familiar peers the student will carry out steps for saying no: criterion to be determined by observing peers (same as peers).
11. With strangers the student will explain steps for saying no: criterion 100%.
12. With strangers the student will carry out steps for saying no: criterion to be determined by observing peers (same as peers).

familiar peers. In contrast, objective 12 presents the requirement that the student carry out the steps of saying no with strangers. (This progression from familiar peers to strangers complements the content because of the situational nature of social competence.) It is the imposition of the horizontal axis, with its behaviors and conditions, that provides the structure needed to use Table 4.1 as a tool for generating objectives, guiding evaluation, and aligning instruction with student needs.

Instructional Objectives.   Most teachers, or students in teacher training programs, have already learned that the curriculum is manifested in the form of instructional objectives. These objectives, which ideally will be sequenced to facilitate the ease and speed of learning, are composed of certain elements. These are seen in Table 4.1 and include statements of *content* (what the student will learn about), statements of *behavior* (what the student will do in order to demonstrate that he or she has learned the content), statements of *conditions* (the circumstances under which the student will demonstrate knowledge), and statements of *criteria* (the level of proficiency expected on the objective). All four of these elements are definitional as they speak directly to key aspects of the objective. If an element is changed, the objective is redefined. For example, compare objective 6—"With familiar peers the student will carry out steps for answering a complaint: Criterion to be determined by observing peers (same as peers)"—with objective 8—"With strangers the student will carry out steps for answering a complaint: Criterion to be determined by observing peers (same as peers)." In this example, a new objective has been produced by only replacing *familiar peers* with *strangers*. Similarly changes in content (e.g., *entering a conversation* for *answering a complaint*), behavior (e.g., *explain* to *carry out*), or criteria (e.g., *100%* to *determined by observing peers* [*same as peers*]) will also change the learning outcome. An objective is unique if some students can do one version but not the other.

There are four steps to designing tables of specifications so that they will produce useful objectives. These same steps apply if you are going to produce objectives without the tables. The steps are identifying content, identifying behavior, identifying conditions, and identifying criteria. Relative to prosocial skills, conditions and criteria present some special problems.

Conditions. The contextual nature of behavior is well established (Stormont & Zentall, 1999; van Geert, 1998). That is why it is important to consider the conditions under which the student is currently behaving as well as the conditions of targeted performance. Other terms for *condition* include *environment, situation,* or *context.* When thinking about conditions, it is important to consider those that are apt to have the greatest impact on the student or the targeted behavior. As Bower (1972) pointed out years ago, these "high-impact" environments may include locations such as the home or school. Other situations can include recess, the workplace, and after-school programs.

Criteria. Part of defining criteria for social skills may include the consideration of concepts such as "appropriate." This problem can be solved two ways. First, the use of concept statements can be avoided. Second, the concepts can be clarified so that they are clear and workable.

One way to clarify a concept is to list behaviors that must be present (essential behaviors) when the concept is illustrated (Engelmann, 1980). Additionally, behaviors that cannot occur (contra behaviors) must be listed. For example, if the concept is "To answer a complaint *appropriately*," dropping your head and mumbling would be contrary (not appropriate). Therefore, these behaviors would signal that your response is inappropriate. Developing short lists of essential and contra behaviors can go a long way toward defining conceptual content.

Finally, as seen in Table 4.1, the average performance of successful peers within a target setting is commonly used for social skill criteria. So, if the goal is to have the student talk appropriately within a work setting, it will be necessary to go to the work setting to determine the appropriate criteria. The same evaluation techniques can be used on a sample of successful individuals (e.g., interval sampling of the target behavior) to fix the criterion (Kaplan, 2000). (Gilbert, 1978). This gives us the wording "determined by observing peers (same as peers)" found under the B and D columns in Table 4.1.

Evaluation

Now that Susan has the curriculum established, she is still not quite ready to teach. Even though the objectives are clearly defined, she does not know exactly which ones should be taught to each student. But before any individual evaluation begins, one needs to consider whether it is even needed. As Aster, Meyer, and Behre (1999) have pointed out, approximately half of classroom behavior problems (not social behavior problems) are produced by only one to 2% of the students in school, and much of that occurs in recognizable locations. For this 1% to 2% of the student population, not much individual student evaluation is warranted. What is needed is an evaluation of the student body and the school. Patterns of ongoing problems can be discovered by reviewing discipline records, mapping the locations where major problems occur, and interviewing students and staff to locate problematic times, places, and students. Once these are approached with logical intercession, the burden of controlling repeated incidents of misbehavior can be relieved. This will allow most teachers more time to pinpoint the needed skills of those few students who show chronic and pervasive patterns of maladaptive, if not dangerous, social behavior. For Susan, however, all of her students fall into this category.

Even for those students who have unique social behavior difficulties, evaluation tools should first be used on academic skills. This is because many inappropriate classroom behaviors, and social problems, are carried out for the function of escaping encounters with academic failure. The evaluation should also include an examination of the classroom management skills and instructional procedures used in the class. This means that Susan may need to examine her own behavior to recognize possible antecedents of student misbehavior.

Next comes the most critical step in any assessment of social skills. One must determine why the student is engaging in the maladaptive behavior. In a curriculum-based model, it is assumed that the student engages in maladaptive behaviors to accomplish some function. The function is the purpose of the maladaptive behavior. In this model there are no maladaptive functions, only maladaptive and adaptive (appropriate) behaviors. Functions are things people want, and students, with even the most severe behavioral problems, want what everyone else wants. Their problem (and Susan's) is that they go about attempting to meet these normal human functions in the wrong way. By identifying the function of a student's action, one is in the position of teaching the student how to get what he or she wants in an appropriate way. You can learn more about the process of functional behavioral evaluation elsewhere in this text (see Chapter 12 by Ervin, Jones, Radford, & Gingerich, this text) and by consulting the Web site for the Center for Effective Collaboration and Practice in Washington, DC.

This course of action is central to the selection of a target behavior. The selection is accomplished by taking the following steps:

1. Specify, in behavioral terms, exactly what the student is doing wrong (e.g., "Says yes to demands that engage her in behaviors that violate social rules").
2. Determine the function (purpose of the maladaptive behavior).
3. Flip the maladaptive behavior over and specify exactly what you would like to see the student doing in his attempts to accomplish the purpose of his behavior (e.g., "Says no to avoid participating when asked to engage in behaviors that violate social rules").
4. Ask a generic set of questions to determine what the student doesn't know, or believe, that is causing her to fail to meet her function appropriately. ("Does the student find it more rewarding to break rules than to follow them?")
5. Summarize what you get and then teach those missing subskills found in the last step.

The process of converting the statement of inadequate behavior into a preferable alternative is *essential* to the processes of evaluation and proactive instruction. The shift in perspective changes the goal from "killing off" undesirable behaviors to building those that are desirable. This simple act removes the problem from control and shifts it to instruction.

In plain terms, what Susan needs to do next is look at Table 4.1 and decide which cells she thinks are important to the process of teaching missing subskills. Then she must look into these cells to determine whether the student does or doesn't have the skills these cells represent. Of course, that is harder to do than it is to state. The best advice is that one take a far-reaching approach by *reviewing* products and records, *interviewing* the student and others, *observing* the student within important environments, and using suitable *tests* (Heartland Education Agency, 1998). Any or all of these processes can be used to focus on a cell in Table 4.1 for the purpose of recognizing the student's status on the objective represented by those cells.

Problem Solving.   One must have a system of evaluation and decision making that is compatible with purpose. For Susan's purpose, this system can follow the scientific method. She must make observations of the students, develop hypotheses about what has been observed, and take the measures needed to support or reject her hypotheses.

In the case of curriculum-based evaluation, the assumed cause for failure at a task is that the student does not have sufficient prior knowledge of subskills of the task (which could include missing expectations or values). Here are some prerequisites that, if missing, might explain why a student does not exhibit appropriate behavior (Howell & Nolet; 2000, Kaplan, 2000). These "generic" sub-skills underlie large numbers of the outcomes generated and clarified by tables of specifications.

- The student can't discriminate the target and maladaptive behaviors from each other and from other behaviors.
- The student can't monitor his or her own behavior well enough to know when he or she is engaging in the target or maladaptive behavior.
- The student can't monitor the environment well enough to recognize events that should prompt the target behavior or inhibit the maladaptive behavior.
- The student doesn't consider the consequences of engaging in a maladaptive behavior to be aversive.
- The student values the maladaptive behavior more than the target behavior.
- The student holds beliefs that are incompatible with the target behavior and compatible with the maladaptive behavior.

Evaluation is not measurement. Measurement is only conducted to get information. Therefore, when all of the other steps have been followed, Susan will need to sit back and arrive at decisions that may help the problem that started her down this path in the first place. She will think of things that are aligned with the student's needs. She will also decide what prior knowledge of the main task the student is missing (this is the knowledge that must be taught first). And then she will check her findings to be sure she has only been thinking about things that can be altered through teaching (other problem-related factors may need to be dealt with by referral or consultation).

The use of adequate preinstruction evaluation should give Susan a clearer understanding of the tasks that she needs to teach. However, Susan may still be unclear about *how* to teach that content. How can she know what type of instructional strategy to employ?

Design and Delivery of Instruction

Instructional Strategies

After determining an objective and recognizing the missing skill/knowledge of the student, a teacher is ready to design a lesson. At this point it is easy to confuse strategies for instructional delivery with specific social skills programs. Strategies for delivering instruction are evident in the teachers' actions. Preprepared social skills programs may or may not be part of these actions. Different teachers may employ various teaching strategies using the same social skills programs. However, no teacher action will work if it does not meet the needs of the student and the task being taught. There are different "types" or approaches to instruction. For example, researchers and practitioners have debated the relative effectiveness of implicit and explicit instructional strategies for years.

Implicit instructional strategies are those that provide students with a rich environment of materials and ideas related to the learning expectation. When these strategies are used, students are expected to generate essential learnings from the environment. Teachers provide little direct initial instruction, but more probing and questioning in order to encourage self-directed learning. Within social skills instruction, the implicit strategies, or extreme version of them, are illustrated by open format discussions, nonevaluated journal writing, communication circles, nondirected "venting," and opportunistic instructional response to misbehavior.

Explicit instructional strategies are those that also provide students with a rich environment for learning. However, this environment includes direct initial instruction on needed skills. This direct instruction is used to provide students with the knowledge necessary for acquiring the desired learning outcome. The instruction is hands-on, and highly structured scaffolds are provided. Explicit teaching is illustrated by heavy use of direct instruction and practice (often through structured role play).

According to Mercer, Lane, Jordan, Allsopp, and Eisele (1996), the decision about an instructional approach should be based on characteristics of the student and the task. For example, if the student already knows a lot about what you will be teaching, if failure to learn the task does not put the student (or others) in danger, and if the student is successful at learning from the very first, you may want to decide on an implicit approach. If failure to learn the task is dangerous, if the student is not highly motivated to work on the problem, if the student finds working on the tasks to be hard, or if there is limited time for the student to learn the task, you should consider an explicit approach.

As one would expect, those teaching social skills commonly prefer lessons that are highly controlled, if not scripted. Moreover, they recognize the need to go beyond knowledge and to teach application of knowledge explicitly. Also, the risk factor makes the argument for teaching directly all the more compelling. However, teachers do not want to mistake explicit instruction for unyielding instruction.

One component of lesson design and delivery is deciding when instruction is *not* advisable. For example, some educators may say that those students who are diagnosed with a mental illness should not receive social skill instruction. That is because the behaviors of students with severe emotional problems and/or mental illness are thought to arise from some form of personal pathology. It may also be harder to predict their behavior. That is assumed to be because these behaviors may not result from an interaction with the immediate geographic environment but rather from the constraints of distorted perceptions, unrealistic expectations, and/or the chronic fear and sadness that can reside in the cognitive environment. At first it may seem difficult to conceptualize and to deal with such factors within an instructional model. For example, how does one plan to teach a student who is behaving out of a preoccupation with some past event? The answer is fairly simple (which is not to imply that it will be easy to employ). In most cases prosocial skills still need to be taught.

However, there are conditions under which one might consider suspending instruction in order to transfer the time spent on instruction to one or more of the other treatment modalities. When students are receiving counseling or medication therapies, there are often still skills they should be taught. But imagine that you have a student who has the anger control skills you teach, as evidenced through monitoring and evaluation procedures, but still goes into rages. Should instruction be stopped? There is a rigorous test for this decision: you must be convinced that the lessons covered the correct skills and were taught well and that the skills were actually learned. Then you can assume that instruction is no longer needed.

The instructional decision in this case should be to suspend instruction on the skills. But this does not mean that the rages should be ignored. The rages need to be dealt with through backup contingencies and plans. These should always be developed along with typical lesson plans. Backup plans go into place when the standard instructional procedures of choice fail (if only for a brief time) and the student engages in a highly intense nonadaptive display of destructive behavior.

Here is one other consideration. Unlike academic behaviors, there may be times when social skill instruction needs to be temporarily suspended during a lesson. Unfortunately, some teachers continue to try and deliver lessons during these intervals. When inappropriate behavior, particularly aggressive or rage behavior, is occurring, teachers should realize that this is not an "instructional moment." They should suspend teaching in favor of containment and reduction of damage. Students need to be taught how to handle these problems either before or after they occur. During the occurrence of extreme behavior, attempts at instruction may actually intensify the problem (Walker, Colvin, & Ramsey, 1995).

Effective Teaching

One can conceptualize a continuum of severity stretching from relatively moderate classroom infractions to severe and intense behavioral outbursts (which may or may not be limited to the classroom setting). It must be clear that a variety of different interventions are required to fully cover the spectrum of social behavior. (See Chapter 10 by Colvin). So how do you pick the right one?

Once a teacher decides that instruction is warranted, then the following steps are often recommended when designing and delivering effective instruction:

1. Select an objective.
2. Plan the lesson.
3. Teach the skill using the parameters outlined in the plan.
4. Monitor the student's skill.
5. Chart the student's progression of skill development.

Select an Objective.   This topic has previously been addressed.

Plan the Lesson.   All effective teachers employ some type of lesson plan. A written plan is frequently best for interventions on the sorts of problems exhibited by Susan's students. The need for a written plan implies a sort of formal preparation that very few experienced teachers actually employ. That is because these teachers automatically incorporate needed routines and lesson components as they teach. However, even the most experienced teacher can start performing like a novice if sufficiently stressed. And there is nothing like aggressive behavior to impose that stress. So, the "maximum/minimum" rule applies here: "Maximum effort for those students with minimum skills." This means the plan will likely need to be written in a more detailed format. At times, when the plan is prepared by a group and is based on a functional behavior assessment, the plan may take on the form of the behavior intervention plan (Gable, Quinn, Rutherford, Howell, & Hoffman, 2000).

The teacher's next step in lesson design is to decide whether a straightforward lesson plan or an "activity plan" is needed. If the student needs initial instruction on a fundamental skill to *learn* a target skill, an explicit teaching strategy will need to be employed. If the student needs to *practice* an already acquired skill, then a more implicit teaching strategy is warranted and an activity plan is needed. This is so that the student can practice and learn to generalize the skill. Price and Nelson (1999) make a clear distinction between these two types of plans because different teacher actions are needed for each type. The components of a lesson plan include (a) lesson objective, (b) presentation of the rationale for the objective, (c) lesson setup, including overview, (d) opening, (d) body (delivery of information), (e) questions, (f) guided and independent activities, (g) feedback as well as correction, (h) closing of the body, (i) extended independent practice and cross-situational practice, and (j) evaluation. The components of an activity play include (a) activity goal, (b) rationale, (c) beginning, (d) middle, and (e) closing. The structure of a lesson plan is considerably more complex than that of a lesson plan. Activity and lesson plans are distinct because each one requires separate teacher actions. The teacher chooses the type of plan based on the student's needs and the skill to be taught. See Boxes 4.1 and 4.2 for example lesson and activity plans.

BOX 4.1

Sample Lesson Plan

    Topic: Interpersonal Skills

Preplanning Tasks

Content Analysis
    Task analysis

1. Identify stranger	3. List steps for answering a complaint
2. Identify complaint	4. Carry out steps by answering complaints made by someone familiar

Objective: The student will carry out the steps presented in class by answering complaints made by strangers. This will be done with 100% accuracy.

(continued)

B O X **4.1**   Continued

Objective rationale: A basic school and community skill is responding appropriately to someone who is making a complaint. Many students who do not exhibit appropriate responses to complaints are isolated from the mainstream of society and therefore miss potential opportunities for academic and social success.

Materials and Logistics: List of the steps. Role-play script to demonstrate skill. Examples and nonexamples of complaints. Access to the cafeteria.

Lesson Setup

The first period bell signifies the beginning of lesson. (signal for attention)

Say, "If you have questions during this lesson, remember to raise your hand and wait until I call on you before speaking." (statement of behavior expectations)

Lesson Opening

Say, "Remember when you practiced using the steps for responding to a complaint made by your peer."

Briefly use the examples and nonexamples to allow a few students to identify a complaint.

Say, "Today you are going to practice using these same steps in the cafeteria when someone you don't know makes a complaint to you."

Lesson Body

Say, "First we are going to review the steps. Say the steps for responding to a complaint to your peer." (check for understanding)

"Now I am going to model the appropriate response when someone makes a complaint to me." The paraprofessional and teacher demonstrate the appropriate response through a role play conducted in front of the class.

"Now I need a volunteer to model appropriate actions in a role play with a student from another class." Teacher chooses a student who will be an appropriate model.

"We will now work with students from another classroom on a role play based on a cafeteria situation." Pair students based on their current social skills. Teachers and paraprofessionals will observe student pairs and give specific feedback.

"Now we are going to the cafeteria for lunch. Someone will make a complaint to you and you will be expected to respond appropriately."

"Go to the cafeteria." Monitor students' behaviors.

Evaluation

Using a progress monitoring data collection form, monitor students' demonstration of each step.

Lesson Closing

Restate the lesson objective: "Today you demonstrated the steps necessary for responding to a complaint made by a stranger."

Review expectations for the rest of the week.

BOX **4.2**

Sample Lesson Plan

Activity: Basketball game with a seventh grade PE class

Activity goal: Students will practice using the steps presented in class by responding to complaints made by strangers.

Activity rationale: Students need to automatically demonstrate appropriate behaviors when responding to complaints made by strangers.

Materials and logistics: Basketballs and PE students

Activity Beginning

Signal for Attention: "I need everyone's attention."

Opening
Say, "Today we are going to play basketball with Ms. Michael's PE class. You all know how to play basketball, and you all remember the steps to follow when someone is making a complaint to you."

Behavior Expectations: "I expect everyone to use the steps we've been practicing in class and in the cafeteria. Students who exhibit appropriate behavior will get to play the remainder of the game."

Activity Middle

State the rules of the basketball game. Let students know how long the game will last. Start the game. Students play basketball with the PE class. Remind students that they have 5 more minutes to play.

Activity Closing

Blow whistle when game is over. Ask one student to collect the ball and put it away. Dismiss students to next class.

One concern among educators is students' lack of generalization of social skills from the classroom context to a more separate societal context. Therefore, generalization must be built in by using activity plans. Often times, students do not get the opportunities necessary to practice those skills.

Teach the Lesson.   Several fundamental characteristics of effective teaching can be considered when delivering a lesson. Some of these seem especially important for the teaching of social skills. We will briefly discuss four of them.

Time.   The impact of time on student learning is well known (Ysseldyke & Christenson, 1996). As a general rule, the more time a person spends studying or working on something, the better he or she will get. This assumes, of course, that the time is well spent. Time is of particular concern to those teaching social skills because, unlike academic skills, a person works on and practices social skill all day. Therefore, students with behavioral problems will often have reached high levels of proficiency on many of their less than desirable behaviors. This means that interventions designed to teach replacement behaviors must be intense and long lasting if they are to be effective, especially with older students.

Time spent on the delivery of information should be greater early in instruction. This is when the strategies you want the student to learn are presented. While it is important that students begin actively using this information (by engaging in activities and answering questions), it is essential that fundamental information be delivered. Therefore, during early stages of instruction, the proportion of time spent on activities is relatively limited.

High Standards.   Some of the strongest effects in the educational literature are those relative to teacher and student standards (Price & Nelson, 1999; Ysseldyke & Christenson, 1996). Higher standards support higher achievement. As a teacher you can support high standards during lessons by being sure that your talk and demeanor reflect interest in the topic, the topic's value, and the need to do the task well.

The standards are laid down during the delivery of information, but they are made real through the responses you give to performance on activities and questions. When responding, place the greatest emphasis on learning, not performance. In other words, avoid praising students for completion of work, and emphasize the effort exhibited and the learning illustrated by a correct answer or activity. When assigning activities, don't fall into the "You have to get this done by recess" trap. The message you want to convey is "Work on this to learn about _____."

The monitoring of student change also provides a chance for the illustration of high standards. This is accomplished by sharing data, ideally in a visual (charted) format, that show where the student started, where the student is now, where she should be, and how well he or she is progressing. Always put the emphasis on overall progress, not performance on individual tasks.

Standards also need to be high during activities. These are the practice sessions that increase the likelihood that learning will be maintained and transferred.

Practice.   Practice typically occurs through work on assigned activities. Cognitive practice may also be promoted through questioning. Therefore, during lesson delivery, you will use a pattern for practice that is the inverse of the pattern for delivery of information. Less practice is used when the student begins to learn a particular skill and increases as instruction and competence progress.

There are also different kinds of practice. By far the most important is *guided practice*, in which the teacher usually demonstrates how to perform the task. Next the teacher will help the student by doing part of the task with the student. Finally, the teacher will help the student work on the task until it can be completed correctly.

During initial lesson delivery, guided practice is used extensively as the teacher demonstrates the desired skills and creates models. The student can use these models later if assistance is needed. Independent practice should not be allowed until the student has reached a high level of proficiency during guided practice. In general, numerous short practice sessions are superior to one long session.

Cognitive Emphasis.   Distinctions are often made between types of knowledge, such as facts, concepts, and strategies. When delivering social skill instruction, the emphasis should be on conceptual and strategic thinking. This emphasis cuts across all other teacher actions. Therefore, a student may state the steps of a strategy for *safe arguing* during delivery, role-play the steps during an activity, and explain the steps, and next get responses feedback on the quality of his or her work, related to them.

Questioning and responding are of particular concern during concept and strategy instruction, as they are very different from the teacher's usual experience with factual instruction. In academics, there are facts such as $2 + 2 = 4$. But in social skills there are few such absolutes. Therefore, questions ought to focus on when and how things should be done. Similarly, responses should include comments like "Good—you recalled the steps and employed them correctly"—not "Good—you got the correct answer."

Monitor the Student's Skill and Chart the Student's Progression of Skill Development. The importance of monitoring and displaying data has been mentioned earlier, and it is also covered in Chapters 1 and 3 of this text. In addition, both of these techniques are so basic to discussions of topics such as behavior management that it is hard to imagine that any reader of this text is not already familiar with them (Kaplan, 2000).

The idea behind both monitoring and display is that one can only judge the effectiveness of an intervention after it has been employed. There are limits to the traditional practice of "front-loading" assessment in which a battery of measures are given prior to the start of instruction and few are given during the course of instruction. The better practice is to treat every initial lesson plan as an intervention to be validated. Begin by employing the most reasonable treatment technique available. Then regulate that procedure as time passes. This is where the data collection and monitoring processes stressed throughout this text come into play. Because the feature being monitored is within the curriculum, the assessment devices (reviews, interviews, observations, and tests) utilized in order to monitor it need to be curriculum based (Heartland Education Agency, 1998). One way to assure that they are is to align them with tables of specifications (like the one in Table 4.1).

During the monitoring procedures, the student's knowledge must be continually summarized in order to allow fine-tuning of the lesson delivery and design. Suppose that the data reveal that the student is not progressing. It might be suspected that the lack of progress is due to limited prior knowledge of the skill being taught. If so, the teacher will need to select a more basic objective or include sufficient adaptations to accommodate for the lack of prior knowledge (although the original objective must eventually be taught and the accommodations must eventually be removed). At this level, there is no difference between evaluation and instruction. The two are fused.

Ms. Sanchez

Susan's principal is pleased with Susan's current skills, but Susan wants to be better. She applies for and receives a $1,000 grant to purchase a social skills program, get inservice training, or buy texts. Take a moment and ask yourself how you would spend the money.

Susan decides not to purchase $1,000 worth of materials but instead:

- pay for a substitute teacher so she can spend a day with a competent social skills instructor developing social skills lessons and materials, using previously purchased materials;
- spend a day reading additional material related to social skills (including the rest of this book);
- spend a day with an expert in curriculum-based evaluation working with evaluating her 10 students to find good social skill objectivess.

Susan does all of this in order to gain a clearer understanding of the skills that her students need. Her overall strategy for helping her students is to use her resources to improve her owns skills and knowledge.

That's usually the best thing to do.

REFERENCES

Aster, A. A., Meyer, H. A., & Behre, W. J. (1999). Unowned places and times: Maps and interviews about violence in high schools. *American Educational Research Journal, 36*(1), 3–42.

Bloom, B. S., Madaus, G. F., & Hastings, J. T. (1981). *Evaluation to improve learning.* New York: McGraw-Hill.

Bower, E. M. (1972). Education as a humanizing process and its relationship to other humanizing processes. In S. E. Golann & C. Eisdorfer (Eds.), *Handbook of community mental health* (pp. 37–49). Englewood Cliffs, NJ: Prentice Hall.

Engelmann, S. (1980). Toward the design of faultless instruction: The theoretical basis of concept analysis. *Educational Technology, 20*(2), 28–36.

Fister, S., Conrad, D., & Kemp, K. (1998). *Cool kids.* Longmont, CO: Sopris West.

Gable R. A., Quinn, M. M., Rutherford, R. B., Howell, K. W., & Hoffman C. C. (2000). *Conducting a functional behavioral assessment* (3rd ed.). Washington, DC: Center for Effective Collaboration and Practice.

Goldstein, A. P. (1997). *Skillstreaming the adolescent* (rev. ed.). Champaign, IL: Research Press.

Hasazi S. B., Furney K. S., & Destefano, L. (1999). Implementing the IDEA transition mandates. *Exceptional Children, 65*(4), 555–566.

Heartland Education Agency. (1998). *Program manual for special education.* Johnston, IA: Heartland Area Education Agency 11.

Howell, K. W., & Nolet, V. (2000). *Curriculum-based evaluation: Teaching and decision making.* Atlanta, GA: Wadsworth.

Johnson, M. (1967). Definitions and models in curriculum theory. *Educational Theory, 7,* 127–140.

Kaplan, J. (2000). *Beyond functional assessment: A social cognitive approach to the evaluation of behavior problems in children and youth.* Austin, TX: Pro-Ed.

Marzano, R. J., Brandt, R. S., Hughes, C. S., Jones, B. F., Presseisen, B. Z., Rankin, S. C., & Suhor, C. (1988). *Dimensions of Thinking: A Framework for Curriculum and Instruction.* Alexandria, VA: Association for Supervision and Curriculum Development.

Mercer, C. D., Lane, H. B., Jordan, L., Allsopp D. H., & Eisele, M. R. (1996). Empowering teachers and students with instructional choices in inclusive settings. *Remedial and Special Education, 17*(4), 226–236.

Price, K. M., & Nelson, K. L. (1999). *Daily planning for today's classroom: A guide for writing lesson and activity plans.* Belmont, CA: Wadsworth.

Sargent, L. R. (1998). *Social skills for school and community: Systematic instruction for children and youth with cognitive delays.* Reston, VA: Division on Mental Retardation and Developmental Delay of the Council for Exceptional Children.

Sheridan, S. (1995). *Tough kid social skills.* Longmont, CO: Sopris West.

Stormont, M., & Zentall, S. S. (1999). Assessment of setting in the behavioral ratings of preschoolers with and without high levels of activity. *Psychology in the Schools, 36*(2), 109–115.

van Geert, P. (1998). A dynamic systems model of basic developmental mechanisms: Piaget, Vygotsky, and beyond. *Psychological Review, 105*(4), 634–644.

Walker, H. M., Colvin, G., & Ramsey, E. (1995). *Antisocial behavior in school: Strategies and best practices.* Pacific Grove, CA: Brooks/Cole.

Ysseldyke, J. E., & Christenson, S. L. (1996). *TIES II: The Instructional Environment System–II.* Longmont, CO: Sopris West.

5 Innovations and Deep Unity

Siegfried Engelmann's Direct Instruction

LANA EDWARDS
Lehigh University

EDWARD J. KAME'ENUI
University of Oregon

Introduction

In this chapter, we examine two prominent but highly elusive words, *Direct Instruction.* While the meanings of these words may appear conspicuously transparent historically, etymologically, and pedagogically to many readers—after all, they have been in the literature for at least 40 years—they are, nonetheless, misunderstood by many in the educational enterprise. To be understood clearly, unmistakably, and substantively, the words *Direct Instruction* must be defined in the context of a singular, prominent individual—Siegfried Engelmann. Throughout the chapter, we highlight selections from Engelmann's passionate and prolific writings to convey his thinking and insights about learning and teaching that serve as the pedagogical and philosophical foundation of Direct Instruction. In addition, we attempt to answer the following questions: What is Direct Instruction? What does Direct Instruction look like when implemented in the classroom? What is the empirical base for Direct Instruction?

Siegfried Engelmann and Direct Instruction

When describing the creative process intrinsic to scientific discoveries, Bronowski (1958) wrote, "Although science and art are a social phenomena, an innovation in either field occurs only when a single mind perceives in disorder a deep new unity" (p. 3). Siegfried Engelmann, originator of Direct Instruction and author of 60 or so commercial curricula, is recognized as the single mind that perceived a revolutionary innovation in instruction. Engelmann's beliefs that all children can learn what they are taught and effective teaching principles transcend diverse learner characteristics reflect a deep unity in how student academic success is perceived. Assumptions such as "There are individual differences between children, but these differences must be expressed in such a way that the teacher can do something about them" (Engelmann, 1969, p. 39) and "The first and most important step in cause finding is to discover *what* the child has failed to learn" (1969, p. 8; italics in original) reveal the philosophical foundation that has contributed to how Direction Instruction has been defined, as well as how it has evolved in the last 30 years.

A critical principle of Direct Instruction is that children's failure to learn is unacceptable and unnecessary if we understand what we want to teach and design the teaching carefully, strategically, and with full consideration of the learner (Kame'enui, Simmons, Chard, & Dickson, 1997). According to Engelmann, *all* children—including students with disabilities, slow readers, disadvantaged learners, poor students, and students with emotional and behavioral disorders—can learn if taught carefully, systematically, and with vigilant attention to the details of instruction (Engelmann, 1980). In other words, "the potential power of instruction in increasing intelligent behavior has *no known limit.* Through better teaching, children can be smarter. Children learn what they are taught" (Becker & Engelmann, 1976, p. 304; italics in original).

What Is Direct Instruction?

According to Engelmann, "Direct Instruction is a system of teaching that attempts to control all the variables that make a difference in the performance of children. The Direct Instruction creed is if the student has not learned, the teacher has not taught" (Adams & Engelmann, 1996, p. 1). Though Engelmann's definition of Direct Instruction focuses on a comprehensive system of teaching that enables students to master academic content and accelerate their learning, previous reviews of Direct Instruction recognize that "a galaxy of meanings assigned to *direct instruction* has indeed been great, perhaps even unwieldy" (Kame'enui, Jitendra, & Darch, 1995, p. 5). A selection of definitions representing a diverse range of conceptualizations is presented in Table 5.1.

When considering the galaxy of meanings associated with discussions of direct instruction, consensus, disagreement, and confusion are evident (e.g., Shannon, 1988; Tarver, 1992). In an article entitled, "Direct Instruction as Eonomine and Contronym," Kame'enui et al. (1995) observe that the words used to define Direct Instruction have historically inspired some while inciting others. This perspective explains in part the authors' reference to Direct Instruction as eonomine and contronym; that is, the words *Direct Instruction* are so elusive they are known only by name, and that name often refers to contradictory things.

TABLE 5.1   Conceptions and Definitions of Direct Instruction

Reference	Definition or Attributes
Rosenshine (1976)	■ Time is structured by the teacher. ■ Students are taught in groups supervised by the teacher. ■ Activities are teacher directed. ■ Teacher poses questions that have a single answer and are academically focused.
Berliner (1981)	■ "A nebulous but semantically rich concept" (p. 217). ■ "A syndrome of classroom variables such as content coverage, opportunity to learn, academic engaged time, allocated time, success rate, etc." (p. 217).
Baumann (1983, 1984, 1988)	■ A direct instruction paradigm for teaching main-idea comprehension involves a four-step procedure: introducing the skill (introduction), providing an (example), providing application and transfer exercises under teacher supervision and corrective feedback (teacher-directed application), and administering practice exercises (independent practice).

Engelmann, too, has noted that "[w]hen teachers, administrators, and university professors discuss Direct Instruction, there is usually confusing (and often loud) disagreement" (Adams & Engelmann, 1996, p. 1). Moving beyond nonproductive, circumlocutory discussions when answering the question "What is Direct Instruction?" requires a clear understanding of what a speaker, writer, or even listener intends Direct Instruction to mean. In their reflections on the question "What does it mean to know a word?" Baumann and Kame'enui (1991) cite the exchange between Humpty Dumpty and Alice in Lewis Carroll's *Through the Looking Glass*

> "When I use a word," Humpty Dumpty said in a rather scornful tone, "it means just what I choose it to mean—neither more or less."
>
> "The question is," said Alice, "whether you can make words mean so many different things."
>
> "The question is," said Humpty Dumpty, "which is to be master—that's all."

Therefore, to ascertain a common understanding of Direct Instruction from such a wide spectrum of interpretations, one must appreciate what is meant by the words *Direct Instruction*. Clarity and consensus in definitions are also established by examining the "structural sameness," or the commonalties associated with critical definitional features of words (Kame'enui, 1991). By examining the structural samenesses of definitions, we can discern what is meant by the words *Direct Instruction*.

When examining the sameness across definitions and conceptualizations, it appears that meanings of direct instruction cluster in three primary ways (Adams & Engelmann, 1996):

Direct Instruction as *direct instruction*

Direct Instruction as *direction instruction* has as its primary focus the behavioral features of a highly structured system of teacher–student interactions (Adams & Engelmann, 1996). Rosenshine's (1976, 1986, 1987) definitions, for example, emphasize the "behavioral" variables of group responses, lesson pacing, and correction of student errors that correlate with student achievement. In addition, direct instruction refers to the amount of student "engaged time" (the time that a student responds to specific tasks presented by the teacher) and the rate of student responses during academic engaged time (Adams & Engelmann, 1996). Overall, *direct instruction* describes a set of instructional variables relating to teacher behavior and classroom organization (Hempenstall, 1999).

Direct Instruction as *Direct Instruction*

This conception of direct instruction was originated by Siegfried Engelmann and his colleagues at the University of Illinois in 1964 and was first described as direct-verbal instruction in the book *Teaching Disadvantaged Children in the Preschool* by Carl Bereiter and Siegfried Engelmann (1966). More than 60 commercial instructional programs were subsequently developed and published by Engelmann and his colleagues at the University of Oregon under the acronym DISTAR, for Direct Instruction System for Teaching and Remediation. The meaning of direct instruction as Direct Instruction has served as the foundation for definitions formulated by education researchers such as Rosenshine (1976, 1987) and Gaskins (1988), as well as Tarver's (1992) view that Direct Instruction represents a "comprehensive system that integrates curriculum design with teaching techniques to produce instructional programs in language, reading, mathematics, spelling, written expression, and science" (p. 141).

Direct Instruction as Teacher-Directed Instruction

Teacher-directed instruction involves a teacher's responsibility for the face-to-face telling, sharing, modeling, demonstrating, and direct leading of academic instruction (Baumann, 1984). Teachers communicate information to students directly and in ways that use instructional time deliberately and efficiently (Kame'enui et al., 1995). When student learning progresses, instruction becomes "less direct" than during initial phases because the teacher gradually gives increased responsibility to the student as the student begins to master more skills.

What Does Direct Instruction Look Like When Implemented in a Classroom?

According to Engelmann (Engelmann & Carnine, 1991; Engelmann & Engelmann, 1966), there are two elements in any learning situation: a teacher and a learner. The following scenario, described in Engelmann and Engelmann's (1966) *Give Your*

Child a Superior Mind, illustrates a learning situation and previews the importance of clear, well-defined, "faultless" instruction:

> Reduce your vocabulary to several hundred of the simplest words, and step into a world of bizarre shapes and sounds. Put a familiar figure—a mother perhaps—in the scene. . . . You can tell by the sound of her voice that she's trying to teach you something. But what? She's walking and saying, "Fast." She's telling you about the room. The room. Now she's walking again, but she looks different. Mad maybe. No, not mad. She tells you about the room again. "Fast," she says. Or is it about her? You thought it was called "walking," not "fast."
>
> Oh well. "Fast," you say.
>
> She smiles. "Slow," she says. But she's *still walking.* Something's not right. . . . You search the room for the slow. It must be around someplace. You're confused. (p. 47; italics in original)

To avoid confusing learning situations like the one just described, Engelmann's theory of instruction emphasizes (a) the design of faultless instructional presentations and lessons, (b) the assumption that students will learn a concept if they receive faultless instruction, (c) the direct and explicit presentation of information to a student while monitoring the student to determine whether the intended concept is learned, and (d) specially designed instruction for unsuccessful students so that the student's capacity to respond to faultless instruction is modified (Engelmann & Carnine, 1991). Avoiding confusing learning situations through the use of faultless communication is a primary intent of Direct Instruction. Yet when Direct Instruction and its inherent faultless communication are implemented in the classroom, what does it really look like?

Depending on whether one watches before-instruction preparations or during-instruction implementation, there are both observable and the "more-difficult-to-observe" features of Direct Instruction. When watching a Direct Instruction lesson, one may see a teacher directly leading activities with a small group of students and students who are actively involved in responding to a fast-paced lesson during which they receive constant feedback (Hempenstall, 1999). While lesson pace, unison responding, and correct feedback are obvious qualities in Direct Instruction implementation, important underlying "architectural" design features also distinguish Direct Instruction from other iterations of direct instruction. Program delivery, program organization, and program design are three primary levels of instructional planning and implementation that define Direct Instruction.

Program Delivery

An analysis of samenesses across definitions clearly reveals that program delivery, what the teacher says and does, is an essential variable in Direct Instruction. Program delivery includes (a) unison oral responding that requires signals from the teacher and allowance for wait or think time, (b) appropriate pacing to engage children's attention and reduce oral responding errors, (c) careful monitoring of students' oral responses and independent seatwork, and (d) strategic diagnosing and correcting of incorrect responses (Carnine, Silbert, & Kame'enui, 1997). Program delivery features are almost exclusively teacher based and are only included in the "during-instruction phase" (Kame'enui & Simmons, 1990). In other words, teachers directly initiate, guide, clarify, respond, and adjust lesson pace *during instruction.*

Program Organization

Program organization, a "before-instruction phase" of Direction Instruction, includes attention to scheduling instruction, the arrangement of the physical setting for instruction, and the organization of teaching materials prior to teaching a lesson (Brophy & Good, 1986; Murphy, Weil, & McGreal; 1986, Rosenshine 1976). Prioritizing instructional time and scheduling instruction so that it is used efficiently and optimally is probably the most important organizational feature of Direct Instruction (Kame'enui et al., 1995). According to Brophy and Good (1986), achievement is maximized when teachers recognize academic instruction as their highest priority, establish high expectations for their students in terms of mastering the curriculum, and allocate the majority of the school day to curriculum-related activities. As Carnine et al. (1997) note:

> Teachers cannot spend 15 minutes getting the students settled in the morning, 5 minutes for transitions between activities, 5 minutes re-explaining assignments and rules that students should understand, and 5 minutes figuring out what to do next while students are waiting. Teachers . . . must carefully schedule activities so that instructional time is well used and enough time is devoted to priority areas. (p. 9)

In addition to the importance of scheduling instruction so that student academic engaged time can be optimized, program organization also requires teachers to attend to the arrangement of the classroom's physical setting and the instructional materials used in a particular lesson (Englert, 1984). Arranging desks so that they are not too close to distractions and organizing lesson materials and student work folders prior to instruction, for example, can facilitate program delivery and maximize engaged time.

Program Design

Despite the critical importance of a teacher's role in direct instruction, Direct Instruction is also about curriculum design (Carnine & Kame'enui, 1992; Carnine et al., 1997; Engelmann & Carnine, 1991; Gersten, Carnine, & White, 1984). In fact, Kame'enui et al. (1995) assert that "the way the information is 'packaged' *before* teacher delivery and the form in which it is available to the learner serve as the basis for Direct Instruction" (p. 257, emphasis added). While it is difficult to distinguish *direct instruction* from *Direct Instruction* when examining teaching techniques, Direct Instruction, as defined as Engelmann's DISTAR programs published by Science Research Associates, can be clearly distinguished from other direct instruction programs on the basis of curriculum components (Tarver, 1992). In essence, curriculum design is no less important than the teacher delivery feature most commonly associated with direct instruction.

Like the program organization features of direct instruction, curriculum design must be considered during a "before-instruction phase" (Carnine et al., 1997; Kame'enui & Simmons, 1990). Unlike observable program organization features and the dynamic teacher role in program delivery, program design features, however, are part of an often more-difficult-to-observe, static curriculum architecture (Tarver, 1992). Program design features include specifying objectives, devising strategies, developing teaching procedures, selecting examples, sequencing examples and skills, and providing practice and review (Carnine et al., 1997).

Although teachers often consider program design features when they select, evaluate, or modify reading programs, rarely do they design complete lessons from beginning to end. Instead, design features are typically part of a program "package" and "worked out *before* the teacher begins the lesson" (Carnine et al., 1997, p. 11; italics in original). In direct instruction, program design is also given its rightful place. Baumann's (1988) direct instruction paradigm includes examples, application exercises, and practice exercises that are similar to the program features of Direct Instruction. However, unlike the direct instruction paradigm, program design for Direct Instruction is based on a unique analysis of the curriculum content (Kame'enui et al., 1995).

What the Research Says about Direct Instruction

Though Engelmann's theoretical vision of Direct Instruction is central to how Direct Instruction has been defined, as well as how the principles of instructional design, planning, and implementation contribute to what Direct Instruction looks like, a substantial empirical base supports the effectiveness of Direct Instruction for a wide range of students. Research has revealed that Direct Instruction contributes to academic success of disadvantaged, at-risk, and average students. In addition, research supports the program design and teacher variables expounded by Engelmann.

Project Follow Through

The empirical integrity and success of Direct Instruction was most dramatically documented in the context of Project Follow Through, a federally funded program in the late 1960s and early 1970s designed to sustain and extend Head Start into the elementary grades. Over 10,000 low-income students in 180 communities were involved in this $500 million project. The overall purpose of Follow Through was to evaluate nine different instructional approaches to educating economically disadvantaged students from kindergarten through grade 3. The nine approaches included in Follow Through were the Behavior Analysis Model developed by Donald Bushell from the University of Kansas, the Direct Instruction Model developed by Siegfried Engelmann and Wes Becker from the University of Oregon, the Language Development (Bilingual) Model from Southwest Educational Development Laboratory, the Cognitively Orientated Curriculum Model from High Scope Foundation, the Florida Parent Education Model from the University of Florida, the Tucson Early Education Model from the University of Arizona, the Bank Street College Model from Bank Street College of Education, the Open Education Model from Education Development Center, and the Responsive Education Model developed by Glenn Nimict from Far West Laboratory.

Each educational model was categorized according to theoretical orientation and degree of academic structure (White, 1973). Theoretical orientation included behavioral, cognitive, and psychodynamic approaches. Behavioral, or basic skills models, were based on the premise that all behaviors are learned and that disadvantaged children were behind because no one was teaching them the necessary social and academic skills. When describing the purpose of the Direct Instruction model, Becker and Engelmann (1978) wrote that "the major goal of the Direct Instruction model was to give disadvantaged children sufficient basic skills to compete with their more advantaged peers for higher education and the opportunities available in our society" (p. 2).

In contrast, models based on the cognitive development approach focused on the developmental sequence that characterized normal cognitive growth. According to cognitive models, disadvantaged children would optimally benefit from interactions with teachers in which language experiences were emphasized and there was exposure to Piagetian-based language, affective, motor, and cognitive instruction. Finally, psychodynamic approaches, or affective skills models, addressed goals relating to socioemotional development and the improvement of children's self-esteem and overall personal growth.

In addition to theoretical orientation, the nine educational models were also categorized according to degree of structure (White, 1973). Models classified as having a high structure included predetermined roles for teachers and students. Teachers, for example, were expected to lead lessons directly as well as provide immediate feedback to students. Implementation of high-structure approaches featured specific educational objectives and consistent implementation across classrooms. Low-structure models gave teachers the freedom to follow their own educational philosophies when implementing instructional activities. The flexibility fostered by the low-structure models led to a diverse range of classroom implementations. Finally, models that were designated as having a middle level of structure were based on broad educational objectives and included a mix of high- and low-structure activities (Stebbins, St. Pierre, Proper, Anderson, & Cerva, 1977).

The data from Project Follow Through were analyzed by Stanford Research Institute (SRI) and Abt Associates (Stebbins et al., 1977) for the U.S. Department of Education. The reports on Project Follow Through have been extensive and, in some cases, controversial (Becker, 1977; Becker, Engelmann, Carnine, & Rhine, 1981; Gersten, Becker, Heiry, & White, 1984; Guthrie, 1977; House, Glass, McLean, & Walker,

1978; Kame'enui & Gersten, 1997). A full and detailed discussion of the results of Follow Through are beyond the scope of this chapter, but a brief summary follows.

The SRI and Abt Associates' longitudinal evaluation examined the impact of the nine different instructional models by comparing Follow Through (FT) model sites with non–Follow Through (NFT) comparison sites. As Becker and Carnine (1980) note, the analysis included 9,255 FT children and 6,485 NFT children, with the nine major educational models represented in 111 of the 139 sites studied. In general, the national evaluation of Project Follow Through found that the Direct Instruction model had a beneficial effect on the achievement of low-income students who participated for 4 years (kindergarten through third grade). At the end of third grade, students taught using the Direct Instruction programs performed at, near, or above the national median in math, language, and spelling. In reading, performance corresponded to the 41st percentile—9 percentile points below the median. Less effective were several nondirective instructional approaches, such as the Open Education Model, the Cognitively Orientated Curriculum Model, the Tucson Early Education Model, and the Bank Street Model. In summary, the Direct Instruction model succeeded in bridging the gap between low-income students and their middle-income peers. Project Follow Through results also provide direct support for the effectiveness of Direct Instruction curriculum programs in language, reading, spelling, and mathematics. (See Gersten et al. 1984 for a secondary analysis of Project Follow Through results.)

Post–Project Follow Through Research

One myth commonly associated with Direct Instruction is that it is only appropriate for at-risk students and low performers. Engelmann notes:

> Because no mistakes or tendencies are unique to lower performers, if one is able to teach a complex skill, such as reading, to lower performers, it is much easier to teach the same skill to higher performers. *Therefore, any instructional sequence that is effective with lower performers would be equally effective with naïve higher performers. . . .* The basic rule is that *if the learning task is the same, we may use the same steps to induce the learning.* (Adams & Engelmann, 1996, pp. 28–29; italics in original)

Direct Instruction Benefits a Diverse Range of Students.   Though the use of Direct Instruction in Project Follow Through contributed to academic gains of economically disadvantaged students in the early grades, research from the 1980s and 1990s explored whether direct instruction would also benefit students at risk of emotional or behavioral disorders, students with learning disabilities, students with developmental disabilities, and regular classroom students. In his recent discussion of Direct Instruction research, Hempenstall (1999) cites several research reviews that refute the myth that Direct Instruction programs are for only low performers and support Engelmann's "all children can learn" assumption (Gersten, 1985; Kavale, 1990; Lockery & Maggs, 1982; White, 1988). In other words, Direct Instruction's emphasis on effective teaching and design principles transcends learner characteristics and has been found to benefit a diverse range of learners (Hempenstall, 1999).

Critical Instructional and Design Features.   Subsequent studies and reviews of the Direct Instruction research have also explored which instructional components contribute to the successful outcomes of Direct Instruction. Instructional intervention research involves experimentally examining the intricate requirements of teaching complex instructional tasks. Studies are designed by (a) identifying component tasks, responses, or knowledge forms that comprise a complex operation; (b) selecting and sequencing examples of the component tasks or knowledge forms; (c) constructing and testing procedures for teaching the component tasks or knowledge forms separately; and (d) linking the teaching procedures of the component tasks or knowledge forms into a systematically integrated teaching sequence (Kame'enui et al., 1997). For example, instructional intervention studies from the Direct Instruction reading literature have examined instructional procedures for teaching students with mild disabilities to simplify and comprehend complex clause constructions (Kame'enui, Carnine, & Maggs, 1980); have investigated instructional strategies for teaching the meanings of unfamiliar vocabulary words to fourth-, fifth-, and sixth-grade students (Kame'enui, Carnine, & Freschi, 1982), and have compared comprehension strategies (Adams, Carnine, & Gersten, 1982; Carnine & Kinder, 1985).

The results of studies comparing interventions support the Direct Instruction approach to teaching reading comprehension and beginning reading. In terms of instructional components, instruction that included the Direct Instruction delivery and design principles—such as teacher-directed lessons in which essential skills, practice, and minimal errors were emphasized—were more likely to enhance students' performance on reading tasks than a range of "control" strategies, which included practice only, the use of traditional basal reading materials, and general, non–Direct Instruction approaches. While the examples of reading studies highlight the broad importance of Direct Instruction principles, research also supports how the specifics of Direct Instruction delivery and design, such as example selection, mastery criterion, and well-defined teacher behaviors, contribute to positive academic outcomes (Carnine, 1980a, 1980b, 1980c; Carnine et al., 1997; Engelmann, 1997; Engelmann & Carnine, 1991; Gersten, 1985; Kryzanowski & Carnine, 1980; Leinhardt, Zigmond, & Cooley, 1981; Williams & Carnine, 1981).

Conclusion: Innovations and Deep Unity

Siegfried Engelmann is the mind that perceived a deep new unity in the "disorder" of often sloppy, confusing instruction and labeling disadvantaged students as "unteachable." With his conceptualization of Direct Instruction, Engelmann created an innovative, comprehensive system of teaching, one that recognized a deep unity in the sense that all children can learn what they are taught. The foundational elements in Engelmann's Direct Instruction can be understood when the structural samenesses of direct instruction definitions are considered and features of program delivery, program organization, and program design (as delineated in Table 5.2) are used to examine what Direct Instruction looks like when implemented in a classroom. Finally, the integrity of Engelmann's innovations in instructional design is supported by substantial empirical findings that indicate Direct Instruction contributes to the academic success of students with a diverse range of learning needs.

TABLE 5.2   "Big Ideas" of Direct Instruction

Critical Feature	Teaching Suggestions
Program delivery	▪ Optimize instructional time by working with students in small groups. Use homogenous groups. Make the group with the higher-performing students the largest and the group with lower-performing students the smallest. ▪ Promote active student engagement with unison group responses. Unison responses also provide the teacher with frequent feedback about each student's progress. ▪ Increase student attentiveness and reduce errors by providing a "fast"-paced lesson presentation. ▪ Teach to mastery criterion; correct all mistakes and repeat an exercise until students can respond to the entire set of questions correctly. Mastery ensures that students will have relatively little difficulty applying learned skills in other situations.
Program organization	▪ Put instructional time to good use. The actual amount of time that students are engaged in instructional activities is critical. ▪ Schedule ample time for instruction and implement the instructional schedule consistently. Ensure that students do not waste substantial amounts of time during group instruction, independent work, or transitions from one activity to another. ▪ Place students in an instructional program that is appropriate to their skill level. They should not be placed in a program that is too easy or too hard. ▪ Arrange classroom work space, lesson materials, and student materials before instructional time.
Program design	▪ Evaluate objectives to ensure that essential skills are taught first. ▪ Teach students to rely on strategies rather than require them to memorize information. ▪ Use an instructional program that includes a lesson format. ▪ Formats should contain the words that a teacher should say during a lesson, instructions on how to correct student errors, and so forth. ▪ Use an instructional program or lessons that include a range of examples (e.g., both positive and negative examples of a concept, rule, principle, or system). ▪ Use an instructional program that emphasizes an optimal order for introducing new information and strategies (e.g., preskills of a strategy are taught before the strategy itself is presented; high utility skills are introduced before less useful ones). ▪ Provide students with ample and strategic opportunities for practicing a skill.

REFERENCES

Adams, A., Carnine, D., & Gersten, R. (1982). Instructional strategies for studying content area texts in the intermediate grades. *Reading Research Quarterly, 17*(1), 27–55.

Adams, G. L., & Engelmann, S. (1996). *Research on direct instruction: 25 years beyond DISTAR.* Seattle, WA: Educational Achievement Systems.

Baumann, J. F. (1983). A generic comprehension instructional strategy. *The Reading Teacher, 44,* 371–372.

Baumann, J. F. (1984, December). *The systematic, intensive instruction of reading comprehension skills.* Paper presented at the annual meeting of the National Reading Conference, St. Petersburg, FL.

Baumann, J. F. (1988). Direct instruction reconsidered. *Journal of Reading, 31*(8), 12–18.

Baumann, J. F., & Kame'enui, E. J. (1991). Vocabulary instruction: Ode to Voltaire. In J. Flood, J. Jensen, D. Lapp, & J. R. Squire (Eds.), *Handbook of research on teaching the English language arts* (pp. 604–632). New York: Macmillan.

Becker, W. C. (1977). Teaching reading and language to the disadvantaged: What we have learned from field research. *Harvard Educational Review, 47,* 518–543.

Becker, W. C., & Carnine, D. W. (1980). Direct instruction: An effective approach to educational intervention with the disadvantaged and low performers. In B. B. Lahey & A. E. Kazdin (Eds.), *Advances in clinical and child psychology* (Vol. 3, pp. 429–473). New York: Plenum.

Becker, W. C., & Engelmann, S. (1976). *Teaching 3: Evaluation of instruction.* Chicago: Science Research Associates.

Becker, W. C., & Engelmann, S. (1978). *Analysis of achievement data on six cohorts of low income children from 20 school districts in the University of Oregon district instruction Follow Through model* (Technical Rep. No. 78-1). Eugene, OR: College of Education.

Becker, W. C., Engelmann, S., Carnine, D. W., & Rhine, R. (1981). The Direct Instruction model. In R. Rhine (Ed.), *Encouraging change in America's schools: A decade of experimentation* (pp. 95–154). New York: Academic Press.

Bereiter, C., & Engelmann, S. (1966). *Teaching disadvantaged children in the preschool.* Englewood Cliffs, NJ: Prentice Hall.

Berliner, D. (1981). Comments on the *NSSE Yearbook:* Philosophy and education. *Educational Theory, 31,* 31–35.

Bronowski, J. (1958). The creative process. In *Readings from* Scientific American: *Scientific genius and creativity* (pp. 3–8). New York: Freeman.

Brophy, J. E., & Good, T. L. (1986). Teacher behavior and student achievement. In M. Wittrock (Ed.), *Third handbook of research on teaching* (pp. 328–375). Chicago, Rand McNally.

Carnine, D. W. (1980a). Relationships between stimulus variation and the formation of misconceptions. *Journal of Educational Research, 74,* 106–110.

Carnine, D. W. (1980b). Three procedures for presenting minimally different positive and negative instances. *Journal of Educational Psychology, 72,* 452–456.

Carnine, D. W. (1980c). Two-letter discrimination sequences: High-confusion alternatives versus low-confusion alternatives first. *Journal of Reading Behavior, 12*(1), 41–47.

Carnine, D. W., & Kame'enui, E. J. (1992). *Higher order thinking: Designing curriculum for mainstreamed students* (pp. 1–22). Austin, TX: Pro-Ed.

Carnine, D. W., & Kinder, D. (1985). Teaching low-performing students to apply generative and schema strategies to narrative and expository material. *Remedial and Special Education, 6*(1), 20–30.

Carnine, D. W., Silbert, J., & Kame'enui, E. J. (1997). *Direct instruction reading* (3rd ed.). Upper Saddle River, NJ: Prentice Hall.

Engelmann, S. (1969). *Preventing failure in the primary grades.* Chicago: Science Research Associates.

Engelmann, S. (1980, February). Toward the design of faultless instruction: The theoretical basis of concept analysis. *Educational Technology,* 28–36.

Engelmann, S. (1997). Theory of mastery and acceleration. In J. W. Lloyd, E. J. Kame'enui, & D. Chard (Eds.), *Issues in educating students with disabilities* (pp. 177–195). Mahwah, NJ: Erlbaum.

Engelmann, S., & Carnine, D. W. (1991). *Theory of instruction: Principles and applications.* Eugene, OR: ADI.

Engelmann, S., & Engelmann, T. (1966). *Give your child a superior mind.* New York: Simon & Schuster.

Englert, C. S. (1984). Examining effective direct instruction practices in special education settings. *Remedial and Special Education, 5,* 38–74.

Gaskins, I. (1988). The missing ingredients: Time ontask, direct instruction, and writing. *Reading Teacher, 41,* 750–755.

Gersten, R. (1985). Direct Instruction with special education students: A review of evaluation research. *Journal of Special Education, 19*(1), 41–58.

Gersten, R., Becker, W. C., Heiry, T. J., & White, W. A. (1984). Entry IQ and yearly growth of children in Direct Instruction programs: A longitudinal study of low SES children. *Educational Evaluation and Policy Analysis, 6,* 109–121.

Gersten, R., Carnine, D. W., & White, W. A. (1984). Direct instruction and applied behavior analysis. In W. Heward et al., (Eds.), *A focus on behavior analysis in education* (pp. 38–57). Columbus, OH: Merrill.

Guthrie, J. T. (1977). Research views—Follow Through: A compensatory education experiment. *Reading Teacher, 3,* 240–244.

Hempenstall, K. (1999). The gulf between educational research and policy: The example of direct instruction and whole language. *Effective School Practices, 18,* 15–29.

House, E. R., Glass, G. V., McLean, L. D., & Walker, D. F. (1978). No simple answer: Critique of the "Follow-Through" evaluation. *Harvard Educational Review, 28,* 128–160.

Kame'enui, E. J. (1991). Toward a scientific pedagogy: A sameness in the message. *Journal of Learning Disabilities, 24,* 364–372.

Kame'enui, E. J., Carnine, D. W., & Freschi, R. (1982). Effects of text construction and instructional procedures for teaching word meanings on comprehension of contrived passages. *Reading Research Quarterly, 17,* 367–388.

Kame'enui, E. J., Carnine, D. W., & Maggs, A. (1980). Instructional procedures for teaching reversible passive-voice and clause constructions to three mildly handicapped children. *The Exceptional Child, 27*(1), 27–40.

Kame'enui, E. J., & Gersten, R. (1997, March 10). *The national evaluation of Project Follow Through: A brief description and summary of results.* Paper invited by the Committee on the Prevention of Reading Difficulties, National Research Council, National Academy of Sciences.

Kame'enui, E. J., Jitendra, A. K., & Darch, C. B. (1995). Direct instruction reading as contronym and eonomine. *Reading and Writing Quarterly: Overcoming Learning Difficulties, 11,* 3–17.

Kame'enui, E. J., & Simmons, D. C. (1990). *Designing instructional strategies: The prevention of academic learning problems.* Columbus, OH: Merrill.

Kame'enui, E. J., Simmons, D. C., Chard, D., & Dickson, S. (1997). Direct-Instruction reading. In S. A. Stahl & D. A. Hayes (Eds.), *Instructional models in reading* (pp. 59–84). Mahwah, NJ: Erlbaum.

Kavale, K. (1990). Variances and verities in learning disabilities interventions. In T. Scruggs & B. Wong (Eds.), *Intervention research in learning disabilities* (pp. 3–33). New York: Springer.

Kryzanowski, J., & Carnine, D. W. (1980). Effects of massed versus spaced formats in teaching sound/symbol correspondences to young children. *Journal of Reading Behavior, 12,* 225–230.

Leinhardt, G., Zigmond, N., & Cooley, W. W. (1981). Reading instruction and its effects. *American Educational Research Journal, 18,* 343–361.

Lockery, L., & Maggs, A. (1982). Direct instruction research in Australia: A ten-year analysis. *Educational Psychology, 2,* 263–288.

Murphy, P. C., Weil, M., & McGreal, T. L. (1986). The basic practice model of instruction. *Elementary School Journal, 87,* 83–95.

Rosenshine, B. (1976). Classroom instruction. In N. L. Gage (Ed.), *The psychology of teaching methods: 75th yearbook for the National Society for the Study of Education* (Part I, pp. 335–372). Chicago: University of Chicago Press.

Rosenshine, B. (1986). Synthesis of research on explicit teaching. *Exceptional Leadership, 43,* 60–69.

Rosenshine, B. (1987). Explicit teaching and teacher training. *Journal of Teacher Education, 38,* 34–36.

Shannon, P. (1988). Can we directly instruct students to be independent in reading? In J. R. Readence & S. Baldwin (Eds.), *Dialogues in literacy research: Thirty-seventh yearbook of the National Reading Conference* (pp. 36–39). Chicago: National Reading Conference.

Stebbins, L. B., St. Pierre, R. G., Proper, E. C., Anderson, R. B., & Cerva, T. R. (1977). *Education as experimentation: A planned variation model* (Vol. IV-A). Cambridge, MA: Abt Associates.

Tarver, S. G. (1992). Controversial issues confronting special education: Divergent perspectives. In W. Stainback & S. Stainback (Eds.), *Direct instruction* (pp. 141–152). Needham Heights, MA: Allyn & Bacon.

White, S. H. (1973). *Federal programs for young children: Review and recommendations* (HEW Service Publication No. OS 74–101). Washington, DC: U.S. Government Printing Office.

White, W. A. T. (1988). A meta-analysis of the effects of higher cognitive questions of student achievement. *Review of Educational Research, 49,* 13–50.

Williams, P. B., & Carnine, D. (1981). Relationship between range of examples and of instruction and attention in concept attainment. *Journal of Educational Research, 74,* 144–148.

6

Reading and Students with E/BD

What Do We Know and Recommend?

CANDACE S. BOS

MAGGIE COLEMAN

SHARON VAUGHN
University of Texas–Austin

Introduction

Students with emotional/behavioral disorders (E/BD) present teachers with a wide variety of instructional and behavioral challenges. As a group, these students exhibit considerable academic difficulties in addition to a myriad of emotional and behavioral problems (see Chapter 1 by O'Shaughnessy, Lane, Gresham, & Beebe-Frankenberger, this text). However, over the years, researchers and practitioners concerned with this population have focused almost exclusively on managing behavior or improving emotional adjustment. Little has been written to guide teachers in how to meet their academic needs, particularly in reading (see Chapter 19 by Lane, Gresham, & O'Shaughnessy, this text). This chapter reviews the descriptive reading research on students with E/BD and the intervention reading research and provides instructional strategies for teaching reading to these students.

What Do We Know about Reading and Students with E/BD?

When you watch a young child reading aloud from a favorite book with fluency, expression, and ease, it is difficult to imagine that reading can be anything but the easiest task to master. Fortunately, for most students reading is a skill that is readily acquired. However, reading researchers view the reading process as a complex one, and though acquired easily by some youngsters, it is only with enormous difficulty and practice that others learn to read (Pressley, 1998). This is particularly true for most of the students who are identified for special education services (Bos & Vaughn, 1998). In particular, students with cognitive impairments such as mental retardation and learning disabilities (LD) are "at risk" for demonstrating significant difficulties in the acquisition of reading skills, with more than 90% of these students requiring special instruction in reading (Lyon, 1995).

Is the case the same for students with E/BD? To assist us in teaching students with E/BD, it is important first to learn what the research says about the reading of students with E/BD. This section explores research relative to students' reading achievement levels, the comparison of reading levels for students with E/BD and students with LD, and the relationship between externalizing behaviors and reading problems.

Reading Levels of Students with E/BD

Only a few studies have documented the reading achievement of students with E/BD. Most of these studies have described reading levels, based on standardized measures, for purposes of comparison with achievement in other subjects or to other groups of students.

The achievement patterns of psychiatric samples, such as students hospitalized for serious behavior disorders, have been studied by Forness and his colleagues, who found moderate levels of reading difficulties. In one study, students were on the average only moderately below grade level on a standardized test of reading achievement despite considerable variability within the sample (Forness, Frankel, Caldon, & Carter, 1980). In a second study, only one-third of a sample of 92 psychiatric inpatients had deficits of more than 1 year in reading when adjusted for IQ (Forness, Bennett, & Tose, 1983). In addition, they displayed a homogeneous pattern of underachievement in reading, spelling, and math, rather than specific deficits in one area. Students in both samples ranged from elementary to middle school (ages 6–14).

Descriptive achievement data have also been obtained on students with E/BD who are in the public schools (Kauffman, Cullinan, & Epstein, 1987). Due to the large age range (7–19), the students were subdivided into younger, middle, and older groups. Almost three-fourths of the sample, regardless of the age group, were functioning 1 to 2 or more years below grade level on reading comprehension.

Another way in which reading achievement has been explored is by studying the intellectual and achievement characteristics of students with E/BD. A review of 25 studies published from 1966 to 1985 in this area (Mastropieri, Jenkins, & Scruggs, 1985) revealed the following:

- Underachievement in reading was noted when actual achievement was compared to intellectual ability levels.
- Support was found for the notion that students with BD are underachieving in all areas of academic functioning with no content-specific deficits, except in some studies that documented more serious problems with math.

■ While other variables have been studied in relation to achievement including attitude toward school subjects, locus of control, impulsivity, and responses to test-taking situations, no causal links between these variables and reading levels were evident.

In summary, the reading levels of students with E/BD *as a group* may be characterized as typically below grade level and moderately deficient. This finding holds across all grade levels. However, as with any categorization or subgroup, there is considerable variability among students with E/BD, with some individuals being excellent readers. Most studies suggest that students with E/BD also exhibit patterns of underachievement when ability levels are taken into consideration.

Comparisons of Students with E/BD and Students with LD

In direct comparisons of the reading levels of students with E/BD with those of students with LD, students with E/BD generally score higher (i.e., are found to be somewhat less deficient) in reading than their counterparts with LD. Four out of five studies with students ranging from ages 6 to 12 documented differences that ranged from slightly higher to significantly higher when statistical comparisons were made (Epstein & Cullinan, 1983; Fuller & Goh, 1981; Harris, King, Reifler, & Rosenberg, 1984; Mastropieri et al., 1985; Scruggs & Mastropieri, 1986). The measures of reading were primarily word recognition and reading comprehension; one study assessed reading rate and found that students with E/BD read at a much higher rate (measured in words per minute) than their LD counterparts (Epstein & Cullinan, 1983).

One study compared the behavioral and academic profiles of students from a special campus for students with LD with those of students from a special campus for students with E/BD and found minimal differences between the two groups (Harris et al., 1984). Students with E/BD had higher total scores on a measure of clinical problems, but students with LD also had inflated scores, well above the average range. As a group, the students with LD were more delayed in reading skills, although not significantly so. Such findings led the authors to conclude that "special services for behavior disorder are needed for the LD group and instruction for specific learning problems are required for the ED group" (p. 431).

Another group of researchers assessed comorbidity, or the presence of LD in children and adolescents admitted to a psychiatric hospital for E/BD (Fessler, Rosenberg, & Rosenberg, 1991). They found that that almost 40% were identified as having LD and almost 18% were identified as having learning problems; the majority of both groups were deficient in all reading areas assessed. Perhaps the statistic of most concern is that fewer than half these students (44%) had received special education services of any type prior to being admitted to the hospital. These statistics would argue for better identification of students with E/BD and for recognizing the coexistence of E/BD with LD.

In sum, the reading achievement of students with E/BD has been documented as highly variable and moderately deficient, probably a little higher when compared with peers with LD. Measures used in these studies represent estimations of reading levels; no diagnostic testing of specific reading skills with this population has been reported. However, research has also investigated the relationship between the reading problems and externalizing behavior disorders as discussed in the next section.

Relationship between Reading Problems and Externalizing Behavior Disorders

Externalizing behavior disorders are prevalent among children and youth with E/BD. Externalizing behaviors are a broad categorization of problem behaviors that are typically defined as including behaviors of an acting-out nature; lying, fighting, cheating, stealing, oppositional behavior, and rule breaking make up one cluster of behaviors often referred to as *antisocial behavior* or *conduct disorder*. Problems with attention, impulsivity, and hyperactivity make up another cluster, usually referred to as *attention deficit hyperactivity disorder*. These two clusters of behavior often overlap; that is, children and youth may both have attentional/ hyperactivity problems and exhibit antisocial behavior (see Chapter 13 by Gresham, Lane, & Lambros, this text). Each cluster will be discussed in the following summary of studies as it relates to research on reading problems.

Both antisocial behavior disorders and severe reading problems persist over time, and both lead to poor adjustment in adolescence and adulthood. The presence of reading difficulties among delinquent populations and others with antisocial or conduct problems has been well documented over the years (e.g., Berger, Yule, & Rutter, 1975; Frick et al., 1991; Hinshaw, 1992; Maguin, Loeber, & Le Mahieu, 1993; McGee, Williams, Share, Anderson, & Silva, 1986), leading researchers and developmental specialists to question whether a causal relationship exists. McMichael (1979) posed this question in the title to her article, "The Hen or the Egg? Which Comes First—Antisocial Emotional Disorders or Reading Disability?"

Researchers in various countries have studied the relationship between externalizing behaviors and severe reading difficulties for 30 years. They conducted a series of epidemiological, longitudinal studies in England (Berger et al., 1975; Rutter & Yule, 1970), New Zealand (McGee et al., 1986), Canada (Stott, 1981), Scotland (McMichael, 1979), and Australia (Jorm, Share, Matthews, & MacLean, 1986). By assessing large numbers of children on behavioral and academic measures early in their school careers, in some cases before any formal instruction took place, and then again years later, researchers were able to ascertain relationships between severe behavior problems and reading problems. More specifically, researchers were able to ascertain whether one preceded the other.

Several findings emerged from these studies that shed some light on the question of "which came first?" and other related issues. First, the New Zealand researchers found that it is helpful to break down externalizing disorders into the two subcategories of attention problems/hyperactivity and antisocial/conduct disorder. The cluster of attention/hyperactivity problems was found to be more closely associated than conduct disorder with reading problems, an association also found by Frick et al. (1991) in a study conducted with boys ages 7 to 12 in the United States. However, in a comprehensive review of literature addressing the relationship between externalizing behavior problems and academic underachievement, Hinshaw (1992) argues that the relationship among the variables may be age related. He makes the case that in younger children, inattention and hyperactivity are stronger correlates of academic underachievement than is aggression, and in older children antisocial behavior and delinquency are more clearly associated with underachievement.

The most salient and important finding from the studies is that externalizing problems, especially inattention and hyperactivity, either predate or coexist with reading problems; there is no evidence to suggest causation in either direction. McMichael (1979) summarizes thus:

> The children who manifested antisocial behavior and reading difficulties at the age of six to seven appeared to have entered school with a constellation of earlier problems connected with delayed linguistic, perceptual, and cognitive development, low self-esteem, and antisocial behavior. The antisocial behavior had not arisen from loss of self-esteem through reading failure so much as accompanied low self-esteem into school. (p. 236)

Hinshaw (1992), in his literature review, confirms that causal relationships have not been established in either direction. He proposes that variables such as the following may be underlying factors contributing to the complex relationship between behavior problems and underachievement in reading:

Socioeconomic status. Socioeconomic status alone does not explain the overlap between externalizing disorders and underachievement; family interaction variables such as parental attitudes toward literacy or listening to the child's reading appear to mediate the relationship between SES and reading attainment.

Familial variables. Research in this area has been hampered by the dearth of studies and by the methodological issue of ascertaining whether family variables are antecedents or consequences of child problems. However, one well-crafted longitudinal study revealed that (a) early adverse family climate did predict specific reading deficits at age 8 even when language deficits and behavior problems were controlled, and (b) maternal depression/anxiety during the child's formative years was also highly predictive of later reading difficulties (Richman, Stevenson, & Graham, 1982).

Subaverage intelligence. Lower intelligence may be a predisposing factor toward both reading difficulties and aggressive or antisocial behavior. However, it is a complex and multifaceted construct and is not the clear causal agent for both.

Language deficits. Recent conceptions of reading failure recognize the role of language deficits, specifically phonologic and linguistic processing difficulties. Additionally, mild to moderate language problems are associated with a number of behavior problems, especially attention deficit hyperactivity disorder. Research to date indicates that early language problems may in fact mediate problems in reading and problems in behavior; however, additional longitudinal research is needed to specify the nature of the association.

Neurodevelopmental delays. Although a few researchers have proposed that neurodevelopmental delays (manifested in delayed maturation of basic perceptual and motor functions) are a causal factor in language deficits, the topic remains controversial. Hinshaw (1992) suggests that neurodevelopmental delay "is a fuzzy construct, badly in need of sharpening" (p. 149), and its role in the association between behavior problems and achievement problems needs further examination.

In summary, many of the studies reviewed by Hinshaw serve to confirm the complex relationships among these variables in the development of both behavioral difficulties and achievement difficulties. According to Hinshaw (1992), attempting to untangle these associations and isolate single factors "is likely to be quite difficult or even misguided" (p. 151).

Based on this research, it may be concluded that although externalizing behavior disorders and reading problems do coexist and have been the subject of much study, there is no evidence for causation in either direction. However, because of the strong and persistent relationship, and given the negative prognosis for each, educators should continue to search for ways to ameliorate both types of problems. One implication of the research is that educators should perhaps intensify efforts to identify attention/hyperactivity problems as early as possible in order to prevent development of both reading problems and related behavior problems in later years.

Conclusion

Overall, three findings from the literature on students with E/BD and reading seem clear:

- Students with E/BD have an established pattern of underachievement in reading.
- Students who demonstrate comorbidity between E/BD and either LD or attention deficit disorder are particularly at risk for reading problems.
- While strong linkages exist between reading difficulties and externalizing behavior, a causal link is not evident.

If reading is problematic, at least for a number of students with E/BD, what strategies or interventions support students with E/BD in overcoming these problems?

What Do We Know about Intervention Research for Students with E/BD?

Unfortunately, we know more about the reading problems of students with E/BD than we do about appropriate interventions to affect reading outcomes for these students. This is less true for students with LD. In a meta-analysis of reading interventions for students with LD conducted by Swanson and Hoskyn (1998), findings revealed high effect sizes for reading comprehension and vocabulary interventions (ES = 0.81 and 0.73, respectively). Furthermore, interventions that included a combined model of direct instruction and strategy instruction yielded the highest effect sizes.

Because a synthesis or review of reading research for E/BD students was not available, Coleman and Vaughn (2000) conducted a synthesis of all of the intervention articles in reading for elementary students with E/BD published between 1975 and 1998. Descriptive constructs that were used in previous research of special education populations (e.g., Vaughn & Klingner, 1998) and selected by the authors as being the most salient to an understanding of reading interventions were used as a means of summarizing the critical information reported. Only eight articles were located, six were articles published in journals, and two were dissertations obtained through *Dissertation Abstracts International*. Five of the eight studies used a single-subject methodology, and three used a group design.

Three of the eight studies examined the influence of cross-age peer tutoring on reading and social outcomes for students with E/BD (Cochran, Feng, Cartledge, & Hamilton, 1993; Resnick, 1987; Shisler, Top, & Osguthorpe, 1986). These studies provided evidence that peer tutoring might be an effective practice for students with E/BD, particularly in the elementary grades. With two of the studies, students with E/BD served as tutors and tutees (Cochran et al., 1993; Resnick, 1987), whereas in one study (Shisler et al., 1986), a sample of general education first graders were tutees and E/BD students were the tutors. Interventions lasted from 8 weeks to 5 months. Improvement in reading skills was found in all three studies on various measures, including increases in sight word acquisition, on standardized reading tests, and on reading inventories. These results are consistent with literature affirming the positive impact of peer tutoring on reading for students with disabilities (Elbaum, Vaughn, Hughes, & Moody, 1999; Mathes & Fuchs, 1994; Scruggs, Mastropieri, & Richter, 1985).

Of the remaining five studies, two addressed sight word acquisition in reading (McCurdy, Cundari, & Lentz, 1990; Skinner, Smith, & McLean, 1994), and two others examined more general interventions, such as reading worksheets to improve reading outcomes (Allyon, Kuhlman, & Warzak, 1982; McLaughlin, 1992). Only one study (Yell, 1992) compared the effects of three specific instructional methods (direct instruction, language master, and independent practice) on sight word reading and on-task behavior. Results revealed that direct instruction demonstrated significantly better results for improving sight word reading.

Since the experimental literature on students with E/BD and reading interventions was limited to eight studies, the authors (Coleman & Vaughn, 2000) conducted a focus group with eight elementary, E/BD teachers who taught reading to determine their views on reading instruction for students with E/BD. These teachers' comments converged around several central topics that included the emotional variability demonstrated by students with E/BD, fear of failure/trust issues, keeping students engaged, instructional practices, assessment/monitoring, and daily reading. Box 6.1 presents the major conclusions.

BOX **6.1**

What Teachers Say about Teaching Reading to Students with E/BD

Emotional Variability of Students

Teachers commented on the complications between students' emotional and behavior problems and their instructional needs. Determining the extent to which a reading problem was separate from students' emotional problems was challenging. Teachers reported that a few of their students were very good readers and even used reading as a means to escape. Most students were identified as having reading difficulties, but these difficulties would be more significant some days than others (depending on their social/emotional problem level that day). Teachers noted that their students tended to make leaps in progress when emotional issues were in check as opposed to slow, steady progress when their emotional problems were more apparent.

Fear of Failure/Trust Issues

Teachers agreed that students' concern with failure and doing something "stupid" had a significant influence on their ability to read or perform reading-related tasks. Teachers reported students selecting books that they could not read just to look like other students their age. Teachers discussed the need first to establish trust with their students before they would be "allowed" to teach them to read.

Keeping Students Engaged

Teachers of their students were aware that instruction in reading would be significantly affected if teachers did not use effective strategies for maintaining student engagement. Teachers acknowledged that maintaining students' interest and motivation was difficult and required effective classroom management techniques. Teachers also recognized that many of the strategies that were most effective were individually tailored to the emotional/behavior needs of each student. Teachers indicated that they used games and incentives to improve motivation and interest.

Instructional Practices Used

Teachers frequently indicated the positive effects from tutoring, especially cross-age tutoring. One teacher revealed that she provided opportunities for her students to be reading tutors for kindergarten students. Teachers also indicated that their students responded well to the reading–writing connection through writing their own books and stories.

Assessment/Monitoring

Teachers recognized the value of ongoing progress monitoring of reading outcomes—especially when students had the opportunity to chart their own progress.

Students Learn to Read by Reading

Several teachers pointed to the importance of their students being able to select their own reading and having time each day to read and discuss what they are reading.

Instructional Practices for Students with E/BD

Given the limited intervention research in reading for students with E/BD (Coleman & Vaughn, 2000), what specific recommendations can we make for teaching reading to these students? The research would support the use of cross-age tutoring (Cochran et al., 1993; Resnick, 1987; Shisler et al., 1986). Substantial gains in reading achievement were noted for both tutors and tutees. The only other area that has received some attention is sight word acquisition (McCurdy et al., 1990; Skinner et al., 1994; Yell, 1992). Of these, only Yell (1992) compared the efficacy of different methods and found direct instruction most beneficial in comparison to using the language master or independent practice writing the word from memory.

With this limited research for students with E/BD, one is left to seek recommendations for instructional practices in the related literature for students with LD. This seems particularly relevant since students who demonstrate comorbidity between E/BD and either LD or attention deficit disorder are particularly at risk for reading problems (Fessler et al., 1991; Hinshaw, 1992). Based on the recent research syntheses of intervention research in reading (Swanson & Hoskyn, 1998), strong evidence suggests that instructional practices are more beneficial if they employ direct, explicit instruction and integrate strategy instruction. Furthermore, for early reading acquisition a strong focus on phonological awareness and the alphabetic principle are important content features. Consequently, this section provides an overview of selected instructional practices for teaching phonological awareness, word recognition, fluency, and reading comprehension that employ these characteristics. Cross-age tutoring, an effective grouping format for promoting reading achievement in students with E/BD, is also described.

Phonological Awareness

The development of phonological awareness and an understanding of the alphabetic principle are critical building blocks for the acquisition of early reading skills (Lyon, 1995; Snow, Burns, & Griffin, 1998). *Phonological awareness* refers to "one's sensitivity to, or explicit awareness of the phonological structure of words in one's language" (Torgesen & Bryant, 1994, p. 1). It includes skills such as separating sentences into words and words into syllables; rhyming words; blending and segmenting words; and deleting, substituting, and manipulating sounds in words. The alphabetic principle provides the basis for understanding that sounds are associated with letters in a systematic manner. Understanding this concept and basic phonic generalizations facilitates students in decoding words (Ehri, 1998; Snow et al., 1998). A number of programs have been developed to support the development of phonological awareness and the alphabetic principle (see Box 6.2). A recent study conducted with first-grade students with externalizing behavior patterns and deficits in early reading skills (Lane, 1999) used the *Phonological Awareness Training for Reading* (PATR) as the supplemental reading instruction to teach phonological awareness.

BOX **6.2**

Selected Programs for Teaching Phonological Awareness

Phonemic Awareness in Young Children: A Classroom, Curriculum by M. J. Adams,
  B. R. Foorman, I. Lundberg, & T. Beeler (1998). Baltimore, MD: Brookes.

Road to the Code: A Phonological Awareness Program for Young Children by B. Blachman,
  E. W. Ball, R. Black, & D. M. Tangel (2000). Baltimore, MD: Brookes.

Sounds Abound by H. Catts & T. Vartianen (1993). East Moline, IL: LinguiSystems.

The Lindamood Phoneme Sequencing Program for Reading, Spelling, and Speech by
  P. Lindamood & P. Lindamood (1998). Austin, TX: Pro-Ed.

Ladders to Literacy: Kindergarten Activity Book by R. E. O'Connor, A. Notari-Syverson,
  & P. Vadasy (1998). Baltimore, MD: Brookes.

Phonological Awareness Training for Reading by J. K. Torgesen & B. Bryant (1994). Austin,
  TX: Pro-Ed.

The PATR is intended to assist students in developing an awareness of the phonological structure of words. The PATR program consists of four activities: warm-up, sound blending, sound segmenting, and reading and spelling. It is organized so that the learning sequence moves children from rhyme awareness through sound comparisons, segmenting, and blending activities to beginning work with letters in reading and spelling. Lane found the results of this program when provided to the students 4 days per week for 30 minutes per session for 6 weeks were mixed in terms of improving early reading skills.

Word Recognition

Key to successful reading is the automatic recognition of words and the ability to use the alphabetic principle and grapheme–phoneme knowledge to decode unknown words. Ehri (1998) suggests that readers read words as they process text using at least five different ways:

- Assembling letters into a blend of sounds, referred to as decoding
- Pronouncing and blending familiar spelling patterns, a more advanced form of decoding
- Using analogy to determine a new word based on a familiar word
- Using context cues to predict words
- Retrieving sight words from memory

The goal is to read words by sight, so that limited effort is expended toward deciphering the print, thus allowing the reader to allocate more effort toward comprehending or constructing the meaning of the print (Gough & Tunmer, 1986; LaBerge & Samuels, 1974). Thus, instructional practices for teaching word recognition should include not only decoding strategies and the use of context cues to recognize unknown words but also strategies for learning words to the automatic level so that they are almost effortlessly retrieved from memory. The features of instruction should incorporate direct instruction and strategy instruction (Swanson & Hoskyn, 1998; Yell, 1992). The features of direct instruction (DI) include a graduated sequence of steps with multiple opportunities for overlearning the content and skills, cumulative review, mass and distributed practice with feedback, and teaching component skills to mastery criterion (Swanson, 1999). Strategy instruction features include discussion given to *why* a strategy facilitates word recognition, *how to* apply the strategy, and *how to check* to see whether the strategy is working (Swanson, 1999).

Selected instructional practices for teaching word recognition include an analogy approach (Ehri & Robbins, 1992), teaching word families (Bloomfield & Barnhart, 1961), systematic structured language or a synthetic phonic approach (Engelmann, Becker, Hanner, & Johnson, 1988, 1989; Gillingham & Stillman, 1973), and the Fernald method (Fernald, 1943).

Using Analogy to Teach Word Recognition and Phonics. The analogy method relies on the students' ability to see the similarities among the words they can already identify and to induce from those words the sound–symbol relationships between oral and written language. The teacher selects a sound–symbol relationship based on the children's needs and the sequence of development (e.g., initial /r/). The teacher and students read aloud a list of known words with the initial /r/ (e.g., *rat, ran, rap,* and *rabbit*) and determine what looks and sounds alike about all the words. The teacher then assists the students as they induce the /r/ sound. When the students come to an unknown word (e.g., *rattle*), the teacher encourages the students to use known words (e.g., *rat* and *battle*) to decipher the new word. While this method emphasizes the alphabetic principle, it does require that the reader have some decoding skills and a sight word vocabulary in order to read words by analogy (Ehri & Robbins, 1992).

Word Families. This approach builds on the rhyming aspects of words and the fact that a number of words are composed of onsets and rimes (e.g., *r-at, f-un,* and *s-ight*). Students are taught word family groups and learn to blend the onset and rimes when decoding the word. For example, students might say /r—at/ and are then cued to "Say it fast" in order to make the word *rat.* This approach is based on the alphabetic principle and capitalizes on the principle of minimal contrast (Bos & Vaughn, 1998).

Structured Language or Synthetic Phonics. With this approach to teaching, students learn a core set of sound–symbol relationships and then are systematically taught how to blend sounds to make words. For example, many programs that use this strategy start by teaching a core set of consonant sounds and several short vowels. The students are taught to construct words blending the sounds and then practicing the words until they recognize them automatically. Programs that use this approach use words and text that are highly controlled so that students are not asked to decode words for which they have not already learned the sound–symbol relationships. These programs provide intensive, systematic instruction in phonics and have demonstrated their efficacy for "difficult to teach" readers (Snow et al., 1998).

Fernald Method.   This method uses a multisensory or a visual-auditory-tactile-kinesthetic approach to teach students to read and write words automatically. Different from the previous methods and approaches that emphasize teaching sound–symbol relationships, this method relies on learning the words as a whole. In the first stage of the method, the students select a word to learn, and the teacher writes it in large print or cursive writing. The teacher then models, saying and tracing the word until it is easy to write from memory. The students then use the same procedure to learn the word. The learned words are then used in stories constructed by the students. As students develop a word bank, sound–symbol relationships are induced through analogy. Empirical evidence lends support for using this method for teaching students with severe reading disabilities (Berres & Eyer, 1970; Fernald, 1943; Thorpe & Borden, 1985).

Fluency

Fluency instruction is designed to increase both word recognition and rate of reading (Bos & Vaughn, 1998). Fluent readers automatically process information at the visual and phonological levels and are therefore able to focus more of their attention on comprehension. One way to enhance fluency is through the use of repeated readings. The general format for this procedure is to have students repeatedly read text segments that range from 50 to 200 words in length until they reach a more fluent reading rate and with adequate word recognition (e.g., 90% accuracy). This procedure has been used with taped books (Carbo, 1978; Chomsky, 1976), with computer assistance (Rashotte & Torgesen, 1985), and with a three-stage method in which the teacher first reads, then the student and teacher read together, and then the student reads independently (Bos, 1982). In general, words that are not automatically recognized by the student are provided by the teacher/tape recording/computer. The use of repeated readings has been shown to be effective with at-risk students and students with LD, but it can also assist students who are learning English as a second language (McCauley & McCauley, 1992).

Reading Comprehension

Comprehension is the ultimate goal of the reading process. It is a process by which the reader interacts with the text to construct meaning by integrating the information provided by the author with his or her background knowledge. Students may have difficulty with reading comprehension for a variety of reasons: word recognition difficulties, limited background knowledge, limited comprehension monitoring, failure to relate what they read to what they already know about the topic, and overall oral and written language differences or delays (Bos & Vaughn, 1998).

Critical to improving comprehension is not only the use of direct instruction but also strategy instruction (Swanson & Hoskyn, 1998). Research with students who have LD have documented the positive effects of strategy instruction in improving such comprehension skills as predicting, questioning, clarifying, paraphrasing or summarizing, and comprehension monitoring. Reciprocal teaching (Palincsar & Brown, 1984, 1986) and collaborative strategic reading (CSR) (Klingner & Vaughn, 1998, 1999; Vaughn, Klingner, & Schumm, 1996) are examples of strategy-based approaches to teaching reading comprehension that have incorporated these skills and strategy instruction.

For reciprocal teaching, the basic procedure is that an adult teacher, working individually or with a small group of students, reads a segment of the text. The teacher (either the adult or student) then leads a discussion that incorporates the four comprehension strategies. For example, the teacher would model a question, summarize the content, clarify any difficult vocabulary or ideas, and finally make a prediction about future content. At first, the adult models the strategies and procedures, but soon control and responsibility are given to the students, with the adult serving as a facilitator. All of these activities are embedded in as natural a dialogue as possible, with the teacher and student giving feedback to each other about how they are using the comprehension strategies (Palincsar & Brown, 1984).

By adding a cooperative learning component to reciprocal teaching and simplifying the cues for the different strategies (see Box 6.3), Vaughn and her colleagues (Klingner & Vaughn, 1996, 1998) developed collaborative strategic reading (CSR).

B O X **6.3**

Cues for Collaborative Strategic Reading

Before Reading
Preview
- Brainstorm: What do we already know about the topic?
- Predict: What do we think we will learn about it when we read?

READ the first paragraph or section

During Reading
Click and Clunk
- Were there any parts that were hard to understand (clunks)?
- How can we fix the clunks? Use fix-up strategies:
  - Reread the sentence and look for key ideas to help you understand the word.
  - Reread the sentence with the clunk and the sentences before or after the clunk looking for the clues.
  - Look for a prefix or suffix in the word.
  - Break the word apart and look for the smaller words.

Getting the Gist
- What is the most important person, place, or thing?
- What is the most important idea about the person, place, or thing?

READ (Repeat Click and Clunks and Get the Gist with all sections in the passage/text.)

After Reading
Wrap Up
- Ask and answer questions to help you understand the most important information.
- Review: What did we learn?

They used CSR to help students read content in textbooks more efficiently and effectively in heterogeneous classrooms in which students with disabilities were included. In the strategy instruction, students learned the procedures and practiced well-defined roles (e.g., encourager, timer, strategy monitor, and reader). Both reciprocal teaching and CSR resulted in improved comprehension. What has not been investigated is the use of either reciprocal teaching or CSR with groups of students having only students with E/BD. A well-structured learning environment would most certainly be one key to success for this instructional grouping.

Cross-Age Tutoring

Research on students with E/BD has demonstrated the effectiveness of cross-age tutoring on reading achievement for both the tutors and tutees (Cochran et al., 1993; Resnick, 1987; Shisler et al., 1986). Key to successful tutoring programs is ample training of the peer tutors. Friend and Bursuck (1999) suggest the following topics for peer tutor training:

- Sensitivity to others' feelings
- Ways to develop positive relationships with tutees
- Effective communication and interaction skills, including directions, being interested, explaining things, and providing feedback, both positive and corrective
- Tutoring procedures and guidelines, including having materials, breaking big steps into smaller ones, demonstrating how to do something, giving tutee time to respond, helping but not doing tutee's work, and reviewing what has been taught
- Procedures for gathering data
- Problem solving about issues
- Tutoring schedule and need for commitment

In general, peer tutoring programs have been used to reinforce skills and strategies that have been taught rather than focusing on initial teaching. Peer tutoring holds promise for students with E/BD since it provides an interesting format for practicing skills and strategies and also emphasize social and communication skills.

Conclusion

While we know that students with E/BD experience problems with reading, little has changed since 1985, when Mastropieri and her colleagues suggested a call to action for further research to identify and refine variables effective in remediating the academic deficits of students with E/BD. This chapter reviewed the research on reading and students with E/BD, including the intervention research. Based on the scarce literature on interventions for these students and the intervention research for students with LD, instructional strategies for teaching phonological awareness, word identification, fluency, and reading comprehension were suggested. However, we agree that a systematic effort is needed to learn more about what works when teaching reading to students with E/BD.

REFERENCES

Adams, M. J., Foorman, B. R., Lundberg, I., & Beeler, T. (1998). *Phonemic awareness in young children: A classroom curriculum.* Baltimore, MD: Brookes.

Allyon, T., Kuhlman, C., & Warzak, W. J. (1982). Programming resource room generalization using lucky charms. *Child & Family Behavior Therapy, 4*(2), 61–67.

Berger, M., Yule, W., & Rutter, M. (1975). Attainment and adjustment in two geographical areas: II. The prevalence of specific reading retardation. *British Journal of Psychiatry, 126,* 510–519.

Berres, R. & Eyer, J. T. (1970). John. In A. J. Harris (Ed.), *Casebook on reading disability* (pp. 25–47). New York: McKay.

Blachman, B., Ball, E. W., Black, R., & Tangel, D. M. (2000). *Road to the code: A phonological awareness program for young children.* Baltimore, MD: Brookes.

Bloomfield, J., & Barnhart, C. L. (1961). *Let's read: A linguistic approach.* Detroit, MI: Wayne State University Press.

Bos, C. S. (1982). Getting past decoding: Using modeled and repeated readings as a remedial method for learning disabled students. *Topics in Learning and LD, 1,* 51–57.

Bos, C. S., & Vaughn, S. (1998). *Strategies for teaching students with learning and behavior problems* (4th ed.). Needham Heights, MA: Allyn & Bacon.

Carbo, M. (1978). Teaching reading with talking books. *The Reading Teacher, 32,* 267–273.

Catts, H. W., & Vartianen, T. (1993). *Sounds abound: Listening, rhyming, and reading.* East Moline, IL: LinguiSystems

Chomsky, C. (1976). After decoding: What? *Language Arts, 53,* 288–296.

Cochran, L., Feng, H., Cartledge, G., & Hamilton, S. (1993). The effects of cross-age tutoring on the academic achievement, social behaviors, and self-perceptions of low-achieving African-American males with behavioral disorders. *Behavioral Disorders, 18*(4), 292–302.

Coleman, M. C., & Vaughn, S. (2000). Reading interventions for students with E/BD. *Behavior Disorders, 25,* 93–104.

Engelmann, S., Becker, W. C., Hanner, S., & Johnson, G. (1989). *Corrective reading.* Chicago: Science Research Associates.

Ehri, L. C. (1998). Grapheme–phoneme knowledge is essential for learning to read. In J. L. Metsala & L. C. Ehri (Eds.), *Word recognition in beginning literacy* (pp. 3–40). Mahwah, NJ: Erlbaum.

Ehri, L. C., & Robbins, C. (1992). Beginners need some decoding skill to read words by analogy. *Reading Research Quarterly, 27,* 12–26.

Elbaum, B., Vaughn, S., Hughes, M. T., & Moody, S. W. (1999). Grouping practices and reading outcomes for students with disabilities. *Exceptional Children, 65,* 399–415.

Epstein, M. H., & Cullinan, D. (1983). Academic performance of behaviorally disordered and learning disabled pupils. *Journal of Special Education, 17*(3), 303–307.

Fernald, G. M. (1943). *Remedial techniques in basic school subjects.* New York: McGraw-Hill.

Fessler, M. A., Rosenberg, M. S., & Rosenberg, L. A. (1991). Concomitant LD and learning problems among students with behavioral/emotional disorders. *Behavioral Disorders, 16*(2), 97–106.

Forness, S. R., Bennett, L., & Tose, J. (1983). Academic deficits in emotionally disturbed children revisited. *Journal of the American Academy of Child Psychiatry, 22*(2), 140–144.

Forness, S. R., Frankel. F., Caldon. P. L., & Carter, M. J. (1980). Achievement gains of students hospitalized for behavior disorders. Severe behavior disorders of children and youth. In R. Rutherford, Jr., C. M. Nelson, & S. R. Forness (Eds.), *Severe behavior disorders of children and youth* (Vol. 3, pp. 34–40). San Diego, CA: College Hill.

Frick, P., Kamphaus, R. W., Lahey, B. B., Loeber, R., Christ, M. G., Hart, E., & Tannenbaum, L. E. (1991). Academic underachievement and the disruptive behavior disorders. *Journal of Consulting and Clinical Psychology, 59,* 289–294.

Friend, M., & Bursuck, W. D. (1999). *Including students with special needs: A practical guide for classroom teachers* (2nd ed.). Needham Hieghts, MA: Allyn & Bacon.

Fuller, G. B., & Goh, D. S. (1981). Intelligence, achievement, and visual-motor performance among learning disabled and emotionally impaired children. *Psychology in the Schools, 18*(3), 261–268.

Gillingham, A., & Stillman, B. (1973). *Remedial training for children with specific disability in reading, spelling, and penmanship.* Cambridge, MA: Educators Publishing Service.

Gough, P., & Tunmer, W. (1986). Decoding, reading, and reading disability. *Remedial and Special Education 7,* 6–10.

Harris, J. C., King, S. L., Reifler, J. P., & Rosenberg, L. A. (1984). Emotional and learning disorders in 6–12-year-old boys attending special schools. *Journal of the American Academy of Child Psychiatry, 23*, 431–437.

Hinshaw, S. P. (1992). Externalizing behavior problems and academic underachievement in childhood and adolescence: Causal relationships and underlying mechanisms. *Psychological Bulletin, 111*(1), 127–155.

Jorm, A. F., Share, D. L., Matthews, R., & MacLean, R. (1986). Behaviour problems in specific reading retarded and general reading backward children: A longitudinal study. *Journal of Child Psychology and Psychiatry, 27*, 33–43.

Kauffman, J. E., Cullinan, D., & Epstein, M. H. (1987). Characteristics of students placed in special programs for the seriously emotionally disturbed. *Behavioral Disorders 12*, 175–184.

Klingner, J. K., & Vaughn, S. (1996). Reciprocal teaching of reading comprehension strategies for students with LD who use English as a second language. *Elementary School Journal, 96*, 275–293.

Klingner, J. K., & Vaughn, S. (1998). Using collaborative strategic reading. *Teaching Exceptional Children, 30*(6), 32–37.

Klingner, J. K., & Vaughn, S. (1999). Promoting reading comprehension, content learning, and English acquisition through collaborative strategic reading (CSR). *The Reading Teacher, 52*, 738–747.

LaBerge, D., & Samuels, J. (1974). Toward a theory of automatic information processing in reading. *Cognitive Psychology, 6*, 293–323.

Lane, K. L. (1999). Young students at risk for antisocial behavior: The utility of academic and social skills interventions. *Journal of Emotional and Behavioral Disorders, 7*, 211–223.

Lindamood, P., & Lindamood, P. (1999). *The Lindamood phoneme sequencing program for reading, spelling, and speech* (3rd ed.). Austin, TX: Pro-Ed.

Lyon, G. R. (1995). Research initiatives in LD: Contributions from scientists supported by the National Institute of Child Health and Development. *Journal of Child Neurology, 10*, S120–S126 (Supplement 1).

Maguin, E., Loeber, R., & LeMahieu, P. G. (1993). Does the relationship between poor reading and delinquency hold for males of different ages and ethnic groups? *Journal of Emotional and Behavioral Disorders, 1*(2), 88–100.

Mastropieri, M., Jenkins, V., & Scruggs, T. (1985). Academic and intellectual characteristics of behavior disordered children and youth. In R. B. Rutherford, Jr. (Ed.), *Severe behavior disorders of children and youth* (Vol. 8, pp. 86–104).

Reston, VA: Council for Children with Behavioral Disorders.

Mathes, P. G., & Fuchs, L. S. (1994). The efficacy of peer tutoring in reading for students with mild disabilities: A best-evidence synthesis. *School Psychology Review, 12*(1), 59–80.

McCauley, J. K., & McCauley, D. S. (1992). Using choral reading to promote language learning for ESL students. *The Reading Teacher, 45*, 526–533.

McCurdy, B. L., Cundari, L., & Lentz, F. E. (1990). Enhancing instructional efficiency: An examination of time delay and the opportunity to observe instruction. *Education and Treatment of Children, 13*(3), 226–238.

McGee, R., Williams, S., Share, D. L., Anderson, J., & Silva, P. A. (1986). The relationship between specific reading retardation, general reading backwardness and behavioral problems in a large sample of Dunedin boys: A longitudinal study from five to eleven years. *Journal of Child Psychology and Psychiatry, 27*, 597–610.

McLaughlin, T. F. (1992). Effects of written feedback in reading on behaviorally disordered students. *Journal of Educational Research, 85*, 312–316.

McMichael, P. (1979). The hen or the egg? Which comes first—antisocial emotional disorders or reading disability? *British Journal of Educational Psychology, 49*, 226–238.

O'Connor, R. E., Notari-Syverson, A., & Vadasy, P. (1998). *Ladders to literacy: Kindergarten activity book*. Baltimore, MD: Brookes.

Palincsar, A. S., & Brown, A. L. (1984). Reciprocal teaching of comprehension fostering and comprehension monitoring activities. *Cognition and Instruction 1*(2), 117–175.

Palincsar, A. S., & Brown, A. L. (1986). Interactive teaching to promote independent learning from text. *The Reading Teacher, 39*, 771–777.

Pressley, M. (1998). *Reading instruction that works: The case for balanced teaching*. New York: Guilford.

Rashotte, C. A., & Torgesen, J. K. (1985). Repeated reading and reading fluency in learning disabled children. *Reading Research Quarterly, 20*, 180–188.

Resnick, M. J. (1987). The use of seriously emotionally disturbed students as peer tutors: Effects of oral reading rates and tutor behaviors. (Doctoral dissertation.) *Dissertation Abstracts International*, order no. 8813441.

Richman, N., Stevenson, J., & Graham, P. (1982). *Preschool to school: A behavioral study*. San Diego, CA: Academic Press.

Rutter, M., & Yule, W. (1970). Reading retardation and antisocial behavior—The nature of the association. In M. Rutter, J. Tizard, & K. Whitmore (Eds.), *Education, health and behaviour* (pp. 240–255). London: Longman.

Scruggs, T. E., & Mastropieri, M. A. (1986). Academic characteristics of behaviorally disordered and learning disabled students. *Behavioral Disorders 11*, 184–190.

Scruggs, T. E., Mastropieri, M. A., & Richter, L. (1985). Peer tutoring with behaviorally disordered students: Social and academic benefits. *Behavioral Disorders, 10*, 283–294.

Shisler, L., Top, B. L., & Osguthorpe, R. T. (1986). Behaviorally disordered students as reverse-role tutors: Increasing social acceptance and reading skills. *Journal of Special Education, 10*, 101–119.

Skinner, C. H., Smith, E. S., & McLean, J. E. (1994). The effects of intertrial interval duration on sight-word learning rates in children with behavioral disorders. *Behavioral Disorders, 19*(2), 98–107.

Snow, C. E., Burns, S. M., & Griffin, P. (1998). *Preventing reading difficulties in young children.* Washington, DC: National Academy Press.

Stott, D. H. (1981). Behaviour disturbance and failure to learn: A study of cause and effect. *Educational Research, 23*(3), 163–172.

Swanson, H. L. (1999). Instructional components that predict treatment outcomes for student with LD: Support for a combined strategy and direct instruction model. *Learning Disabilities Research and Practice, 14*, 129–140.

Swanson, H. L., & Hoskyn, M. (1998). Experimental intervention research on students with Learning Disabilities: A meta-analysis of treatment outcomes. *Review of Educational Research, 68*, 277–321.

Thorpe, H. W., & Borden, K. F. (1985). The effect of multisensory instruction upon the on-task behavior and word reading accuracy of learning disabled students. *Journal of Learning Disabilities, 18*, 279–286.

Torgesen, J. K., & Bryant, B. (1994). *Phonological awareness training for reading.* Austin, TX: Pro-Ed.

Vaughn, S., & Klingner, J. K. (1998). Students' perceptions of inclusion and resource room settings. *Journal of Special Education, 32*, 79–88.

Vaughn, S., Klingner, J. K., & Schumm, J. S. (1996). *Collaborative strategic reading.* Miami: School Based Research, University of Miami.

Yell, M. L. (1992). A comparison of three instructional approaches on task attention, interfering behaviors, and achievement of students with emotional and behavioral disorders. (Doctoral dissertation.) *Dissertation Abstracts International*, order no. 9236987.

7 Teaching Writing to Students with Behavior Disorders

Metaphor and Medium

GERALD TINDAL

LINDY CRAWFORD
University of Oregon

Introduction

According to the U.S. Department of Education's 1994 annual report to Congress, approximately 1% of the school population has been labeled Seriously Emotionally Disturbed (SED) or, using the language of the 1997 Individuals with Disabilities Educational Act, is considered emotionally and behaviorally disturbed (EBD). Nevertheless, as noted by Eber, Nelson, and Miles (1997), these students are present throughout the continuum of educational placements, leading them to conclude that (a) little relationship exists between clinical severity and restrictiveness of education, and, (b) therefore, supports for teachers "are needed across all school settings" (p. 540).

Writing could well be thought of as one of the most important expressive skills for students with behavior disorders or emotional disturbance. As a replacement skill, writing could provide such students with a more appropriate and effective outlet to gain recognition from others and access acceptable events they find reinforcing. In this chapter, we provide a conceptual framework for teaching students with behavior problems effective writing skills, using two critical attributes of writing as a metaphor to describe issues and interventions, both social and academic.

The importance of writing notwithstanding, writing instruction may not be a priority for some teachers of students with severe behavior disorders. Many teachers may believe that it is necessary for students to master appropriate social behaviors before focusing on academic skills even though some researchers in the field of behavior disorders (Coleman, 1986; Glavin, Quay, & Werry, 1971) warn that such a decision is ill formed. For a number of students, difficulty with academic tasks lays the groundwork for the adoption of maladaptive behaviors, while for other students who develop behavior problems early, academic skill deficits only exacerbate their situation. Because of this relationship between behavioral and academic problems, teachers of students with behavior disorders cannot postpone the teaching of academics until other social behaviors are "under control." Instead, academic and behavioral skills need to be taught concurrently. In the case of writing, the focus on an academic skill could well serve as a very powerful medium with which to teach social skills. As we argue in this chapter, writing is communication between teacher–student and student–student dyads, and, as Dyson and Freedman (1991) remind us, these relationships have a strong effect on students.

This communication is inherently social, as Stein (1986) asserts: Most writing tasks are conceived and initiated in social contexts, in which writers have specific goals for communicating via the written word. Pea and Kurland (1987) continue this logic: "[W]riting as communication—to persuade, inform, instruct—is a necessary skill in our society" (p. 280). The broad general goals of informing, explaining, and persuading underlie most acts of writing. Therefore, in analyzing the uses of writing, "it is not writing per se but the sort of social situations in which writing is embedded that determine its ultimate human effects" (Dyson & Freedman, 1991, p. 756).

In summary, writing needs to be considered in a social context with consideration of the purpose, the audience, and the type of discourse. Following the early work of Hayes and Flower (1980), we believe that students need to consider all three of these components simultaneously to engage in a process of translating perspectives into written language.

Writing as a Metaphor and a Medium

We begin our analysis of writing and the development of effective interventions by reference to a conceptual metaphor. Sfard (1998) argues that metaphors provide a basic way of communicating scientific principles using language that is commonly known to help bridge and build new conceptions of knowing. "Indeed, metaphors are the most primitive, most elusive, and yet amazingly informative objects of analysis. Their special power stems from the fact that they often cross the borders between the spontaneous and the scientific, between the intuitive and the formal" (p. 4). She cites Bruner (1986) in describing metaphors as "crutches to help us get up the abstract mountain" (p. 48). For her, the metaphors of acquisition and participation were useful in understanding the current state of disequilibrium in the field of learning. For us, the metaphor of writing as discourse and as strategic metacognition allows bifocal attention to both academic and social skills.

We identify two critical attributes of written expression: (a) different discourse to convey meaning and (b) strategic processes occurring in planning, translating, and revising. In the process of analyzing and intervening with students having behavior disorders, teachers can therefore use writing as a medium to focus on the social nature of both discourse and strategic metacognition.

With discourse analysis, we address both internal and external representations of students and the language used to convey meaning. In the confluence of content with the medium of words, writing perforce is generated with reference to discourse. In considering strategy instruction, we rely on both metacognition as well as task-oriented supports to help students not only learn skills but apply them in specific settings. Both attributes are equally applicable to any consideration of behavior disorders themselves, but we spend a considerable amount of time discussing metacognitive and cognitive strategies because of a diverse research base demonstrating their positive effects on both academic and social behaviors (Kaplan, 1990; Pressley & Woloshyn, 1995). In summary, we use writing as a metaphor to bring both social and academic programming together and address the very issues that are most pertinent for students with behavior disorders.

Early Identification

For interventions to be most effective, early identification and treatment are necessary. In written expression, such early diagnosis is even more important because of the complexity of the skill area. Writing requires the concurrent integration of many different components, all of which must be developed in synchrony. For example, handwriting or computer skills must be sufficient to provide students input. At this level, conventions need to be followed with many rules to consider in correct use of syntax, punctuation, grammar, and spelling. Students also need to have something to write about, requiring attention to topic, audience, and the match between them. Choices need to be made about the type of discourse to use in communicating the topic. Finally, both a macro (coherence) and micro (cohesive) level of organization must be present in the final composition.

Curriculum-Based Measurement in Writing

Any system for early identification must focus on the sensitivity of the assessment system. In the latest report from the National Assessment of Educational Progress (NAEP), 20 years of outcomes are discussed, with the general conclusion being that no progress has been made in writing quality. These findings are mirrored in Oregon, where a similar analytic rubric is used to evaluate writing. Basically, if writing programs are to be effective, students and teachers need to have a scale that is sensitive, using performance indicators not only to identify students who are failing but then provide feedback in a formative, not just summative, manner. For many students with disabilities, the rating scales are not very sensitive. Therefore, we focus on curriculum-based measurement (CBM), primarily because of its sensitivity in early identification and capability of showing growth.

Using standardized procedures that can dovetail into many of the large-scale assessment systems, CBM provides a way of measuring behavior over time that is accessible to all students, even the lowest performers, and that can be used in a formative evaluation system that shows change over time. Developed over the last 20 years within the context of CBM, this system uses objective counts of various writing components, some of which serve directly for targeting interventions and others that are correlated with important components of writing. CBM also is useful in monitoring the progress of interventions using formative evaluation so changes to adjust instruction can be empirically based and maximally individualized. Finally, by focusing on learning gains and frequent feedback, the system we describe provides the kind of instructional focus needed by teachers for students with behavioral problems.

The initial research conducted at the University of Minnesota Institute for Research on Learning Disabilities (IRLD) was conducted to create brief measures of writing that were highly correlated with standardized published achievement tests. A number of studies have published on the criterion validity of various scoring procedures when students were asked to write an imaginative story in response to either picture prompts or story starters (Deno, Mirkin, & Marston, 1982). The number of words written and the number of words spelled correctly appeared to be most highly correlated with (a) the Test of Written Language (Hammill & Larsen, 1988), (b) the Word Usage Subtest of the Stanford Achievement Test (Madden, Gardner, Rudman, Karlsen, & Merwin, 1978), and (c) Lee and Canter's (1971) Development Sentence Scoring (1971). For these two measures, the correlations ranged from .67 to .84. In addition to validity, reliability also has been the focus of several studies. Marston (1989) reports on the alternate form reliability for several measures, with coefficients in the moderate to high range and most above .70. Deno et al., (1980) note that writing samples of various duration all resulted in similar correlations.

In an effort to find a more sensitive measure and one that would be connected to the writing process, Videen, Deno, and Marston (1982) counted the number of correct word sequences and found high correlations with both measures of production (total words written and total spelled correctly), as well as with holistic ratings by teachers and the Test of Written Language. Correlations with Developmental Sentence Scoring were only moderate. Tindal and Parker (1991) generally confirmed these results with intermediate elementary students, though the correlations were quite a bit lower with the SAT (1982 edition with Gardner, Rudman, Karlsen, & Merwin) but the same for teacher ratings. In another study with middle-secondary students by Tindal and Parker (1989), such quantitative measures were not as highly correlated with teachers' ratings. With scores converted to the percentages, however, for both words spelled correctly and words in correct sequence, the correlations were again moderate. Parker, Tindal, and Hasbrouck (1991) confirmed this relationship with a large number of students ranging from both elementary and secondary school grades: Both the percentage of words spelled correctly and in correct sequence were most appropriate for screening and eligibility determination. Watkinson and Lee (1992) also found group differences between general and special education students when both the number and the percentage of words and correct word sequences were computed. Such criterion validity for secondary students also has been examined by Espin, Scierka, Skare, and Halverson (1999) using correct word sequences and mean length of correct word sequences, as well as several computer-generated metrics such as words written, spelled correctly, characters written, characters per word, and sentences written. They found that a combination of measures correlate the highest with the language subtests of the California Achievement Test (CTB/McGraw-Hill, 1985). Finally, Marston, Lowry, Deno, and Mirkin (1981) and Deno, Marston, Mirkin, Lowry, Sindelar, and Jenkins (1982) have examined the sensitivity to change for several writing measures, including the total number of words written and the number of words spelled correctly. Both over grade levels and within a grade level from fall to spring, these two measures showed consistent increases for students in general education.

In summary, many of the indices studied as part of CBM in writing focus on quantifiable indices that can detect small amounts of behavior and show change over time while being used to evaluate instructional programs formatively. In reflecting on these two features, students with low production and proficiency can be included meaningfully in assessment and show growth. This feature is what allows us to bridge the characteristics of early writers with those of more advanced writers. Any early identification system needs to identify not only who is having problems but also what their performance should be like. Using the novice–expert literature allows us to focus on both identification and remediation.

Novice versus Expert Writers

Although early identification is necessary, it often is difficult to accomplish. In part, the very complexity of writing means that the differences between good and poor writers are only visible after years. Nevertheless, the research that has been done between these two groups has been consistent with two major differences apparent between novices and experts:

1. Novices' writing is writer oriented with less thought given to the eventual reader, while experts' writing is more reader oriented as they plan and generate ideas (Flower, 1979; Flower & Hayes, 1977). In identifying students with writing problems, it is therefore important to focus on discourse or perspective.
2. Novices revise at the word level and make changes in form, while experts revise at the discourse levels and make meaning changes (Bridwell, 1980; Sommers 1980).

This literature allows us to approach the process of writing strategically and build a bridge that connects early writing to later, more advanced writing. Interventions can then be developed that move students through phases of proficiency with the product evaluated on the degree of expertness. Therefore, using these two features, we focus the remainder of the chapter on discourse and metacognition, the areas in which writing interventions should be most emphasized, particularly for novices.

Discourse Analysis

We use Hicks's (1995–1996) definition of the term *discourse* as implying "communication that is socially situated and that sustains social 'positionings': relations between participants in face-to-face interaction or between author and reader in written texts" (p. 49). As such, *discourse* implies a dialectic of both linguistic form and social communicative practices. One can talk of "discourse in terms of oral and written text that can be examined after the fact and socially situated practices that are constructed in moment to moment interaction" (p. 51).

Hillocks (1995) describes the writing process as purposive; people write for specific reasons, and without a clear purpose, writing falters. He challenges current approaches to writing instruction that focus on declarative knowledge of discourse modes before exploring more general purposes for writing, stating that people write to fulfill a purpose and choose to write in a particular mode of discourse that meets their intended purpose. The question of purpose is a very real one for students. "Why are we doing this?" is an all-too-common question for students of all grade and skill levels. Student motivation for writing may be increased when they are able to collaborate with their teachers in defining the purpose for writing, well in advance of any prewriting activities.

Most young people complete the majority of their writing at school. However, as students age, the number of school audiences increases. Much of the writing literature discusses the importance of audience in students' writing, yet researchers report inconsistent results. Although instructional techniques that promote audience awareness do not always result in better-quality writing (Schriver, 1993), audience awareness seems to increase students' sense of purpose and motivate them to improve the quality of their written compositions, as facilitated through use of structured peer feedback (Mentzell, Ryder, Vander Lei, & Roen, 1998) and writing conferences (Bowen, 1993). Therefore, teachers of younger students or students with writing challenges may want to create multiple audiences, allowing students the opportunity to realize its importance.

When teaching students to compose in different modes of discourse, teachers should rely on the elements of scaffolding or gradually faded prompts and explicitly defined dimensions. *Scaffolding* is an instructional technique that provides students with adequate models and opportunities to create while slowly decreasing the level of assistance provided to students, whereas *explicitly defined dimensions* provide students with the substantive knowledge related to characteristics of different discourse modes, which can then be evaluated using scoring guidelines that are specific to the particular mode of discourse.

In summary, teaching students about discourse serves as a model for making choices that are sensitive to audience awareness, which also is paramount in the demonstration of appropriate behaviors. Behavioral expectations differ according to various settings, and students' ability to analyze the audience and its expectations affords them the opportunity to exhibit acceptable behaviors within that particular microcosm.

The Strategic Nature of the Writing Process and Metacognition

Writing is typically viewed as composed of many processes that are not fixed in any particular order: planning, transcribing, and reviewing. It also is typically regarded as hierarchically organized, goal directed, and problem-solving oriented (Dyson & Freedman, 1991).

The most popular approach is the *natural process approach* in which students plan, write, and revise (Hillocks, 1984). Students initiate interactions, proceed at their own pace, and seek feedback when necessary. This approach is by far the most common across educational classrooms. Bereiter and Scardamalia (1982) describe this process with teacher support as "procedural facilitation," in which cognitive and strategic coaching is provided to students with less attention given to the content of their text.

Yet, in Hillocks's meta-analysis, this approach was not very successful. In contrast, an *environmental approach* was more effective, in which students were directed to develop goals, content, and procedures needed for a composition cooperatively. Both content and process need to have been directly taught, and students need to have been "taught" how to work together as well as how to work independently. Again, in the integration of academic with social behavior instruction, the metaphor is clear.

Probably Flower and Hayes (1981) have proffered the most compelling model of the writing process. They analyzed writing in terms of three major elements: (a) the task environment (the rhetorical problem to be solved, the evolving text, the writer's tools, and the information sources), (b) the long-term memory of the writer (topic, audience, and strategies), and (c) the process (planning, writing, and reviewing/revising). Within this cognitive model, most researchers view writing as a decision-making process composed of various stages (Flower & Hayes, 1981). The most accepted definition of the writing process includes three stages: planning, writing, and revising. These stages are viewed as recursive because writers are believed to move back and forth between them in a nonlinear manner. For example, writers may begin their compositions with planning but revisit this stage as the written text develops.

Evaluation is a component not included in most discussions of the writing process, but very applicable to writing completed in school settings. We see this as part of the writing process because teachers are increasingly engaging students in the evaluation of their own work as well as the work of others. Therefore, we describe the majority of school writing as consisting of four stages: planning, writing, reviewing/revising, and evaluating (see Box 7.1).

For writing to be effective, the process must be strategic. The different writing stages provide a structure, or framework, that students internalize and apply to different writing situations. As is true with any strategy, the writing process needs to be explicitly taught with students provided numerous opportunities for practice. Once students have mastered the writing process, however, they need to be empowered to complete various writing tasks independently.

BOX 7.1

Writing as a Recursive Process

We argue, that, to move efficiently through each stage of the writing process and complete these various writing tasks requires strategies, which can be separated into two categories: metacognition or self-regulation strategies (Harris & Graham, 1996; Howell, Fox, & Morehead, 1993) and task-specific strategies. *Metacognitive* refers to skills that are "relatively content free and revolve around people's ability to reflect on and control their own thinking processes" (Stein, 1986, p. 232). In contrast, task-specific strategies are very context-specific and provide procedural knowledge on the writing process, and although necessary, they may be less generalizable. In writing, examples of such strategies include topical brainstorming activities, outlining, and revision strategies.

To the greatest extent possible, strategy instruction should focus on metacognition even though both metacognitive as well as task-specific strategies have been researched and found to be successful in the development of expressive writing skills (Graham & Harris, 1989). The multifaceted needs of students with academic and behavioral difficulties require teachers to be as efficient as possible in their choice of strategies. Efficiency is possible by teaching students metacognitive strategies that enable them to increase their abilities to perform independently in a multitude of settings. Examples of these strategies include self-monitoring and self-evaluation, both of which can be used across various settings with different discourse and audience.

Although the effectiveness of strategy instruction permeates much of the special education and school psychology literature, it rarely is applied across academic and behavioral fields of study. In this section of the chapter, we illustrate the effectiveness of various learning strategies, and other research-based interventions, in improving students' academic and behavioral skills. Again the metaphor applies: Many metacognitive strategies applied during writing are equally as effective when applied to behavioral tasks. For example, the use of self-monitoring has been demonstrated to improve the quality of a writer's message (Graham & Harris, 1989), as well as promote generalization of appropriate social skills (Kiburz, Miller, & Morrow, 1985). It is these strategies that we emphasize. However, effective writing also requires fluency with task-specific strategies. Therefore, in our discussion of the four stages of the writing process, we also describe strategies specific only to the writing process.

Stage 1: Planning and Using Gateway Activities

In the classroom, the first phase of the writing process often consists of planning. As is true for all stages of the writing process, planning is affected by a student's level of procedural and substantive knowledge. *Procedural* knowledge provides information related to the "how" of writing, and *substantive* knowledge provides information related to the "what" of writing. Both procedural and substantive knowledge can be facilitated by use of metacognitive and task-specific strategies.

The importance of procedural knowledge cannot be underestimated. Students with disabilities can learn procedures for completing tasks when they receive explicit instruction, ample modeling, many opportunities to practice, and teacher feedback (Swanson & Hoskyn, 1998). Without the correct procedures for composing various types of writing, students will not have the tools necessary to convey meaning. Task-specific planning strategies serve as examples of procedural knowledge, such as topical brainstorming, clustering, or mapping of ideas prior to writing. Procedural knowledge of this type is relatively easy to teach, and writing interventions focusing on procedural knowledge have been demonstrated to be very effective (Hillocks, 1984).

Although procedural knowledge is critical to completing writing tasks, teachers cannot overlook the importance of substantive knowledge, without which students will have nothing to write about. In extending the meaning of writer- versus reader-based strategies, Stein (1986) argues for the need first to use writing as a communication act in which an evaluation is made of the type and amount of information needed to manage cognitive change. Assuming the content (of information) is adequate, the process can continue with further planning and revising. Consequently, it is clear that writing serves two main purposes: (a) to help the writer clarify and understand what is known about a topic and (b) to inform, teach, or persuade others with reference to particular ideas.

Stein (1986) then further articulates an evaluation process that focuses on two possible reasons for skill deficits in writing. The first reason is a lack of skill in strategies, or how the writing process should proceed (e.g., planning, writing, revising, and evaluating). The second reason is a lack of substantive knowledge about the topic or the type of discourse best suited to accomplish a purpose. To her, many writing difficulties arise from student lack of specific content knowledge; in essence she argues against any notion of a general writing ability. Rather, writing skills need to be considered as context-dependent and rely on the acquisition of substantive knowledge. Teaching must include not only the structural aspects of writing but the content that is embedded in the discourse, whether it use forms such as stories, arguments, descriptions, essays, expositions, summaries, and so forth.

Planning activities such as topical brainstorming, clustering, or mapping are ineffective if students (a) do not have any prior knowledge to brainstorm, or ideas to cluster, or (b) are not familiar with particular discourse demands of the task. The content used for most school-related writing tasks relies on students' prior knowledge but young students, and students with restricted life experiences, have limited prior knowledge. Planning activities for these students should not neglect the importance of substantive knowledge but rather consist of activities that either build on students' prior knowledge or provide them with the substantive information needed to write.

Students lacking substantive knowledge have been shown to benefit from in-depth inquiry activities during the planning process, as well as directed research activities to assist in the generation of ideas and content (Hillocks, 1995). *Gateway activities*, in particular, are one way of increasing substantive knowledge (Hillocks) and have been demonstrated to generate student inquiry. These activities are fairly complex and demand more time than the perfunctory 5 to 10 minutes allotted for prewriting activities. They are not brief, teacher-led lessons designed to teach isolated writing skills. Instead, they are fairly lengthy, well-planned excursions into a particular subject matter meant to engage students in meaningful inquiry. During these activities, teachers and students collaborate and exchange ideas related to the content of the writing piece, as well as the elements inherent in the particular genre. Following is an abbreviated example of a gateway activity, for the creation of a fable, as provided by Hillocks.

The first step in a gateway activity is to identify the critical features of a particular writing task. Once these features are identified, strategies can be designed to support students as they learn about, and apply, critical features in creating their own piece of writing. For example, a fable can be described as having three critical features: (a) animals that exhibit human characteristics, (b) one animal that has a unique character trait, and (c) a moral concluding the fable. Consideration of these features lays a partial foundation for creation of an appropriate gateway activity. The remainder of the foundation relies on an awareness of the learner's prior knowledge. The activity is designed to teach students the critical features of the writing genre by building on their level of prior knowledge and range of interests.

For example, a gateway activity might begin with brainstorming to identify interesting personality traits of famous people (e.g., musicians, actors, or authors). Hillocks suggests this as a starting place as opposed to brainstorming possible morals. He shares that many students overrely on familiar morals and are less creative than when they begin the activity by brainstorming personality traits. Once developed, the list of traits should be discussed until a clear picture is established. For example, teachers may want to ask students to elaborate on particular personality traits. How are these traits manifested? What do the students believe are the underlying motives behind certain behaviors?

Next, students brainstorm possible animals that exemplify these particular traits. Again, students are challenged to describe why an animal personifies a particular trait. Is it in the way that the animal looks or sounds? Or is it in the way the animal behaves in its own habitat or in an unknown environment? Teachers engage students in discussions, challenging them to extend their ideas and elaborate on them. This may be accomplished in whole-class or small-group discussions, depending on the skill level of students. Throughout this process, however, the focus is on providing substantive knowledge.

Once a suitable animal is chosen, a plot needs to be developed. This is more challenging with fables than with personal narratives because they are mostly imaginative and not merely retellings of actual events in the lives of students (Hillocks, 1995). Finally, students develop a one-line moral to the story that acts as a self-contained lesson. Hillocks briefly discusses three types of morals that students can create depending on their skill level and their previous practice with creating fables: direct statements of the obvious, subtle generalizations about behavior, or intricate word plays.

Gateway activities are one way to facilitate substantive knowledge, and their use could easily be extended into the teaching of appropriate behaviors. Students with behavioral difficulties may lack substantive information that provides the examples and knowledge needed to differentiate between appropriate and inappropriate behavior. Students with behavioral difficulties also may be missing the procedural knowledge needed to respond in accordance with the demands of various social situations. Obviously, procedural and substantive knowledge are critical in the development of appropriate social behaviors, and early assessment of these types of knowledge in academic and behavioral realms will help focus instruction, increasing its efficiency.

Stage 2: Writing

Once a student completes a certain level of planning, the next step is generating text by writing rough drafts. Instructional approaches to the teaching of writing are varied, roughly divided between two opposing factions. Some theorists promote a constructivist approach, or as Hillocks (1984) defines it in his meta-analysis, a "natural process" approach, in which teacher direction is minimal, an externally imposed structure is absent, and students are free to create unique compositions. According to this model, explicit instruction suffocates creativity, and does not result in meaningful learning (McCabe, 1971; Novak, 1990). Writing is synonymous with inspiration, or as Hillocks (1995) states, "invoking the muse" (p. 77). Other researchers believe that students best learn to write when exposed to highly structured, teacher-led instruction. In this model, instruction is explicit, and students practice discrete skills that are introduced hierarchically and thoroughly mastered before the next level of writing is taught. In this model, sentence construction is learned to mastery before the completion of paragraphs, and paragraphs before the creation of larger text units. An example of a program adhering to this model is Expressive Writing (Engelmann & Silbert, 1983).

Many researchers in the field of writing embrace elements contained in both of the models just described, emphasizing the importance of writing as a creative endeavor while still realizing the necessity of explicit instruction, modeling, sufficient opportunities to respond, and corrective feedback. It is this view that we endorse. "Writing is complex. It's part thought, part passion, part structure" (Spandel & Stiggins, 1990, p. 34). Learning to write cannot be fully conceptualized as mastery of a set of discrete skills to be taught in a bottom-up fashion; neither can it be viewed as divine inspiration, a natural talent that cannot be taught. We believe that the best approach for students with learning or behavioral problems is one that combines both models discussed here.

According to Isaacson (1989), students with learning and behavioral problems may need more support than their peers because their lack of secretarial skills may limit their ability to concentrate on their skills as authors. In other words, their lack of automaticity with procedural knowledge interferes with the writing process. Therefore, writing is best viewed as a collaborative process consisting of as much teacher support and guidance as necessary to ensure that students have the necessary tools to write. The amount of teacher support varies with the skill level of students and is gradually withdrawn until students are writing independently.

Scaffolding provides students with needed support while strategy instruction encourages them to participate actively in their own learning. Perhaps more than any other component, strategy use enables students to become independent learners and provides them with the tools necessary to be successful in writing as well as in interacting with others. Metacognitive and task-specific strategies are used by students to create coherent and cohesive text. These strategies focus primarily on procedural knowledge.

Due to the wealth of possible strategies, teachers need to be discriminating in choosing strategies that are effective as well as highly efficient when working with students who have academic and behavioral skill deficits. We suggest two guidelines for teachers to follow when deciding which strategies to teach: (a) choose strategies according to individual student needs and characteristics, and

(b) teach generalizable strategies. Students benefit when metacognitive strategies are learned because they allow for increased practice opportunities as well as opportunities to generalize to different settings. Finally, teachers benefit because generalizable metacognitive strategies are much more efficient than task-specific strategies.

Stage 3: Revising

Perhaps the most challenging stage of the writing process is the revision stage. Revising one's own work is a daunting task, and frequently students do not revise very well. Researchers have found that student revisions do not necessarily improve their writing, and they sometimes actually reduce overall quality (Perl, 1979; Scardamalia & Bereiter, 1983). Furthermore, inexperienced writers have been found to revise less frequently than more advanced writers (Faigley & Witte, 1981), and their revisions are of poorer quality than the revisions of more experienced writers (Faigley & Witte, 1981; Stoddard & MacArthur, 1993). Quality differences also are apparent in the types of revisions students make. Students who are not "good" writers make more surface-level revisions than meaning-level revisions, concerning themselves more with form than with substance (Bridwell, 1980).

It is important to note that much of the research on revision has been conducted with older students, and caution is warranted when generalizing findings from one group to another group of students with widely different characteristics. Students with disabilities in written language typically have not been included in many of these studies and generalization to other subgroups may be unwarranted (Kame'enui & Simmons, 1990).

In response to the need for students to become more adept at critically evaluating and revising their work, research has been conducted exploring the effectiveness of peer feedback. Using peers during this phase of the writing process (Stoddard & MacArthur, 1993), and using peer response groups during revision activities is highly recommended (DiPardo & Freedman, 1988), resulting in a positive impact.

The use of peers can be incorporated during revision activities in a variety of ways. For example, Perl (1983) suggests the method of "active listening" to provide a strategy or structure for students while they revise each other's work. Using this model, students work with a partner, with each student reading a section of his or her partner's work and then paraphrasing the section in his or her own words. Listening to their partner, the composer is able to hear whether the text made sense to the reader and is better able to generate meaning-level revisions.

Peer collaboration can also be structured to provide more specific feedback. Depending on the skills of the students, teachers may want to generate a list of steps for students to follow when revising each other's work. These steps prompt students to remain focused on the activity and encourage them to be neither too critical of each other's work nor too accepting. For example, when teaching students with disabilities to work in pairs on revision activities, Stoddard and MacArthur (1993) designed a task-specific strategy, consisting of five explicitly defined steps, and taught this strategy to students. Students were successful in applying the strategy as evidenced by an increase in the quality of their written texts.

The parallel between the importance of peers in the writing process and the importance of peers in acquiring and displaying new social behaviors is obvious. "Writing instruction doesn't take place in a vacuum. Rather instruction takes place in the context of school: a context that is both physical and social" (Harris & Graham, 1996, p. 189). Peers are powerful role models, and their presence often inspires students to learn and maintain new behaviors. Furthermore, as is the case with strategy instruction, skills that students learn for appropriate interactions with peers often are generalizable to a multitude of academic as well as behavioral settings. Teaching students how to collaborate successfully with their peers during the writing process should generalize to other settings that emphasize other interactive behaviors, once again resulting in more efficient use of instructional time.

Stage 4: Evaluation

The final phase of the writing process is evaluation. Students need to learn to critically assess their own work (Spandel & Stiggins, 1990), and expressive writing provides them with this opportunity. Self-assessment is a metacognitive strategy and is generalizable to other settings as well. However, as with revision, self-assessment of one's writing is not easy. Rather, writing is highly personal and "filled with emotion" (Meichenbaum, 1996, p. 12). As with all behaviors, it is hard to step back and critically appraise one's work. Therefore, peers should not be responsible for the final evaluation of students' written work. Instead, assessment should rest with the student writer and the teacher.

Experience has shown us that many students with academic and/or behavioral difficulties judge themselves far too harshly when engaging in self-evaluation, while a smaller portion of the students are not constructive enough. Because self-evaluation is not an easy task, many authors believe that self-evaluation should center on the writing process as opposed to the writing product (Harris & Graham, 1996; Newcomer, Nodine, & Barenbaum, 1988). By focusing on completion of the stages of the writing process, students are less driven by the need to create a perfect piece of writing and may find it easier to engage in self-assessment that is constructive as opposed to destructive.

We propose use of analytic trait scoring to evaluate students' writing across different discourse modes. Analytic scales consist of explicit scoring criteria that can be shared with students at all stages of the writing process. As previously discussed, traits in an analytic scale can be aligned with more precise measures of writing (e.g., total words written, mean sentence length), to provide a more sensitive measurement system when needed (see Box 7.2). For the majority of students, however, analytic scales will suffice, providing students with explicit feedback on

BOX **7.2**

Qualitative Dimensions for Scoring Writing Cross-Mapped to CBM Indices

Content

Number of words written (include common symbols and numbers in count)

Thought units or sentences relating to the prompt (do not include sentence fragments in total)

Number of story grammar words (e.g., character, setting, plot, problem, solution)

Number of large or mature words (words totaling seven letters or more)

Thought units/sentences relating to topic sentences (percentage calculated for each paragraph)

Organization

Number of paragraphs and/or topic sentences (total only those that relate to the prompt)

Number of story grammar words

Number (or percentage) of transition words or sentences

Mean length of correct word sequences (compute the average length of consecutive correct word sequences to evaluate text cohesiveness)

Style

Number of words written

Number of unique or infrequent words (count words that appear only once in composition)

Number of large or mature words

Variety of sentence types (number or percentage of simple, compound, or complex sentences)

Mean length of thought units/sentences

Mechanics or Conventions

Correct word sequences (adjacent words with correct grammar, spelling, and punctuation)

Number of words written

Percentage of words spelled correctly

what is expected as well as how they are progressing toward these expectations. In the end, teachers need to evaluate students' written products using thoughtfully developed scoring rubrics that are fair and explicit.

Many teachers model their scoring rubrics after those used in large-scale writing assessments. These are general rubrics applied to writing composed for a variety of purposes. Some researchers question the usefulness of the same scoring rubric across various modes of discourse (Cooper, 1999). Research into the quality of writing within different modes of discourse demonstrates that students' writing varies according to discourse mode, partly because of the cognitive and task demands and partly because of the amount of experience they have with different discourse modes (Quellmalz, Capell, & Chou, 1982). Although general scoring rubrics are helpful, they may not be explicit enough when attempting to engage students in different types of writing. For example, a scoring rubric that focuses on general organization and content without also considering assertions or counter-arguments in the production of a persuasive piece of writing may not be explicit enough for students with academic or behavioral difficulties.

For students with behavioral challenges, the strength of analytic scales is in their explicitness and their stability of expectations. Scoring rubrics also provide students with fair and frequent feedback related to the elements of the writing process. Students learning to write need to be provided guidelines that define "good writing." It is this substantive knowledge that makes it clear for students the criteria as well as the exact expectations for them to meet. Students cannot apply metacognitive strategies and other procedural knowledge if they are unclear of their eventual goals.

Creation and implementation of scoring rubrics across academic and behavioral tasks increases the consistency of students' school environments, an obvious need for students with behavioral problems. Rubrics can be modified for use in a variety of educational settings once students become familiar with their general organization. As discussed previously in this chapter, students complete higher-level tasks more effectively when the lower-level tasks are learned to automaticity. Once the structure of the rubric is familiar to students and they have reached a level of mastery in its use, they are freed to concentrate on meeting academic or behavioral expectations as opposed to navigating an unknown system of evaluation.

Summary

We have focused on interventions and assessment in writing for students with behavior disorders and have listed them in Box 7.3. We believe writing is a natural medium to address many of the issues, as it is relevant for both academic and social behaviors. After focusing initially on early identification, we used two specific attributes of writing to convey our perspective: (a) discourse analysis and

BOX **7.3**

Recommended Steps for Teaching and Assessing Writing

Written Expression: Teaching Recommendations

Step 1   **Establish a clear purpose** for writing, including audience awareness. Provide students with ample opportunities to meet intended purposes by composing in various discourse modes.

Step 2   **Provide students with prior knowledge** needed to engage in creative writing activities. When necessary, engage students in elaborate prewriting, or gateway, activities before beginning formal planning activities.

Step 3   **Use explicit instruction to teach critical subskills** (spelling; sentence structure), but do not postpone opportunities for students to write creatively until subskills are mastered.

Step 4   **Teach the stages of the writing process** while encouraging students to use metacognitive strategies to monitor movement in and out of each stage.

Step 5   **Focus on procedural knowledge** (how to write) and substantive knowledge (what to write).

Step 6   **Encourage peer feedback** by creating structured formats for students to follow when assisting each other in all stages of the writing process.

Step 7   **Teach metacognitve strategies** (self-monitoring; self-evaluation) to enhance generalization of skills across academic and social settings.

Written Expression: Assessment Recommendations

Step 1   **Collect brief samples of students' writing** (5–15 minutes). Use CBM indices to monitor students' writing progress on a monthly basis.

Step 2   **Focus most evaluative efforts on the writing process** and strategy use, as opposed to the writing product, creating a positive environment that fosters skill development and strategy use.

Step 3   **Adopt or create explicitly defined analytic scales.** Share analytic scales with students before they begin writing. Rely on scales to provide students with clear, objective feedback about their writing performance.

Step 4   **Formally evaluate writing products quarterly,** and use the information to focus instruction.

(b) strategic metacognition. In both attributes, writing serves as a metaphor and a medium. For students with behavioral disorders, discourse focuses on the language of communication and perspective taking, providing them alternatives to the ineffective systems they currently are using. By addressing metacognition, we attend to long-term effects with internalized rule structures that are not stipulated to specific settings.

REFERENCES

Bereiter, C., & Scardamalia, M. (1982). From conversation to composition. In R. Glaser (Ed.), *Advances in instructional psychology* (Vol. 2). Hillsdale, NJ: Erlbaum.

Bowen, B. A. (1993). Using conferences to support the writing process. In A. M. Penrose & B. M. Sitko (Eds.), *Hearing ourselves think: Cognitive research in the college writing classroom.* New York: Oxford University Press. (pp. 188–200).

Bridwell, L. (1980). Revising strategies in 12th grade students' transactional writing. *Research in the Teaching of English, 3,* 197–222.

Bruner, J. (1986). *Actual minds, possible worlds.* Cambridge, MA: Harvard University Press.

Coleman, M. C. (1986). *Behavior disorders: Theory and practice.* Englewood Cliffs, NJ: Prentice Hall.

Cooper, C. R. (1999). What we know about genres, and how it can help us assign and evaluate writing. In C. R. Cooper & L. Odell (Eds.), *Evaluating writing: The role of teachers' knowledge about text, learning and culture* (pp. 23–52). Urbana IL: National Council of Teachers of English.

CTB/McGraw-Hill. (1985). *California Achievement Test.* Monterey, CA: Author.

Deno, S. L., Marston, D., Mirkin, P., Lowry, L., Sindelar, P., & Jenkins, J. (1982). *The use of standard tasks to measure achievement in reading spelling and written expression: A normative and developmental study* (Research Report No. 87). Minneapolis: University of Minnesota, Institute for Research on Learning Disabilities.

Deno, S. L., Mirkin, P. L., & Marston, D. (1980). *Relationships among simple measures of written expression and performance on standardized achievement tests* (Research Report No. 22). Minneapolis: University of Minnesota Institute for Research on Learning Disabilities.

Deno, S. L., Mirkin, P. L., & Marston, D. (1982). Valid measurement procedures: Continuous evaluation of written expression. *Exceptional Children, 48,* 368–371.

DiPardo, N., & Freedman, S. W. (1988). Peer response groups in the writing classroom: Theoretic foundations and new directions. *Review of Educational Research, 58*(2), 119–149.

Dyson, A. H., & Freedman, S. W. (1991). Writing. In J. Flood, J. J. Jensen, D. Lapp, & J. Squire (Eds.), *Handbook of research on teaching the English language arts.* New York: Macmillan.

Eber, L., Nelson, C. M., & Miles, P. (1997). School-based wraparound for students with emotional and behavioral challenges. *Exceptional Children, 63*(4), 539–555.

Engelmann, S., & Silbert, J. (1983). *Teacher presentation book: Expressive Writing I.* Tigard, OR: C. C. Publications.

Espin, C. A., Scierka, B. J., Skare, S., & Halverson, N. (1999). Curriculum measures in writing for secondary students. *Reading and Writing Quarterly, 15,* 5.

Faigley, L., & Witte, S. (1981). Analyzing revision. *College Composition and Communication, 32,* 400–414.

Flower, L. (1979). Writer-based prose: A cognitive basis for problems in writing. *College English, 41,* 19–37.

Flower, L., & Hayes, J. R. (1977). Problem-solving strategies and the writing process. *College English, 39*(4), 449–461.

Flower, L., & Hayes, J. R. (1981). A cognitive process theory of writing. *College Composition and Communication, 32,* 365–387.

Gardner, E. F., Rudman, H. C., Karlsen, B., & Merwin, J. C. (1982). *Stanford Achievement Test—Primary 3.* Austin, TX: Harcourt, Brace, Jovanovich.

Glavin, J. P., Quay, H. C., & Werry, J. S. (1971). Behavioral and academic gains of conduct problem children in different classroom settings. *Exceptional Children, 37,* 441–446.

Graham, S., & Harris, K. R. (1989). Improving learning disabled students' skills at composing essays: Self-instructional strategy training. *Exceptional Children, 56,* 201–214.

Hammill, D., & Larsen, S. (1988). *Tests of written language—2.* Austin, TX: Pro-Ed.

Harris, K. R., & Graham, S. (1996). *Making the writing process work: Strategies for composition and self-regulation.* Cambridge, MA: Brookline.

Hayes, J. R., & Flower, L. S. (1980). Writing as problem solving. *Visible Language, 14*(4), 388–399.

Hicks, D. (1995–1996). Discourse, learning, and teaching. In M. W. Apple (Ed.), *Review of research in education* (Vol. 21, pp. 49–95). Washington, DC: American Education Research Association.

Hillocks, G., Jr. (1984). What works in teaching composition: A meta-analysis in experimental treatment studies. *American Journal of Education, 93*(1), 107–132.

Hillocks, G., Jr. (1995). *Teaching writing as reflective practice.* New York: Teachers College Press.

Howell, K. W., Fox, S. L., & Morehead, M. K. (1993). *Curriculum-based evaluation: teaching and decision making* (2nd ed.). Pacific Grove, CA: Brooks/Cole.

Isaacson, S. (1989). Role of secretary vs. author: Resolving the conflict in writing instruction. *Learning Disability Quarterly, 12,* 209–217.

Kame'enui, E. J., & Simmons, D. C. (1990). *Designing Instructional Strategies: The prevention of academic learning problems.* Englewood Cliffs, NJ: Macmillan.

Kaplan, J. (1990). *Beyond behavior modification* (2nd ed.) Austin, TX: Pro-Ed.

Kiburz, C. S., Miller, S. R., & Morrow, L. W. (1985). Structured learning using self-monitoring to promote maintenance and generalization of social skills across settings for a behaviorally disordered adolescent. *Behavioral Disorders, 11,* 47–55.

Lee, L., & Canter, S. M. (1971). Developmental sentence scoring. *Journal of Speech and Hearing Disorders, 36,* 335–340.

Madden, R., Gardner, E. F., Rudman, H. C., Karlsen, B., & Merwin, J. C. (1978). *Stanford achievement test.* New York: Harcourt, Brace, Jovanovich.

Marston, D. (1989). A curriculum-based measurement approach to assessing academic performance: What it is and why do it. In M. Shinn (Ed.), *Curriculum-based measurement assessing special children* (pp. 18–78). New York: Guilford.

Marston, D., Lowry, L., Deno, S. L., & Mirkin, P. (1981). *An analysis of learning trends in simple measures of reading, spelling, and written expression: A longitudinal study* (Research Report No. 49). Minneapolis: University of Minnesota, Institute for Research on Learning Disabilities.

McCabe, B. J. (1971). The composing process: A theory. In G. Hillocks, B. J. McCabe, & J. F. McCampbell (Eds.), *The dynamics of English instruction: Grades 7–12* (pp. 516–529). New York: Random House.

Meichenbaum, D. (1996). Foreword. In K. R. Harris & S. Graham (Eds.), *Making the writing process work: Strategies for composition and self-regulation* (pp. xii–xiii). Cambridge, MA: Brookline.

Mentzell Ryder, P., Vander Lei, E., & Roen, D. H. (1998). Audience considerations for evaluating writing. In C. R. Cooper & L. Odell (Eds.), *Evaluating writing: The role of teachers' knowledge about text, learning, and culture* (pp. 53–71). Urbana, IL: National Council of Teachers of English.

Newcomer, P., Nodine, B., & Barenbaum, E. (1988). Teaching writing to exceptional children: Reac-

tion and recommendations. *Exceptional Children, 54,* 559–564.

Novak, J. D. (1990). Concept mapping: A useful tool for science education. *Journal of Research in Science Teaching, 27,* 937–949.

Parker, R., Tindal, G., & Hasbrouck, J. (1991). Countable indices of writing quality: Their suitability for screening-eligibility decisions. *Exceptionality, 2,* 1–17.

Pea, R. D., & Kurland, D. M. (1987). Cognitive technologies for writing. In E. Z. Rothkopf (Ed.), *Review of Research in Education* (Vol. 14, pp. 277–326). Washington, DC: American Educational Research Association.

Perl, S. (1979). The composing process of unskilled college writers. *Research in the Teaching of English, 13,* 317–333.

Perl, S. (1983). How teachers teach the writing process: Overview of an ethnographic research project. *Elementary School Journal, 84,* 19–24.

Pressley, M., & Woloshyn, V. (1995). *Cognitive strategy instruction that really improves Children's Academic Performance.* Cambridge, MA: Brookline.

Quellmalz, E., Capell, F. J., & Chou, C. (1982). Effects of discourse and response mode on the measurement of writing competence. *Journal of Educational Measurement, 19,* 241–258.

Scardamalia, M., & Bereiter, C. (1983). The development of evaluative, diagnostic and remedial capabilities in children's composing. In M. Marlew (Ed.), *Psychology of written language: A developmental and educational perspective* (pp. 67–96). New York: Wiley.

Schriver, K. A. (1993). Revising for readers: Audience awareness in the writing classroom. In A. M. Penrose & B. M. Sitko (Eds.), *Hearing ourselves think: Cognitive research in the college writing classroom* (pp. 147–169). New York: Oxford University Press.

Sfard, N. (1998). On two metaphors for learning and the dangers of choosing just one. *Educational Researcher, 27*(2), 4–13.

Sommers, N. (1980). Revision strategies of student writers and experienced adult writers. *College Composition and Communication, 31,* 378–388.

Spandel, V., & Stiggins, R. J. (1990). *Creating writers: Linking writing assessment and instruction.* New York: Longman.

Stein, N. (1986). Knowledge and process in the acquisition of writing skills. In E. Rothkopf (Ed.), *Review of research in education* (pp. 225–258).

Washington, DC: American Educational Research Association.

Stoddard, B., & MacArthur, C. A. (1993). A peer editor strategy: Guiding learning-disabled students in response and revision. *Research in the Teaching of English, 27,* 76–103.

Swanson, H. L., & Hoskyn, M. (1998). Experimental intervention research on students with learning disabilities: A meta-analysis of treatment outcomes. *Review of Educational Research, 68*(3), 277–321.

Tindal, G., & Parker, R. (1989). Assessment of written expression for students in compensatory and special education programs. *Journal of Special Education, 23,* 169–183.

Tindal, G., & Parker, R. (1991). Identifying measures for evaluating written expression. *Learning Disabilities Research & Practice, 6,* 211–218.

U.S. Department of Education (1994). *19th annual report to Congress* (1994). Washington, DC: Author.

Videen, J., Deno, S. L., & Marston, D. (1982). *Correct word sequences: A valid indicator of proficiency in written expression* (Research Report No. 84). Minneapolis: University of Minnesota, Institute for Research on Learning Disabilities.

Watkinson, J. T., & Lee, S. W. (1992). Curriculum-based measures of written expression for learning-disabled and non-disabled students. *Psychology in the schools, 29,* 184–191.

R E C O M M E N D E D   R E A D I N G S

Calkins, L. (1994). *The art of teaching writing.* Portsmouth, NH: Heinemann.

Calkins uses personal and professional examples to relay the message that writing is more than a set of skills but a way of being in the world. Separate chapters are devoted to different developmental stages of writing. The book's contents center around using the writing workshop to teach students at all grade levels (nursery school through high school). Many chapters conclude with extensive bibliographies, describing books to be read by teachers and by students.

Graves, D. (1988). *Writing: Teachers and children at work.* Portsmouth, NH: Heinemann.

Using dozens of stories about students' writing experiences, actual samples of student writing, and a collection of transcripts from actual conversations between teachers and students about the writing process, Graves describes how to create a classroom where writing is encouraged by teachers and embraced by students. He suggests that teachers listen and learn from children; structure classrooms for writing activities, engage students in the writing process, conduct writing conferences, and publish children's work. This book is a good resource for beginning writing teachers, containing explicitly detailed instructional lessons and useful evaluation tools.

Graves, D. (1994). *A fresh look at writing.* Portsmouth, NH: Heinemann.

A text designed for teachers of students in the primary and intermediate grades, Donald Graves describes this text as more "assertive" than his previous books on teaching writing, noting that today's teachers need to be extremely efficient with their instructional time. The text is separated into four sections, emphasizing the importance of listening to children, modeling one's thoughts during the generation of text, providing students opportunities to read and interact with self-generated text, and organizing classrooms to enhance the writing process. One section of the book is devoted to teaching the fundamentals of writing (including spelling and conventions), and a separate chapter describes how to work with parents and administrators.

Harris, K., & Graham, S. (1996). *Making the writing process work: Strategies for composition and self-regulation.* Cambridge, MA: Brookline.

A book written for teachers of students at all ages, focusing on teaching students how to use cognitive and metacognitive strategies to improve their writing. Authors emphasize the importance of teaching students to use self-regulation and other metacognitive strategies to monitor their writing activities. Readers also are provided with detailed descriptions of specific writing strategies designed to help students plan, write, edit, and evaluate their written products.

Murray, D. (1999). *Write to learn* (6th ed.).

Murray has written another highly engaging book designed for secondary students and adults with varying levels of writing skills. Best described as a guidebook, Murray uses chapters of the book to walk the reader through the steps of the writing process, while providing numerous suggestions for overcoming obstacles that one might face at every step along the way. The inside covers of the book act as an index to questions frequently posed by all writers (For example, "How do I find the voice for my writing?" "What should I do if I can't write?") This guidebook is a wonderful resource for older writers.

Sebranek, P., Meyer, V., & Kemper, D. (1995). *Write source 2000: A guide to writing, thinking, and learning.* Wilmington, MA: Great Source Education Group.

A student handbook filled with reference information related to the writing process, including writing for different purposes and audiences, as well as the fundamental rules for writing. The authors state that the handbook is designed for students of all ages, but it seems most appropriate for use by students in the intermediate grades. This book is a user-friendly resource for student writers, providing information about writing as well as information about strategic learning. It provides the reader with procedural as well as substantive knowledge, including world maps and historical documents (e.g., U.S. Constitution).

Spandel, V. (1994). *Seeing with new eyes: A guidebook on teaching and assessing beginning writers.* (2nd ed.). Portland, OR: Northwest Regional Educational Laboratory.

Three primary themes are inherent in this guidebook designed for use by primary teachers (grades K–3): (a) use of a six-trait model to teach important aspects of the writing process, (b) use of rubrics to assess students' writing, and (c) instructional and assessment strategies for different writing genres. This guidebook focuses primarily on instruction, but it also discusses assessment strategies for evaluating children's writing. Spandel provides many writing samples generated by young children to focus discussion about writing traits and different genres.

Spandel, V. & Stiggins, R. (1997). *Creating writers: Linking writing assessment and instruction* (2nd ed.). New York: Longman.

A teacher's guide to designing classroom-based instruction and assessment of student writing. Authors describe how to use the Six-Trait Analytical Scoring Guide that they developed for use in writing classrooms. Traits include voice, ideas, organization, sentence fluency, conventions, and word choice. Suggestions for using writing conferences and peer reviews are also provided.

8

Mathematics

Screening, Assessment, and Intervention

**GEORGE H. NOELL AND
KRISTIN A. GANSLE**
Louisiana State University

Introduction

Students in American schools are increasingly required to think quantitatively and use quantitative technologies such as calculators and computers. The challenges confronting mathematics education are growing in the data-rich information age (National Council of Teachers of Mathematics [NCTM], 1998). Although the need to educate students to understand and function in this environment is obvious, research indicates that many students' mathematics skills are deficient. For example, the National Assessment of Educational Progress (1997; NAEP) indicates that in 1996, only 21% of fourth graders performed at a proficient level in the four basic arithmetic operations. The study also found that major corporations experienced difficulty filling entry-level positions due to applicants having insufficient skills and that these corporations were expending capital to provide remedial mathematics instruction to employees.

In addition to the broader societal implications of mathematical incompetence, research supports the importance of mathematical competence for individual students in several ways. First, greater mathematical knowledge is associated with greater earnings in the workplace (Condition of Education, 1996). Second, research indicates that individuals' preferences tend to shift from less successful activities toward activities in which they are more successful (Osipow & Scheid, 1971). Finally, data indicate that strengthening academic responding is an effective means of decreasing problematic behavior (Ayllon & Roberts, 1974).

The benefits of mathematical competence may be particularly important for students who exhibit or who are at risk of exhibiting behavioral disorders. Effective mathematics instruction and intervention can potentially decrease students' challenging behavior in mathematics classes, increase their preference for mathematics learning, and provide students with a competitive advantage after they graduate. Additionally, to the extent that academic failure and frustration set the occasion for disruptive antisocial behavior, educational programs that occasion success provide a form of primary prevention for challenging behaviors.

The balance of this chapter describes a process for supporting mathematics success for all students. The process includes three main elements. The first element is routine screening of student achievement to permit early identification of students who need additional instructional support. The second element is using assessment to guide development of an intervention to meet individual student needs. The final element is intervention implementation and progress monitoring.

Screening

Mathematics is a core academic content area that is central to students' educational, vocational, and life success. Mathematics is similar to language arts in that they both use arbitrary symbols to convey ideas and relationships, they function according to rules, and in mastering them, students must learn basic skills before applying them to more conceptual, theoretical, or abstract problems (Howell, Fox, & Morehead, 1993). It is important that educators employ reliable, valid procedures to measure student learning and screen for students who are not learning core content. However, before screening can take place, agreement must be reached regarding what comprises "mathematics" and what constitutes acceptable performance standards in this area. The definition of mathematics curricular content, weighting of the relative importance of content, and standards for performance vary widely. Information provided within the local curricula, from local education agency (LEA) content standards, and from NCTM can all potentially contribute to the design of progress monitoring and screening procedures.

NCTM Standards

In 1989, NCTM published the *Curriculum and Evaluation Standards for School Mathematics* (NCTM, 1989). It was NCTM's first formal adoption of standards for mathematics instruction in the United States. Its intent was to ensure quality, to indicate goals, and to promote change in the American education system (NCTM, 1998). That document is currently undergoing revision. The working document, *Principles and Standards for School Mathematics: Discussion Draft* (NCTM, 1998), provides five mathematical content standards for student learning and five mathematical process standards through which students should obtain and utilize their mathematical knowledge. These standards are designed to apply to *all* students, from prekindergarten to 12th grade, regardless of their level of expertise with mathematical skills, operations, or concepts. Central to the foundation of *Standards* is that *all* students can and should learn mathematics. Within each standard, a small number of focus areas are identified for each grade, and the relationship of focus areas between grades is clarified (NCTM, 1998). Mathematical content standards include Number and Operation; Patterns, Functions, and Algebra; Geometry and Spatial Sense; Measurement; and Data Analysis, Statistics, and Probability. The mathematical process standards include Problem Solving, Reasoning and Proof, Communication, Connections, and Representation. These standards emphasize the applied and conceptual elements of mathematics. For additional details, refer to the NCTM *Standards* (1998).

A cursory examination of the *Standards* indicates that NCTM considers mathematics instruction to be focused on much more than memorization of number facts, computation, and mathematical procedures. Students who are well schooled in mathematics must be competent in applying number facts and computation at a more conceptual level. In other words, students must know not only *how* to add but *when* and *why* to add.

Curriculum

Although it provides principles and standards for the teaching of mathematics in the schools, NCTM does not make recommendations regarding specific curricula. Instead, they suggest that each LEA draw on materials appropriate to and for its students, teachers, and administrators, with the caveat that curriculum should be designed "to systematically provide students with mathematical experiences that progressively become broader and deeper" (NCTM, 1998, p. 30).

Despite substantive criticisms of spiral curricula (e.g., Cawley, Baker-Kroczynski, & Urban, 1992; Carnine, 1991), most available mathematics texts are based on a spiral curriculum. These curricula typically present a little of this and a little of that, returning to this and returning to that at different times in the skill sequence (Cawley & Parmar, 1991). The progression through content emphasizes the developmental readiness construct rather than mastery of skills. The same skill is taught at varying degrees of depth and complexity at different times that can be separated by years between presentations. Because curricula vary in the depth of coverage and sequencing of concepts, examination of the students' curriculum is an important first step in devising a screening and progress monitoring plan. In order for the screening device to be maximally informative, it should examine what students were taught and expected to learn.

Selecting and Devising Screening Tools

It is crucial when selecting or devising instruments to screen mathematics skills that the procedures capture all core content areas. Unlike reading, in which fluency predicts comprehension and a variety of reading-relevant outcomes (for a discussion, see Marston, 1989), good scores in one area of mathematics do not necessarily predict good scores in other areas of mathematics (Shapiro, 1989). Students may subtract well but be unable to tell time or understand disjoint sets but be unable to identify appropriate units of measurement for length. The screening tool should reflect what was taught, what was most important among the skills taught, and the expected level of student proficiency with those skills. Ideally, the proficiency standards will be defined for the entire LEA and will include both accuracy and fluency. (Issues related to the development of accuracy and fluency standards are discussed near the conclusion of the screening section.) In addition to being reliable, valid, and instructionally relevant, an optimal screening device would be brief, easily scored, and inexpensive and would have numerous parallel forms to permit repeated administration. The two primary choices available to educators (published instruments and curriculum based assessment) for the repeated screening of mathematics achievement differ in their cost, utility, and general suitability as a screen.

Norm-Referenced Tests.   Norm-referenced tests typically have adequate data to support their reliability and validity and require little or no preparation time. Unfortunately, they typically are relatively expensive to administer, may not match instruction, and have little utility for instructional planning (Witt, Elliott, Daly, Gresham, & Kramer, 1998). Additionally, parallel forms are not consistently available, and when they are, they are typically few in number. This presents a major barrier to the frequent screening that is necessary for early detection and intervention. Norm-referenced tests also return data that can be more misleading than informative. Grade equivalence scores appear to describe students' readiness for grade-appropriate materials; however, grade equivalency scores do not accurately describe students' readiness for instructional materials or tasks (Witt et al., 1998). Although using grade-equivalent statements to make placement decisions is a patently unsound practice, some tests do collect useful samples of mathematics skills (Howell et al., 1993). In order for them to be used effectively, however, the items used on the test must be cross-referenced with the sequence of skills taught in the relevant curriculum.

Despite their limitations, some research examining norm-referenced tests as potential screening devices has been published. Flanagan and colleagues (1997) compared university students' scores on the Kaufman Functional Academic Skills Test (K-FAST; Kaufman & Kaufman, 1994), the Woodcock-McGrew-Werder Mini-Battery of Achievement (MBA; Woodcock, McGrew, & Werder, 1994), and the Wide Range Achievement Test—3 (WRAT-3; Wilkinson, 1993), and they determined that the mathematics scores from the three batteries were consistently correlated, supporting the validity of the measures. However, that study did not investigate the validity of using those instruments with elementary or secondary students, and it did not provide evidence that they were valid for the purpose of screening proficiency in any given curriculum. Time to administer varies among this group, parallel forms are unavailable, and the cost may be a significant consideration when screening large groups of students.

Additionally, adaptations of the Stanford Achievement Test (SAT; Psychological Corporation, 1989) have been developed for use as screening devices. Holt (1995) developed screening procedures for use with students with hearing disabilities, and McBride (1989) pilot-tested a computerized screening test based on the

SAT. Unfortunately, no brief screening device based on the SAT is currently commercially available. Using the full SAT as a screening device appears to be impractical due to the administration time (45 minutes), number of forms available per level (two), and the cost of test forms and answer booklets.

It is also worth noting that LEAs commonly administer well-validated normative instruments for reasons other than screening. Many school districts will administer tests such as the Iowa Tests of Basic Skills (Riverside Publishing, 1996) or the Metropolitan Achievement Test (MAT; Durost, Bixler, Wrightstone, Prescott, & Balow, 1971) to all students in particular grade levels. Although these tests are not practical screening devices due to cost and infrequent administration, they provide useful data. Minimally, results from tests such as the ITBS and MAT can be reviewed to help identify students who are struggling in one or more broad domains of mathematics. These data in turn can signal the need for additional assessment.

Basic Skill Builders.   Basic Skill Builders (formerly Precision Teaching; Conrad, Anderson, & Beck, 1995), is a program designed to build and maintain fluency in basic skills in a number of areas. The mathematics set provides skill builder sheets that may be used for frequent progress monitoring. They require only a few minutes to administer, have multiple parallel forms, and are easy to score. These materials could be more aptly described as samples of various mathematics tasks rather than as a formal instrument.

Curriculum-Based Measurement.   Curriculum-based measurement (CBM) provides an alternative to norm-referenced tests that is inexpensive, tied to the curriculum, and instructionally relevant and can provide an unlimited number of parallel forms (Shapiro, 1990). Additionally, standardized procedures for developing, administering, and scoring tests (typically referred to as *probes*) have been developed whose reliability and validity are known to be adequate (Deno, 1985; Shinn, 1989). In reviewing several validity studies for CBM mathematics, Marston (1989) reported validity coefficients across studies that ranged from .26 to .65. The median correlation reported with the Problem-Solving section of the MAT was .425 and .54 with MAT Math Operations. In addition to demonstrating criterion validity, CBM is a particularly useful form of screening and progress monitoring because of its treatment validity. CBM can be used to develop educational interventions that improve student outcomes (Deno, 1985; Shinn, Collins, & Gallagher, 1998).

Typically, a CBM mathematics assessment is based on a series of 2-minute tests called *probes*. Probes consist of math computation problems and may include a mixture of problem types or a single type of computation. Probes are scored for the number of digits students completed correctly during the probe. A simple subtraction fact may require only one digit to complete, while a long division problem can require 35 digits to complete. Digits correct is used as the metric within CBM mathematics because it provides a consistent metric across tasks of varying difficulty, it is more sensitive to growth than problems correct, and it has demonstrated adequate reliability and validity (Marston, 1989). Even though it is not the standard metric, the percentage of problems completed correctly can also be useful in intervention planning. Interested readers can consult Shapiro (1989) and Shinn (1989) for detailed information regarding the design, administration, scoring, and interpretation of CBM probe data.

Numerous advantages are associated with using routine CBM probes to monitor student progress and screen students for mathematics difficulties. Preparation time for fact or calculation probes is modest and may not be greater than other routine teacher-prepared tests used during regular lessons. CBM probes potentially can be integrated into the routine of teaching. Scoring is easily learned, and feedback can be almost immediate. In addition, scoring need not be entirely dependent on teachers. Initial research indicates that students as young as second graders can be taught to score probes accurately (Dufrene & Noell, 1999). CBM probes are brief (2 minutes per probe), an infinite number of parallel forms can be readily prepared, and the cost of materials and administration is low. Fully implemented examples exist for using local CBM norms, curriculum-based assessment, and problem solving as a school-system-wide approach for addressing referral concerns for students who are at risk and identified as having handicapping conditions (Ikeda, Tilly, Stumme, Volmer, & Allison, 1996).

Arguably, the most important limitation of CBM in the area of mathematics is that it is not designed to assess directly some of the more abstract, integrated, or conceptual mathematics behaviors emphasized in the NCTM (1998) *Standards.* However, this does not preclude an LEA from supplementing a CBM assessment strategy with brief tests examining more complex mathematical behaviors. For example, a probe could be developed based on one or several word problems that require estimation, rounding, the selection of units of measurement, and a multiple-step mathematics operation. Although any single probe may not be sufficiently broad, a well-designed series of probes can capture a range of mathematics behaviors and can be used to identify students who are at risk for mathematics failure. Probe design and procedures can be adapted to meet a range of needs.

Establishing Performance Standards

Using screening data to identify at-risk students and guide instructional decision making requires that the data be evaluated. Evaluating screening data will raise questions about what level of performance or progress is adequate and what is not. For example, is 90% accuracy on a particular task sufficient? Unfortunately, no generally accepted source for assigning performance criteria exists. Additionally, performance standards are dependent on the task being assessed and the grade level of the students. Although 90% accuracy may be adequate for some mathematics skills at some points in instruction, it is clearly inadequate for fundamental mathematics skills such as counting, reading mathematical symbols, or multiplying (White & Harring, 1982). It is crucial that students master these fundamental skills with 100% accuracy because they are critical building blocks for the development of a conceptual and applied knowledge of mathematics. Lesser standards place students at a tremendous disadvantage for learning more complex tasks. For example, if students learn basic fact operations to 90% accuracy and then use those facts to solve four-step problems, fact errors alone will result in students completing only 66% of those operations accurately.

Setting accuracy criteria for complex multielement tasks and for less fundamental tasks is more challenging. Although no generally accepted standards are available, at least two approaches are possible based on information available within schools. First, if minimum performance criteria are specified by the school district (e.g., percentage correct for a passing grade), the performance criterion should exceed this standard. However, passing grades may set standards that are too low to prepare the student to be successful with future applications of that skill. A second approach is to set criteria based on the performance of successful students. This approach is particularly practical in schools due to the availability of students who have already mastered the content. These students can be identified by teacher nomination or by identifying students who successfully apply the skill to new contexts or problems. This approach may require collecting data from students in more advanced grades to set standards.

Optimally, performance standards in mathematics will include fluency standards in addition to accuracy standards. Fluency (i.e., sustained quick accurate responding) is an important part of academic competence because academic work is typically time limited and fluency is important in preparing students to retain and apply skills (Daly, Martens, Kilmer, & Massie, 1996; Wolery, Bailey, & Sugai, 1988). Fluency standards are typically defined as a number of problems, operations, or digits completed correctly within a specified time period.

Despite the importance of academic fluency, generally accepted standards for fluency have not been developed. Proposed mastery criteria actually vary rather widely, with ranges of 20 (Shapiro, 1989; for third-grade students) to 80 (Howell et al., 1993; addition facts) digits correct per minute appearing in standard references. Developing fluency standards is further complicated by the diverse array of activities that constitutes mathematics. Students will need to achieve a higher fluency in reading numbers than in solving for one unknown within linear equations.

Three general approaches appear to be most practical for setting fluency standards. First, accept standards established by the student's school district or curriculum publisher when they are available. Second, consult a standard educational assessment reference that provides criterion standards; Howell et al. (1993) is useful for this purpose. Third, develop a standard based on the performance of competent individuals. Assess the fluency of several students who have mastered the skill and use the lowest fluency as your criterion.

Interpreting Screening and Progress Monitoring Data

When screening and progress monitoring data are evaluated by comparison to performance standards the results can be *roughly* divided into three general outcomes (Witt, Daly, & Noell, 2000). First, all students are functioning at acceptable levels and are exhibiting acceptable progress. No follow-up action is indicated other than appropriate recognition of the students' and teachers' achievement. Second, most students have not learned instructed material and are exhibiting little progress. Stated differently, the current curriculum and instruction are ineffective for most students. In this situation, numerous individual interventions are an inefficient approach to address a systemic need. This problem may be evident in a classroom, school building, or entire school system. This outcome indicates the need for a critical assessment of current curriculum and instruction with the goal of identifying modifications that are likely to address the needs of many students. Readers confronting this type of outcome might choose to begin this process by examining Chapters 4 (Howell & Kelley) and 5 (Edwards & Kame'enui) within this volume that address instructional design. Third, most students are functioning adequately, but one or several students are outliers who are not learning the material. This assessment outcome indicates the need for individualized assessment of the student or students who are not progressing satisfactorily.

Assessment for Intervention Design

Classwide screening and progress monitoring are invaluable for identifying students who are not learning core mathematics concepts, but they are insufficient for developing an intervention. Screening procedures may identify students who are not completing measurement problems accurately, but they will not clarify whether the problem is in the domain of motivation, multiplication, numeration, units of measurement, or the accurate use of measurement tools. Screening procedures provide too limited a sample of student functioning to serve as the sole basis for developing an intervention. This section describes a series of assessment activities that can be used to guide the development of an individualized intervention. These assessment activities are designed to examine the possibility that poor student performance is the result of measurement error, poor motivation, a deficiency in a subordinate skill, or a deficiency in the integration of skills. Each stage in the assessment process provides data regarding a potential explanation for poor student performance and is linked to intervention needs. Figure 8.1 describes the assessment activities, potential assessment outcomes, and the implications for intervention or further assessment. The following sections describe each stage of this assessment process in some detail. After the process has been described, two case examples are provided to illustrate this approach to assessment and intervention design.

Measurement Error

All assessment data include measurement error. Anything that changes scores on a mathematics screening measure other than mathematics skill is a source of error. Students' scores on the screening measure could have been depressed because they were sleep deprived, sick, distracted by peers, or confused by the directions. Additionally, scores can be influenced by problems with the administration and scoring of the probes. Before devoting resources to an individualized intervention, an alternate form of the screening device should be administered under carefully con-

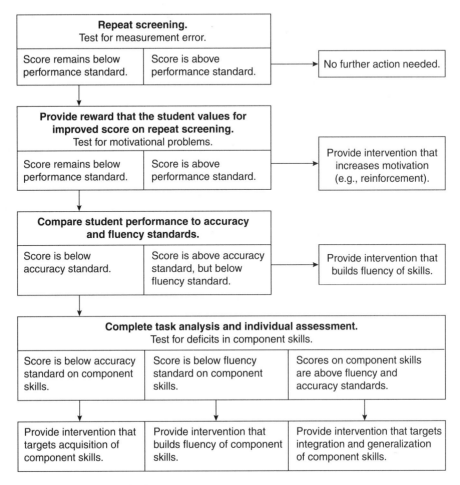

FIGURE 8.1 Individual Assessment

trolled conditions to confirm the original deficit and to reduce the risk that a low score or a series of low scores is attributable to measurement error. If students perform acceptably on the rescreening, then no additional action is indicated in this instance. If students frequently fail the routine screenings and subsequently pass the alternate form, administration and scoring procedures should be reviewed for potential problems. If students fail both the initial screening and the alternate form of the screen, additional assessment is needed.

Motivation

Although a range of factors can contribute to poor academic performance, inadequate skills and motivation are key possibilities (Daly, Witt, Martens, & Dool, 1997; Skinner, 1998). Gresham (1981) emphasizes the importance of this distinction for the assessment of children's social skills, describing social competence problems as resulting from either inadequate skills, a *skill deficit,* or from the inadequate performance of the skills within the individual's repertoire, a *performance deficit.* Testing the impact of motivational manipulations within an individualized assessment can provide valuable data for treatment programming.

Several recent studies have described a practical assessment approach that can be adapted to a range of academic concerns and examines motivation (e.g., Mortenson & Witt, 1998; Noell, Witt, Gilbertson, Ranier, & Freeland, 1997). This assessment can be described as including three phases. First, student performance data are collected under either standardized or typical conditions. Second, student performance is measured under conditions that eliminate or reduce the availability of potential reinforcement for other behaviors and provide a salient consequence for improved performance. Typically this consequence will be access to some highly valued activity or reward. Finally, the data from the two assessment occasions are compared. If students perform substantially better when the incentive is available and this improved performance is within an acceptable range, then the deficit can be described as a performance deficit or motivational problem. This result would suggest the need to program consequences that will increase student motivation to use their skills he or she possesses. Reinforcement-based interventions have been used in a number of published studies to increase student performance of mathematics (Pereira & Winton, 1991). It may also be useful to clarify for students *why* it is important that they complete this activity and master this particular skill.

Component Skills Assessment

If students did not perform the task successfully when a strong incentive was present and reinforcement for other behaviors was limited, additional assessment of skills is indicated. The assessment approach described in this chapter is based on developing a task analysis for the problematic activity and evaluating assessment data within the conceptual heuristic of the Instructional Hierarchy (IH) (Daly, Lentz, & Boyer, 1996; Haring, Lovitt, Eaton, & Hansen, 1978). The IH provides a conceptual link between instructional strategies and students' skills. The IH describes students as initially acquiring skills and then developing fluency with those skills. Fluency (i.e., sustained quick accurate responding) will be emphasized in the assessment process because of the importance of time in academic work and the importance of fluency in preparing students to retain and apply skills (Daly et al., 1996; Wolery et al., 1988). Once students have developed fluency, they are ready to generalize the skill to novel contexts and adapt the skill to novel demands. The goal of this process is to break the problematic activity down into its constituent parts and determine the student's level of skill development within those constituents.

Task Analysis. A task analysis is the process of breaking down a complex behavior into a series of discrete, measurable, and teachable components (Cooper, Heron

& Heward, 1987). For example, completing multiplication problems requires that students read the numbers, read the operation sign, identify the correct answer, and write the correct answer. Similarly, completing a word problem will include at least a reading component, identification of the question being asked, identification of relevant data, selection of appropriate operations, completion of those operations, and written reporting of the correct answer.

Several strategies for completing a task analysis are possible. One approach is to watch and carefully record the behavior of several competent individuals. Asking the competent individual then to explain each step in the process can potentially enhance this approach. This can permit the task analysis to include more subtle aspects of the task that the observer may have initially overlooked. This approach to task analysis can be readily accomplished in educational contexts because of the availability of competent students who are not the focus of the referral. A second approach is to consult an expert. In the context of an educational assessment this could be accomplished by discussing the skill and its components with the teacher and examining instructional guides relevant to the skill. A third approach is simply to perform the task and record each of the steps needed to complete the task. Interested readers can consult Cooper et al. (1987) for a more extensive and detailed description of task analysis techniques.

Assessment of the Component Skills.   Component skills will be assessed to determine whether the referral concern can be reasonably attributed to deficits in one or more component skills. Once the component skills have been identified through the task analysis, assessment can examine these skills sequentially to identify any deficiencies. For example, completing addition fact problems accurately requires reading the problem accurately, selecting the correct answer, and writing the answer. Teachers will typically emphasize selection of the correct answer (e.g., responding to 3 + 4 with 7) as the component being instructed when students are learning addition facts. However, written practice of addition facts includes reading and writing components. Students are only prepared for this form of practice to the extent that they can read and write numbers and mathematical symbols accurately and fluently.

Based on the three-step task analysis described earlier, an assessment for addition fact problems would include three elements. First, the accuracy and fluency with which students can read problems would be assessed. Students would be asked to read addition problems aloud much as students do in the context of CBM reading probes (Shinn, 1989). Second, the accuracy and fluency with which students can *orally* provide answers to problems would be assessed. Students would read problems and say the correct answers without having to write them. This activity is intended to separate selecting the correct answer from potential problems with writing. Third, the accuracy and fluency with which the student can write dictated numbers would be assessed. This activity is designed to assess the possibility that the difficulty with the target task is primarily a writing problem.

Evaluating Component Skills Assessment Data

Once student performance data for the component skills have been collected, the data can be evaluated by comparison to accuracy and fluency standards. However, standards may not be available for all of the skills that were assessed. If the skill being assessed was also a screening target, then accuracy and fluency standards should be readily available. If the skill being assessed was not part of the routine screening, standards may not be available for that skill. In these cases, the most practical approaches are likely to be developing standards based on the behavior of nonreferred competent students or consulting references that provide standards for academic tasks (e.g., Howell et al., 1993).

The goal of the evaluation stage of the process is to identify appropriate instructional targets and clarify intervention needs for those target skills. The process for identifying targets and instructional needs draws from the conceptual heuristic of the IH (Haring et al., 1978). If the assessment data fall below either accuracy or fluency standards, then that skill should be targeted for intervention. Students will not be prepared to master the more complex skill targeted in the screening until they have mastered its component skills. The initial focus of the intervention will be determined by the assessment data. If student responding is below the accuracy standard developed for that skill, then the initial intervention target will be establishing accurate responding. If the responding is accurate but slow, then the instructional need is to develop fluency. Once students have mastered the component skills, they will be ready to master the skill that was initially screened.

In some instances students will complete all of the subordinate skills fluently but still be unable to complete the criterion task accurately. This outcome can be described as a problem with the integration and generalization of the previously mastered subordinate skills (Daly et al., 1996; Haring et al., 1978). For example, students may have all of the requisite reading and mathematics skills needed to complete word problems but be unable to integrate these skills to complete assigned problems. In this case the intervention would target the complete task (e.g., word problems), and the instructional need would be facilitate the generalization and integration of the component skills. In some instances the criterion task will be completed accurately but too slowly. In this case the target will be developing fluency with the complete task. The outcomes of the data evaluation process and the relevant instructional needs are presented at the bottom of Figure 8.1.

Developing an Intervention Based on the Assessment Data

The assessment process just described will lead to the identification of specific target behaviors and intervention goals. The goal will be to develop accurate responding, to encourage fluent responding, or to facilitate the generalization and integration of skills. The incredible diversity of mathematics tasks precludes an exhaustive presentation of methods to achieve those outcomes for all potential areas of concern. The following discussion describes fundamental methods for enhancing students' accuracy, fluency, and generalization. The intent is to provide the reader with fundamental information that can be adapted to a wide range of mathematics tasks.

Accuracy. Establishing accurate responding requires at least two fundamental instructional components. Instructional cues must be provided that permit students to make correct responses consistently, and a sufficient number of complete learning trials must be provided. Prompts or models can be used to cue students to practice correct rather than incorrect responses. The classic show-tell-do instructional sequence begins with modeling the correct response. Students are initially shown how to complete the task, are then told what they are expected to do, and are then provided the opportunity to complete the task. Similarly, the cover-copy-compare instructional procedure begins by providing students with a model of the correct response (Skinner, Bamberg, Smith, & Powell, 1993).

Constant time-delayed prompting (Wolery et al., 1992) is another procedure for providing instructional cues that both facilitates correct responding and reduces student errors. In this procedure students are presented with an instructional demand such as "What is 7 times 8?" A predefined period of time is allowed to pass (e.g., 4 seconds; Cybriwsky & Schuster, 1990). If students do not respond before the end of that interval, then the correct answer is provided as a prompt for students to imitate. Interested readers can consult Wolery et al. (1992) or Handen and Zane (1987) for a detailed and comparative review of prompting procedures.

The second crucial element of establishing accurate responding is to provide sufficient complete learning trials (CLTs) to master the material. A complete learning trial consists of a response opportunity (e.g., a question), a student response, and feedback. It is vital that the delay between student response and instructor feedback be short enough that students can learn from the feedback. Generally, younger students and students who are in the initial stages of learning a skill need more immediate feedback. Some students who fail the screening measure will exhibit adequate progress if they are provided more CLTs. Procedures such as choral responding (Heward, Courson, & Narayan, 1989) and reciprocal peer tutoring (Fantuzzo, King, & Heller, 1992) can be used to increase the number of student CLTs and provide timely feedback.

Fluency. Once students learn to respond accurately, they are ready to develop fluency with the skill. The core element of developing fluency is intensive practice that emphasizes working quickly. Immediate instructional feedback for each response is less crucial at this stage because the student has already learned to respond accurately. Students will need feedback that allows them to see the extent to which they are progressing toward their fluency goal. Because developing fluency is hard work, it is important that fluency-building exercises include motivational elements such as embedding the practice in a game or reinforcement for more fluent performance (Noell et al., 1998) to help maintain student motivation.

Integration and Generalization. Once students have mastered the component skills for a task, they are ready to learn to integrate these skills to complete the target task. The integration and generalization of skills can be particularly challenging for complex tasks such as real-life mathematics applications or word problems. Educators can facilitate student generalization by providing models, offering strategy instruction, and teaching students to use self-monitoring strategies. A model can help students generalize and integrate skills by making it clear to them how they can combine their skills and abilities to solve a new challenge. The efficacy of modeling potentially can be enhanced if students have the opportunity to imitate the model as the model progresses through the process and instructional feedback is provided following imitation.

Strategy instruction emphasizes teaching the student how to combine previously mastered skills and the process of solving the problem (Howell et al., 1993). Strategy instruction will frequently include "verbal mediation" in which the students learn to talk themselves through the process of solving the problem (Davis & Hajicek, 1985). Strategy instruction has been used to teach mathematics skills to students with behavioral disorders (e.g., Davis & Hajicek, 1985). Self-monitoring is similar to strategy instruction in that the emphasis is on providing students with behavioral tools to mediate the use of skills they have developed previously. Self-monitoring as an instructional support is typically accomplished by giving students a written guide that cues them to complete specific parts of the task and can require completing the tasks in a particular order. The written materials also provide a place for students to record their progress as they complete each part of the task. Self-monitoring procedures have been used to teach students a range of mathematics skills (e.g., Dunlap & Dunlap, 1989).

Two Examples

Eddie was a third-grade student who was referred for assistance due to disruptive behavior and academic failure. He had been retained the previous year. The most severe immediate academic concern was in mathematics. Although systematic progress monitoring and screening data were not being gathered, Eddie's teacher did collect products such as worksheets. Review of these assignments revealed that Eddie did not consistently complete his assignments, and the accuracy of his work was poor. His average percentage correct on a collection of assignments reviewed at the point of referral was 53%.

The repeated screening step in the assessment was omitted due to Eddie's repeated failure on in-class assignments and the absence of standardized procedures for completing assignments. To test the possibility that Eddie's poor performance was the result of poor motivation, a recently failed assignment was readministered with a reward for doing his "best work." Eddie quickly completed the assignment with 95% accuracy. This result was above the teacher's performance standard. The motivational manipulation was repeated with another failed worksheet, and a reward standard of 80% correct was used. Eddie completed this assignment in less than half the allotted time and exceeded the reward criterion. Based on this assessment result, an intervention was designed that provided Eddie with programmed rewards for exceeding specific academic goals. This intervention resulted in improved behavior and an average score on daily mathematics assignments of 78% correct.

Traci was a fourth-grade student who was receiving mathematics instruction in a self-contained special education program.[1] Traci's teacher had been working with her in a small group on solving simple word problems, but Traci had made minimal progress. The text of the word problems was typically two sentences, and they could be solved using a single addition or subtraction operation. Traci's teacher used a 10-minute timed test containing five simple word problems one to two times per week to monitor students' progress. The teacher's goal was that students would complete all five problems correctly in 10 minutes. Traci's peers were approaching this goal.

Several progress-monitoring probes were obtained from the teacher to complete the initial part of the assessment. First, the screening was repeated. A probe was administered to Traci in a quiet office following the procedures typically used in the classroom. Traci completed four problems, but only one of those was correct. The assessment continued because her score was substantially below her teacher's performance standard. Second, a reward was provided for improved performance. A new probe was administered, but Traci could earn a choice among several rewards if she got at least four problems correct. She finished the entire probe but only completed two problems correctly. Traci's score remained below both accuracy and fluency expectations.

This result indicated the need to complete a task analysis for word problems. The task analysis was completed with Traci's teacher and consisted of reading the problem, identifying the question, constructing a number sentence that answers that question, and solving the problem. Assessment then shifted to these component skills. Traci was able to read the problems fluently and readily stated the question being asked. Both of these skills were judged to be accurate and fluent. Review of past progress monitoring data indicated that Traci had already mastered addition and subtraction operations through two digits by two digits addition and subtraction without regrouping. These were the most advanced operations required by the problems.

When Traci was asked to work through several probes and write the number sentence that would complete the problem, she made numerous errors. She did not consistently choose the correct operation, she transcribed numbers into the sentence incorrectly, and for those problems that included irrelevant data, she did not consistently select the correct data. An intervention was developed for Traci that focused on establishing correct construction of number sentences to complete word problems. The intervention initially targeted word problems without irrelevant data and then progressed to problems including irrelevant data. The intervention included modeling, coaching, immediate feedback, and error correction.

---

[1]The case description of Traci was adapted from the several cases for purposes of illustration.

Follow-up on Intervention Implementation

The most important element of intervention is monitoring the implementation of the intervention and the students' progress. Progress monitoring that includes examination of plan implementation provides an important procedural safeguard for students (Noell & Witt, 1999). Too often in education intervention plans are developed but not actually implemented (Happe, 1982). The resulting documentation indicates that students were not progressing adequately in general education, an individualized intervention was provided, and students did not benefit from that, either. Unfortunately, this documentation supports students' need for more intensive/restrictive services when the efficacy of intervention in general education is still unknown. Documenting intervention implementation can also lead to needed program modifications for interventions that prove to be impractical or were not well understood. They also permit decisions regarding intervention efficacy to be appropriately influenced by implementation data.

Progress monitoring data should be collected more frequently for students who are struggling than the routine screenings that are provided to all students. Fuchs and Fuchs's (1986) meta-analysis supported the adequacy of twice-weekly progress monitoring. They found that the effect size for twice-weekly progress monitoring was not statistically significantly different from the effect size for daily progress monitoring. Progress monitoring also creates a feedback loop that permits the iterative correction of the intervention plan. This provides a mechanism to correct mistakes made in the assessment or intervention design stages. Additionally, effective interventions will result in student progress that requires shifting the targets and goals of the intervention. For example, students may progress from acquiring a skill to fluency building or from mastery of component skills to learning to integrate skills. Students' progress will require changes in instructional goals and, as a result, changes in instructional strategies. Finally, progress monitoring provides an empirical basis for terminating the intervention when the students have achieved sufficient progress.

Summary

Mathematics is an increasingly important instructional demand for all students; success in this skill domain conveys a competitive advantage in the workplace. To the extent that instruction results in student success, it is likely to increase students' preference for mathematics and decrease problematic behavior (Ayllon & Roberts, 1974; Osipow & Scheid, 1971). Despite the importance of mathematics, many students experience frequent failure and frustration in mathematics class.

This chapter outlined an approach designed to enhance academic success in mathematics for all students. The core element of this approach is frequent, routine screening/progress monitoring of all students to permit early identification of students who are in need of additional instructional support. The development of screening measures should also occasion specification of core curricular content and student performance standards for that content. The second major element described herein is an individual assessment process in which the problematic activity is broken into its component skills. The individualized assessment is then designed to examine the student's level of skill development within those skills. The intent of this assessment is to match an instructional approach to key intervention targets and facilitate student achievement. The assessment and intervention model was guided by the IH and emphasized student skills as progressing from acquisition to fluency and finally to skill integration and generalization. The final and most important element of the process is delivering the intervention, monitoring its implementation, and measuring student outcomes.

SUPPLEMENTAL READINGS

Englemann, S., & Carnine, D. (1991). *Connecting math concepts.* Chicago: Science Research Associates.

Howell, K. W., Fox, S. L., & Morehead, M. K. (1993). *Curriculum-based evaluation: Teaching and decision making.* Pacific Grove, CA: Brooks/Cole.

Shapiro, E. S. (1996). *Academic skills problems: Direct assessment and intervention* (2nd ed.). New York: Guilford.

Stoner, G., Shinn, M. R., & Walker, H. M. (Eds.). (1991). *Interventions for achievement and behavior problems.* Silver Spring, MD: National Association of School Psychologists.

Wolery, M., Bailey, D. B., & Sugai, G. M. (1988). *Principles and procedures of applied behavior analysis with exceptional children.* Needham Heights, MA: Allyn & Bacon.

REFERENCES

Ayllon, T., & Roberts, M. D. (1974). Eliminating discipline problems by strengthening academic performance. *Journal of Applied Behavior Analysis, 7,* 71–76.

Carnine, D. (1991). Reforming mathematics instruction: The role of curriculum materials. *Journal of Behavioral Education, 1,* 37–58.

Cawley, J. F., Baker-Kroczynski, S., & Urban, A. (1992). Seeking excellence in mathematics education for students with mild disabilities. *Teaching Exceptional Children, 24,* 40–43.

Cawley, J. F., & Parmar, R. S. (1991). Maximizing mathematics success in the regular classroom. In G. Stoner, M. R. Shinn, & H. M. Walker (Eds.), *Interventions for achievement and behavior problems* (pp. 415–438). Silver Spring, MD: National Association of School Psychologists.

Condition of Education. (1996). *Third International Mathematics and Science Study* (NCES Publication No. 97255). Washington, DC: National Center for Educational Statistics.

Conrad, D., Anderson, P., & Beck, R. (1995). *Basic skill builders.* Longmont, CO: Sopris West.

Cooper, J. O., Heron, T. E., & Heward, W. L. (1987). *Applied behavior analysis.* Upper Saddle River, NJ: Prentice Hall.

Cybriwsky, C. A., & Schuster, J. W. (1990). Using constant time delay procedures to teach multiplication facts. *RASE: Remedial and Special Education, 11,* 54–59.

Daly, E. J., III, Lentz, F. E., & Boyer, J. (1996). The instructional hierarchy: A conceptual model for understanding the components of reading interventions. *School Psychology Quarterly, 11,* 369–386.

Daly, E. J., III, Martens, B. K., Kilmer, A., & Massie, D. R. (1996). The effects of instructional match and content overlap on generalized reading performance. *Journal of Applied Behavior Analysis, 29,* 507–518.

Daly, E. J., III, Witt, J. C., Martens, B. K., & Dool, E. J. (1997). A model for conducting functional analysis of academic performance problems. *School Psychology Review, 26,* 554–574.

Davis, R. W., & Hajicek, J. O. (1985). Effects of self-instructional training and strategy training on a mathematics task with severely behaviorally disordered students. *Behavioral Disorders, 10,* 275–282.

Deno, S. L. (1985). Curriculum-based measurement: The emerging alternative. *Exceptional Children, 52,* 219–232.

Dufrene, B., & Noell, G. H. (1999). [The use of performance feedback to increase the integrity with which students implement a peer tutoring procedure]. Unpublished raw data.

Dunlap, L. K., & Dunlap, G. (1989). A self-monitoring package for teaching subtraction with regrouping to students with learning disabilities. *Journal of Applied Behavior Analysis, 22,* 309–314.

Durost, W. N., Bixler, H. H., Wrightstone, J. W., Prescott, G. A., & Balow, I. (1971). *Metropolitan Achievement Test.* New York: Harcourt, Brace, & Jovanovich.

Englemann, S., & Carnine, D. (1991). *Connecting math concepts.* Chicago: Science Research Associates.

Fantuzzo, J. F., King, J. A., & Heller, L. R. (1992). Effects of reciprocal peer tutoring on mathematics and school adjustment: A component analysis. *Journal of Educational Psychology, 84,* 331–339.

Flanagan, D. P., McGrew, K. S., Abramowitz, E., Lehner, L., Untiedt, S., Berger, D., & Armstrong, H. (1997). Improvement in academic screening instruments? A concurrent validity investigation of the K-FAST, MBA, and WRAT-3. *Journal of Psychoeducational Assessment, 15,* 99–112.

Fuchs, L. S., & Fuchs, D. (1986). Curriculum-based assessment of progress toward long- and short-term goals. *Journal of Special Education, 20,* 69–82.

Gresham, F. M. (1981). Assessment of children's social skills. *Journal of School Psychology, 19,* 120–133.

Handen, B. L., & Zane, T. (1987). Delayed prompting: A review of procedural variations and results. *Research in Developmental Disabilities, 8,* 307–330.

Happe, D. (1982). Behavioral intervention: It doesn't do any good in your briefcase. In J. Grimes, (Ed.), *Psychological approaches to problems of children and adolescents* (pp. 15–41). Des Moines: Iowa Department of Public Instruction.

Haring, N. G., Lovitt, T. C., Eaton, M. D., & Hansen, C. L. (1978). *The fourth R: Research in the classroom.* Columbus, OH: Merrill.

Heward, W. L., Courson, F. H., & Narayan, J. S. (1989). Using choral responding to increase active student response during group instruction. *Teaching Exceptional Children, 21,* 72–75.

Holt, J. A. (1995). Efficiency of screening procedures for assigning levels of the Stanford Achievement Test (eighth edition) to students who are deaf or hard of hearing. *American Annals of the Deaf, 140,* 23–27.

Howell, K. W., Fox, S. L., & Morehead, M. K. (1993). *Curriculum-based evaluation: Teaching and decision making.* Pacific Grove, CA: Brooks/Cole.

Ikeda, M. J., Tilly, W. D., Stumme, J., Volmer, L., & Allison, R. (1996). Agency-wide implementation of problem solving consultation: Foundations, current implementation, and future directions. *School Psychology Quarterly, 11,* 228–243.

Kaufman, A. S., & Kaufman, N. L. (1994). *Kaufman Functional Academic Skills Test.* Circle Pines, MN: American Guidance Service.

Marston, D. B. (1989). A curriculum-based measurement approach to assessing academic performance: What it is and why do it. In M. R. Shinn (Ed.), *Curriculum-based measurement: Assessing special children* (pp. 18–78). New York: Guilford.

McBride, J. R. (1989, November). *A computerized adaptive mathematics screening test: A pilot study.* Paper presented at the Annual Meeting of the California Educational Research Association, Burlingame, CA.

Mortenson, B. P., & Witt, J. C. (1998). The use of weekly performance feedback to increase teacher implementation of a prereferral academic intervention. *School Psychology Review, 27,* 613–627.

National Assessment of Educational Progress. (1997). *Digest of educational statistics: International comparison of education* (Publication No. 98–105). Washington, DC: Bureau of Labor Statistics.

National Council of Teachers of Mathematics. (1989). *Curriculum and evaluation standards for school mathematics.* Reston, VA: Author.

National Council of Teachers of Mathematics. (1998). *Principles and standards for school mathematics: Discussion draft.* Reston, VA: Author.

Noell, G. H., Gansle, K. A., Witt, J. C., Whitmarsh, E. L., Freeland, J. T., LaFleur, L. H., Gilbertson, D. A., & Northup, J. (1998). Effects of contingent reward and instruction on oral reading performance at differing levels of passage difficulty. *Journal of Applied Behavior Analysis, 31,* 659–664.

Noell, G. H., & Witt, J. C. (1999). When does consultation lead to intervention implementation? Critical issues for research and practice. *Journal of Special Education, 33,* 29–35.

Noell, G. H., Witt, J. C., Gilbertson, D. N., Ranier, D. D., & Freeland, J. T. (1997). Increasing teacher intervention implementation in general education settings through consultation and performance feedback. *School Psychology Quarterly, 12,* 77–88.

Osipow, S. H., & Scheid, A. B. (1971). The effect of manipulated success ratios on task preference. *Journal of Vocational Behavior, 1,* 93–98.

Pereira, J. A., & Winton, A. S. W. (1991). Teaching and remediation of mathematics: A review of behavioral research. *Journal of Behavioral Education, 1,* 5–36.

Psychological Corporation. (1989). *Stanford Achievement Test.* San Antonio, TX: Author.

Riverside Publishing. (1996). *Iowa Tests of Basic Skills.* Itasca, IL: Author.

Shapiro, E. S. (1989). *Academic skills problems: Direct assessment and intervention.* New York: Guilford.

Shapiro, E. S. (1990). An integrated model for curriculum-based assessment. *School Psychology Review, 19,* 331–349.

Shapiro, E. S. (1996). *Academic skills problems: Direct assessment and intervention* (2nd ed.). New York: Guilford.

Shinn, M. R. (Ed.). (1989). *Curriculum-based measurement: Assessing special children.* New York: Guilford.

Shinn, M. R., Collins, V. L., & Gallagher, S. (1998). Curriculum-based measurement and its use in a problem-solving model with students from minority backgrounds. In M. R. Shinn (Ed.), *Advanced applications of curriculum-based measurement* (pp. 143–174). New York: Guilford.

Skinner, C. H. (1998). Preventing academic skill deficits. In T. S. Watson & F. M. Gresham (Eds.), *Handbook of child behavior therapy* (pp. 61–82). New York: Plenum.

Skinner, C. H., Bamberg, J. W., Smith, E. S., & Powell, S. S. (1993). Cognitive cover, copy, and compare: Subvocal responding to increase rates of accurate division responding. *RASE: Remedial and Special Education, 14,* 49–56.

Stoner, G., Shinn, M. R., & Walker, H. M. (Eds.). (1991). *Interventions for achievement and behavior problems.* Silver Spring, MD: National Association of School Psychologists.

White, O. R., & Harring, N. G. (1982). *Exceptional teaching* (2nd ed.). Columbus, OH: Merrill.

Wilkinson, G. S. (1993). *Wide Range Achievement Test— 3.* Austin, TX: Pro-Ed.

Witt, J. C., Daly, E. J., III, & Noell, G. H. (2000). *Functional assessment: A step-by-step guide to solving academic and behavior problems.* Longmont, CO: Sopris West.

Witt, J. C., Elliott, S. N., Daly, E. J., III, Gresham, F. M., & Kramer, J. J. (1998). *Assessment of at-risk and special needs children* (2nd ed.). New York: McGraw-Hill.

Wolery, M., Bailey, D. B., & Sugai, G. M. (1988). *Principles and procedures of applied behavior analysis with exceptional children.* Boston: Allyn & Bacon.

Wolery, M., Holcombe, A., Cybriwsky, C., Doyle, P. M., Schuster, J. W., Ault, M. J., & Gast, D. L. (1992). Constant time delay with discrete responses: A review of effectiveness and demographic, procedural, and methodological parameters. *Research in Developmental Disabilities, 13,* 239–266.

Woodcock, R. W., McGrew, K. S., & Werder, J. K. (1994). *Woodcock-McGrew-Werder Mini-Battery of Achievement.* Itasca, IL: Riverside.

9 Homework and Students with Emotional and Behavioral Disorders

EDWARD J. SABORNIE

North Carolina State University

Introduction

It should not be surprising to practitioners that scant, if any, attention is directed to homework in the special and regular education teacher preparation programs across the United States (Epstein, Polloway, Foley, & Patton, 1993; Heller, Spooner, Anderson, & Mims, 1988; Patton, 1994). Despite this lack of attention, homework is a common practice in educational environments serving all age levels of students with and without disabilities. Homework comprises up to 20% of the time students spend on school-related academic tasks (Cooper & Nye, 1994). Completing academic tasks such as homework assists students in taking responsibility and in personally managing their school-related activities (Bryan & Sullivan-Burstein, 1997). Homework completion and increased academic achievement are correlated in a positive direction, and having parents involved with homework assists in students' attitude toward school (Cooper, 1989; Epstein, 1985, 1987). Moreover, with ever-increasing numbers of students with emotional and behavioral disorders (E/BD) spending time in regular education classrooms, the importance of homework and its accurate completion for general education course credit cannot be overemphasized. If educators want students with E/BD to exhibit appropriate self-determination as an independent adult, then completing homework is one way of practicing such behavior while still in school.

Homework functions in many ways. Epstein (1988) provides seven different *purposes* of homework, including (a) *practice*—so skill speed and maintenance are enhanced; (b) *participation*—so that students increase their involvement with assigned tasks; (c) *personal development*—so students can augment their responsibility in academic tasks; (d) *parent–child relations*—to improve communication between parents and students concerning school matters; (e) *policy*—to function under school or district regulations concerning homework; (f) *public relations*—so that schools can inform parents of activities; and (g) *punishment*—to keep students in compliance with school or district academic and behavioral requirements.

While doing homework can be a positive, worthwhile experience for some students (Cooper, 1989), like most other academic tasks in the lives of students with learning and behavior problems, it has created some problems. These problems are not endemic only to students—parents and teachers of all types of students in different educational arrangements have expressed difficulty and confusion related to homework. Elementary-level students with high incidence disabilities (i.e., E/BD, learning disabilities [LD], mild mental disability [MMD]) are more likely *not* to do homework when compared to similar nondisabled peers in general education (Bryan & Nelson, 1994). Students with E/BD and LD experience more problems with homework than do their nondisabled peers (Epstein et al., 1993; Polloway, Epstein, & Foley, 1992). Students with high incidence disabilities (a) need to be reminded about homework completion, (b) often daydream for long periods while doing homework, and (c) frequently procrastinate regarding homework (Epstein et al., 1993).

Jayanthi and colleagues (i.e., Jayanthi, Nelson, Sawyer, Bursuck, & Epstein, 1995; Jayanthi, Sawyer, Nelson, Bursuck, & Epstein, 1995) showed that school-to-home communication problems are rampant in homework assigned to students with high-incidence disabilities by general education teachers. Teachers and parents in the Jayanthi et al. studies reported having limited time and opportunity to communicate concerning homework. Parents appreciate when general education teachers provide a list of the major assignments to be completed for the school year (Epstein, Munk, Bursuck, Polloway, & Jayanthi, 1999).

Lastly, only about one-third of U.S. school districts have written policies regarding homework and, of those districts with policies, about 64% report the possibility of homework modifications for students with disabilities (Roderique, Polloway, Cumblad, Epstein, & Bursuck, 1994). The problems related to homework of students with E/BD therefore, are far-reaching and more than worthy of additional attention.

The intent of this chapter is to review the available research and other literature concerning homework of students with E/BD and to suggest ways to eliminate some of the problems associated with this long-lived educational practice. In reviewing both areas, the reader will be able to understand why these two domains are so important in the effective school treatment of students with E/BD.

Homework Research

The research concerning homework and students with E/BD can be classified into two types: (a) a few studies polling students for their perceptions toward homework and (b) several investigations concerning teachers' and parents' perspectives on the matter. One additional study (Roderique et al., 1994) examined national policies of school districts concerning homework and whether specific modifications with students with disabilities were made.

Research with Students

Bryan and Nelson (1994) examined the homework experiences of elementary and junior high school students in regular education classrooms, resource rooms, and self-contained special education environments. Thirty-six of the 1,527 participants in this study were identified as having E/BD, and 28 additional students were labeled LD/E/BD. Other students with high-incidence disabilities were also included (LD, $n = 158$; MMD, $n = 46$). Students were surveyed concerning (a) how often they received homework, (b) how much time they spent doing homework, (c) types of homework assigned, (d) the conditions under which they completed homework, (e) the amount of assistance provided by family members in completing homework, (f) teacher practices related to homework, and (g) consequences for not completing homework. Results indicated that elementary students with high-incidence disabilities in self-contained classes were assigned less homework than their nondisabled counterparts in regular education and their peers in resource room programs, but middle school students with disabilities in self-contained classes reported receiving *more* homework than comparison participants in both regular education (i.e., nondisabled) and resource rooms. Other important findings pertaining to students with high-incidence disabilities included (a) those in self-contained classes were less likely to receive help from friends than those in regular education or resource rooms, (b) participants in resource rooms were less likely to complete assigned homework than were nondisabled peers in regular education, and (c) students in self-contained classrooms claimed to learn more from homework than those in regular education and resource rooms. The authors concluded that if special educators expect students to complete homework, then such teachers are responsible for ensuring that their students comprehend its rationale and benefits.

Nelson, Epstein, Bursuck, Jayanthi, and Sawyer (1998) asked middle school students for their perceptions concerning various homework adaptations found in general education classrooms. The Student Preferences for Homework Adaptations Questionnaire (SPHAQ) was administered to participants that consisted of 211 students, including 17 students with high-incidence disabilities (i.e., E/BD, $n = 2$; LD, $n = 15$). Sample queries on the SPHAQ include "give assignments that are finished at school," "allow extra credit assignments," "give shorter, more frequent assignments," "allow oral rather than written answers," and "require use of assignment notebook," and students rate each item using a Likert scale ranging from dislike (1) to high preference (4). Results showed that students with high-incidence disabilities rated the homework adaptations found on the SPHAQ lower than any other group except those who were very high achieving (i.e., other groups were low achieving, average achieving, high achieving, or very high achieving). Nelson et al. suggest that teachers listen carefully to students when constructing and allowing for adaptations in homework. Some adaptations, while in the best interest of students, may not be to their liking.

Homework Research with Parents and Teachers

Research Using the Homework Problem Checklist (HPC).   Epstein et al. (1993) administered the HPC (Anesko, Sholock, Ramirez, & Levine, 1987) to teachers and parents of students with E/BD, LD, and those who were nondisabled. A total of 82 dyads of teachers and parent(s) completed the HPC on students with E/BD in grades K through 12. The 20 items on the HPC range from "denies having homework assignment," "procrastinates, puts off homework," "fails to complete homework," to "produces messy or sloppy homework," and respondents rate each item using a Likert scale that ranges from never (0) to very often (3). Results showed that teacher ratings of students with E/BD and LD were significantly higher (i.e., higher score = more relative problems) than those for the nondisabled comparison sample. The ratings offered by teachers and parents did not differ significantly, and the differences between the samples with E/BD and LD also did not differ significantly. The authors suggest that examinations of the role of homework in the school lives of students with E/BD should acquire greater importance because of the recent tendency to place increasing numbers of such students in general education classes in which homework is frequent.

In another study that surveyed the perceptions of teachers and parents of secondary-level students with E/BD and those who were nondisabled, Soderlund, Bursuck, Polloway, and Foley (1995) also used the HPC with participants. Twenty pairs of general and special education teachers participated, as well as equal numbers of parents of students who were E/BD or nondisabled. A parent and a special education teacher completed the HPC for a selected student with E/BD, and regular education teachers and parents of nondisabled students completed the HPC for a matched nondisabled participant. The results showed that the homework difficulties of adolescents with E/BD are far more pervasive than those demonstrated by the nondisabled on *all* items of the HPC. Parents identified procrastination and distractibility as the most problematic homework-related behaviors of those with E/BD, and teachers mentioned analogous problems. Similar to other researchers, Soderlund et al. conclude that adolescents with E/BD need assistance both at home and at school in order to alleviate the plethora of homework problems.

Epstein, Foley, and Polloway (1995) also used scores on the HPC as the dependent measure to examine the homework problems of students with E/BD from the perspective of teachers and parents. Forty-two pairs of students who were nondisabled or were identified as E/BD were matched, and their special and regular education teachers, along with a parent, rated relevant homework problems. Remarkably, students with E/BD were rated—by both teachers and parents—as having three times the number of homework problems as the matched nondisabled students. Epstein et al. note that students with E/BD need specific interventions (e.g., a homework "diary" signed by parents) in order to decrease the number of homework problems evident in their school experiences.

Homework Communication Research. Polloway, Epstein, Bursuck, Jayanthi, and Cumblad (1994) examined the homework practices of a national sample of elementary- and secondary- level teachers serving students with disabilities in general education classrooms. The entire group of teacher respondents ($n = 427$) stated that they had familiarity teaching a wide variety of students with disabilities, but the exact percentage of teachers with experience instructing students with E/BD was not provided. Teachers completed a four-page survey related to homework and its (a) frequency, (b) amount, (c) type, (d) teaching strategies pre- and postcompletion, (e) adaptations, (f) strategies for communicating with families, and (g) professional responsibility for adaptations. Teachers answered the survey queries in Likert-scale fashion. Results showed that homework assigned two to four times per week is the most common occurrence level across grade levels, and assignments that require less than 30 minutes are most widespread. Teachers stated that providing additional assistance and aids such as a peer tutor, checking frequently for student understanding, and allowing for compensatory response patterns among students with disabilities were the most helpful. Moreover, teachers cited that talking to students was most beneficial when homework assignments were incomplete and that publicly posting students names was the least effective way of dealing with homework noncompliance. Approximately 61% of the respondents said that they (regular education teachers) are most responsible for making homework adaptations for pupils with disabilities in general education classrooms. Polloway et al. conclude that homework that is not complex or novel is probably the best type assigned to pupils with disabilities in inclusive environments.

Jayanthi, Nelson, et al. (1995) attempted to identify the types of communication problems that exist between parents and teachers of students with high-incidence disabilities in regular education classes. The researchers formed nine focus groups (three with special education teachers, three with regular education teachers, and three with parents of students with disabilities) to examine the impact that homework had on the various constituents. The exact number of parents of students with E/BD was not provided. The results showed that the major problems involved with home–school homework communication include (a) problems with initiating communication, (b) problems with timeliness of communication, (c) consistency and frequency of communication, (d) lack of follow-through with communication, and (e) clarity and usefulness of communication. The focus groups also identified additional factors that contribute to homework communication problems. These include (a) lack of time and opportunity to communicate; (b) lack of knowledge, understanding, and awareness; (c) attitudes, abilities, and behaviors of students, parents, and teachers; and (d) parent–teacher expectations and perceptions. Homework communication problems also seemed to become progressively worse as students grew older. Jayanthi, Nelson, et al. conclude that teacher ambivalence toward taking responsibility for homework communication with parents needs great attention.

Jayanthi, Sawyer, et al. (1995) attempted to find solutions to the communication problems shown by educators and parents of students with E/BD. Participants included 8 parents of students high incidence disability, 13 special education teachers of students with E/BD, LD and other disabilities, and 11 regular educators who served students with disabilities in general education. Focus groups were used again to elicit recommendations from the stakeholders concerning how to eliminate homework communication problems across teachers and parents. Numerous recommendations were generated from the focus groups, including (a) use technology (e.g., computer networks) to improve communication between parents and teachers; (b) change teacher schedules or providing release time for teachers to communicate with each other and parents; (c) teachers should "mentor" good communication skill for students to model; (d) teachers should provide written communication to parents concerning homework; and (e) provide a list of teachers to parents with how and when to contact them regarding homework issues. The authors conclude that while some of the recommendations lacked feasibility and validity (e.g., providing additional pay to teachers to communicate with each other and with parents), more user-friendly ways must be found to improve homework-related communication between teachers and parents.

Buck, Bursuck, Polloway, Nelson, Jayanthi, and Whitehouse (1996) examined a national sample of special education teachers to obtain their perspectives on homework communication problems. A total of 576 teachers were participants; all grade levels and teachers with numerous types of licensure in special education were represented. Similar to the findings shown in Jayanthi, Nelson, et al. (1995), special education teachers cited numerous communication problems associated with homework, including (a) poor communication between special and regular education teachers, (b) a lack of time spent communicating with parents on homework matters, (c) a less than desirable attitude of parents toward homework, and (d) a lack of accountability across regular and special educators regarding ownership of homework communication. It is clear that communication across individuals involved in homework assignment and completion for students with disabilities is in great need of repair.

Epstein et al. (1999), in a national survey, attempted to determine the effectiveness of strategies to improve homework communication that were uncovered in Jayanthi, Sawyer, et al. (1995). The participants were 639 general education teachers, and 84% of these educators had experience teaching students with E/BD. Respondents were instructed to rank recommendations on improving homework communication from most to least effective in seven separate areas. A few of the highest-ranked recommendations in terms of effectiveness were (a) teachers should provide parents with a list of major homework assignments at the beginning of the school year; (b) parents should call teachers early in the day so that teachers can return calls before the end of the school day; (c) schools should provide parents with teachers' home and work telephone numbers, as well as when parents are to call teachers; (d) students should keep daily homework assignment books; (e) assignments should be put on audiotape, available via phone, so that parents can call to check on homework, and (f) general and special education teachers should have their classrooms in close proximity so that brief meetings and communication can occur. The authors stated that the highest-ranked recommendations reflect the sentiment that most students with disabilities can complete homework assignments.

Other Research. In a qualitative study, Baumgartner, Bryan, Donahue, and Nelson (1993) examined parents' unstructured ideas and comments regarding homework, tests, and grades. Some of the respondents had children served in special education resource rooms ($n = 45$), and others had offspring in self-contained classrooms ($n = 13$). Parents were not asked to provide information on what type of disability was true for their son or daughter while in school. It is not possible, therefore, to determine how exact the results of this study are for parents and students with E/BD. Nevertheless, the findings indicated that complaints about homework, teachers, school, curricula, and parent–teacher communication were abundant, and parent compliments about homework, teachers, school, curricula, and parent–teacher communication were fewest. Baumgartner et al. conclude that parents wanted homework to be more consistent (e.g., some teachers give plenty; others, very little) and that parents are undecided about the overall amount of homework given to their offspring in special education.

Roderique et al. (1994) examined policies of school districts toward homework and modifications made in homework procedures for students with disabilities. A national sample of 267 districts was surveyed. Modifications necessary for success of students with disabilities ranged from (a) specific homework strategies noted on a student's IEP to (b) any that a teacher deemed necessary for completion and accuracy of responses. Even though Roderique et al. reported that only a small minority of school districts had formal policies toward homework, the authors were encouraged to find that modifications were available for students with disabilities.

Summary.   While homework for pupils with E/BD may not be "a dirty word" (Check & Ziebell, 1980), it is evident that problems exist in (a) students' ability to complete assignments in a timely manner and their attention to task while completing homework, (b) communication among all parties involved, and (c) teacher responsibility for homework assignment and completion. The next section addresses some suggestions for alleviating homework problems among those with E/BD.

Strategies to Improve Homework Problems

The literature concerning improving homework problems among students with disabilities is not as voluminous as that with the nondisabled. Moreover, the literature that suggests corrections to the homework problems for students with E/BD is not as abundant as the number of studies that uncovered their homework-related problems. Most of the strategies to alleviate homework difficulties originate with directives aimed at no one particular type of disability. Many of the ideas presented here for making homework less problematic, therefore, may need additional adaptations to be totally efficacious for those with E/BD.

Jenson, Sheridan, Olympia, and Andrews (1994) provide a thorough explication of the many ways in which to make homework more meaningful for those with behavior disorders and learning disabilities. These authors consider homework difficulties for students with high-incidence disabilities with variables under teacher, family, and student control. First, under teacher control, they suggest that a comprehensive explanation of the homework assignment should be performed as well as giving students the opportunity to begin the task while still in class. Teachers also need to be aware of the need to grade, edit if necessary, and return assignments to students in a timely fashion. Grading students' homework has been shown to affect student productivity (Walberg, Paschal, & Weinstein, 1985), but valid generalization of this research awaits application to pupils with E/BD. Homework assignments need to reflect the daily instructional goals and objectives, and a direct link between what is covered in class and what is presented in homework must be established. Lastly, consideration must be given to the length of time expected for completion of the homework assignment. Jenson et al. suggest between 10 and 45 minutes is sufficient for homework completion among students in the primary grades, between 45 to 90 minutes per night for students in grades 4 through 6, 1 to 2 hours per night is recommended for seventh through ninth graders, and 1.5 to 2.5 hours of completion time is sufficient for students in grades 10 to 12.

The family variables that interact with homework in Jenson et al.'s (1994) study include socioeconomic status, level of education of primary caregivers, and home conditions. The authors suggest that mandatory times for homework completion must be enforced for students with behavior and learning problems, and such students need to be supervised during this time to ensure attention to task. The mandatory time for homework completion (and television watching or on-line computer time) should be kept consistent, and this is seen as more important than parents checking and signing completed homework.

The most important student variable related to homework, according to Jenson et al. (1994), is time on task—an issue that is particularly relevant to students with E/BD. Without consistent time on task, the benefits of increasing academic achievement through homework provision are lost. With distractibility seemingly ubiquitous among those with externalizing E/BD, Jenson et al. suggest that caregivers provide reinforcement to children and youth for consistently increasing time on task devoted to homework.

A robust contribution to help eliminate homework problems was provided by Olympia and colleagues in three separate curricula: *Study Buddies: A Parent-to-Child Tutoring Program in Reading, Math, and Spelling* (Bowen, Olympia, & Jenson, 1995); *Homework Teams: Homework Management Strategies for the Classroom* (Olympia, Andrews, Valum, & Jenson, 1993); and *Sanity Savers for Parents: Tips for Tackling Homework* (Olympia, Jenson, & Neville, 1995). In *Study Buddies*, parents are trained to become effective tutors of their children in traditional academic subjects. In *Homework Teams*, classroom teachers are taught how to use cooperative learning groups (teams) to facilitate accuracy and completion of homework while students are at school. It should be noted that this is the only curriculum of the three to be field tested with students who were at risk for school failure. *Sanity Savers* attempts to show parents ways in which to improve their child's homework performance in a 5-week program. In week 1, parents assess homework difficulties; week 2 involves communication with the teacher and constructing an effective homework environment; week 3 introduces a reinforcement program to motivate students; during week 4, students are instructed in homework self-management procedures; and week 5 is used for troubleshooting homework problems (e.g., incomplete, messy, or missing homework). All three of the Olympia et al. homework assistance programs are worth consideration, for each one is based on research-validated procedures. Additional research is necessary, however, to determine the efficacy of each program with students identified as E/BD.

Patton (1994) presents practical suggestions for using homework with students with high incidence disabilities that are worthy of consideration by educational practitioners and parents of students with E/BD. These recommendations are divided into four categories: (a) management considerations, (b) assignment considerations, (c) student competencies, and (d) parent involvement issues. Again, some of these recommendations await research validation with students identified as E/BD, but they are worthy of discussion here because such students are still receiving homework assignments, and practitioners and parents need additional information in this matter. Management considerations found in Patton (1994) are presented here; interested readers are encouraged to examine the original source for suggestions related to other issues.

Patton (1994) suggests the following regarding management of homework: (a) assess students' homework skills; (b) involve parents from the very beginning of the school year, and teachers should assign homework from the very beginning; (c) teachers need to establish routines for assigning, collecting, and grading homework (see chapter 10 by Colvin); (d) have consequences if students show noncompliance with homework assignments; (e) attempt to minimize the amount of teacher time homework comprises, and coordinate homework assignments with other teachers; (f) present homework instructions clearly, and verify that students understand; (g) allow students to begin homework in class, and students should use homework folders to organize their efforts; (h) use reinforcement to help students comply with homework directives; (i) have parents sign homework folders; and (j) always grade homework assignments. By using these management recommendations consistently, practitioners will approach homework practices in a systematic way, and students, parents, and teachers should benefit.

In addition to the research already reviewed, Jayanthi and colleagues (Jayanthi, Bursuck, Epstein, & Polloway, 1997) also provide a wide range of homework strategies for teachers, administrators, parents, and students with high-incidence disabilities. Much of what Jayanthi et al. (1997) suggest is a result of the focus group research that found many procedures that can help the people involved with homework of students with disabilities (see Jayanthi, Nelson, et al. 1995; Jayanthi, Sawyer, et al., 1995). All teachers serving a student with a high-incidence disability, for example, should communicate regularly so that such pupils are not excessively burdened with too much homework on a given night. Additional suggestions for parents that originated with the Jayanthi et al. focus group research includes checking with their children every night to assure that the homework assigned receives attention. The entire list of suggestions to correct homework difficulties presented in Jayanthi et al. (1997) is provided in Box 9.1.

Jayanthi, Nelson, et al. (1995) also provide data on what homework adaptations were most and least preferred by actual seventh- and eighth-grade students with E/BD and LD. Student preferences in this study are worthy of inspection simply because if teachers assign homework with a few student-preferred adaptations included, then chances are the assignment will be completed as requested. The most preferred homework adaptations mentioned by the students were (a) give assignments that are finished in school; (b) allow extra-credit assignments; (c) begin homework assignments in class, and check for understanding; and (d) give more reminders about completion dates. The four least preferred homework adaptations, from the perspective of actual students, were (a) give fewer assignments than are given to other students, (b) give shorter assignments than are given other students,

BOX **9.1**
Jayanthi, Bursuck, Epstein, and Polloway (1997) Recommendations for Successful Homework Experiences of Students with High Incidence Disabilities

Group	Strategy
Teachers	Provide progress reports to parents about their child's homework performance.
	Communicate with parents using written forms of communication.
	At the beginning of a school session, give parents information on the assignments for the semester, adaptations available for completion, and policies regarding missed assignments and extra credit.
	Attempt to have frequent face-to-face communications with parents and other teachers concerning homework.
	Understand that homework may not be a high priority for some families compared with other matters at home.
	Remind and help students in completing homework on time.
Administrators	Use homework hot lines or answering machines so that students and parents can access assignments at home.
	Change teachers' schedules to facilitate communication across teachers serving the same student(s).
	Provide release time for teachers to communicate with each other and with students and parents.
	Develop school- or districtwide policies on homework and home–school communication.
	Encourage students to use assignment notebooks for recording of homework assignments.
	Provide communication opportunities by holding evening conferences for working parents.
	Hold workshops, conferences, and support group meetings to increase the knowledge of teachers and parents concerning homework.
	Provide parents with a list of teachers, and indicate how and when they can be contacted.
	Have family nights to promote communication between teachers and parents.
	Provide a telephone in every classroom to facilitate communication among homework stakeholders.
	Have teachers who are skilled communicators mentor other teachers and new educators with limited skills in communication.
	Make assignments available in public libraries.
	Allow students the opportunity to complete homework in school.
	Do not give homework to students whose family situation will hinder homework completion.
	Provide release time for teachers to communicate with other teachers and with students and parents.

(continued)

BOX **9.1**   Continued

Parents	Call teachers early in the morning so that they can return the call later in the day.
	Communicate expectations regarding homework with teachers and students.
	Make every attempt to attend face-to-face meetings.
	Check with children about homework every night.
	Establish consequences when children do not complete homework, and follow through with consequences.
	Provide teachers with phone numbers and times when they can be reached.
Students	Take responsibility for completing and submitting homework on time.
	Act as a contact between home and school.
	Maintain an assignment book, and have the book available during and after school.

Source: Jayanthi, M., Bursuck, W., Epstein, M. H., & Polloway, E. A. (1997). Strategies for successful homework. *Teaching Exceptional Children, 30*(1), 4–5. Copyright © 1997 by The Council for Exceptional Children. Reprinted with permission.

(c) arrange for another student to help with assignments, and (d) grade assignments more easily than for other students. It is clear from the list of least preferred homework adaptations that middle school students with E/BD and LD would like to be treated just like any other student when homework is assigned. Moreover, students also cited fairness as an issue in whether an adaptation was preferred.

Bryan and Sullivan-Burstein (1997), as part of a 2-year funded project sponsored by the U.S. Department of Education, attempted to solve the homework problems of students with high-incidence disabilities. Another goal of their project was to assist students with disabilities in connecting what occurs in school with what students do in their lives outside school, with homework being just one student activity that takes place beyond school walls. The project also worked with elementary school teachers in regular and special education to design ways in which teachers can facilitate completion of homework and use of study skills. Among the suggestions that Bryan and Sullivan-Burstein found are (a) parents should provide a special time and place, with the necessary supplies, for homework activities; (b) parents need to monitor students' television watching so that it does not interfere with homework completion; and (c) teachers need to instruct students in study skills so that homework has a greater probability of accurate completion. Other suggestions concerning homework were organized under developing innovative assignments, using a homework planner, teaching study skills, and working with parents; the complete list of homework-related suggestions found in Bryan and Sullivan-Burstein is presented in Box 9.2.

BOX 9.2
Strategies to Improve Homework for Students with Disabilities

Topic	Recommendation
Develop innovative homework assignments	1. Teachers should work together to develop similar homework practices. 2. Use games and fun activities as homework activities. 3. Remember that effective homework assignments are relevant to the child's life outside the classroom, and help make the connection between what is learned in school and what is reality in the students' lives outside school. 4. Give students rewards for homework completion.
Use a homework planner	1. Use the planner to help improve students' organizational skills. 2. Use the planner to communicate with parents. 3. Show students how to graph their homework achievement progress in the planner.
Teach study skills	1. Help students to (a) identify a time and place for doing homework, (b) have the necessary materials, (c) place completed work in a safe place, (d) remember to bring homework to school, and (e) recognize and eliminate distractions by other family members, pets, television, and so forth. 2. Teach students to recognize when they are fatigued and lacking appropriate attention and ways in which to deal with such matters. 3. Teach students how to take notes and use mnemonic devices to increase memory skills.
Working with parents	1. Communicate with parents regarding how much homework is assigned. 2. Help parents learn how to see discrepancies between the teacher's expectations on the homework task and the actual achievement shown by the child. 3. Suggest activities that parents can do with their children that are related to the homework. 4. Determine whether parents are comfortable in working with their child on homework. 5. Ask the parent to play the role of the student, with the child playing the role of the teacher. 6. Ask the parent to sign the completed homework. 7. Encourage parents to speak with their child regarding what happened during the school day. 8. Encourage parents to reinforce their child for accurate homework completion. 9. If problems persist, ask the parent to keep a log of what occurred around homework time.

Source: Bryan, T., & Sullivan-Burstein, K. (1997). Homework how-to's. *Teaching Exceptional Children,* 29(6), 32–37. Copyright © 1997 by The Council for Exceptional Children. Reprinted with permission.

Homework and Technology

A multitude of Web sites are devoted to homework with assistance not only for students but also for teachers and parents (e.g., school.discovery.com/students/homeworkhelp/bjpinchbeck/). Most of these sites, unfortunately, do not address research-proven strategies for students with E/BD. New technology does exist, however, that will be of great assistance to students, parents, and teachers involved with homework.

Homework posting systems provide a central location where homework information is found, and students and parents phone or log in to the control center to retrieve assignments. The homework posting systems available at present are meant to prevent some of the communication problems that exist across teachers, students, and parents. A posting system developed by Telad Enterprises (1999) includes access by phone, and teachers simply record their homework assignments daily or weekly. Students and parents call a toll-free number, 24 hours a day, to access assignments. Parents never have to be worried that their child missed an assignment, for the homework information is always available.

Another homework posting program that is becoming popular—for many reasons—is Homework Hero (no date). This type of program is the fastest-growing Internet-based homework service, and many school districts are now using it with ease and success. With Homework Hero (and similar services), teachers post homework assignments on a password-protected Web site, and students and parents simply log on to the Internet, enter the site, and see homework assignments. With some homework assignments, students do not have to bring homework from school, for the entire task is posted in worksheet fashion via scanning the text and uploading the document to the Web site. Students then have the choice of either completing the assignment using their computer or printing the document and finishing it in traditional pencil-and-paper manner. Teachers can post homework (and other) grades on-line so that parents are completely informed about their child's performance. Students complete their assignments and then email their finished work back to the teacher, or bring it to school. Homework Hero's basic service is free to schools, but it (and other, similar programs) also offers a fee-based "deluxe plan" that includes more than just the basic homework posting service.

Homework posting programs do involve some extra work for instructors and school administrators. Teachers must be organized and know in advance what homework they want posted, and they also need to know how to upload documents to a server. Administrators must provide enough computers so that many teachers can post homework at the same time, and specialists must be hired for information technology maintenance. One advantage of Internet-based homework posting services is that it is available anywhere a student or a parent can access the Internet. Perhaps if more students with E/BD and their parents had access to home computers and Internet service providers, this approach could relieve many of the home–school communication problems that are evident with homework.

Summary

This chapter reviewed some of the homework literature associated with students having E/BD. While the research concerned with homework and students with E/BD is not as voluminous as the empiricism covering other topics in this text (e.g., social skills [Chapter 15], internalizing behaviors [Chapter 14], etc.), the amount of research is sufficient for a few accurate generalizations. The research reviewed herein indicates that many problems exist surrounding homework and pupils with E/BD. Nonetheless, many strategies are also available to eliminate homework difficulties. Teachers and parents of students with E/BD must not ignore the problems associated with homework, just as they should not eschew the many solutions available for all concerned. With sufficient attention and application of some of the procedures suggested here, homework need not become the disaster that many teachers and parents have called it. Homework can be beneficial to students with E/BD in advancing their academic achievement—a worthy goal of any special or general educator.

REFERENCES

Anesko, K. M., Sholock, G., Ramirez, R., & Levine, F. M. (1987). The homework problem checklist: Assessing children's homework difficulties. *Behavioral Assessment, 9,* 179–185.

Baumgartner, D., Bryan, T., Donahue, M., & Nelson, C. (1993). Thanks for asking: Parent comments about homework, tests, and grades. *Exceptionality, 4,* 177–185.

Bowen, J., Olympia, D., & Jenson, W. R. (1995). *Study buddies: A parent-to-child tutoring program in reading, math, and spelling.* Longmont, CO: Sopris West.

Bryan, T., & Nelson, C. (1994). Doing homework: Perspectives of elementary and junior high school students. *Journal of Learning Disabilities, 27,* 488–499.

Bryan, T., & Sullivan-Burstein, K. (1997). Homework how-to's. *Teaching Exceptional Children, 29*(6), 32–37.

Buck, G. H., Bursuck, W. D., Polloway, E. A., Nelson, J., Jayanthi, M., & Whitehouse, F. A. (1996). Homework-related communication problems: Perspectives of special educators. *Journal of Emotional and Behavioral Disorders, 4,* 105–113.

Check, J. F., & Ziebell, D. G. (1980). Homework: A dirty word. *The Clearing House, 54,* 439–441.

Cooper, H. M. (1989). *Homework.* White Plains, NY: Longman.

Cooper, H., & Nye, B. (1994). Homework for students with learning disabilities: The implications of research for policy and practice. *Journal of Learning Disabilities, 27,* 470–480.

Epstein, J. L. (1985). Home and school connections in schools of the future: Implications of research on parent involvement. *Peabody Journal of Education, 62,* 18–41.

Epstein, J. L. (1987). Parent involvement: What research says to administrators. *Education and Urban Society, 19,* 119–136.

Epstein, J. L. (1988). *Homework practices, achievements and behaviors of elementary school students* (Report No. 27). Baltimore, MD: Johns Hopkins University, Center for Research on Elementary and Middle Schools.

Epstein, M. H., Foley, R. M., & Polloway, E. A. (1995). Homework problems: A comparison of students identified as behaviorally disordered with nonhandicapped students. *Preventing School Failure, 40*(1), 14–18.

Epstein, M. H., Munk, D. D., Bursuck, W. D., Polloway, E. A., & Jayanthi, M. (1999). Strategies for improving home–school communication about homework for students with disabilities. *Journal of Special Education, 33,* 166–176.

Epstein, M. H., Polloway, E. A., Foley, R. M., & Patton, J. R. (1993). Homework: A comparison of teachers' and parents' perceptions of the problems experienced by students identified as having behavioral disorders, learning disabilities, or no disabilities. *Remedial and Special Education, 14*(5), 40–50.

Heller, H. W., Spooner, F., Anderson, D., & Mims, A. (1988). Homework: A review of special education practices in the Southwest. *Teacher Education and Special Education, 11*(2), 43–51.

Homework Hero. (no date). *Homework Hero* [Online]. Available: http://www.homeworkhero.com/ [2000, June 1].

Jayanthi, M., Bursuck, W., Epstein, M. H., & Polloway, E. A. (1997). Strategies for successful homework. *Teaching Exceptional Children, 30*(1), 4–7.

Jayanthi, M., Nelson, J. S., Sawyer, V., Bursuck, W. D., & Epstein, M. H. (1995). Homework-communication problems among parents, classroom teachers, and special education teachers. *Remedial and Special Education, 16,* 102–116.

Jayanthi, M., Sawyer, V., Nelson, J. S., Bursuck, W. D., & Epstein, M. H. (1995). Recommendations for homework-communication problems from parents, classroom teachers, and special education teachers. *Remedial and Special Education, 16,* 212–225.

Jenson, W. J., Sheridan, S. M., Olympia, D., & Andrews, D. (1994). Homework and students with learning disabilities and behavior disorders: A practical, parent-based approach. *Journal of Learning Disabilities, 27,* 538–548.

Nelson, J. S., Epstein, M. H., Bursuck, W. D., Jayanthi, M., & Sawyer, V. (1998). The preferences of middle school students for homework adaptations made by general education teachers. *Learning Disabilities Research & Practice, 13,* 109–117.

Olympia, D., Andrews, D., Valum, J. L., & Jenson, W. R. (1993). *Team homework: Cooperative student management of daily homework.* Longmont, CO: Sopris West.

Olympia, D., Jenson, W. R., & Neville, M. (1995). *Do it yourself homework manual: A sanity saver for parents.* Longmont, CO: Sopris West.

Patton, J. R. (1994). Practical recommendations for using homework with students with learning disabilities. *Journal of Learning Disabilities, 27,* 570–578.

Polloway, E. A., Epstein, M. H., Bursuck, W. D., Jayanthi, M., & Cumblad, C. (1994). Homework practices of general education teachers. *Journal of Learning Disabilities, 27,* 500–509.

Polloway, E. A., Epstein, M. H., & Foley, R. (1992). A comparison of the homework problems of students with learning disabilities and nonhandicapped students. *Learning Disabilities Research and Practice, 7,* 203–209.

Roderique, T. W., Polloway, E. A., Cumblad, C., Epstein, M. H., & Bursuck, W. D. (1994). Homework: A survey of policies in the United States. *Journal of Learning Disabilities, 27,* 481–487.

Soderlund, J., Bursuck, B., Polloway, E. A., & Foley, R. A. (1995). A comparison of the homework problems of secondary school students with behavior disorders and nondisabled peers. *Journal of Emotional and Behavioral Disorders, 3*(3), 150–155.

Telad Enterprises. (1999). *The Telad Homework Advisor* [Online]. Available: http://www.teladenterprises.com/index.htm [2000, January 17].

Walberg, H. J., Paschal, R. A., & Weinstein, T. (1985). Homework's powerful effects on learning. *Educational Leadership, 42,* 76–79.

10 Designing Classroom Organization and Structure

GEOFF COLVIN

University of Oregon
Behavior Associates, Eugene

Introduction

Mary-Ellen was one of the most promising students in the teachers' certification program at Menghis Hall University. Her grades were close to a 4.0, she received excellent reports for her practice teaching assignments, and she was very inspired by the opportunity of playing a significant role in the lives of many students. However, when she obtained her first teaching position at O'Malley Middle School, her dreams slowly evaporated. Instead of actively engaging her students in her subject specialty of math, she spent most of her time trying to secure the students' attention, get them seated, and start their work; instead of establishing a positive, productive relationship with her students, she felt more like a police officer trying to establish order, separating noisy students, dealing with students coming in late, and addressing student profanities and other forms of misbehavior. The most discouraging aspect of her first-year teaching was that she felt that the students did not respect her. Yet, she made every effort to make classes meaningful and tried to relate to them in positive ways.

Unfortunately, Mary-Ellen's experience in her first year of teaching is relatively common. The solution, however, is far from simple. Many factors could be contributing to these problems over which Mary-Ellen has very little control, such as the inadequacy of a schoolwide behavior management system in which serious discipline problems occur in most of the school settings; the location of the school in a neighborhood that has a very high crime rate, and the school experiences spillover effects, which can be very disruptive; or totally insufficient special education services and other support systems. Clearly, these system variables need to be addressed in order for classroom teachers to maintain a satisfactory level of instruction and management.

However, in addition to system factors that may need to be addressed, teachers can control directly a number of classroom variables to ensure that effective instruction takes place in their classrooms. These factors include appropriate student assessment and placement, curriculum choices and implementation, research-based classroom and individual management techniques, instructional methodologies, and classroom structure (Emmer, Evertson, Clements, & Worsham, 1994; Evertson, Emmer, Clements, & Worsham, 1994; Hofmeister & Lubke, 1990; Wong & Wong, 1991).

The purpose of this chapter is to describe a well-documented proactive strategy for preventing problem behavior and for setting the stage for quality instruction that teachers can directly control and implement and that is *classroom organization* (Colvin & Lazar, 1997; Colvin & Sugai, 1988; Paine, Radicchi, Rosellini, Deutchman, & Darch, 1983; Sprick, Garrison & Howard, 1998; Walker, Colvin & Ramsey, 1995). The simple assumption is that if the classroom is reasonably well organized, students are more likely to behave more appropriately and to engage in instruction more readily. Namely, classroom organization helps ensure that activities in the classroom are stable and predictable for students, helping them understand how the classroom operates. For example, when we walk into a restaurant, several features indicate that this restaurant is ready to serve people in a pleasant, inviting, and well-designed layout. The atmosphere sets the occasion for the diners to have a relaxing and tasteful meal. Similarly, in the classroom, the level of organization and planning sets the stage for learning and acceptable behavior to occur. Conversely, poorly designed classroom organization increases the likelihood for chaos and disruption and less opportunity for learning.

The specific topics of classroom organization that will be described are (a) designing the classroom space, (b) setting a practical schedule, (c) establishing classroom expectations, and (d) determining classroom procedures. Checklists are included for each topic.

Designing Classroom Space

Many functions take place in today's classrooms. Some activities occur on a regular basis, while others occur infrequently. The success or failure of these activities in achieving their intended goals will, by and large, depend on the way in which the classroom is designed (Colvin & Lazar, 1997; Paine et al., 1983; Sprick et al., 1998). Two steps are typically used to organize classroom space (see Box 10.1). First, clearly identify the full range of functions and activities that are likely to occur in the classroom. Second, carefully arrange the room to ensure that each of these functions may be accomplished. Obviously the specific activities for each classroom will vary depending on the age group and the subject matter. The following list of functions with guidelines for classroom design is relatively common to all classrooms.

Independent work requires an area with minimum distractions. It is best to have individual desks or as much space as possible to separate students. Areas for independent work should be in a low-traffic section away from materials and from time-out and free-time activity areas.

BOX **10.1**

Checklist 1: Organization of Classroom Space

Activity	Completion Date	Notes
1. Locate specific classroom areas for:		
a. Independent work	__/__/__	_____
b. Group work	__/__/__	_____
c. Free choice activity	__/__/__	_____
d. Time out	__/__/__	_____
e. Material's storage	__/__/__	_____
f. Notice board	__/__/__	_____
g. Quiet area	__/__/__	_____
h. Other	__/__/__	_____
2. Draw up seating plans:		
a. Rows	__/__/__	
b. Clusters	__/__/__	
c. Semicircular	__/__/__	
d. Combinations	__/__/__	
e. Other	__/__/__	
3. Identify other classroom design tasks:	__/__/__	
_____		
_____		
_____		
_____		

Group work areas should ensure that students are able to attend easily to the teacher and each other. A semicircle or row configuration of desks can facilitate group-oriented instruction.

If some students are engaged in group work and others are in different activities, such as working independently, the group instruction should always be conducted in front of the class so the teacher can readily supervise the entire classroom. The teacher should take care to keep his or voice moderately low during group instruction to prevent students not in the group from being unnecessarily distracted.

Choice activities are sometimes for students who finish their work early or as a reward for special achievement. Restrict this activity to a quiet location behind the instructional areas. Specific rules of behavior governing the use of these activities should be in effect.

A *time-out or penalty area* is used in the classroom for a student whose behavior is unacceptable. This area could consist of a desk in the corner of the room, a small table facing the back of the room, or a desk at the side of the classroom. This consequence also serves as a signal to all students that the behavior is not acceptable in the classroom. Select an area that isolates the student from the other students to limit their interactions. If more than one student is isolated at one time, they need to be separated.

Storage materials and supplies are located in low-traffic areas to avoid distraction and allow easy access. Ensure that materials are neatly arranged and that they do not obstruct supervision or the students' view.

The *teacher's desk* is placed out of the path and flow of instruction. It should be located in an area that will safeguard personal property and confidential material.

The *notice board* should be highly visible in the room in a high-traffic area but so that it does not divert student attention during instruction. Divide the notice board into sections for specific communication, such as news, special projects, and rules.

Supervision is maximized by arranging the room so that *all* students are in sight. Be careful of high objects, such as bookshelves, that may obstruct supervision.

Quiet time area is used, by some teachers, to provide students an opportunity to calm down when they experience stress or become agitated. This area needs to be as isolated as possible to prevent interactions with other students and staff.

The *seating arrangement* can vary considerably. The key is flexibility. Use the following guidelines in developing a seating plan (given there is sufficient space):

1. Ensure all students can easily see presentations during whole-group instruction.
2. Minimize distractions.
3. Use clusters for small-group instruction.
4. Change the seating chart on a periodic basis so that students are placed next to different students.
5. Involve the students in the seating plans as appropriate. It's better for the teacher to assign seating at the beginning of the school year and involve student participation at a later date.
6. Vary the seating arrangement on a periodic basis (rows, semicircular arrangements, and clusters). Three common examples of classroom arrangements are
   a. whole-class instruction,
   b. small-group activities, and
   c. small-group instruction combined with independent work.

Summary

Classroom instruction and discipline are considerably enhanced when a teacher pays careful attention to the multiple elements involved in the physical arrangement of the classroom. Teaching is a very complex task, and one way a teacher can minimize this complexity is to plan in advance the design of the classroom. Emmer et al. (1994) have identified five summary keys for making decisions in designing the classroom arrangement: (a) Use a room arrangement consistent with your instructional goals and activities, (b) keep high-traffic areas free of congestion, (c) be sure students are easily seen by the teacher, (d) keep frequently used teaching materials and student supplies readily accessible, and (e) be certain students can easily see instructional presentations and displays.

Setting a Practical Schedule

One of the surest strategies for establishing a stable and predictable classroom environment for learning and appropriate behavior is to develop a practical schedule (see Box 10.2). Cotton (1990), in an extensive review of research literature, reports that schedules should be regarded as flexible time management tools that are designed to best serve the educational needs of students. However, developing a schedule is not an easy task since many blocks of time that have to be accommodated, such as lunch time, recess, core subjects, elective subjects, specialist's periods, team teaching periods, and district events. The classroom teacher needs to allow priority time at the start of the school year before the students return to develop a well-organized schedule.

Typically, secondary teachers have little flexibility in developing a schedule in relation to the master schedule as the periods or blocks are determined by the master schedule based on subjects. Given that most secondary schools have adopted

---

BOX 10.2

Checklist 2: Developing a Practical Classroom Schedule

Activity	Completion Date	Notes
1. Identify schoolwide fixed schedules for:		_____
a. Start of school day	__/__/__	_____
b. Morning recess	__/__/__	_____
c. Lunch	__/__/__	_____
d. Afternoon recess	__/__/__	_____
e. End of school day	__/__/__	_____
f. Other	__/__/__	_____
2. Identify specialists' schedule:		_____
a. Music	__/__/__	_____
b. Art	__/__/__	
c. Library	__/__/__	
d. Physical education	__/__/__	
e. Labs	__/__/__	
f. Other	__/__/__	
3. Identify team teaching periods.	__/__/__	
4. Develop a classroom schedule for:		
a. Master schedule	__/__/__	
b. First day	__/__/__	
c. First week	__/__/__	
d. First month	__/__/__	

block scheduling involving 90- to 120-minute periods, teachers need to manage their use of time carefully within these blocks to maximize learning and minimize problem behavior.

Elementary teachers, on the other hand, typically have more opportunity to construct a schedule after the schoolwide activities and specialist teacher periods have been identified. The following suggestions are providing for developing schedules at the elementary and secondary levels.

Developing Schedules at the Elementary Level

The basic approach for constructing the schedule is, first, to identify the fixed *external* periods that need to be accommodated, such as lunch or a specialist's period, and, second, to organize their schedule within the remaining periods of time.

Step 1: Make a list of all the schoolwide events that have fixed schedules, such as the start and end of the school day, pledge and school announcements, recess, lunch, assemblies, and special events (e.g., school assemblies).

Step 2: List the predetermined periods that are allocated to specialist teachers, such as music, art, physical education, library, media room, and computer lab. If specialist teachers are not available for these content areas, schedule these subjects within your own classroom timetable. In addition, the schedule for special education students who receive instruction in the resource room may impact on the classroom schedule.

Step 3: If some subjects are taught on a team teaching basis, plan the schedule with participating teachers. A particular time slot is agreed on, such as the first 45 minutes after recess. This time slot becomes fixed so that the teacher builds the individual classroom schedule around this period.

Step 4: Once the fixed scheduled events have been accommodated, develop an order for subjects and activities that are taught and conducted in the classroom itself. However, pay particular attention to the order of these subjects. For example, the basic skill subjects (reading, writing, math, and spelling) should be scheduled as early as possible in the school day. Students are typically fresher and more cooperative at this time, and these subjects are crucial for the students' success in school. Other activities such as projects, hands-on tasks, and high-interest lessons can be scheduled for the latter part of the day. In general, prioritize the subjects and activities to be conducted in your classroom.

Step 5: Construct a master classroom schedule for the term to include periods for the major content areas within the classroom, schoolwide programs, and specialist subjects. The master schedule will vary from day to day to accommodate specialist subjects, but try to ensure that the schedule is stable on a weekly basis. Schedule basic skill subjects for fixed times each day. Also, use the master schedule as a basis to develop other schedules (first day, first week, and first month).

Schedule for the First Three Days.   Build the specific first-day activities into the master schedule. For example, take part of the reading period to teach the classroom behavioral expectations. Spread the activities for the first day throughout the periods of the master schedule to prevent giving the students an overdose of information.

The primary emphasis for the first day is *orientation.* The main activities center on (a) making the students welcome, (b) teaching the class behavioral expectations, (c) explaining the critical class classroom procedures, (d) providing an overview of the class content and activities, (e) explaining the use of the classroom and the building, (f) motivating the students to have a great year, and (g) testing for team teaching and student grouping where appropriate.

Schedule for the First Week and First Month.   Use the remainder of the first week to continue teaching and practicing classroom procedures, explaining behavioral expectations, and completing testing. At the close of the first week, begin to phase into the master schedule that should be operating for the remainder of the month.

Managing Block Schedules at the Secondary Level

It is not within the scope of this chapter to present an in-depth evaluation of block scheduling or the logistics in developing block schedules. Rather, the assumption is that most secondary schools operate on block schedules; consequently, guidelines are presented here for beginning teachers on how to manage the long block periods effectively and efficiently.

Block scheduling arose as part of the restructuring process undertaken by many school systems in response to the continued problems facing secondary schools, such as low student achievement; curriculum fragmentation; the impersonal nature of large high schools; gaps between skills needed in the workforce; high rates of suspensions, expulsions, and students dropping out of school; and the sustained pressure from teaching and learning in the five to six 50-minute periods a day.

In a seminal work on the subject, Canady and Rettig (1995) define block scheduling as introducing larger blocks of time (more than 60 minutes) to allow flexibility for a diversity of instructional activities. Typically, high schools begin with a master schedule and then make many minor adjustments to accommodate their unique needs.

Perhaps the best strategy for a new teacher to manage a block schedule is to understand the intent and advantages of this relatively recent system for scheduling in most secondary schools. Once these advantages are understood, the teacher can develop specific lesson plans and strategies to maximize student learning (Cawelti, 1994; Irmsher, 1996).

Acknowledging Students Learn at Their Own Rate.   The longer period of time for instruction gives more opportunity for *all* students to learn the targeted skills of the instructional period. This means that the teacher needs to design the lesson with a clear picture of the instructional objectives and develop techniques for assessing student mastery. To this end, move around the classroom, checking student responses and designing tasks, questions, activities, or problems to determine whether the students have learned the targeted skill. Make plans for the students who have learned or completed the work while others are still engaged completing the instructional tasks. Provide more assistance and practice for the students who have not grasped the skill.

Creating Active Learners.   With short periods teachers, felt they were directing most of the instruction while the students were relatively passive. With blocks, however, there is more time to include a full range of instructional activities creating more opportunities for students to be active learners.

Moreover, teachers are able to pay particular attention to frequent transitions and new activities to keep students' attention. Otherwise, they may become bored with the longer periods. Plan for at least three different activities per block. Different activities include group work, individual seatwork, oral or listening activities, video segments, guest speakers, lectures, or student board work. Students with lower abilities might need more activities than classes of students with higher abilities.

Establishing Relationships with the Students.   The longer block periods with changing activities enable teachers to get to know their students in a much more personal manner and to establish a deeper working relationship with them. Also, teachers are able to take steps to learn their students' learning styles and behavioral patterns and adjust instruction accordingly. Typically, students are more responsive and become more motivated learners when they sense that their teacher is in tune with them, cares for them, and takes extra measures to help them learn and be successful.

Catching Up.   One reason that students drop out of school is that they get behind in their work and consequently fall behind in the number of credits needed for graduation. The longer block periods provide students with an opportunity to catch up on missed assignments or obtain assistance to complete assignments. Provide time and a system for students to catch up on their work should they fall behind. Keep tracking records that are readily accessible to identify student progress within the term or semester.

Providing Cooperative Learning Opportunities.   Cooperative learning is an established instructional tool with sound documentation for its effectiveness in elementary classrooms for many years (Johnson, Johnson, & Holubec, 1990; Slavin, 1988). The long periods used in block scheduling enables teachers to utilize cooperative techniques learning.

Essentially cooperative learning is an activity-based instructional strategy whereby students work in small groups. Typically the teacher presents an instructional task with guidelines to the students, and the student groups work together to complete the task and master the objectives. Keep in mind that cooperative learning does not just happen overnight. Unless careful planning and structuring take place, the students may neither cooperate nor learn. To establish successful groups, (a) develop clear procedures for forming the groups; (b) carefully describe the specific activities for the groups to engage in for task completion; (c) clarify objectives and outcomes, especially if a product is required; (d) establish group rules for behavior and teach these rules; and (e) develop times and time lines for activities within the group.

In general, block scheduling has become the norm in most secondary schools. Beginning teachers have the opportunity to utilize a wide range of instructional strategies to provide opportunities to their students for acceleration, remediation, and individualization in a relaxed and student-centered environment (Irmesher, 1996).

In planning for a 60- to 90-minute block period, the teacher needs to develop a schedule within this period. Canady and Rettig (1995) recommend that teachers utilize a variety of specific instructional activities and allocate a set amount of time for each activity.

Summary.   A well-designed schedule is essential for ensuring quality instruction and desirable behavior. While aspects of a schedule are already predetermined, the classroom teacher needs to orchestrate carefully the time slots that are available within the school day. A well-planned schedule serves as a road map for students, providing them with a necessary structure for effective instruction.

Establishing Classroom Expectations

Perhaps one of the most undisputed beliefs regarding teaching and learning is the strong relationship between teacher expectations and student achievement and social behavior (Evertson et al., 1994; Kauffman, Mostert, Trent, & Hallahan, 1998; Sprick et al., 1998; Walker et al., 1995; Wong & Wong, 1991). Simply put, if the teacher expects the students to achieve and behave appropriately, then they will. Conversely, if the teacher expects the students to achieve poorly and behave inappropriately, then they will.

Hofmeister and Lubke (1990) report that the task of setting expectations is relatively easy since the majority of students know the rules in the first place. However, establishing the expectations is a more complex task that requires careful planning, long-term commitment, and systematic implementation. To establish classroom expectations, the following steps are recommended: (a) understand the function of teacher expectations, (b) utilize best-practice procedures for selecting expectations, and (c) systematically teach the expectations (see Box 10.3).

B O X **10.3**

Checklist 3: Establishing Classroom Expectations

Subject	Completion Date	Notes
1. Identify classroom expectations: a. b. c. d. e.		
2. Develop schedule for teaching behavioral expectations: a. First day b. First week c. First month		
3. Develop procedures for teaching behavioral expectations.		
4. Develop procedures for communicating behavioral expectations: a. Classroom display b. Parents c. Other		
5. Other		

Understanding the Function of Teacher Expectations

Teachers must believe that their students can achieve high expectations in both academic skills and social behavior as a function of their instruction. However, an important discrimination needs to be made. There is a significant difference between high standards and high expectations (Kauffman et al., 1998). *Standards* refer to a group response, defining the level of achievement, academically and socially, for the majority of students. *Expectations,* on the other hand, focus on individual progress. In this sense, when a teacher sets high expectations, this means that every student is challenged to achieve academically and socially to his or her greatest potential.

Utilizing Best-Practice Procedures for Selecting Expectations

Classroom expectations are designed to provide students with clear information on the academic and social responses required of them so that instruction and learning take place. A simple relationship is taught: appropriate behavior results in positive consequences, and inappropriate behavior leads to their absence or withdrawal. Some steps can be used to establish this essential relationship:

Explicitly state rules so it is clear to anyone (teacher, student, or observer) when a rule has been kept or broken. For this reason, rules should be precise, practical, and behaviorally expressed.

Select functional rules that focus on student behaviors that facilitate instruction and learning such as coming to class prepared and on time, following teacher directions, participating in class, doing your best work, staying on task, and completing assignments.

Establish the behavioral expectation immediately on the first day of the new school year because any downtime usually makes it more difficult to establish them later.

Rehearse and review the behavioral expectations regularly during the classroom schedule so students are constantly reminded of the rules. In this way, teachers, as well as students, can identify which rules are not working or need further clarification.

Practice frequently broken behavioral expectations by simulating situations and providing practice. Some teachers prefer to involve the students in the development of these expectations, in which case the teacher should have an outline of expectations and some clarification of what he or she expects.

Utilize positive practices to reinforce students who demonstrate expected behavior.

Involve the students in the process as appropriate. Some teachers prefer to involve the students in the development of rules and classroom expectations to obtain more commitment. In such cases, teachers should have an outline of the expectations and procedures in mind for clarifying them.

Individualize expectations as appropriate. In some cases the classroom expectations may be too high for some students and too low for others. Most teachers have two sets of expectations, (a) a general set of rules or expectations that are required of all students and (b) a classroom understanding that in special cases exceptions will be made. Students can be taught to understand that they are not all the same and that they have different needs at different times. It is on these occasions that the teacher makes a specific accommodation with the student(s) as needed.

Schedule for teaching classroom behavioral expectations. List and schedule the behavioral expectations to be taught the first day of school and the first week. Be sure to schedule review sessions throughout the first month of school.

Systematically Teaching the Expectations

Cotton (1990), in her research on effective discipline practices, concludes that behavioral expectations need to be directly taught. "Children below fourth grade require a great deal of instruction and practice in classroom rules and procedures. . . . [E]ffective management, especially in the early grades, is more . . . instructional than a disciplinary enterprise" (p. 8).

Similarly, she reports that older students need reminders and supervision. "With older students, researchers have noted that the best results are obtained through vigilantly reminding students about the rules and procedures of the classroom and monitoring their compliance with them" (p. 8). Colvin, Kame'enui, and Sugai (1993) found that when staff provided systematic feedback to their students in addition to reminders and supervision, behavior improved significantly.

Effective strategies for establishing behavioral expectations and for managing problem behavior emphasize directly teaching social behaviors (Colvin & Sugai, 1988; Cummings, 1983; Evertson et al., 1994; Kame'enui & Darch, 1994; Sprick, 1985). As an example, an instructional plan for use by elementary teachers will be described next, followed by a description of adaptations for use by secondary teachers.

An Instructional Plan for Teaching Classroom Expectations for Elementary Teachers

Use five steps to teach classroom expectations: (a) explain, (b) specify student behaviors, (c) practice, (d) monitor, and (e) review (Colvin & Lazar, 1997).

Step 1: Explain.   Provide adequate reasons and purposes for the particular classroom procedure. Make provisions for discussion to clarify the need, provide an opportunity for student input, answer questions, and develop strategies. Foster student involvement in the development of strategies to ensure understanding and to facilitate cooperation. At the close of the discussion, ask questions related to the purpose of the classroom procedure and the specific strategies that will be adopted. Student responses will indicate their level of understanding.

Step 2: Specify Student Behaviors.   Clearly specify the behaviors that are required of the students. These behaviors should be *discrete, sequential* and *observable.* For example, when students transition from the classroom to the gym for PE, they are required to put their materials away, push in their chairs, line up quietly at the door, and wait for the signal to leave. The level of detail and order often varies from class to class and from teacher to teacher. Establish sufficient detail in the behaviors to ensure that the purpose of the classroom procedure is accomplished.

Step 3: Practice.   Teachers typically use practice to develop fluency in skill development. Schedule practice sessions. Model the first example of the skill to ensure that the students observe a correct example. Next, call on the students to role-play. Use small groups of students to demonstrate the classroom procedure. Ensure that *all* students have an opportunity to demonstrate and practice the classroom procedure. Do not require the students to exhibit the classroom procedure independently in the real situation until they have demonstrated proficiency in the practice sessions.

Step 4: Monitor.   Once the students have had the opportunity to practice the classroom procedure, provide them with opportunities to exhibit the classroom procedure independently in the real situation. *Carefully monitor* the students' performance, especially in the early stages. Catch problems early; provide praise or reinforcement to students who follow the classroom procedure correctly; and offer prompts, correction, and encouragement to students who may be making errors. Give feedback to the students on their performance at the completion of the classroom procedure.

Step 5: Review.   Develop a system to review periodically the students' performance on the classroom procedure. Include formal observation of the students' behavior to assess how many of the students are following the classroom procedure, how long the procedure takes, and what kinds of errors are occurring. If errors occur, briefly introduce steps 1, 2, 3, and 4 (i.e., explain, specify student behaviors, practice, and monitor) before the next opportunity to demonstrate the classroom procedure. Note that more structure is usually needed for younger students, larger groups of students, and classes composed of students with significant problem behaviors.

Adaptations for Teaching Classroom Expectations for Secondary Teachers

The main difference between teaching behavior to secondary students and elementary students is that there usually is less need for the practice step at the secondary level (step 4). Moreover, in most cases the students may know and understand the classroom expectations. However, at the start of the school year or at the beginning of a new semester, plan to spend time on steps 1 and 2, explaining the expectations and specifying the expected behaviors. Once the term is under way, these two steps will be replaced with reminders. Continue to implement steps 4 and 5 (monitor and review, respectively) throughout the term. Do not underestimate the student need for ongoing reminders, supervision, and feedback in order to establish the classroom expectations.

Summary

Classroom rules and expectations are a necessary foundation for effective instruction and classroom management. The old adage "What you expect is what you get" is perfectly true when it comes to classroom behavior. There are three keys for establishing classroom expectations: (a) develop a systematic process for selecting a short list of expectations, (b) systematically teach the list, and (c) be prepared to implement the procedures consistently over the full course of the school year.

Determining Classroom Procedures

Classroom procedures refer to those routine activities that are completed by students with minimum assistance from the teacher. Essentially, the goal is to have the students manage these tasks by themselves. These classroom procedures usually consist of a number of sequential behaviors or routines tied to specific activities conducted in the classroom (see Box 10.4). For example, a teacher may expect the students to turn in completed assignments and products at a specific place in the room, return to their desk, and begin another activity without prompting from the teacher.

Many benefits to instruction and management result once a teacher has established the classroom procedures and routines: students learn self-management skills, instructional time is managed more efficiently, disruptions are minimized, and the classroom assumes a relaxed and orderly environment very conducive to teaching and learning (Colvin & Lazar, 1997; Jones & Jones, 1986; Kame'enui & Darch, 1994).

BOX **10.4**

Checklist 4: Classroom Procedures and Teaching Schedule

List of Classroom Procedures

1. _____   6. _____
2. _____   7. _____
3. _____   8. _____
4. _____   9. _____
5. _____   10. _____

Teaching Schedule for Each Procedure

First Day   Procedures to Teach
                                 1. _____
                                 2. _____
                                 3. _____

First Week   Procedures to Teach
                                 4. _____
                                 5. _____
                                 6. _____
                                 7. _____

First Month   Procedures to Teach
                                 8. _____
                                 9. _____
                                 10. _____

Essentially, classroom procedures are simply a set of specific classroom expectations directly related to student tasks and responsibilities. Consequently, teachers use the same five instructional strategies for teaching classroom expectations described earlier in this chapter (i.e., explain, specify the student behaviors, practice, monitor, and review.)

A very important decision teachers need to make is to identify the procedures they wish to establish in their classroom. In effect, teachers develop their own list of classroom routines with appropriate levels of detail to suit their purposes and needs. The critical step in establishing these procedures is to be quite clear on the behaviors expected of the students and to teach the routines formally early in the school year. For example, one elementary teacher wanted to establish a routine for starting the school day. The following specific student behaviors were identified:

> Put hats, coats, bags, and lunch boxes in designated areas.
> Turn in homework or products to appropriate places.
> Put instructional materials in their desks.
> Sharpen pencils and gather necessary materials for class.
> Be in their seat ready to start class by the time 5 minutes is up.

In addition, the teacher taught this routine in the first week of class, tried to be consistent with implementation, and reviewed student progress periodically.

Common routines that have been implemented by teachers include entering the classroom, working independently, using the drinking fountain, using the rest rooms, sending work home, securing teacher or student assistance, moving around the classroom and accessing materials, establishing classroom helpers, organizing assignments, conducting tests and quizzes, meeting individual student needs, and managing dead time.

Summary

Researchers report that teachers spend from 40% to 75% of available instructional time in activities other than instruction (Goodlad, 1984; Hoffmeister & Lubke, 1990; Walker et al., 1995). One strategy for increasing instructional time is to firmly establish classroom routines and procedures. Once the procedures become automatic, students can take an independent role with several responsibilities in the classroom, thereby freeing the teacher to attend to other critical aspects of instruction.

Conclusion

As the diversity of classrooms increases dramatically, teachers face greater pressures to teach and manage their students effectively and efficiently. Cangelosi (1992) appropriately claims, "As a teacher you are confronted with more variables to concurrently manipulate than is expected in any other profession" (p. 8). Moreover, public schools are leaning more toward positive and proactive procedures that emphasize preventing problem behavior. In this chapter, information was presented on the use of a specific prevention procedure, classroom organization, related to the design and proper functioning of the classroom environment. By systematically utilizing these strategies, teachers provide students with a stable, predictable environment that will generally facilitate desirable behavior and will minimize problem behavior. A classroom environment is thus established that is conducive to providing quality instruction and teaching desirable social behavior.

REFERENCES

Canady, R. L., & Rettig, M. D. (1995). *Block scheduling: A catalyst for change in high schools.* Princeton, NJ: Eye on Education.

Cangelosi, J. S. (1992). *Systematic teaching strategies.* New York: Longman.

Cawelti, G. (1994). *High school restructuring: A national study.* Arlington, VA: Educational Research Service.

Colvin, G., & Lazar, M. (1997). *The effective elementary classroom: Managing for success.* Longmont, CO: Sopris West.

Colvin, G., Kame'enui, E., & Sugai, G. (1993). School-wide and classroom management: Reconceptualizing the integration and management of students with behavior problems in general education. *Education and Treatment of Children, 16,* 361–381.

Colvin, G., & Sugai, G. (1988). Proactive strategies for managing social behavior problems. *Education and Treatment of Children, 11*(4), 341–348.

Cotton, K. (1990). Schoolwide and classroom discipline. *School improvement research series: Close up #9.* Portland, OR: Northwest Regional Educational Laboratory.

Cummings, C. (1983). *Managing to teach* (3rd ed.). Edmonds, WA: Teaching Inc.

Emmer, E. T., Evertson, C. M., Clements, B. S., & Worsham, M. E. (1994). *Classroom management for secondary teachers* (3rd ed.). Needham Heights, MA: Allyn & Bacon.

Evertson, C. M., Emmer, E. T., Clements, B. S., & Worsham, M. E. (1994). *Classroom management for elementary teachers* (3rd ed.). Needham Heights, MA: Allyn & Bacon.

Goodlad, J. I. (1984). *A place called school: Prospects for the future.* New York: McGraw-Hill.

Hofmeister, A., & Lubke, M. (1990). *Research into practice: Implementing effective teaching strategies.* Needham Heights, MA: Allyn & Bacon.

Irmsher, K. (1996). *Block scheduling in high schools.* Eugene: Oregon School Study Council, University of Oregon.

Johnson, D. W., Johnson, R. T., & Holubec, E. J. (1990). *Cooperation in the classroom* (rev. ed.). Edina, MN: Interaction.

Jones, V., & Jones, L. (1986). *Comprehensive classroom management: Creating positive learning environments.* Needham Heights, MA: Allyn & Bacon.

Kame'enui, E., & Darch, C. (1994). *Classroom management.* White Plains, NY: Merrill.

Kauffman, J., Mostert, M. P., Trent, S. C., & Hallahan, D. P. (1998). *Managing classroom behavior: A reflective case-based approach* (2nd ed). Needham Heights, MA: Allyn & Bacon.

Paine, S. C., Radicchi, J., Rosellini, L. C., Deutchman, L., & Darch, C. B. (1983). *Structuring your classroom for academic success.* Champaign, IL: Research Press.

Slavin, R. (1988). Cooperative learning and student achievement. *Educational Leadership, 46*(2), 31–33.

Sprick, R. (1985). *Discipline in the secondary classroom.* New York: Center for Applied Research in Education.

Sprick, R., Garrison, M., & Howard, L. (1998). *CHAMPs: A proactive and positive approach to classroom management.* Longmont, CO: Sopris West.

Walker, H. M., Colvin, G., & Ramsey, E. (1995). *Antisocial behavior in school: Strategies and best practices.* Pacific Grove, CA: Brooks/Cole.

Wong, K. K., & Wong, R. T. (1991). *The first days of school: How to be an effective teacher.* Sunnyvale, CA: Wong.

PART THREE

Managing Challenging Behaviors

11 Developmental Prevention of At-Risk Outcomes for Vulnerable Antisocial Children and Youth

HILL M. WALKER
University of Oregon

HERBERT H. SEVERSON
Oregon Research Institute
Eugene, Oregon

Introduction

This chapter makes a case for the achievement of desirable, school-based outcomes for vulnerable children and youth, especially those who are at risk for developing antisocial behavior patterns, through coordinated early intervention approaches. In the past several decades, a number of highly effective intervention approaches have been developed that have the potential to achieve true prevention goals in this domain (see Greenberg, Domitrovich, & Bumbarger, 1999; Loeber & Farrington, 1998). Longitudinal studies evaluating these interventions across multiple school years document their effectiveness and suggest that the earlier and more comprehensively intervention occurs, the greater the return on the investment (Hawkins, Catalano, Kosterman, Abbott, & Hill, 1999; Zigler, Taussig, & Black, 1992). However, these proven interventions, which represent cost-effective best practices, are typically not in evidence within family, preschool, school, and community contexts.

We need to take the long view toward achieving true prevention as opposed to continuing to address youth problems reactively at the point where they become most salient and problematic (e.g., school dropout, adolescent offending, drug and alcohol use, etc.). We should also address these problems before the behavior of the child exceeds the tolerance limits of schools and communities and results in punitive sanctions. Policies and practices that will produce these desirable outcomes are currently known, but the will to adopt them has been largely absent due to such factors as concerns about costs, skepticism about prevention outcomes, threats of redistribution of existing resources, reluctance to identify at-risk children and youth because of potentially stigmatizing effects, territorial imperatives and claims, and philosophical objections (Kauffman, 1999). Unless we do indeed take the long view and effectively address these barriers and other obstacles to the adoption and implementation of evidence-based, proven interventions, we run the risk of continuing to tread water, at best, and to see further deterioration in the lives of our vulnerable children and youth, at worst. The social and economic costs to our society, institutions, families, and at-risk children and youth of failing to address this growing problem proactively and comprehensively are potentially exponential.

The Current Landscape

Growing up in our society today is risky business. Thousands of vulnerable children and youth are at risk for a host of negative developmental outcomes. Many of them are currently embarked on destructive pathways that longitudinal studies clearly show lead to unfortunate outcomes such as school failure and dropout, alcohol and substance abuse, delinquency, social rejection, victimization, and sometimes violence (Loeber & Farrington, 1998; Patterson, Reid, & Dishion, 1992). In spite of recent reports of declining crime rates for juveniles and adults, the United States continues, by wide margins, to lead all developed nations in violent criminal acts (robbery, rape, aggravated assault, and murder) as well as homicide deaths of 15- to 24-year-old males (Osofsky, 1997). The risk factors and societal forces that contribute so strongly to these negative outcomes continue largely unabated, are overwhelming in their pervasiveness, and are generally not adequately addressed by prevention efforts. They include, among others, poverty, racial discrimination, neglect and abuse (domestic, sexual, emotional), alcohol and substance abuse, pervasive images of violence in the media and our daily lives, social fragmentation, and, most important, a diminished capacity to raise and socialize our children safely (American Psychological Association, 1993).

Realistically, impacting many of these forces and conditions of risk, in a meaningful way, is well beyond the reach of most social, educational, and judicial institutions. Furthermore, many of these factors operate outside the school setting, and most have already begun to register their destructive effects on the developing child prior to school entry. It is critically important to address and enhance protective factors (social competence, supportive peers, mentors, attachment and bonding to schooling, etc.) that can buffer and offset the damaging effects of these risk factors. Box 11.1 lists factors that contribute to risk and buffering-offsetting protective factors that operate across child, family, school, and community-cultural contexts.

BOX **11.1**

Risk and Protective Factors Associated with Antisocial and Criminal Behavior

Risk Factors

Child Factors	Family Factors	School Context	Community and Cultural Factors
Prematurity	*Parental characteristics:*	School failure	Socioeconomic disadvantage
Low birth weight	Teenage mothers	Normative beliefs about aggression	Population density and housing conditions
Disability	Single parents		
Prenatal brain damage	Psychiatric disorder, especially depression	Deviant peer group	Urban area
Birth injury	Substance abuse		Neighborhood violence and crime
Low intelligence	Criminality	Bullying	
Difficult temperament	Antisocial models	Peer rejection	Cultural norms
Chronic illness	*Family environment:*	Poor attachment to school	Concerning violence as acceptable response to frustration
Insecure attachment	Family violence and disharmony	Inadequate behavior management	
Poor problem solving	Marital discord		
Beliefs about aggression	Disorganized		Media portrayal of violence
Attributions	Negative interaction/ social isolation		Lack of support services
Poor social skills	Large family size		Social or cultural discrimination
Low self-esteem	Father absence		
Lack of empathy	Long-term parental unemployment		
Alienation	*Parenting style:*		
Hyperactivity/ disruptive behavior	Poor supervision and monitoring of child		
Impulsivity	Discipline style (harsh or inconsistent)		
	Rejection of child		
	Abuse		
	Lack of warmth and affection		
	Low involvement in child's activities		
	Neglect		

(continued)

BOX **11.1**   Continued

Protective Factors

Child Factors	Family Factors	School Context	Community and Cultural Factors
Social competence	Supportive, caring parents	Positive school climate	Access to support services
Social skills	Family harmony	Prosocial peer group	Community networking
Above-average intelligence	More than 2 years between siblings	Responsibility and required helpfulness	Attachment to the community
Attachment to family	Responsibility for chores or required helpfulness	Sense of belonging/bonding	Participation in church or other community group
Empathy			
Problem solving			
Optimism	Secure and stable family	Opportunities for some success at school and recognition of achievement	Community/cultural norms against violence
School achievement			
Easy temperament	Supportive relationship with other adult		Strong cultural identity and ethnic pride
Internal locus of control			
Moral beliefs	Small family size	School norms concerning violence	
Values	Strong family norms and morality		
Self-related cognitions			
Good coping style			

National trends regarding the risk factors and background conditions that large numbers of our children and youth face daily are being increasingly recognized as destructive forces in their lives and school performances. The nonschool experiences of children and youth have everything to do with how they perform in school and react to the experience of schooling (see Steinberg, 1996). All too often these experiences and conditions impair school performance and contribute to school failure. Schools can be central players in buffering and offsetting the damaging effects of this kind of exposure; however, to do so, they have to be adequately funded and be willing to enter into true collaborative partnerships with families, public safety, juvenile courts, and both public and private agencies. Too often, schools have been viewed as detached, unwilling participants in this regard.

The state of Oregon mirrors the national profile of risk factors and conditions to which children and youth are exposed daily in the United States. In its 2000 annual report on the welfare of the state's children, Children First of Oregon examines child welfare in four areas: health, well-being of the family, child care and early education, and community involvement. The report estimates that at least one-fourth of Oregon's children, aged 0 to 8, are at substantial risk in one or more of these areas. Following are some of the report's major findings:

1. One in five Oregon children are born to mothers with less than a high school education.
2. One in six children live at or below the federal poverty level of $1,157 monthly for a family of three.
3. One in six children have witnessed or heard domestic violence in the home within the past year.
4. One in 55 children under age 8 are known victims of serious abuse or neglect.

Our society needs to renew ever more forcefully its commitment to protecting its children and youth from the influence of these toxic conditions of risk. Our generic approach for dealing with these challenges should also undergo an examination or audit in terms of the strategies used to cope with them and the manner in which we allocate resources for this purpose. Currently, our policies and practices, particularly in regard to addressing school failure and delinquency, are concentrated heavily at the point where at-risk youth begin committing arrestable offenses and disengaging from schooling (i.e., early adolescence). We are greatly in need of a more balanced approach in which key risk factors, which put vulnerable children on a pathway to later destructive outcomes, especially delinquency, are addressed much earlier in the developmental age span, when their social impact and cost effectiveness can be maximized. As noted earlier, schools are ideally positioned to take a key leadership role, in collaboration with other agencies, institutions, and social systems, in forging partnerships and making such a balanced approach an effective reality.

It is never too late to intervene or too early to engage in prevention efforts. Critical transition points exist at key stages along the early developmental continuum where intervention resources can be concentrated to great effect and in which a substantial return on investment can be realized. While successful intervention programs have been validated for the full age–grade range (K–12), a large number of experts seem to agree that earlier is better in terms of exposing at-risk children to proven, evidence-based interventions (Eddy, Reid, & Fetrow, 2000; Greenwood, 1999; Reid, 1993; Zigler et al., 1992). The remainder of this chapter describes issues, key findings, and promising practices involving effective developmental prevention.

Achieving Developmental Prevention through Early Intervention

There is considerable disagreement, and some confusion, among professionals about the relationship between prevention and intervention. *Prevention* is an outcome that is achieved by different types of intervention strategies. In contrast, *intervention* is a process or an approach that is a means to achieving that end. There are three types of prevention: (a) *primary prevention,* whose goal is to prevent harm; (b) *secondary prevention,* whose goal is to reverse harm; and (c) *tertiary prevention,* whose goal is to reduce harm (see Chapter 1 by O'Shaughnessy, Lane, & Gresham, this text). Primary prevention efforts usually rely on universal interventions for achieving broad-based outcomes across large groups of individuals who either are not at risk or experience very mild levels of risk. In contrast, secondary prevention relies on specialized intervention approaches designed for use with individuals or small groups who show the clear signs of prior or continuing exposure to risk factors. Finally, tertiary prevention is concerned with those extremely at-risk individuals for whom neither universal nor targeted, specialized interventions work. Generally, the focus of tertiary prevention is on comprehensive case management and wraparound strategies and processes. Schools are an ideal setting for implementing a coordinated and integrated approach to achieving these three types of prevention outcomes. The role of schools as a host setting for coordinating these three types of prevention has been previously addressed by Walker and his colleagues (1996).

Figure 11.1 illustrates the changing relationship among primary, secondary, and tertiary prevention outcomes over the 0- to 18-year developmental age span. Because we typically do not intervene early as problems begin emerging, when they can often be solved through less expensive universal interventions, costs escalate dramatically as one progresses upward through the developmental age span. As a general rule, the longer one waits, the more resistant are problems to solution, the greater the costs, and the more negative the impact on at-risk individuals, their families, and society. Most seriously, the impact of intervention in solving these intractable and long-standing problems is likely to be attenuated.

Just as we cannot fiscally afford a health care system in which a family's first contact with medical services is the emergency room, since their disease by this time is likely to be at a relatively advanced stage and emergency room care is one of the most expensive forms of medical treatment, we similarly cannot afford to wait until youth develop antisocial behavior patterns, fail school, and begin committing delinquent acts before intervening. We currently have the ability to identify, early in their lives and school careers, those vulnerable children and youth who are following a pathway or trajectory toward delinquency, school failure, and sometimes violence. Longitudinal research has identified the markers and characteristics (e.g., well-developed, early antisocial behavior patterns that are behaviorally diverse, occur at high rates, and are in evidence across a range of settings) that are strongly associated with later school adjustment problems (i.e., rejection by teachers and peers, depression, low academic achievement, disciplinary referrals, etc.) and delinquency (Loeber & Farrington, 1998; Patterson et al., 1992).

Figure 11.2 illustrates the path or trajectory that increasing numbers of children and youth are now on due to the social and economic risks to which they are exposed on a daily basis. The longer one is on this path, the more likely it is that short-term and/or long-term negative outcomes will be encountered. Evidence exists that at-risk children who get on this path early in their lives, and who do not receive needed intervention and supports, are likely to manifest antisocial tendencies throughout their lives (Moffitt, 1994). Eddy and colleagues (2000) argue persuasively that our best treatment options are, first, to prevent at-risk children from

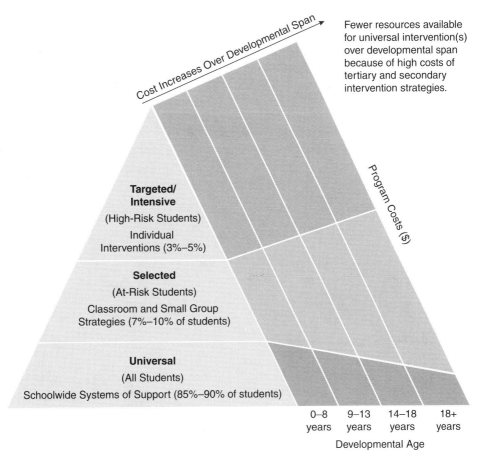

Cost Increases Over Developmental Span

Fewer resources available for universal intervention(s) over developmental span because of high costs of tertiary and secondary intervention strategies.

Program Costs ($)

Targeted/ Intensive

(High-Risk Students)

Individual Interventions (3%–5%)

Selected

(At-Risk Students)

Classroom and Small Group Strategies (7%–10% of students)

Universal

(All Students)

Schoolwide Systems of Support (85%–90% of students)

| 0–8 years | 9–13 years | 14–18 years | 18+ years |

Developmental Age

FIGURE 11.1   Relationship between Costs and Prevention Type Across the 0–18 Developmental Age Span

Source: Adapted from Figure 2, Preventing violent and destructive behavior in schools: primary, secondary, and tertiary systems of prevention (p. 71) from Walker, H. M., and Sprague, J. R. (1999). *The path to school failure, delinquency, and violence: Causal factors and some potential solutions. Intervention in School and Clinic,* 35 (2), 67–73.

getting on this path and, second, to get them off it quickly if we fail to do so. Early intervention that is comprehensive in nature, and that specifically addresses key risk factors for antisocial behavior and related destructive outcomes, is an excellent vehicle for realizing developmental prevention. (See Hawkins et al., 1999, for an excellent, recent example.)

Achieving developmental prevention outcomes through early intervention means addressing the *precursors* of delinquency, school failure, and dropout *prior* to the onset of these outcomes. There are some significant developmental opportunities in which to mount such interventions with great effect (i.e., prenatal, infancy, early childhood, and middle childhood). The strategies used, their focus, and the

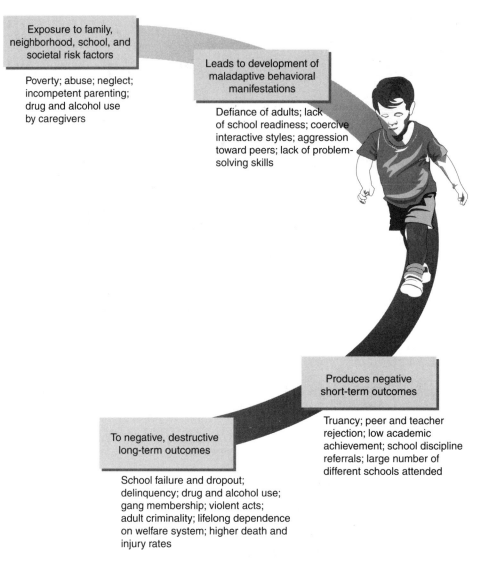

Exposure to family, neighborhood, school, and societal risk factors

Poverty; abuse; neglect; incompetent parenting; drug and alcohol use by caregivers

Leads to development of maladaptive behavioral manifestations

Defiance of adults; lack of school readiness; coercive interactive styles; aggression toward peers; lack of problem-solving skills

Produces negative short-term outcomes

Truancy; peer and teacher rejection; low academic achievement; school discipline referrals; large number of different schools attended

To negative, destructive long-term outcomes

School failure and dropout; delinquency; drug and alcohol use; gang membership; violent acts; adult criminality; lifelong dependence on welfare system; higher death and injury rates

FIGURE 11.2   The path to long-term negative outcomes for at-risk children and youth
Source: Walker, H. M. and Sprague, J. R. The path to school failure, delinquency, and violence: Causal factors and some potential solutions. *Intervention in School and Clinic,* 35, 67–73. Copyright © 1999 by Pro-Ed, Inc. Reprinted with permission.

targets of these efforts will differ to some extent across these transition points and developmental stages. Figure 11.3 illustrates a developmental model that explains how antisocial, dysfunctional behavior emerges out of an at-risk environment, responds to contributing influencing factors, and progresses over the 0 to 18 age span (Reid & Eddy, 1997).

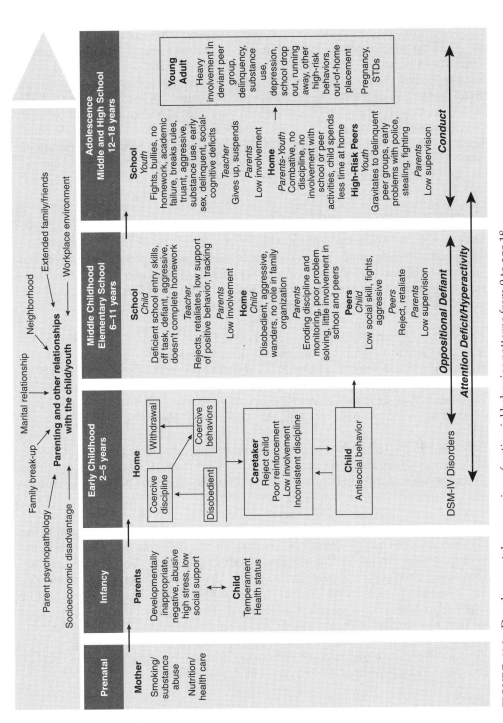

FIGURE 11.3 Developmental progression of antisocial behavior patterns from 0 to age 18

Source: Reid, J. B., & Eddy, J. M. "The prevention of antisocial behavior: Some considerations in the search for effective interventions." In D. M. Stoff, J. Breiling, & J. D. Maser (eds.). Copyright © 1997 *The handbook of antisocial behavior* (pp. 343–356). This material is used by permission of John Wiley & Sons, Inc.

The progression shown in Figure 11.3 has been confirmed many times over by longitudinal studies conducted in the United States, Europe, Canada, and Australia. (See Loeber & Farrington, 1998, for an overview.) This figure also provides a road map that guides implementation of early intervention strategies at critical transition points and developmental stages. To address potential risks effectively and to develop offsetting protective factors, it is essential to coordinate intervention strategies across prenatal, infancy (0–2), early childhood (2–5), and middle childhood (6–11) developmental stages. It is also critical to create a seamless continuum of tracking, supports, and services across each of these developmental stages so vulnerable children do not fall through the cracks and get onto a destructive pathway.

Promising Programs and Practices

Described in the following sections are some promising practices and intervention approaches that should be considered in developing a comprehensive network of supports and services for addressing risk factors within and across these four developmental stages (i.e., prenatal to age 11). All have solid research evidence underlying them that supports their effectiveness.

Prenatal.   Healthy Start and the Olds Nurse Home Visitation Model both work with pregnant at-risk mothers in order to address risk factors and to develop protective factors and social supports. Both of these programs continue their involvement and family supports after the birth of the child through systematic home visitations. Each is highly cost-effective, and the Olds model has been shown to prevent later delinquency (see Olds, Hill, & Rumsey, 1998).

Infancy.   Early Head Start and systematic parent education efforts in effective child care and parenting practices are important for the welfare of at-risk infants at this developmental level. Parent training instruction can often be delivered in concert with participation in Early Head Start.

Early Childhood.   Enrollment in Regular Head Start is of critical importance for all children who qualify. Currently, less than half of Oregon's children who legitimately qualify can access Regular Head Start Programs, and only 4% of eligible Oregon children currently participate in Early Head Start. Of equal importance, all families with children in the 0 to 6 age range, who warrant crisis intervention and support services, should be able to access them. Finally, school readiness programs such as the First Step to Success home and school intervention for aggressive, antisocial kindergartners and first graders should be available for all who qualify for them to help ensure that at-risk children get off to the best start possible in school (Walker, Kavanagh, Stiller, Golly, Severson, & Feil, 1998).

Middle Childhood.   The importance of getting off to the best possible start in school and fully engaging and bonding with the schooling process thereafter cannot be overestimated. School attachment, commitment, and full engagement with schooling serve as very strong protective factors for all students and especially those from at-risk backgrounds. A recently published, longitudinal study by Hawkins et al. (1999) shows that attachment to and engagement with the schooling process serves as a protective factor years later for a host of destructive outcomes, including drug and alcohol use, antisocial behavior, and delinquency. At this developmental stage, every student, but especially at-risk students, should be taught mastery of the following critical sets of skills: how to make and hold friends; how to avoid challenging, disruptive, or aggressive forms of behavior; how to apply study and organizational skills essential for school success; and how to achieve social goals without resorting to bullying, intimidation of others, or coercion. Finally, teaching rule-governed behavior and violence prevention skills (empathy, anger management, conflict resolution, and impulse control) as part of the regular school curriculum is essential for the healthy development of all students and for establishing a positive, safe, and respectful school climate.

Implementing a seamless continuum of this type would buffer and partially offset many of the risk factors that help account for delinquency, school failure, and dropout. It would require a significant investment of resources to implement this model fully, but the long-term recapture of the initial investments would likely be robust if it were implemented with integrity. The cost benefits of early intervention have been the subject of economic analyses by a number of analysts over the past two decades (Barnett, 1985; Barnett & Escobar, 1992; Greenwood, 1999). Results of these studies are consistent in showing that the return on investment of early interventions that address key risk factors and are implemented with integrity can produce long-term savings that generally exceed the original investment in today's dollars.

Schools have a very important role to play in a prevention initiative of this type, with their greatest involvement likely occurring in the preschool and school-age developmental stages. It is especially critical that all children be evaluated at the point of school entry on two important dimensions that have everything to do with a successful school career. These are (a) the presence of challenging forms of behavior and (b) lack of school readiness associated with learning to read. Children who manifest aggressive, coercive behavior patterns suffer terribly in school and victimize peers, teachers, and other adults. They are often pushed out of school in late middle school or beginning high school because of their aversive, noxious behavior. Children who fail to learn to read, or read to the best of their abilities, constantly receive the message that they are a failure in school. The cumulative effect of this negative messaging often results in their dropping out of school during this same period. Those with reading failure *and* challenging behavior are severely at risk, both in and out of school, and are likely to experience a low overall quality of life.

What the Research Evidence Indicates

Substantial numbers of cross sectional and longitudinal studies have been conducted over the past three decades examining the risk factors, and their progression over time, that are associated with antisocial behavior, delinquency, and adult crime. (See Loeber & Farrington, 1998, for a comprehensive treatment of this topic.) They converge remarkably well in support of the following statements:

1. Risk factors are cumulative, and their negative impact increases with exposure to greater numbers of them.
2. Different as well as overlapping sets of risk factors are associated with certain negative, destructive outcomes.
3. Risk factors can combine and interact in very destructive ways on the developing child or youth.
4. Early intervention approaches that address key risk factors are highly effective in preventing delinquency years later.
5. Economic analysis studies of long-term follow-ups of early intervention participants show superior prevention effects, compared to nonparticipating controls, on a broad range of outcomes, including delinquency and violent acts.
6. The savings from comprehensive early intervention in preschool settings lasting two school years, for disadvantaged children, can range up to approximately $11,000 per case depending on the number of outcomes assessed and the length of the follow-up period.

It is absolutely essential that early intervention efforts, which seek to prevent later delinquency and other destructive, long-term outcomes, address the known risk factors predictive of such outcomes. The focus should also be on targeting and coordinating the critical roles of the three most important social agents in a child's life within the intervention: parents, teachers, and peers (Reid, 1993).

School-Based Prevention of Antisocial Behavior Outcomes

School personnel now have available to them a broad array of options for addressing antisocial behavior patterns within the context of schooling. Compendiums of evidence-based intervention programs suitable for this purpose have been provided recently by Greenberg et al. (1999), the American Institutes for Research (2000), Elliott (1998), and Kingery (2000). These compendia describe school-based prevention programs that are proven to work and that have strong evidence to support this claim. The reader is urged to consult these sources before designing and/or selecting intervention approaches to address antisocial behavior in children and youth in the context of schooling.

Illustrated next are intervention approaches, designed to achieve primary, secondary, and tertiary prevention outcomes, that collectively address antisocial behavior patterns, interpersonal violence, school failure, and delinquency. Each of these interventions requires the establishment of collaborative partnerships between school personnel and families. In one case (tertiary prevention), activities and roles of professionals from a range of agencies, and family members, are coordinated by a case manager (i.e., child welfare, mental health, schools, corrections, and family court). They exemplify the findings of Greenberg et al. (1999) that multicomponent interventions involving social agents from across multiple settings are much more likely to be effective than those that do not fit this profile.

Primary Prevention. As noted earlier, the purpose of primary prevention approaches is to prevent the occurrence or onset of problems. Implementing schoolwide discipline programs and fluoridating a community's water supply are two examples of universal interventions designed, respectively, to prevent school-based behavior problems and the development of dental caries. Universal interventions are implemented in a fashion such that all who are exposed to them receive the same intervention in the same manner at the same dosage level.

The *Second Step Violence Prevention Curriculum* (Committee for Children, 1992) is a universal intervention designed to teach violence prevention skills in the preschool–grade 9 range. Second Step is taught as part of the regular school curriculum and uses the same instructional methods as those for teaching language, math, science, and so forth. The curriculum teaches four skills that are known to be associated with violence prevention: empathy, impulse control, anger management, and conflict resolution. Teaching strategies used by the Second Step program include discussion, video representations of social scenarios, role playing, debriefing, and feedback. Parents are also involved in the teaching and practice of target skills at home.

The Second Step program was independently evaluated as to its effectiveness in a randomized control trial (Grossman et al., 1997). Results indicated that, for treatment students, as compared to nontreatment participants, levels of aggression decreased and prosocial behavior increased, as determined by in vivo behavioral observations recorded by trained observers ($p = .03$ and $.04$, respectively). These effects were largely in evidence 6 months later, according to the authors.

The Second Step program is a cost-effective intervention popular with teachers and other school personnel. It also contributes to establishing and maintaining a positive school climate in addition to addressing the precursors of violence. It is recommended as a best practice for making schools safer and violence-free.

Secondary Prevention. Intervention approaches for achieving this type of prevention are focused on either an individual or a small group of at-risk individuals. They tend to be more time-consuming, intensive, and expensive than universal interventions; they are concerned with reversing the harm that has been caused by exposure to risk factors rather than preventing it.

The *First Step to Success* early intervention program is a collaborative home and school intervention that addresses secondary prevention goals. It is designed to address emerging antisocial behavior patterns and to assist target children in getting off to the best start possible in school (Walker et al., 1997). The First Step program is coordinated by a behavioral coach (i.e., counselor, school psychologist, early interventionist, or resource specialist) who sets up the school-based part of the intervention, operates it initially, and then turns it over to the regular kindergarten or first-grade teacher. The coach then works with the target child's parents and caregivers to teach them how to instruct their child in school success skills (i.e., cooperation, accepting limits, being ready for school, completing work, etc.). A parent handbook, weekly training sessions conducted in the parents' home, and frequent telephone contact and follow-up visits by the First Step coach are used to achieve caregiver mastery of this program component. At the same time, teachers recognize and reinforce these skills at school. Peers are also enlisted in the intervention as special helpers, and they tend to be very supportive of the target child's efforts to change.

First Step consists of three interconnected modules: screening and identification, school intervention, and HomeBase parent training. The program is applied to one target child at a time and requires approximately 3 months from start to finish. First Step was developed through a 4-year grant to the senior author from the U.S. Department of Education. A randomized trial, involving 46 kindergartners, and a wait-list control group design was used to evaluate the First Step program's impact (Walker et al., 1998). Across five evaluation measures (four teacher rating measures and one direct observational measure), the calculated effect size for the pre-/postchanges, compared to wait-list control participants, was .86, which is considered to be a robust magnitude of impact. The original cohorts 1 ($N = 24$) and 2 ($N = 22$) on whom the First Step program was originally tested and evaluated were recently followed up into grades 6 and 5, respectively. The initial behavioral gains produced through exposure to the program, when they were in kindergarten, have proven to be surprisingly durable over this time span (see Epstein & Walker, in press).

The First Step program has now been adopted in 12 states and three Canadian provinces in addition to Australia and New Zealand. Like Second Step, it is a popular program with educators and costs approximately $400 per case to implement in terms of professional time and cost of materials.

Tertiary Prevention.   The most severely at-risk students within a school's population are generally candidates for tertiary prevention strategies. Interventions and supports used to achieve this kind of prevention can be extremely expensive (i.e., upward of $200,000 annually) depending on the array of services required.

An outstanding example of an effective tertiary intervention is the *Multisystemic Therapy* (MST) model developed by Scott Henggeler and his colleagues (Henggeler, 1998), which is one of 10 "blueprint" violence prevention programs validated as effective by Del Elliott and his associates at the Center for the Study and Prevention of Violence at the University of Colorado. MST is highly effective with severely at-risk youth who have been or are about to be incarcerated for committing arrestable offenses, often of a violent nature. It is a social-ecological intervention that addresses risk factors in family, individual, school, and community contexts. The MST intervention process is delivered by a team of master's-level therapists, supervised by a Ph.D.-level psychologist, who are all systematically trained in the MST model by its developers.

MST is a superb example of a complex intervention that addresses key risk factors and coordinates multiple systems of care, support, and treatment. It has proven to be highly effective in preventing recidivism of severely at-risk and involved adolescents and also in reducing antisocial behavior (Henggeler, Melton, & Smith, 1992; Schoenwald, Brown, & Henggeler, 2000). It is recommended as a proven intervention for delinquent and potentially violent adolescents. The program is not designed for, and does not work with, adolescents who are sex offenders or are mentally ill.

Conclusion

Antisocial behavior continues to be a dangerous social toxin in our schools and communities. Early investment in this unfortunate behavior pattern carries substantial downstream risks for at-risk youth, their families, and support networks. The negative, destructive outcomes associated long-term with antisocial behavior are extremely costly to the individual and society and have been well documented (Kazdin, 1987; Loeber & Farrington, 1998; Patterson et al., 1992; Zigler et al., 1992).

Very promising practices and interventions currently exist that, if adopted and carefully implemented, will substantially impact this behavior pattern with the potential to divert at-risk children from the path that so often leads inexorably toward school failure and dropout, delinquency, sometimes violence, and adult crime. Schools have to be a central player in any comprehensive strategy that will be successful in changing the landscape in relation to this societal challenge. The interventions and practices described herein can be used for this purpose. However, they will not be effective unless they are adequately funded, are implemented with integrity, are coordinated and delivered skillfully, address key risk factors predictive of later destructive outcomes, and are scaled up and applied with sufficient intensity to impact the target youth's problems.

Additional Recommended Resources

Listed in the appendix are some recommended resources on the topics dealt with herein. In addition, some articles are cited that provide important information on interventions and approaches that work in diverting vulnerable, at-risk children from a path leading to delinquency and a host of related, destructive outcomes.

REFERENCES

American Institutes for Research. (2000). *Safeguarding our children: An action guide.* Washington, DC: U.S. Department of Education.

American Psychological Association. (1993). *Violence and youth: Psychology's response. Volume I: Summary report of the American Psychological Association Commission on Violence and Youth.* Washington, DC: Author.

Barnett, W. S. (1985). Benefit–cost analysis of the Perry Preschool program and its policy implications. *Educational Evaluation & Policy Analysis, 7*(4), 333–342.

Barnett, W. S., & Escobar, C. M. (1992). Economic costs and benefits of early intervention. In S. J. Meisels & J. P. Shonkoff (Eds.), *Handbook of early childhood intervention* (pp. 560–582). New York: Cambridge University Press.

Committee for Children. (1992). *Second Step: Violence prevention curriculum for preschool–grade 9.* Seattle: Author.

Eddy, J. M., Reid, J. B., & Fetrow, R. A. (2000). A prevention program to decrease youth violence and delinquency: Linking the Interests of Families and Teachers (LIFT). *Journal of Emotional and Behavioral Disorders, 8*(3) 165–176.

Elliott, D. S. (Ed.). (1998). *Blueprints for violence prevention.* Boulder, CO: Center for the Study and Prevention of Violence.

Epstein, M. H., & Walker, H. M. (Eds.). (in press). Special education: Best practices and First Step to Success. In B. Burns, K. Hoagwood, & M. English (Eds.), *Community-based interventions for youth with serious emotional disorders.* Cary, NC: Oxford University Press.

Greenberg, M. T., Domitrovich, C., & Bumbarger, B. (1999). *Preventing mental disorders in school-age children: A review of the effectiveness of prevention programs.* State College: Prevention Research Center for the Promotion of Human Development, College of Health and Human Development, Pennsylvania State University.

Greenwood, P. W. (1999). *Costs and benefits of early childhood intervention.* (OJJDP Fact Sheet 94.) Washington, DC: U.S. Department of Justice, Office of Justice Programs.

Grossman, D. C., Neckerman, H. J., Capsule, T. D., Liu, P. Y., Asher, K. N., Beland, K., Frey, K., & Rivera, F. P. (1997). Effectiveness of a violence prevention curriculum among children in elementary school: A randomized controlled trial. *Journal of the American Medical Association, 277*(20), 1605–1611.

Hawkins, J. D., Catalano, R. F., Kosterman, R., Abbott, R., & Hill, K. G. (1999). Preventing adolescent health-risk behaviors by strengthening protection during childhood. *Archives of Pediatrics & Adolescent Medicine, 153,* 226–234.

Henggeler, S. W. (1998). Multisystemic therapy. In D. S. Elliott (Ed.), *Blueprints for violence prevention.* Boulder, CO: Center for the Study and Prevention of Violence.

Henggeler, S. W., Melton, G. B., & Smith, L. A. (1992). Family preservation using multisystemic therapy: An effective alternative to incarcerating serious juvenile offenders. *Journal of Consulting and Clinical Psychology, 60,* 953–961.

Hunt, T. (Ed.). (1999). *Status of Oregon's children—Special focus: Early childhood.* Available from Children First for Oregon, 523 S. E. Stark Street, Portland, OR 97214–1127.

Kauffman, J. M. (1999). How we prevent the prevention of emotional and behavioral disorders. *Exceptional Children, 65*(4), 448–468.

Kazdin, A. (1987). *Conduct disorders in childhood and adolescence.* London: Sage.

Kingery, P. (2000). *Effective violence prevention programs.* Washington, DC: Hamilton Fish National Institute on School and Community Violence, George Washington University.

Loeber, R., & Farrington, D. P. (Eds.). (1998). *Serious and violent juvenile offenders: Risk factors and successful interventions.* Thousand Oaks, CA: Sage.

Moffitt, T. (1994). Adolescence-limited and life-course-persistent antisocial behavior: A developmental taxonomy. *Psychological Review, 100*(4), 674–701.

Olds, D., Hill, P., & Rumsey, E. (1998). *Prenatal and early childhood nurse home visitation* (Juvenile Justice Bulletin NCJ172875). Washington, DC: U.S. Department of Justice, Office of Juvenile Justice & Delinquency Prevention.

Osofsky, J. D. (Ed.). (1997). *Children in a violent society.* New York: Guilford.

Patterson, G. R., Reid, J. B., & Dishion, T. J. (1992). *Antisocial boys.* Eugene, OR: Castalia.

Reid, J. (1993). Prevention of conduct disorder before and after school entry: Relating interventions to developmental findings. *Development and Psychopathology, 5*(1/2), 243–262.

Reid, J. B., & Eddy, J. M. (1997). The prevention of antisocial behavior: Some considerations in the search for effective interventions. In D. M. Stoff, J. Breiling, & J. D. Maser (Eds.), *The handbook of antisocial behavior* (pp. 343–356). New York: Wiley.

Schoenwald, S., Brown, T., & Henggeler, S. W. (2000). Inside Multisystemic Therapy: Therapist, supervisory, and program practices. *Journal of Emotional and Behavioral Disorders, 8*(2), 113–127.

Steinberg, L. (1996). *Why school reform has failed and what parents need to do.* New York: Simon & Schuster.

Walker, H. M., Horner, R. H., Sugai, G., Bullis, M., Sprague, J. R., Bricker, D., & Kaufman, M. J. (1996). Integrated approaches to preventing antisocial behavior patterns among school-age children and youth. *Journal of Emotional and Behavioral Disorders, 4,* 193–256.

Walker, H. M., Kavanagh, K., Stiller, B., Golly, A., Severson, H. H., & Feil, E., (1998). First Step to Success: An early intervention approach for preventing school antisocial behavior. *Journal of Emotional and Behavioral Disorders, 6*(2), 66–80.

Zigler, E., Taussig, C., & Black, K. (1992). Early childhood intervention: A promising preventative for juvenile delinquency. *American Psychologist, 47*(8), 997–1006.

APPENDIX

Recommended Resources on Preventing Antisocial Behavior and Delinquency

Books

Walker, H. M., Colvin, G., & Ramsey, E. (1995). *Antisocial behavior in schools: Strategies and best practices.* Pacific Grove, CA: Brooks/Cole.

Walker, H. M., & Epstein, M. (Eds.). (2000). *Making schools safer and violence free.* Austin, TX: Pro-Ed.

Chapters

Gottfredson, D. C. (1997). School-based crime prevention. In L. Sherman, D. Gottfredson, D. Mackenzie, J. Eck, P. Reuter, & S. Bushway (Eds.), *Preventing crime: What works, what doesn't, what's promising* (pp. 5-1–5-74). College Park, MD: Department of Criminology and Criminal Justice.

Journal Articles

Barnett, W. S. (1993). Economic evaluation of home visiting programs. *The Future of Children, 3*(3), 93–112.

Barnett, W. S. (1988). The economics of early intervention under P.L. 99-457. *Topics in Early Childhood Special Education, 8*(1), 12–23.

Barnett, W. S. (1986). Methodological issues in economic evaluation of early intervention programs. *Early Childhood Research Quarterly, 1*(3), 249–268.

Barnett, W. S. (1985). *The Perry Preschool program and its long-term effects: A benefit–cost analysis.* High/Scope Early Childhood Policy Papers (No. 2). Ypsilanti, MI: High/Scope.

Constantino, J. N. (1992). On the prevention of conduct disorder: A rationale for initiating preventive efforts in infancy. *Infants and Young Children, 5*(2), 29–41.

Embry, D. D., Flannery, D., Vazsonyi, A., Powell, K., & Atha, H. (1996). Peacebuilders: A theoretically driven, school-based model for early violence prevention. *American Journal of Preventive Medicine, 12,* 91–100.

Furlong, M. J., & Morrison, G. M. (Eds.). (1994). School violence and safety in perspective (9-article miniseries). *School Psychology Review, 23*(2), 139–261.

Greenberg, M. T., Kusche, C. A., Cook, E. T., & Quamma, J. P. (1995). Promoting emotional competence in school-aged children: The effects of the PATHS curriculum. *Development and Psychopathology, 7,* 117–136.

Greenwood, P. W. (1999). Prevention: The cost effectiveness of early intervention as a strategy for reducing violent crime. In E. L. Rubin (Ed.), *Minimizing harm: A new crime policy for modern America* (pp. 67–89). Boulder, CO: Westview.

Hughes, J., & Hasbrouck, J. (1996). Television violence: Implications for violence prevention. *School Psychology Review, 25*(2), 134–151.

Maguin, E., & Loeber, R. (1996). Academic performance and delinquency. In M. Tonry (Ed.), *Crime and Justice: A Review of Research, 20,* 145–264.

Patterson, G. R., Crosby, L., & Vuchinich, S. (1992). Predicting risk for early police arrest. *Journal of Quantitative Criminology, 8*(4), 335–355.

Sprague, J. R., & Walker, H. M. (2000). Early identification and treatment of antisocial and violent youth. In R. Skiba & R. L. Peterson (Eds.), *Building safe and responsive schools: Perspectives on school discipline and school violence* [Special issue]. *Exceptional Children, 66*(3), 367–379.

Walker, H. M., Forness, S. R., Kauffman, J. M., Epstein, M. H., Gresham, F. M., Nelson, C. M., & Strain, P. S. (1998). Macro-social validation: Referencing outcomes in behavioral disorders to societal issues and problems. *Behavioral Disorders, 24*(1), 7–18.

Walker, H. M., & Gresham, F. M. (1997). Making schools safer and violence free. *Intervention in School and Clinic, 32*(4), 199–204.

Walker, H. M., Irvin, L. K., & Sprague, J. R. (1997, Fall). Violence prevention and school safety: Issues, problems, approaches, and recommended solutions. *OSSC Bulletin, 41*(1). Eugene: Oregon School Study Council, College of Education, University of Oregon.

Walker, H. M., Kavanagh, K., Stiller, B., Golly, A., Severson, H. H., & Feil, E. G. (1998). First Step to Success: An early intervention approach for preventing school antisocial behavior. *Journal of Emotional and Behavioral Disorders, 6*(2), 66–80.

Walker, H. M., & Sprague, J. R. (1999). The path to school failure, delinquency and violence: Causal factors and some potential solutions. *Intervention in School and Clinic, 35*(2), 67–73.

Walker, H. M., & Sylwester, R. (1998). Reducing students' refusal and resistance. *Teaching Exceptional Children, 30*(6), 52–58.

Reports

Anderson, B. (1998). *Colorado Even Start: 1997–1998 progress report* (ERIC No. ED428869). Denver: Colorado State Department of Education.

Dwyer, K., Osher, D., & Warger, C. (1998). *Early warning, timely response: A guide to safe schools.* Washington, DC: U.S. Department of Education.

Greenwood, P. W., Model, K. E., Rydell, C. P., & Chiesa, J. (1996). *Diverting children from a life of crime.* Santa Monica, CA: RAND.

Reid, J. B., Eddy, J. M., Fetrow, R. A., & Stoolmiller, M. (1998). *A prevention program to decrease youth violence and delinquency: Linking the Interests of Families and Teachers (LIFT).* Eugene: Oregon Social Learning Center.

12 Proactive and Preventative Assessment, Intervention Selection, and Progress Monitoring Practices for Students With or At Risk for ADHD

RUTH A. ERVIN
Western Michigan University

KEVIN M. JONES
Eastern Illinois University

PAMELA M. RADFORD

MARGARITA GINGERICH
Western Michigan University

Introduction

Attention deficit hyperactivity disorder (ADHD; American Psychiatric Association, 1994) is recognized as a disorder characterized by pervasive problems with sustained attention, impulsivity, and overactivity. This diagnosis is fairly common, affecting approximately 3% to 5% of school-aged children. Typically, children are identified with this disorder upon entrance to or within the first few years of entering the school system (Safer, Zito, & Fine, 1996). According to the U.S. Census Bureau (1998), 1.4 to 2.3 million students are diagnosed with ADHD, and this number is increasing (Safer & Zito, 2000; Safer et al., 1996).

The characteristic pattern of deficits in behavioral control and self-regulation that is the hallmark of ADHD often leads to difficulties in school. Within the classroom, students generally are expected to respond to the teacher's verbal instructions and not to competing stimuli (e.g., a noise in the hallway) and/or contingencies for inappropriate behavior (e.g., talking to a peer or calling out). For children with ADHD whose problem behaviors have sometimes been conceptualized in terms of poor stimulus control and deficient rule-governed behavior (Barkley, 1989), compliance to teacher instructions and general classroom rules is an arduous task. Although not all children diagnosed with ADHD exhibit significant problems in school, it is more likely that they do. When problems persist, children with ADHD are at significant risk for academic failure and limited educational attainment (Barkley, 1998; DuPaul & Stoner, 1994).

Children and adolescents who receive a diagnosis of ADHD are more likely than are students without a diagnosis to exhibit noncompliant and defiant behaviors in schools. It has been well documented that up to 40% of children and 65% of adolescents with ADHD develop sufficient levels of noncompliance, oppositional behavior, or defiance to meet full diagnostic criteria for oppositional defiant disorder (ODD; American Psychiatric Association, 1994) (Barkley, DuPaul, & McMurray, 1990; Barkley, Fischer, Edelbrock, & Smallish, 1990). For children with ADHD and ODD, negative long-term outcomes are even more probable (Barkley et al., 1990). A substantial literature base supports the linkage between ODD and later development of conduct disorder (CD; American Psychiatric Association, 1994) and antisocial behavior (Patterson, Reid, & Dishion, 1992). Thus, it is not surprising that approximately 20% to 30% of children and between 40% to 60% of adolescents with ADHD will exhibit sufficient signs of antisocial behavior to receive a diagnosis of CD (Barkley et al., 1990). Research indicates the development of CD in children with ADHD can be attributed to the ODD seen in childhood (Barkley, 1998). Recurring academic failure and rejection by parents, teachers, and normal peers often lead children with ODD to associate with a deviant peer group, which increases the probability of later delinquency, truancy, and substance abuse (Patterson et al., 1992). For those who develop CD, longitudinal studies have indicated that antisocial children have trouble staying employed as adults, tend to be downwardly mobile, lack social skills, and are at risk for being arrested (Patterson et al., 1992; see also chapter 13 by Gresham, Lane, & Lambros, this text).

Recent research has demonstrated the critical need for early intervention if the progression from mild (noncompliance) to more serious forms of antisocial behavior (aggression) is to be curtailed. Unfortunately, "persistent and pervasive patterns of antisocial behavior are likely if proactive, early prevention and intervention strategies, and comprehensive intervention approaches are not implemented" (Sprague, Sugai, & Walker, 1998, p. 471). Because the presence of defiant or noncompliant behaviors in children with ADHD negatively impacts later life outcomes, the development of proactive and preventative classroom intervention strategies is an essential treatment consideration.

School-Based Interventions for Students with ADHD

Preventative and efficacious intervention services are warranted for those children who, because of deficiencies associated with the symptoms of ADHD, are at risk of school failure and increased potential for the development of more severe behavior problems. Effective interventions are those interventions that are not specific to the diagnosis, per se, but to the individual needs of the child (DuPaul, Eckert, & McGooey, 1997; DuPaul & Ervin, 1996). More specifically, effective interventions are developed through careful assessments that are functional in nature and lead to the selection of intervention strategies that are proactive and closely monitored for their success. Unfortunately, current practice does not always mirror empirically derived best practices, and this also is true for intervention services for students with ADHD.

Educational assessment and intervention services employed for students with ADHD typically include traditional special education, pharmacological interventions (e.g., methylphenidate), and/or behavioral interventions (e.g., time-out) (Reid, Maag, Vasa, & Wright, 1994). In the following sections, we will describe the current status of school-based service delivery practices for students with ADHD, highlighting the need for a more proactive and preventative model. Next, we will present an alternative model.

Current Practices

Researchers have pointed to a general lack of information regarding "the type of services students with ADHD are receiving, the extent to which these students are identified under existing handicapping categories, and the type of placement or educational treatments they receive" (Reid, Maag, & Vasa, 1994, p. 118). In part, this is due to the fact that children with ADHD are a heterogeneous population in need of an individualized approach to treatment (DuPaul & Ervin, 1996; DuPaul et al., 1997).

According to the 1999 Rules and Regulations regarding the 1997 amendments to the Individuals with Disabilities Act (IDEA), students with ADHD *may* qualify for special education services under existing categories. Alternatively, these students *may* qualify for services through the requirements of section 504 of the Rehabilitation Act of 1973 (Section 504) and its implementing regulation in 34 CFR Part 104. It is important to note, however, that "no child is eligible for services under the Act merely because the child is identified as being in a particular disability category. Children identified as ADD/ADHD are no different, and are eligible for services only if they meet the criteria of one of the disability categories, and because of their impairment, need special education and related services" (*Federal Register*, 1999, Part II, p. 12543). A student is eligible for services under IDEA or Section 504 solely on the fact their disability results in an educational impairment that entitles them to those services and not on the basis of the diagnosis alone. Despite over a decade of debating the merit of including ADHD as a separate disability category, the 1997 amendments to IDEA upheld the position that children with ADHD, like other children, are eligible for special education services only under existing categories. For example, students with ADHD qualify under the category of "other health impairment" (OHI) when the presence of ADHD adversely affects academic performance.

Studies indicate that students with ADHD are referred for special education at high rates, with 50% (range, 44.8%–66.8%) eligible and receiving special education services (e.g., Bohline, 1985; Sandoval & Lambert, 1984–85). In one survey, Reid and colleagues (1994) obtained specific demographic information and examined the presence of other disabilities, type of placements and related services, academic achievement, and interventions employed for students with ADHD. Reid et al. (1994) reported that in one school district serving 14,229 students, 136 students were clinically diagnosed with ADHD, and 57% ($n = 77$) of those diagnosed were receiving special education services. When students who were not identified under IDEA were considered, the vast majority of students with ADHD spent most if not all of their time in general education classrooms. These statistics mirror the current practices of inclusion in which over 80% of students served through IDEA spend time in general education settings (U.S. Department of Education, 1990). Thus, general education teachers must know how to assist the needs of students with ADHD effectively in inclusive settings. Unfortunately, teachers reported they lacked the knowledge and skills to do so (Reid et al., 1994).

When approaches to interventions were considered, 90% of students with ADHD (including 47% who were not receiving special education services through IDEA) were medicated (Reid et al., 1994). Of those medicated, 94.3% received at least one dosage at school, yet, according to reports from school nurses, in 50.9% of these cases there was no physician contact regarding monitoring. These findings are not surprising given recently reported findings from regional and national databases that indicate "on average, there has been a 2.5-fold increase in the prevalence of methylphenidate treatment of youth with ADD between 1990 and 1995" and, "in all, approximately 2.8% (or 1.5 million) of U.S. youths aged 5 to 18 were receiving this medication in mid-1995" (Safer et al., 1996, p. 1084).

According to the empirical literature, both pharmacological (e.g., stimulant medication) and behavioral interventions (e.g., contingency management, token reinforcement, response cost, etc.) have been found to reduce symptoms of ADHD while enhancing behavior control and academic performance for a majority of children (Barkley, 1998; DuPaul & Eckert, 1997; MTA Cooperative Group, 1999a). However, *individual differences* in response to various treatments and/or their combinations or potencies have been noted (Whalen & Henker, 1991). Furthermore, the degree to which comorbid disorders/disabilities are present may impact the success of interventions and warrant multimodal approaches to treatment (Barkley, 1998). In these cases, the need for classroom intervention is markedly increased. According to a recent, large-scale, 14-month, comparative study conducted by a national consortium of researchers, "medication management, alone or combined with intensive behavioral treatment, was superior to behavioral treatment and community care in reducing ADHD symptoms; but only combined treatment showed consistently greater benefit than community care across other outcome domains (disruptive and internalizing symptoms, achievement, parent-child relations, and social skills)" (MTA Cooperative Group, 1999b, p. 1088). According to the MTA Cooperative Group (1999b), "conclusions suggest the relative strength of medication-based interventions across 14 months of treatment for ADHD-related symptoms and the modest superiority of combined treatment for both oppositional/aggressive symptoms and specific functional domains" (p. 1096).

Problems with Existing Practices and Rationale for an Alternative Model

Given the heterogeneity of children with ADHD and the range of school-based treatment options (e.g., special education placement; pharmacological intervention; behavioral interventions), school personnel must determine which techniques or combinations of techniques would work best for a specific student with ADHD (DuPaul & Eckert, 1997; DuPaul et al., 1997; DuPaul & Ervin, 1996). Several researchers (e.g., DuPaul et al., 1997; DuPaul & Ervin, 1996; Kratochwill & McGivern, 1996; Zentall & Javorsky, 1995) have pointed to a need for a more individualized approach to treatment selection for students with ADHD, such as functional assessment. Essentially, functional assessment is a structured problem-solving process through which a broad range of information is gathered to identify environmental variables related to a target behavior (O'Neill et al., 1997). Information obtained through a functional assessment is examined to develop hypotheses regarding behavior function and treatment (e.g., Dunlap & Kern, 1996; O'Neill et al., 1997; Vollmer & Northup, 1996). Traditionally, functional assessment has focused on the manipulation of consequences or antecedent variables in analog conditions (i.e., Iwata, Dorsey, Slifer, Bauman, & Richman, 1982/1994) for the primary purpose of determining the function of behavior problems (i.e., self-injurious behavior or aggression) exhibited by persons with developmental disabilities. More recently, these procedures have been adapted to include manipulations of instructional variables (e.g., Dunlap, et al. 1993) for the primary purpose of intervention selection (e.g., Dunlap et al., 1993; Kern, Childs, Dunlap, Clarke, & Falk, 1994). Several recent studies have demonstrated the role of environmental variables in the maintenance of problem behaviors exhibited by students with ADHD (e.g., Broussard & Northup, 1995; 1997; Ervin, DuPaul, Kern, & Friman, 1998; Lewis & Sugai, 1996; Northup, Broussard, Jones, George, Vollmer, & Herring, 1995). Research has demonstrated that classroom problem behaviors exhibited by children with ADHD are systematically related to a variety of classroom variables. These include but are not limited to peer attention (Broussard & Northup, 1997; Ervin et al., 1998; Lewis & Sugai, 1996; Northup et al., 1995; Umbreit, 1995), teacher attention (Lewis & Sugai, 1996), and escape from academic tasks (Broussard & Northup, 1995; Ervin et al., 1998; Umbreit, 1995). These studies provide promising data regarding the utility of functional assessment as an intervention selection process.

Proactive and Preventative Model for ADHD

A multimodal treatment approach is recommended for students with ADHD (Barkley, 1998; DuPaul & Stoner, 1994). This approach addresses four major domains, including educational accommodations, promoting appropriate behavior, medical management, and ancillary support services for children and parents (e.g., counseling, parental support groups). A wealth of empirical knowledge exists in the field of applied behavior analysis that can be utilized in a proactive and preventative manner to serve students with ADHD. To help students be successful, school personnel need to know how to (a) proactively screen for the early identification of problems that place students at risk for the development of more severe problems associated with ADHD; (b) utilize assessment strategies to match interventions to the needs of individual students, existing curriculum, and classroom ecology; (c) arrange educational environments to provide sufficient learning opportunities and contingencies to support the development of academic, prosocial, and behavioral skills so that students are maintained in inclusive settings; (d) monitor progress and evaluate outcomes so intervention modifications can be made in a timely fashion; (e) implement systemwide models of service delivery within school settings; and, (f) collaborate with families and coordinate services.

To be proactive, we must first identify students with ADHD who are at risk of the development of more severe problems *early* (Sprague et al., 1998). Various screening devices have been supported as valid methods for early identification of students at risk of both internalizing (withdrawn) and externalizing (acting-out) behavior problems (e.g., Walker & Severson, 1992; Walker, Severson, & Feil, 1995). Unfortunately, these screening tools do *not* provide direction for a specific course of intervention. We recommend the use of screening devices to identify at-risk students with ADHD (e.g., Walker & Severson, 1992) who should be recipients of functional assessments and direct intervention (i.e., the model presented here).

The model we will describe in this chapter will focus on the assessment, intervention selection, and progress-monitoring components of the broader, comprehensive service model for students with ADHD described earlier. Although we recognize the importance of early screening, the implementation of a systemwide model, and collaboration across service providers, these topics are beyond the scope of this chapter (see Chapter 1 by O'Shaughnessy, Lane, Gresham, & Beebe-Frankenberger and Chapter 3 by Severson & Walker, this text). Instead, we will present a model focused on linking assessment to intervention that is based on the functional assessment literature but organized in a manner that includes practitioner-friendly language to describe the basic concepts (Friman, 2000).

Conceptual Framework for Matching Assessment to Intervention

Once students are identified (through screening or teacher referral) as being at risk of school failure related to ADHD, it is imperative that school staff address presenting concerns, symptoms, and risk behaviors. School practitioners have an enormous database of intervention strategies from which to choose. Selecting strategies that are likely to work with each student is often a difficult undertaking and requires some basic understanding of how problems develop and persist over time. Before we can begin to discuss how to change existing behaviors, we must first understand how children learn. With a thorough grasp of the principles of learning, we are better equipped to teach alternative behaviors and to structure environments conducive to supporting desirable or "appropriate" behaviors. Although this knowledge base is essential to effective problem solving, it is not sufficient. Translating basic learning principles into effective practice also will require effective communication across various service providers.

According to Bijou (1993), "an individual interacts continuously and endlessly with his or her environment. In other words, behavior affects the environment and the environment affects behavior" (p. 12). Figure 12.1 presents a model for understanding how this person–environment interaction influences learning. This model is *not* new in the behavior analysis literature (e.g., Bijou, Peterson, & Ault,

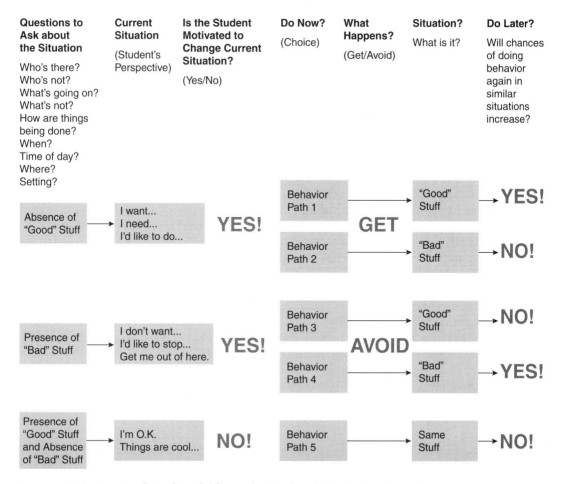

FIGURE 12.1   A nontechnical model for understanding behavior learning paths

1968). Figure 12.1 presents the basic principles of learning and behavior (i.e., reinforcement, punishment, and establishing operations) in a nontechnical manner. It is the basic premise of behavior analysis, and our belief, that all children learn in this manner, including children with disabilities such as ADHD.

The model presents learning paths in a simplified manner to illustrate the scientific "laws" denoting relations between environmental events (x) and behavior (y)—what happens in the environment and what children learn. According to Millenson (1967), "when a functional law exists between x [environmental events] and y [behavior], knowing the value of x we may predict the value of y" (p. 361). According to this model, in any given situation, we need to consider *situational variables*, meaning the "stuff" that exists in the environment (e.g., materials, task, classroom structure, instructional format, social interactions, physical environment, access to tangible items, etc.). In addition, we need to consider *student variables*, meaning all of the possible behaviors that the student is capable of emitting, as well as student preferences, skills, and physiological states (e.g., medication status). Finally, we need to consider how different situations produce motivation to change access to the stuff that is available and how engaging in different behaviors is likely to be associated with different *outcomes*. More specifically, different behaviors will act on the environment in any number of ways, producing various outcomes. Outcomes in this model are defined as changes in access to the stuff (i.e., "good" or "bad") that exists in the environment (Friman, 2000). Some behaviors will change the current situation by *gaining access* to stuff or *losing access* to stuff, whereas other behaviors will not result in any substantial change (i.e., stuff will *remain the same*).

What behavior or set of behaviors a student is likely or unlikely to emit in any given situation is dependent in part on the motivation produced by the current situation and in part on the student's previous history with the connection between different behaviors and their effect on the stuff that exists in the environment (i.e., functional relations). According to basic learning principles, behaviors that lead to access to good stuff (i.e., positive reinforcement) or avoidance of bad stuff (i.e., negative reinforcement) are strengthened (i.e., more likely to occur again in similar situations). In contrast, behaviors that lead to access to bad stuff (i.e., positive punishment) or removal/denial of good stuff (i.e., negative punishment) are weakened (i.e., less likely to occur again). Whether or not stuff is defined as good or bad is dependent on person variables (e.g., likes/dislikes) as well as current levels of access to or restriction from that stuff (i.e., establishing operations) and aspects of the environment that may signal the potential access or removal of stuff when certain behaviors are emitted (i.e., discriminative stimuli).

For example, based on your personal preference, you may agree with the authors that Key lime pie is good stuff. This definition, however, is not just dependent on personal preference but also subject to situational variables. If you have just finished a very large piece of Key lime pie (because you generally consider Key lime pie to be good stuff), for instance, an additional piece of Key lime pie may be aversive and now considered bad stuff. Furthermore, other stuff in the environment may influence how you define what stuff is good or bad. In the Key lime pie example, other factors may include time of day, what else you have eaten and how recently, and the immediacy of a scheduled workout routine. All of these factors would come into play if we were trying to predict or influence whether someone would engage in behaviors likely to lead to access to or avoidance of Key lime pie.

The more information we obtain about a person's preferences, current situation, and previous history with respect to making choices to engage in behaviors that result in access to or avoidance of certain stuff, the better we are able to make predictions about, and subsequently influence, their choices (e.g., to eat or not eat Key lime pie). When educators are informed about why a student with ADHD is engaging in a problem behavior, then they can carefully match intervention strategies to address the reason the problem is occurring in the first place—rather than attempting to implement interventions in a trial-and-error fashion. It is important to note, however, that "scientific laws give an accurate representation of nature only when certain conditions are met . . . but no scientific law is true under all conditions" (Millenson, 1967, p. 361). Our predictions about behavior are not absolute; thus, neither are our controls over what choices are made. We do, however, have a greater likelihood of influencing someone's choices when we have more information about these controlling factors.

When a student with ADHD engages in an inappropriate behavior such as "calling out" in the classroom setting, he or she is more or less likely to be doing so for a variety of reasons or functions. A student may call out because, in the past, calling out has been followed by access to attention from adults or peers, access to a preferred object or activity, or access to sensory stimulation. Alternatively, calling out may have previously resulted in the removal or avoidance of task demands, unpleasant sensory stimulation, or social interaction. If we do not consider why the problem is occurring in the first place, then, depending on the means through which we intervene, we run the risk of inadvertently strengthening inappropriate behaviors.

For example, a student with ADHD might perceive periods in which social interactions with the teacher are infrequent (e.g., independent seatwork) as a state of deprivation from social attention (i.e., absence of good stuff in Figure 12.1). The student in this situation will be motivated to change the existing situation and may learn that calling out will result in teacher attention (i.e., behavior path 1 in Figure 12.1). If calling out is more likely to produce teacher attention than waiting quietly or raising one's hand, then calling out may be more likely to be strengthened. It is important to note, however, that, although behavior is a function of its *previous* connection to access or avoidance of good or bad stuff (e.g., teacher attention), future behavior is a function of the *present* connection and can therefore be altered.

Given this scenario, interventions that are likely to be successful will address the function of the behavior in one of three ways. First, functional interventions *reduce the motivation for the behavior by changing the situation.* In this example, the situation involves a perceived state of deprivation from teacher attention that might be alleviated by adding more frequent or scheduled teacher attention. Second, functional interventions *teach alternative behaviors that result in the same outcome or function.* A student who calls out to gain access to teacher attention might be taught to signal for teacher attention in a more acceptable manner (e.g., raising hand). Third, functional interventions *weaken the connection between the problem behavior* (calling out) *and access to good stuff* (teacher attention). If calling out results in access to teacher attention, then the teacher might be taught to ignore such behavior (i.e., extinction).

When the removal or avoidance of stuff/situations strengthens problem behaviors (avoiding bad stuff, behavior path 4 in Figure 12.1), functional interventions work in much the same way. For example, a student with ADHD who has difficulty with phonics may be motivated to escape or avoid choral reading activities. If the student learns that calling out results in a period of removal from class activities (e.g., teacher sends student to the time-out chair), then calling out may inadvertently be strengthened because it results in removal of the task (behavior path 4 in Figure 12.1). A teacher who gathers information to understand the behavior path prior to selecting an intervention would be in a better position to develop a functional intervention strategy. A functional intervention for an escape/avoidance motivated behavior would include methods for *altering the stuff from which the student is motivated to escape/avoid*. In this example, the teacher might reduce the difficulty of reading material and/or change the instructional demands to make the task less aversive. In addition, a second intervention approach would be to place an emphasis on *teaching the student a more acceptable means of avoiding the aversive situation* such as asking for help or requesting brief breaks from reading and/or working on improving phonics skills. Finally, a functional intervention would work to *weaken the connection between the problem behavior* (calling out) *and escape /avoidance of the task*. In this example, the teacher would *not* send the student to time-out for calling out, and, instead, the student might earn brief breaks for periods of task engagement.

Procedural Guidelines for Matching Assessment to Intervention

Understanding basic learning principles is a first step to establishing a more proactive and preventative intervention model for students with ADHD. It also is important for school personnel to utilize sound methods for gathering information to make *informed* (i.e., evidence-based) choices based on basic learning principles. A technology for conducting functional assessments has been developed that includes a list of steps to guide the process (e.g., Dunlap & Kern, 1996). The major components of the model include problem identification, problem analysis, intervention design, and intervention evaluation progress monitoring/follow-up.

Problem Identification.   For students with ADHD who may exhibit a variety of problem behaviors in the classroom, it is important to start the problem-solving process by defining the problem, validating its existence, and establishing a tentative behavioral goal. Because behaviors serve different functions and there may be more than one problem behavior of concern, it is important to know which behaviors (appropriate and inappropriate classroom deportment; academic performance; social interactions) will be targeted for intervention. Furthermore, to be accountable, evidence should be gathered to confirm the existence of target behaviors (i.e., validate referral concern). Behaviors must be prioritized and clearly defined. Problems should be defined in objective, observable, and measurable terms to ensure that careful documentation of their occurrence and nonoccurrence is possible. For example, rather than defining a problem as "defiance," the problem definition should include a description of specific overt behaviors that constitute what defiance "looks" like (e.g., talking back; throwing objects; failure to begin a task within 5 seconds of a request). Whether the problem is academic, social, or a matter of classroom deportment, problem definition is a critical component in this process.

Part of problem identification includes careful assessment of "how much" behavior is occurring in relation to various environmental events. In order for a behavior to be quantified, it is important to think in terms of frequency, latency, duration, and magnitude. There are many ways to measure behaviors (appropriate and inappropriate) to determine when they are likely and unlikely to occur and to what degree (frequency, magnitude, etc.). There also are many practical constraints to doing so in applied settings. We recommend practitioners and applied researchers consider a variety of measurement techniques and select one based on its precision, objectivity, practicality, and social validity (for a practical guide, see Poling, Methot, & LeSage, 1995).

Problem Analysis.   Once a problem behavior has been identified and clearly defined, it is important to gather information from various sources (e.g., teacher; parent; student; administrator; observer) through a variety of assessment tools (e.g., direct observation; anecdotal reports; rating scales; semistructured interviews; record reviews) in an attempt to understand why the problem behavior persists. Throughout this information-gathering process, the objective is to identify patterns of relations between behaviors and environmental events (behavior paths from Figure 12.1). This process should emphasize the collection of *empirical evidence* regarding these relations and the environmental conditions in which these relations hold true. For example, we are interested in evidence that suggests a functional relation (link) between disruptive behavior and access to teacher attention, but we also are concerned with the conditions under which this relation is robust such as activities in which teacher attention is low (e.g., independent seatwork; teacher helping another student).

In this process of collecting and identifying patterns of relations between problem behavior and environmental events, it is important to gather information to rule out the influence of variables that may not be under the school's control. Although we recommend that school-based interventions focus on events that we can change (e.g., instructional accommodations, teaching strategies, materials, and feedback), we recognize the fact that outside factors (e.g., medical conditions and stressful life events) may play a role in the development and maintenance of problem behaviors. Thus, when working with a student with ADHD, it is important to address the potential role of outside factors through the involvement of persons able to provide relevant information (e.g., parents/legal guardians; physicians; outside agencies). More specifically, when a medical condition is thought to play a role (e.g., allergies; illness), school personnel will need to consult with medical professionals to obtain evidence regarding the relation between the medical condition and the occurrence of problem behaviors. Similarly, when extraordinary life events are suspected to play a role (e.g., death in the family; divorce), it is important to obtain evidence regarding the relation between these events and problem behavior. Finally, if a skill deficit is suspected (e.g., poor reading fluency), then it is important to obtain evidence to support or refute its relation to the occurrence of problem behaviors.

During the problem analysis stage, efforts are focused on gathering evidence (through data collection) to measure directly relations between problem behavior and situations or events. Asking questions such as when, where, with whom, and during which activities problem behaviors are likely and unlikely to occur can guide this process. A critical feature of this stage in problem solving is the need to have *evidence* in the form of *objective data* to confirm or disconfirm the relations that exist between problem behaviors and environmental events. For example, during an interview, the student's teacher may report disruptive behaviors occur more frequently in the afternoon, during independent seatwork. If direct observations also indicate this to be true, then we have two pieces of evidence to suggest this relation. Although we recognize our limitations in determining these relations in an absolute manner, we can select methods of assessment that are likely to provide reliable and valid evidence. When a variety of sources suggest the same relation and when we can assume greater objectivity of the source, we are better equipped to make informed hypotheses about functional relations and, subsequently, better able to select effective educational accommodations/interventions that address these functional relations.

Intervention Design.   When evidence collected during problem analysis suggests that outside factors (e.g., medication conditions; stressful life events) play a significant functional role in the maintenance of problem behaviors, it is important to make appropriate referrals to and collaborate with agencies that can directly address those issues (e.g., pediatricians; community mental health agencies). If during problem analysis sufficient evidence suggests a functional relation between problem behavior and environmental events that are directly under the control of school personnel, efforts can turn toward the selection of an intervention strategy. Proactive and functional interventions will directly address the behavior path by (a) reducing the motivation for the behavior by addressing the context/situations in which the behavior is likely to occur, (b) teaching an alternative behavior that is acceptable and serves the same purpose, and (c) weakening the functional relation between problem behavior and maintaining environmental events (disconnecting the existing behavior path). Working from this model and these three strategies for addressing function, many specific intervention tactics might be used (for examples of specific intervention tactics, see Reid, 1999). School staff should involve key stakeholders (parents, students, teachers, and administrators) when selecting specific interventions. Careful consideration should be given to how the intervention addresses functional relations, as well as to practical constraints, individual preference, and social validity.

Intervention Evaluation and Progress Monitoring/Follow-up. Once appropriate interventions have been identified, it is important to ensure they are implemented as planned (Witt, 1997). This is true regardless of whether the intervention will address outside factors and involve external agencies or will be restricted to classroom interventions conducted by school personnel. School staff, parents, and other service providers should develop a comprehensive and concise behavior support plan with specific goals, objectives, activities, roles and responsibilities, and methods of evaluation. When medication is part of the intervention package, monitoring its effects on target behavior(s) in the school setting is imperative. Furthermore, the school team should determine the adequacy of existing resources and the need for additional resources in plan development. Finally, time lines for implementing objectives and achieving desired goals should be specified. At follow-up, the school team should review the plan, consider evaluation data, and revise the plan as needed. Continuous monitoring and evaluation of the plan is essential. As with other phases of the model, evidence should be gathered to determine whether plans are effective (i.e., change behavior in the direction of the goal), practical (i.e., relatively easy to implement with integrity), and acceptable. To ensure that the intervention was responsible for the observed change in behavior, it is important to compare "how much" problem behavior occurred during the intervention relative to when the intervention was not in place. Poling et al. (1995) provide practical descriptions of various experimental designs (e.g., withdrawal; multiple baseline) that can be employed to make these comparisons.

REFERENCES

American Psychiatric Association. (1994). Diagnostic and statistical manual of mental disorders (4th ed.). Washington, DC: Author.

Barkley, R. A. (1998). *Attention-deficit hyperactivity disorder: A handbook for diagnosis and treatment* (2nd ed.). New York: Guilford.

Barkley, R. A. (1989). The problem of stimulus control and rule-governed behavior in attention deficit disorder with hyperactivity. In L. M. Bloomingdale & J. M. Swanson (Eds.), *Attention deficit disorder: Volume IV. Current concepts and immerging trends in attentional and behavioral disorders of childhood.* Oxford: Pergamon.

Barkley, R. A., DuPaul, G. J., & McMurray, M. B. (1990). Comprehensive evaluation of attention deficit disorder with and without hyperactivity as defined by research criteria. *Journal of Consulting and Clinical Psychology, 58,* 775–789.

Barkley, R. A., Fischer, M., Edelbrock, C. S., & Smallish, L. (1990). The adolescent outcome of hyperactive children diagnosed by research criteria: I. An 8-year prospective follow-up study. *Journal of the American Academy of Child and Adolescent Psychiatry, 29,* 546–557.

Bijou, S. W. (1993). *Behavior analysis of child development* (rev. ed.). Reno, NV: Context.

Bijou, S. W., Peterson, R. F., & Ault, M. H. (1968). A method to integrate descriptive and experimental field studies at the level of data and empirical concepts. *Journal of Applied Behavior Analysis, 1,* 175–191.

Bohline, D. S. (1985). Intellectual and affective characteristics of attention deficit disordered children. *Journal of Learning Disabilities, 18,* 604–608.

Broussard, C. D., & Northup, J. (1995). An approach to functional assessment and analysis of disruptive behavior in regular education classrooms. *School Psychology Quarterly, 10,* 151–164.

Broussard, C. D., & Northup, J. (1997). The use of functional analysis to develop peer interventions for disruptive behavior. *School Psychology Quarterly, 12,* 65–76.

Dunlap, G., & Kern, L. (1996). Modifying instructional activities to promote desirable behaviors: A conceptual and practical framework. *School Psychology Quarterly, 11,* 297–312.

Dunlap, G., Kern, L., deParzel, M., Clarke. S., Wilson, D., Childs, K. E., White, R., & Falk, G. D. (1993). Functional analysis of classroom variables for students with emotional and behavioral disorders. *Behavioral Disorders, 18*, 275–291.

DuPaul, G. J., & Eckert, T. L. (1997). The effects of school-based interventions for attention deficit hyperactivity disorder: A meta-analysis. *School Psychology Review, 26*, 5–27.

DuPaul, G. J., Eckert, T. L., & McGooey, K. E. (1997). Interventions for students with attention-deficit/hyperactivity disorder: One size does not fit all. *School Psychology Review, 26*, 369–381.

DuPaul, G. J., & Ervin, R. A. (1996). Functional assessment of behaviors related to attention-deficit/hyperactivity disorder: Linking assessment to intervention design. *Behavior Therapy, 27*, 601–622.

DuPaul, G. & Stoner, G. (1994). *ADHD in the schools: Assessment and practice.* New York: Guilford.

Ervin, R. A., DuPaul, G. J., Kern, L., & Friman, P. C. (1998). Classroom-based functional and adjunctive assessments: Proactive approaches to intervention selection for adolescents with attention-deficit/hyperactivity disorder. *Journal of Applied Behavior Analysis, 31*, 65–78.

Friman, P. C. (2000, June). *Developmental learning and behavioral issues for students with ADHD.* Paper presented at the 2000 ADHD Summer Institute in Kalamazoo, MI.

Iwata, B., Dorsey, M., Slifer, K., Bauman, K., & Richman, G. (1994). Toward a functional analysis of self-injury. *Journal of Applied Behavior Analysis, 27*, 197–209. (Reprinted from *Analysis and Intervention in Developmental Disabilities, 2*, 3–20, 1982.)

Kern, L., Childs, K. E., Dunlap, G., Clarke, S., & Falk, G. D. (1994). Using assessment-based curricular intervention to improve the classroom behaviors of a student with emotional and behavioral challenges. *Journal of Applied Behavior Analysis, 27*, 7–19.

Kratochwill, T. R., & McGivern, J. E. (1996). Clinical diagnosis, behavioral assessment, and functional analysis: Examining the connection between assessment and intervention. *School Psychology Review, 25*, 342–355.

Lewis, T. J., & Sugai, G. (1996). Functional assessment of problem behavior: A pilot investigation of the comparative and interactive effects of teacher and peer social attention on students in general education settings. *School Psychology Quarterly, 11*, 1–19.

Millenson, J. R. (1967). *Principles of behavior analysis.* New York: Macmillan.

MTA Cooperative Group. (1999b). Moderators and mediators of treatment response for children with attention-deficit/hyperactivity disorder: The multimodal treatment study of children with attention-deficit/hyperactivity disorder. *Archives of General Psychiatry, 56*, 1088–1096.

Northup, J., Broussard, C. D., Jones, K., George, T., Vollmer, T. R., & Herring, M. (1995). The differential effects of teacher and peer attention on the disruptive classroom behavior of three children with a diagnosis of attention deficit hyperactivity disorder. *Journal of Applied Behavior Analysis, 28*, 227–228.

O'Neill, R. E., Horner, R. H., Albin, R. W., Sprague, J. R., Storey, K., & Newton, J. S. (1997). *Functional assessment and program development for problem behavior: A practical handbook* (2nd ed.). Pacific Grove, CA: Brooks/Cole.

Patterson, G. R., Reid, J. B., & Dishion, T. J. (1992). *Antisocial boys.* Eugene, OR: Castalia.

Poling, A., Methot, L. L., & LeSage, M. G. (1995). *Fundamentals of behavior analytic research.* New York: Plenum.

Reid, R. (1999, December). Attention deficit hyperactivity disorder: Effective methods for the classroom. *Focus on Exceptional Children, 32*, 1–20.

Reid, R., Maag, J. W., & Vasa, S. F. (1994). Attention deficit hyperactivity disorder as a disability category: A critique. *Exceptional Children, 60*, 198–214.

Reid, R., Maag, J. W., Vasa, S. F., & Wright, G. (1994). Who are the children with attention deficit-hyperactivity disorder? A school-based survey. *Journal of Special Education, 28*, 117–137.

Safer, D., & Zito, J. M. (2000). Pharmacoepidemiology of methylphenidate and other stimulants for the treatment of attention deficit hyperactivity disorder. In L. L. Greenhill & B. B. Osman (Eds.), *Ritalin theory and practice* (pp. 7–26). New York: Liebert.

Safer, D. J., Zito, J. M., & Fine, E. M. (1996). Increased methylphenidate usage for attention deficit disorder in the 1990's. *Pediatrics, 98*, 1084–1088.

Sandoval, J., & Lambert, N. M. (1984–85). Hyperactive and learning disabled children: Who gets help? *Journal of Special Education, 18*, 495–503.

Sprague, J., Sugai, G., & Walker, H. (1998). Antisocial behavior in schools. In T. S. Watson & F. M.

Gresham (Eds.), *Handbook of child behavior therapy* (pp. 451–474). New York: Plenum.

MTA Cooperative Group. (1999a). A 14-month randomized clinical trial of treatment strategies for attention-deficit/hyperactivity disorder. *Archives of General Psychiatry, 56,* 1073–1086.

Umbreit, J. (1995). Functional assessment and intervention in a regular classroom setting for the disruptive behavior of a student with attention deficit hyperactivity disorder. *Behavioral Disorders, 20,* 267–278.

U.S. Census Bureau. (1998). *School enrollment—Social and economic characteristics of students: October 1996 (Update).* Washington, DC: U.S. Government Printing Office.

U.S. Department of Education. (1990). *To assure the free and appropriate public education of all handicapped children: Twelfth annual report to Congress on the implementation of the Education of the Handicapped Act.* Washington, DC: U.S. Government Printing Office.

Vollmer, T. R., & Northup, J. (1996). Some implications of functional analysis for school psychology. *School Psychology Quarterly, 11,* 76–92.

Walker, H. M., & Severson, H. H. (1992). *Systematic Screening for Behavior Disorders (SSBD): User's guide and administration manual.* Longmont, CO: Sopris West.

Walker, H. M., & Severson, H. H., & Feil, E. G. (1995). *The Early Screening Project: A proven child-find process.* Longmont, CO: Sopris West.

Whalen, C. K., & Henker, B. (1991). Therapies for hyperactive children: Comparisons, combinations, and compromises. *Journal of Consulting and Clinical Psychology, 59,* 126–137.

Witt, J. C. (1997). Talk is not cheap. *School Psychology Quarterly, 12,* 281–292.

Zentall, S. S., & Javorsky, J. (1995). Functional and clinical assessment of ADHD: Implications of DSM-IV in the schools. *Journal of Psychoeducational Assessment* (Monograph Series: Special ADHD Issue), 22–41.

Author Note

The authors would like to acknowledge and thank Patrick C. Friman, Ph.D., for his contribution to this chapter. In particular, Dr. Friman is credited with inspiring the first two authors to espouse a nontechnical approach to explaining basic principles of behavior analysis in an effort to enhance the lives of the children, parents, and teachers with whom they work. Manuscript preparation was partially supported by the United States Department of Education Grant (Award Number H023N80017). Correspondence regarding this manuscript should be addressed to Ruth A. Ervin, Ph.D., School Psychology Program, Department of Psychology, Western Michigan University, Kalamazoo, MI 49008-5195; e-mail: Ruth.Ervin@wmich.edu.

13 Children with Conduct and Hyperactivity-Impulsivity-Attention Problems

Identification, Assessment, and Intervention

FRANK M. GRESHAM
University of California–Riverside

KATHLEEN L. LANE
Peabody College of Vanderbilt University

KATINA M. LAMBROS
University of California–Riverside

Introduction

The rising rate of violent crimes committed by children and adolescents in the United States is alarming. The prevalence of antisocial behavior among preschoolers ranges from 4% to 9%. Six percent to 12% of school-age children display aggressive or antisocial acts; however behavior problems of a more severe nature occur in 2% to 4 % of children (Frick, 1998). Approximately 55% of all crimes are committed by juvenile delinquents (Foley, Carlton, & Howell, 1996). In 1993, Federal Bureau of Investigation (FBI) statistics indicated that juvenile arrests constituted 15% of all violent crimes. It is important to note however, that juvenile crime rates are increasing not only for males but for females as well. In fact, between 1986 and 1995, female juvenile arrest rates grew more rapidly relative to male juvenile arrest rates. Specifically, females were responsible for 20% of the growth in arrest rates pertaining to violent crimes and 89% of the growth in arrests due to property destruction (Office of Juvenile Justice and Delinquency Prevention, 1997). While these statistics are quite disturbing, they are not surprising given that very young children who demonstrate behaviors predictive of antisocial behavior are largely ignored until their behavior becomes explosive and unpredictable.

Too often, today's children enter the school system equipped with antisocial behaviors, such as aggression, defiance, and impulsivity. These behaviors, coupled with deficits in prosocial and adaptive skills, negatively impact teacher and peer relationships (Walker, Colvin, & Ramsey, 1995; Walker & Gresham, 1997). These children tend to misinterpret neutral cues as confrontational or hostile (Dodge, 1986). This inability to read social situations accurately and their lack of prosocial problem-solving skills prompt antisocial children to respond aggressively to situations that the child views to be threatening. The interaction among (a) a pattern of reactive aggression; (b) lack of appropriate problem-solving skills; (c) easy access to drugs, alcohol, and weapons; and (d) media that seduce youth with violence and early sexuality (Kauffman, 1999) results in a dangerous set of circumstances that puts society at risk for intense forms of violence (Gresham, Lane, & Lambros, 2000).

Antisocial behavior, the cornerstone for conduct disordered behavior, can be defined as persistent violations of socially acceptable behavior patterns and is inclusive of, but not limited to, verbal and physical hostility toward others, defiance toward authority figures, and aggressive, coercive behaviors. Prevalence rates of antisocial behavior in nonclinical populations range from 2% to 6%, representing 1.3 to 3.8 million school-age children (Kazdin, 1993; Walker et al., 1995). In fact, adolescents with antisocial, aggressive behavior patterns constitute between one-third and one-half of referrals for mental health services (Achenbach, 1985; Rogers, Johansen, Chang, & Salekin, 1997).

The numbers of children with or at risk for antisocial behavior are staggering. Given the educational system's reactive approach to serving children with behavioral problems, numerous children with behavioral problems will go undetected and, subsequently, unserved during their early elementary years (Lane, 1999). Because the schools are ill prepared to serve this group of challenging children, it is possible for children with extreme antisocial behaviors to pose serious risks to adults and peers in the educational systems (see Chapter 11 by Walker & Severson, this text).

Recently, the research community has identified a group of children who are at high risk for developing lasting, insidious pattern of antisocial and delinquent behavior. These children are characterized by hyperactivity-impulsivity-inattention and conduct problems. Specific examples of behaviors include theft, truancy, noncompliance, deception, physical aggression, and arguing. Under the psychiatric classification system, these children would be diagnosed as having both attention deficit hyperactivity disorder (ADHD) and conduct disorder (CD)(Diagnostic and Statistical Manual-IV, American Psychiatric Association, 1994). Lynam (1996) refers to these children as "fledgling psychopaths."

Although the term *fledging psychopath* has been used to refer to an empirically validated population of children, the term has invoked a strong reaction from some members of the research community (see Leone, 2001). In an effort to introduce a term that captures the behavioral characteristics of this population, but in such a manner that does not offend and alienate those in need of support, Lane, Gresham, MacMillan, and Bocian (in press) refer to these children as having *antisocial behavior + hyperactivity* (ABH).

The intent of this chapter is twofold. First, we will provide a brief review of the literature on this group of children focusing on issues of epidemiology and prognosis. Second, we will introduce a set of procedures for detecting and assessing this group of students.

Terminology and Behavioral Characteristics

Although a variety of behavior problems capture teachers' attention, the two most common types of behavior problems likely to result in a referral to mental health services are aggressive, antisocial conduct and hyperactivity-implusivity-inattention (Hinshaw, 1987). Mental health professions have different classifications for these disorders in the *Diagnostic and Statistical Manual of Mental Disorders* (DSM-IV)—namely, CD and ADHD, respectively. Yet, there has been considerable debate as to whether these two disorders represent separate entities (Barkley, 1982; Loney & Milich, 1982) given that a substantial degree of overlap exists between the two disorders. In a comprehensive review of the literature, Hinshaw (1987) notes that 30% to 90% of children in with one diagnosis could also be classified as having the other diagnosis.

As mentioned earlier, Lynam (1996) has identified a subtype of conduct problems that he refers to as the "fledgling psychopaths." Fledgling psychopathy, or antisocial behavior + hyperactivity (ABH), consists of children with conduct problems (CP) and hyperactivity-impulsivity-inattention (HIA). *Psychopathy* refers to a behavior pattern marked by risk-taking behavior coupled with criminal activities. A psychopathic individual may be described as self-centered, manipulative, lacking empathy, and forceful. In contrast to popular opinion, these individuals do not suffer from low self-esteem; in fact, they have an inflated sense of self-esteem (Gresham, Lane, MacMillan, & Bocian, 1999). Hare (1981) indicates that psychopathic criminals actually commit more thefts, robberies, and assaults and escape more often that nonpsychopathic criminals.

Clearly, children with CP+HIA tend to be characterized by the worst features of both domains. In comparison to children who have either CP or HIA in isolation, these children tend to exhibit more physical aggression, display greater achievement deficits, and experience higher levels of peer rejection. Children with CP+HIA are also at heightened risk for the development of psychopathology in adulthood along with several other undesirable outcomes such as substance abuse, unemployment, motor vehicle accidents, divorce, and welfare dependency (Walker, Lahey, Hynd, & Frame, 1987). Unfortunately for the schools, these students are highly resistant to interventions aimed at increasing appropriate behaviors and decreasing inappropriate behaviors. Research by Kazdin (1987) suggests that if we do not intervene with children antisocial behavior patterns prior to age 8, the goal of prevention is not attainable. After age 8, the focus of interventions shifts to remediation—helping children live with the disorder they possess. Therefore, early identification and detection are critical.

When one considers the behavioral and academic profile of children with ABH coupled with the fact that the behavior pattern becomes relatively stable after age 8 and that there is a poor prognosis for remediation (Kazdin, 1987; Walker et al., 1995), the picture is, at best, bleak if not frightening. The question comes to mind: How did these children become fledgling psychopaths?

Causal Pathways

The research community has identified three causal models to explain the development of a group of children with both CP and HIA: risk factor model, stepping stone model, and subtype model. The risk factor model suggests that HIA is one factor among several risk factors that leads to negative consequences for children that propel them into antisocial behavior patterns. For instance, Patterson, DeBaryshe, and Ramsey (1989) introduced a model suggesting that disruptive child-rearing practices (e.g., harsh and inconsistent discipline, low levels of involvement, and poor supervision) set the stage for the development of antisocial behavior problems. Unskilled parents who are raising children with difficult temperaments unintentionally train their children to acquire aggressive and coercive behaviors via negative reinforcement. Patterson's (1982) Microsocial Coercive Family Processes model indicates that parents attempt to use aggressive and coercive tactics to shape their child's behavior. The child, in turn, learns that arguing and manipulation can help them escape undesirable circumstances (i.e., following parent directions; taking out the trash; completing homework). This coercive cycle is repeated literally *thousands* of times throughout the child's early years. Consequently, when the child enters the school setting, he or she is equipped with oppositional defiant behaviors that negatively impact the child's peer and adult relationships (Coie & Jacobs, 1993). If the child is not successful in mediating peer and adult relationships, he or she is likely to experience a host of negative outcomes, two of which include social rejection and academic underachievement (Bullis & Walker, 1994; Walker, Irvin, Noell, & Singer, 1992). Over time, the child's antisocial behaviors increase in magnitude, ultimately resulting in extreme conduct problems. In this model, HIA is but one risk factor among others (e.g., poor parenting skills, academic underachievement, and social rejection) that contributes to the development of CP.

The stepping stone model, in contrast to the risk factor model, indicates that the presence of HIA early in a child's life leads to oppositional defiant disorder (ODD), which may then escalate into CD. In this developmental model, the early onset of HIA problems in combination with environmental factors produces a chain of aversive and oppositional interactions between the child and his or her parent, teacher, and peers. For example, Moffitt (1993), like Patterson (1982), proposes that a difficult temperament at birth prompts an escalating chain of negative parent–child interactions that impede the child's social and academic development. This pattern of antisocial behavior becomes embedded in the child's daily routines and increases in intensity and frequency, eventually magnifying into severe conduct problems. The stepping stone model further suggests that early detection and intervention of children with HIA can break the behavioral chain and therefore prevent early HIA problems from intensifying into ODD and CD (Lynam, 1996). The recommended method of intervention, from this perspective, includes a combination of stimulant medication and parent management training (Barkley, 1990) (see Chapter 12 by Ervin, Jones, Radford, & Gingerich, this text).

Although there is support for both the risk factor and the stepping stone models, neither model explains why children with HIA only have more deficits in sustained attention than do the HIA + CP and CP only groups. The subtype model suggests that children with both HIA and CP constitute a unique subgroup—the fledgling psychopaths (Lynam, 1996). Research by Lynam (1996) suggests that this subgroup of children have deficits in the ability to incorporate new information while engaging in goal-directed behavior. For example, children with ABH would struggle in social situations that shifted from being hostile to neutral or positive. This difficulty may stem from failure to attend to shifts in social cues. Accordingly, these children are apt to continue engaging in a confrontational manner despite a peer attempting to be more positive in a given social interaction. Furthermore, these children are low in "constraint," which may explain, in part, why these children tend to exhibit impulsive and sensation-seeking behaviors. Lynam (1996) speculates that children fitting the ABH profile start out with low levels of constraint that, in turn, make it difficult for them to interpret feedback from the environment accurately. Early on these children demonstrate signs of HIA that expands into ODD because the parents, albeit unintentionally, interfere with the child's goal-directed behavior. When the child enters the school setting, he or she substantially deviates from the model behavior profile expected by most teachers (Walker et al., 1992) in that the child has trouble staying quiet, remaining seated, complying with teacher directions, and transitioning between activities.

In summary, it appears that neither the risk factor nor stepping stone model fully explains how children develop behaviors characteristic of ABH. The subtype model appears to be a more accurate model; however, it is speculative at this time. Clearly, additional research on identification and intervention is warranted to test the viability of this model (Lynam, 1996). Before the teaching and research communities can effectively intervene with this group of youngsters, there needs to be an accurate and reliable method for identifying students at risk for ABH. Therefore, we contend that an important first step is to develop a comprehensive screening procedure that incorporates psychometrically sound assessment tools in order to identify children at risk for ABH accurately and reliably. Then, once the identification procedures are in place, the focus can shift to intervention.

Early Detection and Assessment

In light of the poor prognosis for remediation and the numerous long-term negative consequences facing children who exhibit antisocial behavior patterns coupled with characteristics of HIA, early identification of these children is paramount. The question is, How do we effectively identify students at risk for "fledgling psychopathy"? Walker and colleagues (1995) suggest that effective early identification procedures contain the following features. First, screening procedures should be proactive, rather than reactive, in an effort to identify to children who are at risk for antisocial behavior patterns. Second, screening should take place as early as possible, preferably upon initial school entry when students are more amenable to intervention (Kazdin, 1987). Third, teacher nominations and rankings, which are effective procedures, should be supplemented with more specific and precise measures (e.g., behavior rating scale and direct observations) in subsequent stages of the screening process. Fourth, assessment of student behavior should be based on the principle of multioperationalism, meaning that students should be evaluated in more than one setting (e.g., classroom, playground, and home) by more than one source (e.g., teachers, parents, peers, and self) using more than one method (e.g., behavior rating scales, direct observation, interviews, sociometrics, and school record reviews). Additionally, assessment information should then be used to design idiographic interventions specific to the child's needs (Gresham et al., 2000). By linking assessment information to intervention procedures, appropriate interventions based on the child's acquisition and performance deficits can be constructed and implemented with the proper intensity and integrity.

Gresham and colleagues (2000) propose a multiple gating process, Early Identification of Antisocial Behavior + Hyperactivity (EIABH), similar to the Systematic Screening for Behavior Disorders (SSBD; Walker & Severson, 1992) for use in identifying students at risk for ABH (see Gresham et al., 2000 for a detailed description). In this system, they describe some of the current procedures and tools available for screening for this population. As with the SSBD, EIABH involves a set of assessment tools and procedures that increase in intensity, diagnostic precision, and costs. The EIABH consists of four key stages: teacher nomination, multi-informant ratings, intensive assessment, and resistance to intervention used to identify children at risk for ABH (see Figure 13.1).

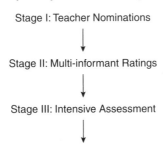

Early Identification of Antisocial Behavior + Hyperactivity (EIABH): An Empirically Based Screening System

Stage I: Teacher Nominations

Stage II: Multi-informant Ratings

Stage III: Intensive Assessment

Stage IV: Resistance to Intervention

FIGURE 13.1 Early Identification of Antisocial Behavior + Hyperactivity: An Empirically Based Screening System.

Source: Adapted from Gresham, F. M., Lane, K. L., & Lambros, K. L. (2000). Comorbidity of conduct problems and ADHD: Identification of "fledgling psychopaths." *Journal of Emotional and Behavioral Disorders, 8,* 83–93.

BOX **13.1**

A Behavioral Definition of Antisocial Behavior + Hyperactivity

Antisocial Behavior + Hyperactivity: Behavioral Profile
This behavior profile refers to aggressive, coercive, impulsive behaviors exhibited by children toward the social environment. Children fitting this behavior pattern show signs of hyperactivity, impulsivity, inattention, defiance, and aggressive behaviors that are frequently accompanied by a lack of remorse or empathy toward others."

Source: Adapted from Gresham, F. M., Lane, K. L., & Lambros, K. (2000). Comorbidity of conduct and attention deficit hyperactivity problems: Issues of identification and intervention with "fledgling psychopaths." *Journal of Emotional and Behavioral Disorders, 8*(2), 83–93.

Stage I: Teacher Nomination

It is possible for teachers to identify children at risk for ABH. For example, if provided with a clear, operational definition of antisocial behavior + hyperactivity (see Box 13.1 for a behavioral definition), teachers could be asked to identify seven to eight children who most closely match the behavioral profile of ABH. This list of children is then rank ordered from most like (1) to least like (8). Students who are ranked 1 to 3 then pass through the first gate.

Stage II: Multi-informant Ratings

In Stage II, a wide variety of people who are familiar with the child are asked to provide information regarding the child's behavior. We support using existing behavior rating scales that have excellent psychometric properties such as: the Teacher Rating Form (TRF; Achenbach, 1991), the Child Behavior Checklist (CBCL; Achenbach, 1991), and the Critical Events Index (CEI; Walker & Severson, 1992). The TRF, which is completed by teachers, and CBCL, which is completed by parents, each have subscales—Delinquent Behavior, Aggressive Behavior, and Attention Problems—that have been successfully used to differentiate the FP population from CP-only and HIA-only groups (Lambros, 1999). The CEI is a nationally standardized, 33-item checklist that measures high-intensity, low-frequency behaviors (i.e., sets fires; steals; physically assaults others). Recent investigations have shown the CEI, which is completed by teachers, to be highly accurate in identifying students at risk for emotional and behavioral disorders (Gresham, MacMillan, & Bocian, 1996).

We suggest that the following 11 behaviors identified on the CEI would be useful in identifying children at risk for ABH: steals, sets fires, has tantrums, is physically assaults an adult, is physically aggressive with other students or adults, damages others' property, attempts to seriously injure others, ignores teacher warnings and reprimands, uses obscene language, makes lewd or obscene gestures, and exhibits cruelty to animals. Students who have high ratings on two or more of these instruments would then pass through the second gate.

Stage III: Intensive Assessment

Stage III can be characterized as a more labor- and time-intensive assessment relative to Stage I or II. The assessment procedures in this stage include (a) direct observation, (b) sociometric assessment, and (c) functional assessment interviews. Each method will be briefly described next.

Direct Observation.   Direct observations, in a perfect world, would occur in both the classroom and playground settings in an effort to obtain a representative sample of student behavior. For the classroom observations, we recommend observing academic engaged time (AET) and total disruptive behaviors (TDBs). Similarly, two categories of behavior should also be observed on the playground: total negative social interaction (TNSI) and time spent alone (TSA). See Box 13.2 for an operational definition of each behavior along with directions on how to record behavior.

B O X **13.2**

Direct Observation Measures

Academic Engaged Time (AET)
AET refers to attending to the material and task, making the appropriate motor response, and asking for assistance in an appropriate manner.

Total Disruptive Behavior (TDB)
TDB is a class of behaviors that disturbs the classroom ecology and interferes with instruction. Examples of disruptive behaviors include being out of seat without permission, not complying with teacher instruction, hitting, biting, making any audible noises or vocalizations that disrupt the environment, yelling, cursing, and taking others' property.

Total Negative Social Interaction (TNSI)
TNSI is defined as behaviors that disturb ongoing play activities and involves physical or verbal aggression. Examples of these disruptive behaviors include hitting, biting, cursing, threatening, and grabbing.

Time Spent Alone (TSA)
TSA is defined as when the target student is *not* within 10 feet of any other children, is *not* socially engaged, and is *not* participating in any activity with other children.

Duration Recording Procedures
- Select at 15- to 20-minute intervals of time.
- Start a stopwatch whenever a student is engaging in the target behavior.
- Stop the stopwatch whenever a student is not engaged in the target behavior.
- At the end of the interval, compute the percentage of the time spent in the target behavior by dividing the total amount of time spent engaging in the target behavior, dividing it by the total time observed, and them multiplying by 100.

Note: Each target behavior (AET, TDB, NSI, ALONE) should be collected in separate observations sessions.

Adapted from Walker and Severson's (1992) Systematic Screening for Behavior Disorders

Sociometric Assessment. Quite often teachers are not privy to peer culture (Sheridan, 1995). Consequently, it is important to obtain information on how at-risk children are viewed by their peers. There are a number of psychometric procedures available, which have met with varying degrees of success. We support the use of the peer nomination procedures described by Coie, Dodge, and Coppotelli (1982). In this method, students in the classroom are asked to select from a roster the three classmates whom they like most and the three classmates whom they like least. The number of nominations in each category is then summed to yield Liked Most (LM) and Liked Least (LL) scores. From these scores Social Preference (SP) and Social Impact (SI) scores can be calculated. These scores are standardized within each classroom by converting each score to a z score ($M = 0$; $SD = 1$). These standard scores can be used to identify students who are rejected or not rejected. Being rejected by one's peers in elementary school has consistently been predictive of future antisocial behavior patterns (Asher & Coie, 1990; Coie et al., 1982; Walker et al., 1995). Students who earn a "rejected" label from their peers and have high rates of TDB, TNSI, and TSA coupled with low rates of AET pass through this gate.

Functional Assessment Interviews. Prior to passing into the fourth stage, we recommend conducting functional assessment interviews (FAIs). The functional assessment interview is designed to (a) identify and define specific antisocial behaviors, (b) gain initial information regarding the function of the inappropriate, antisocial behavior in the form of behavioral hypotheses; and (c) identify appropriate replacements behaviors (see Chapter 13 by Ervin, Jones, Radford, & Gingerich, this text). FAIs can be conducted with teachers, parents, and the target students to obtain a complete picture of the child's behavior. A variety of FAI protocols are currently in print. We recommend O'Neill, Horner, Albin, Sprague, Storey, and Childs' (1994) protocol for use with parents and teachers and Kern and Dunlap's (in press) Student-Assisted Functional Assessment for use with students.

Stage IV: Resistance to Intervention

The final phase of this multiple gating approach to early identification involves conceptualizing students as being at risk for ABH based on the notion of resistance to intervention. In other words, it is possible to identify students who are at risk for ABH by virtue of the fact that they do not respond to interventions that have previously been effective in altering other students' inappropriate behavior. Resistance to intervention refers to the lack of change in a given behavior as a function of intervention (Gresham, 1991, 1998; Gresham et al., 2000). The purpose of all interventions is to change behaviors. Specifically, interventions are designed to create a discrepancy between baseline and postintervention levels of performance. If this discrepancy does not occur, even when the intervention was implemented as originally designed, with integrity (Gresham, 1989), this lack of change can be used as one justification for providing additional support for a student or for making a determination that the child may be eligible for special education services. If the inappropriate behavior continues despite the fact that an appropriate intervention was implemented with integrity, it is quite possible that the student might need

(a) the same intervention implemented more frequently with greater intensity (e.g., five times a week rather than three times a week), (b) a stronger, more intensive intervention, or (c) an alternative placement.

The literature on antisocial behavior, in general, indicates that these students have high rates of maladaptive behaviors and low rates of prosocial behaviors. Further, these students are extremely resistant to intervention. In particular, interventions that are not based on empirically established best practices and those that are not implemented with a high degree of integrity are likely to be ineffective with this group of children (Gresham, 1989; Lane, 1999; Lipsey & Wilson, 1998; Walker et al., 1995). Best practices suggest that a variety of interventions with varying degrees of intensity may be necessary to change maladaptive behaviors that have been well established.

A useful model to follow, which is based on the notion of resistance to intervention, when providing intervention support to children who are at risk for ABH involves three levels of intervention (see Chapter 11 by Walker & Severson, this text). The first level of intervention is primary intervention. Primary intervention strategies, also referred to as *universal interventions*, are delivered to all students in a given school. Examples of universal interventions included schoolwide discipline plans, a social skills curriculum, conflict resolutions programs, and drug education classes. The majority of general education students will respond to these interventions. Students who are unresponsive to primary interventions will need additional support—namely, secondary interventions. Secondary interventions, also referred to as *selected interventions*, are interventions provided to a subset of children who are believed to be at risk in either an academic or behavioral domain. Examples of secondary interventions include social skills instruction and academic remediation or tutoring. Students who do not respond to secondary interventions will need even more support in the form of a tertiary intervention. Tertiary interventions are based on the implementation of indicated interventions such as parent training, functional assessment based interventions, or one-to-one instruction in a given academic area. (For a more detailed discussion, see Bullis & Walker, 1994; Lipsey & Wilson, 1998; Walker et al., 1995).

Conclusion

In this chapter, we have discussed issues related to the identification, assessment, and intervention of children at risk for HIA and CP—antisocial behavior + hyperactivity. This group of children demonstrates more frequent, severe, and stable maladaptive behavior patterns that are coupled with an impulsive response style that makes their behavior erratic and unpredictable. The prognosis for these students is poor as their maladaptive behaviors become increasingly resistant to intervention over time (Hinshaw, 1987; Kazdin, 1987; Lynam, 1996). These children are at risk for many unpleasant outcomes in adulthood: substance abuse, unemployment, divorce, motor vehicle accidents, welfare dependency, and criminality (Loeber, 1982; Loeber, Brinthaupt, & Green, 1990).

Clearly, early identification and intervention with students at risk for ABH is imperative. As previously discussed, Kazdin (1987) suggests that if we, as educators, do not effectively intervene with this population prior to age 8 (third grade), we cannot hope to prevent the development of antisocial behaviors. After age 8, our focus will shift to one of remediation—or risk management. At such time, antisocial behavior can then be considered comparable to a chronic illness such as diabetes. It can be managed with the necessary supports, but it cannot be cured (Kazdin, 1987).

The multiple gating screening process proposed in this chapter can be useful in identifying students at risk for ABH. This process incorporates well-established, validated instruments such as the SSBD (Walker & Severson, 1992), the TRF (Achenbach, 1991), CBCL (Achenbach, 1991), and peer nominations (Coie et al., 1982). However, this work is in the beginning stages. To date, the combination of procedures discussed is merely a theoretical model, not an empirically validated model.

As is the case with all early detection efforts, the issues of incorrectly identifying, or not identifying, students need to be addressed. Specifically, the issues of false positives, false negatives, and base rates must be examined. A *false positive* occurs when a student is identified as at risk for a given problem when, in reality, he or she does not have the problem under consideration (e.g., saying a child is at risk for ABH when, in fact, the child is not). A *false negative* occurs when a student actually is at risk but is not identified (e.g., saying a child is *not* at risk for ABH when he or she actually is at risk). *Base rate* refers to the prevalence of a problem in a population (e.g., the total number of children at risk for ABH in a given population).

In the initial stages of screening, high levels of false positives are acceptable because, in this particular instance, a false negative would be a much more serious error than a false positive. However, as students pass through subsequent gates, the false-positive rate should decrease as a result of more stringent criteria characteristic of the remaining gates. Because false-positive and false-negative rates exist on a continuum, as the number of false positives decrease, the number of false negatives will necessarily increase.

A final issue to consider is that of base rate. If the base rate for a particular problem is 50%, a person could correctly identify those individuals having the problem by chance alone (e.g., flipping a coin). However, the challenge of correctly identifying children at risk for ABH is more formidable. Namely, because the base rate of ABH is very low, the process of identification is much less accurate than if the base rate for this population were higher.

REFERENCES

Achenbach, T. (1985). *Assessment and taxonomy of child and adolescent psychopathology.* Beverly Hills, CA: Sage.

Achenbach, T. M. (1991). *The child behavior checklist: Manual for the teacher's report form.* Burlington: University of Vermont, Department of Psychiatry.

American Psychiatric Association. (1994). *Diagnostic and statistical manual of mental disorders* (4th ed.). Washington, DC: Author.

Asher, S. R., & Coie, J. D. (1990). (Eds.). *Peer rejection in childhood.* New York: Cambridge University Press.

Barkley, R. (1982). Guidelines for defining hyperactivity. In B. B. Lahey & A. E. Kazdin (Eds.), *Advances in clinical child psychology* (pp. 137–175). New York: Plenum.

Barkley, R. (1990). *Attention deficit hyperactivity disorder: A handbook for diagnosis and treatment.* New York: Guilford.

Bullis, M., & Walker, H. M. (1994). *Comprehensive school-based systems for troubled youth.* Eugene: University of Oregon, Center on Human Development.

Coie, J. D., Dodge, K. A., & Coppotelli, H. (1982). Dimensions and types of social status: A cross-age perspective. *Developmental Psychology, 18,* 557–570.

Coie, J. D., & Jacobs, M. (1993). The role of social context in the prevention of conduct disorder. *Development and Psychopathology, 5,* 263–275.

Dodge, K. (1986). A social information process model of social competence in children. In M. Perlmutter (Ed.), *Minneapolis symposia on child psychology* (Vol. 18., pp. 77–125). Hillsdale, NJ: Erlbaum.

Federal Bureau of Investigation. (1993). *Age-specific arrest rates and race-specific arrest rates for selected offenses: 1965–1992.* Washington, DC: U.S. Government Printing Office.

Foley, H., Carlton, C., & Howell, R. (1996). The relationship of attention deficit hyperactivity disorder and conduct disorder to juvenile delinquency: Legal implications. *Bulletin of the American Academy of Psychiatry and Law, 24*(3), 333–345.

Frick, P. J. (1998). *Conduct disorders and severe antisocial behavior.* New York: Plenum.

Gresham, F. M. (1989). Assessment of treatment integrity in school consultation and prereferral intervention. *School Psychology Review, 18,* 37–50.

Gresham, F. M. (1991). Conceptualizing behavior disorders in terms of resistance to intervention. *School Psychology Review, 20*(1), 23–36.

Gresham, F. M. (1998). Designs for evaluating behavioral change: Conceptual principles of single case methodology. In T. Watson & F. Gresham (Eds.), *Handbook of child behavior therapy* (pp. 23–40). New York: Plenum.

Gresham, F. M., Lane, K. L., & Lambros, K. L. (2000). Comorbidity of conduct problems and ADHD: Identification of "fledgling psychopaths." *Journal of Emotional and Behavioral Disorders, 8,* 83–93.

Gresham, F. M., Lane, K. L., MacMillan, D. L, & Bocian, K. M. (1999). Social and academic profiles of externalizing and internalizing groups: Risk factors for emotional and behavioral disorders. *Behavior Disorders, 24,* 231–241.

Gresham, F. M., MacMillan, D. L., & Bocian, K. M. (1996). Behavioral earthquakes: Low frequency, salient behavioral events that differ-

entiate students at-risk for behavioral disorders. *Behavioral Disorders, 21,* 277–292.

Hare, R. (1981). Psychopathy and violence. In J. R. Hayes, T. K. Roberts, & K. S. Solway (Eds.), *Violence and the violent individual* (pp. 53–74). Jamaica, NY: Spectrum.

Hinshaw, S. P. (1987). On the distinction between attentional deficits/hyperactivity and conduct problems/aggression in child psychopathology. *Psychological Bulletin, 101,* 443–463.

Kauffman, J. M. (1999). How we prevent the prevention of emotional and behavioral disorders. *Exceptional Children, 65,* 448–468.

Kazdin, A. (1987). *Conduct disorders in childhood and adolescence.* London: Sage.

Kazdin, A. (1993). Treatment of conduct disorder: Progress and directions in psychotherapy research. *Development and Psychopathology, 5,* 1–2, 277–310.

Kern, L., & Dunlap, G. (in press). Assessment-based interventions for children with emotional and behavioral disorders. In A. C. Repp & R. H. Horner (Eds.), *Functional analysis of problem behavior: From effective assessment to effective support.* Monterey, CA: Brooks/Cole.

Lambros, K. M. (1999). *Examination of conduct problems and hyperactivity-impulsivity-inattention problems as correlates of fledgling psychopathy: A longitudinal perspective of children at risk.* Unpublished doctoral dissertation, University of California–Riverside.

Lane, K. L. (1999). Young students at risk for antisocial behavior: The utility of academic and social skills interventions. *Journal of Emotional and Behavioral Disorders, 7*(4), 211–223.

Lane, K. L., Gresham, F. M., MacMillan, D., & Bocian, K. (in press). Early detection of students with antisocial behavior and hyperactivity problems. *Education and Treatment of Children.*

Leone, P. (2001). Letter to the editor, *Journal of Emotional and Behavioral Disorders 9*(2), 82–83.

Lipsey, M. W., & Wilson, D. (1998). Effective intervention for the serious juvenile offenders: A synthesis of research. In R. Loeber & D. Farrington (Eds.), *Serious and violent juvenile offenders: Risk factors and successful interventions* (pp. 313–345). Thousand Oaks, CA: Sage.

Loeber, R. (1982). The stability of antisocial behavior and delinquent child behavior: A review. *Child Development, 53,* 1431–1436.

Loeber, R., Brinthaupt, V., & Green, S. (1990). Attention deficits, impulsivity, and hyperactivity with or without conduct problems: Relationships to delinquency and unique contextual factors. In R. J. McMahon & R. D. Peters (Eds.), *Behavioral disorders of adolescence: Research, intervention, and policy in clinical and school settings* (pp. 39–61). New York: Plenum.

Loney, J., & Milich, R. (1982). Hyperactivity, inattention, and aggression in clinical practice. In M. Wolraich & D. Routh (Eds.), *Advances in developmental and behavioral pediatrics* (Vol. 3, pp. 113–147). Greenwich, CT: JAI.

Lynam, D. R. (1996). Early identification of chronic offenders: Who is the fledgling psychopath? *Pscyhological Bulletin, 120,* 209–234.

Moffit, T. M. (1993). Adolescent-limited and life-course persistent antisocial behavior: A developmental taxonomy. *Psychological Review, 100,* 674–701.

O'Neill, R. E., Horner, R. H., Albin, R. W., Storey, K., & Sprague, J. R. (1990). *Functional analysis of problem behavior: A practical assessment guide.* Sycamore, IL: Sycamore.

Office of Juvenile Justice and Delinquency Prevention. (1997). *Crime in the United States.* Washington, DC: U.S. Government Printing Office.

Patterson, G. (1982). *Coercive family processes.* Eugene, OR: Castilia.

Patterson, G., DeBaryshe, B. D., & Ramsey, E. (1989). A developmental perspective on antisocial behavior. *American Psychologist, 44,* 329–335.

Rogers, R., Johansen, J., Chang, J., & Salekin, R. (1997). Predictors of adolescent psychopathy: oppositional and conduct-disordered symptoms. *Journal of the American Academy of Psychiatry and Law, 25*(3), 261–271.

Sheridan, S. M. (1995). Building social skills in the classroom. In S. Goldstein, L. Braswell, M. Goldstein, S. Sheridan, & S. Zentall (Eds.), *Understanding and managing children's classroom behavior* (pp. 375–396). New York: Wiley.

Walker, H. M., Colvin, G., & Ramsey, E. (1995). *Antisocial behavior in school: Strategies and best practices.* Pacific Grove, CA: Brooks/Cole.

Walker, H. M., & Gresham, F. M. (1997). Making schools safer and violence free. *Intervention in Schools and Clinic, 32,* 199–204.

Walker, H. M., Irvin, L. K., Noell, J., & Singer, G. H. S. (1992). A construct score approach to the assessment of social competence: Rationale, technological considerations, and anticipated outcomes. *Behavior Modification, 16,* 448–474.

Walker, J. L., Lahey, B. B., Hynd, G. W., & Frame, C. L. (1987). Comparison of specific patterns of antisocial behavior in children with conduct disorder with or without coexisting hyperactivity. *Journal of Consulting and Clinical Psychology, 55,* 910–913.

Walker, H. M., & Severson, H. (1992). *Systematic Screening for Behavior Disorders (SSBD): User's guide and technical manual.* Longmont, CO: Sopris West.

14 Internalizing Behavior Disorders

RICHARD J. MORRIS
University of Arizona
School Psychology Program
Tucson, Arizona

KETKI SHAH
University of Arizona
School Psychology Program
Tucson, Arizona

YVONNE P. MORRIS
Private Practice
Tucson, Arizona

Introduction

Concern with the assessment, diagnosis, and treatment of internalizing behavior disorders in children and adolescents has increased tremendously over the past three decades (Kendall & Morris, 1991; Morris & Kratochwill, 1998a, 1998b). These childhood behavior disorders refer to those behaviors and related thoughts that typically are overcontrolled, are often covert, and include the following types of behavioral difficulties: fears, phobias, and related anxieties (e.g., separation anxiety, reading and math anxiety, test anxiety, and public speaking anxiety); childhood depression (with the possible presence of social isolation or social withdrawal and feelings of alienation from others); and obsessive-compulsive disorder and related overemphasis on perfectionism. These disorders often create high levels of personal discomfort and frustration in a child or adolescent and can negatively affect his or her learning, development, and socialization.

Incidence and Prevalence Data

Internalizing disorders are found in children from early childhood through adolescence. Those disorders seen in early childhood, such as fears, phobias, and related anxieties, are usually in reaction to something taking place in the child's environment (Morris & Kratochwill, 1983). As the child becomes older and enters school, his or her fears and related anxieties broaden and may involve imaginary figures or sleeping or staying alone. With increasing age, the child may become fearful of particular objects, places, or people as well as the future (e.g., an upcoming test at school or a class presentation) and bodily injury (Morris & Kratochwill, 1998a).

In terms of the prevalence of fears, phobias, and related anxieties, the literature suggests that between 3.5% and 8% of children and adolescents referred for treatment to a mental health professional or clinic manifest intense or severe fears or anxieties—with girls having these disorders more often than boys (Morris & Kratochwill, 1998a). Among adolescents, in particular, approximately 3.5% of these youth have experienced a specific clinical phobia sometime during their life, with the peak time period for developing this type of phobia being between 10 and 14 years of age (Essau, Conradt, & Peterman, 2000). Panic attacks associated with various phobias and fears are rare in preadolescent children, whereas in adolescents, such attacks, if present, are usually of short duration (King, Ollendick, & Mattis, 1994). Regarding school phobia, estimates of the prevalence rates vary greatly—from .04% to 8% of children referred to clinics, based on the definition of the disorder (Morris & Kratochwill, 1998a).

With respect to childhood depression, it is estimated that approximately one out of six children (16.66%) who are seen in a psychiatric setting have the diagnosis of depression (Reynolds, 1990). Among elementary school-age and prepubescent children, there does not appear to be a difference in prevalence rates between males and females; however, for adolescents, females tend to have more depressive symptoms than males. Researchers have also reported that depressed youth are 20 to 80 times more likely to experience at least one other coexisting (or comorbid) internalizing disorder (e.g., Angold & Costello, 1993). In this regard, a number of researchers have reported that many youths who are diagnosed with depression have had a history of anxiety-related symptoms and that a substantial number of these children also have low self-esteem (e.g., Cole, Peeke, Martin, Truglio, & Seroczynski, 1998; Kaslow, Morris, & Rehm, 1998; Stark, Dempsey, & Christopher, 1993). In addition, other behavior problems that may coexist with depression include substance-related disorders, panic disorder, obsessive-compulsive disorder, eating disorders (e.g., anorexia and bulimia), hypersensitivity and self-consciousness, social withdrawal and isolation, attention deficit hyperactivity disorder (ADHD), and borderline personality disorder (American Psychiatric Association, 1994; Kendall & Chu, 2000; Orvaschel & Weissman, 1986).

Prevalence data on obsessive-compulsive disorder (OCD) in children suggest that it is not as rare as once thought—with estimates being between 2% and 4% of those seen in psychiatric settings. The sex ratio regarding the frequency of OCD is approximately equal for males and females (e.g., Riddle et al., 1990), with the mean age of onset for boys being 9 years and the mean onset age for girls being 11 years. Prevalence studies also report that male children are two times more likely than females to be diagnosed with this disorder before 10 years of age (e.g., March, Leonard, & Swedo, 1995).

Children diagnosed with OCD before 6 to 8 years tend to show more compulsions than obsessions. Moreover, these children do not appear to experience a sudden onset of their symptoms, and the nature of the symptoms tend to change as the child grows older—with the severity of the symptoms often linked to stress (Milby, Robinson, & Saniel, 1998). In terms of comorbidity issues, many children have comorbid diagnoses of depression, eating disorder, or social or other phobias and related anxiety disorders, and 5% to 7% of OCD children have also been diagnosed with Tourette's disorder (e.g., Milby et al., 1998; Riddle, et al., 1990).

The epidemiological literature suggests that children having internalizing disorders tend to be impaired in various social and school activities, as well as in their perceived self-competence (e.g., Benjamin, Costello, & Warren, 1990; Messer & Beidel, 1994). Kendall and Chu (2000) have also indicated that such disorders can have long-term implications for adult functioning (p. 209) since the research literature suggests that the symptomatology associated with many of these disorders may intensify over time.

Assessment of Children's Internalizing Behavior Disorders

Unlike adults, children and adolescents are not always viewed by mental health professionals as the most reliable and valid sources of information regarding the symptomatology, frequency, severity, and settings associated with their respective behavior disorders. In fact, it is often the case that socialization agents—such as parents, teachers, and other school or day care personnel—bring the child to the attention of a mental health service provider in the school or clinic setting. This is because children may not view their behavioral symptoms as problematic or may not feel that their behavioral or emotional difficulties are as problematic as their parents or teachers believe them to be (Kendall & Morris, 1991; Morris & Morris, 2000). These factors may therefore affect the reliability and validity of an evaluation of a particular child's behavior disorder if the assessment procedures used rely solely on the child versus including parent(s) and/or teacher(s) responses in the assessment process (Lachar, 1993).

To understand the nature of a child's internalizing disorder, a mental health professional must first conduct a psychological assessment of the child and her or his family. Whenever possible, the assessment process should also include the child's teacher(s). In addition, assessment procedures need to consider the age and developmental stage of the child being assessed, as well as issues pertaining to cultural and individual diversity and, where appropriate, the child's level of acculturalization to, and assimilation in, the dominant culture (e.g., Morris & Morris, 2000).

Assessment of childhood behavior disorders generally include the following: (a) identification of circumstances and/or settings in which the behavior problem occurs, as well as those conditions under which it does not occur; (b) frequency of occurrence of the problematic behavior(s); (c) duration of the problem and chronicity of the problem over time; (d) severity level; (e) whether the problem has improved or become worse over time; (f) developmental appropriateness of the behavior being demonstrated by the child, as well as its social and cultural appropriateness;

(g) child's/family members'/teachers' level of personal distress regarding the behavior; (h) the child's/family members'/teacher's history of previous attempts at remedying the problem; and (i) developmental history related to the nature of the problem. This assessment approach not only assists the child mental health professional and teacher in fully understanding and diagnosing the child's behavior difficulties but also helps him or her in identifying target issues and/or behaviors that need to be addressed in therapy, determining the constraints on the therapy implementation plan, and deciding who needs to be in therapy and whether significant others, including teachers, need to be consulted as treatment progresses.

A number of methods can be used to assess various internalizing disorders. The most common methods are direct observation, self-monitoring, interview, and use of behavior checklists and rating scales. These methods are on a continuum ranging from direct to indirect measures. Direct measures (e.g., direct observation and self-monitoring) assess a child's behavior at the same point in time that it is occurring, while indirect measures (e.g., interviews and behavior checklists and rating scales) assess a behavior at a time following its occurrence. While the use of these different methods and sources of information may make the diagnostic process more complex and time-consuming, they can also make it more accurate and reliable. Each method has the potential of providing the child therapist, parent, or teacher with reliable information regarding the frequency, duration, severity, and developmental appropriateness of the various behaviors comprising a child's internalizing behavior disorder. In Box 14.1 we have listed some guidelines that child therapists and school-based mental health professionals and teachers might consider when assessing a child's internalizing disorder.

BOX **14.1**

Helpful Hints Regarding Assessing Students with Internalizing Behavior Disorders

1. Since each assessment method provides helpful information, both direct and indirect assessment methods should be used.
2. If possible, observe the child at different times during the day and on different days. This will minimize the effects of either the child or observer having a particularly good or bad day on the data that are gathered.
3. Direct observation can be done in the classroom as well as in nonclassroom and simulated settings. Before implementing any observation, it is important to define operationally the behaviors that are of concern to the teacher and other school personnel—that is, to specify in observable terms the student's behavior problem(s). The observer should also be sensitive to the impact of his or her presence on the frequency, duration, and intensity of the child's problem behavior(s).
4. Direct observations in simulated settings may be necessary when it is not possible to obtain accurate data in the child's classroom or other setting and when the behavior problem(s) is (are) infrequent, unpredictable, unlikely, difficult, or too dangerous to record in actual settings.

Treating Internalizing Behavior Disorders

Although, historically, the most prominent form of child psychotherapy involved psychoanalysis, more contemporary views of the development and understanding of children's behavior disorders, as well as the emerging research literature on child therapy, have led to an expansion of the list of types child therapy procedures available. Specifically, the expanded list now includes child psychoanalysis, behavior modification (or behavior therapy) and cognitive behavior therapy, Adlerian child therapy, family systems therapy systems, client-centered (humanistic) therapy, reality therapy, and ecological and consultation approaches (see, e.g., Kratochwill & Morris, 1993), with behavioral, cognitive, eclectic, psychodynamic, and family therapies being rated as "most useful" by some child-oriented psychologists and psychiatrists (Kazdin, Siegel, & Bass, 1990).

If one focuses on empirically based psychological intervention practices in school and clinic settings, one finds in the research literature a major emphasis on the use of *behavior therapy* and *cognitive behavior therapy* approaches to treat internalizing disorders and a deemphasis on such child therapies as psychoanalysis, client-centered therapy, family systems approaches, and Adlerian child therapy (see, e.g., Bear, Minke, & Thomas, 1997; Kratochwill & Morris, 1993; Morris & Kratochwill, 1998b; Witt, Elliott, & Gresham, 1988). Behavior therapy and cognitive behavior therapy emerged largely from experimental psychology laboratories and are based on theories concerning how people learn to perform various acts or engage in particular behaviors (Bandura, 1969; Bijou, 1955; Mowrer, 1960; Pavlov, 1927; Skinner, 1938; Wolpe, 1958). The underlying assumptions of these therapy approaches are that internalizing disorders are learned behaviors that occur in response to various circumstances or stimuli taking place in a person's life and that more appropriate or desirable behaviors can be learned in response to the same stimuli.

Consistent with this theoretical emphasis, in the remainder of this chapter we describe behavior therapy and cognitive behavior therapy approaches that have been frequently used in the treatment of three categories of internalizing disorders: fears, phobias, and related anxieties; childhood depression; and obsessive-compulsive disorder. The effectiveness of each of the methods described is influenced by numerous factors, including (a) the presence of comorbid (or coexisting) internalizing or externalizing disorders in the child—that is, the presence of comorbid behavior disorders may complicate or extend the application of the intervention program; (b) the support, receptivity, and willingness of teachers and/or parents to participate, where necessary, in the intervention program—that is, involving teachers and/or parents in the intervention process often assists the child in maximally generalizing treatment outcome to a variety of settings; and (c) the nature and quality of the therapeutic relationship—that is, child therapy should always be conducted within the framework of a positive and respectful therapeutic relationship (e.g., Kendall & Morris, 1991; Morris & Nicholson, 1993).

Fears, Phobias, and Related Anxieties

Definition and Characteristics.   A variety of terms have been used in the literature to refer to fears, phobias, and related anxieties. *Fears* are often considered abnormal reactions to real or perceived threats and involve avoidance of a threatening stimulus (e.g., moving away from a barking dog), thoughts of being scared (e.g., saying to oneself, "That dog scares me! "), and physiological changes (e.g., increased heart rate) as a result of being exposed to the stimulus (Morris & Kratochwill, 1998a). *Phobias* are a subclassification of fears and are defined as a persistent, illogical, and involuntary avoidance reaction to a threatening stimulus. In addition, phobias—unlike most fears—are not specific to a child's age or developmental stage (Coleman, 1996; Morris & Kratochwill, 1998a). *Anxieties* are reactions to a host of diverse stimuli in a person's life that cause the same type of thoughts, physiological changes, and motoric actions that fears and phobias do. Although some writers have tried to differentiate these three terms, in many cases they have been used interchangeably within the child therapy and behavior disorders literature. Terms such as *stress* and *worry* have also been used interchangeably with *fears, phobias,* and *anxieties* (Morris & Kratochwill, 1983, 1998a). A guide for teachers is presented in Box 14.2 regarding characteristics to look for in a child or adolescent who may have a fear, phobia, or related anxiety and to help determine whether he or she should be referred for a psychological evaluation.

Treatment Methods.   There are four major behavior therapy methods that have been used on a regular basis to treat children experiencing fears, phobias, and related anxieties: systematic desensitization and its variations, contingency

---

BOX 14.2

What Teachers Should Be Looking For in Deciding Whether Children or Adolescents Should Be Referred for a Psychological Evaluation for Fears, Phobias, and Related Anxieties

The behaviors, thoughts, and feelings associated with children's fears, phobias, and related anxieties typically

- are not proportional to situational demands in or outside the classroom;
- cannot be removed or explained away on the basis of discussions with the student;
- are beyond the student's voluntary control (i.e., he or she cannot voluntarily stop);
- lead to the avoidance of feared or anxiety-provoking situations;
- are not age- or developmental stage–specific;
- persist over an extended period of time;
- are often associated with worrying thoughts and feelings whenever the anxiety-provoking or feared stimulus is near the student or the student anticipates being exposed to the stimulus.

Source: Morris and Kratochwill (1998a).

management procedures, modeling methods, and self-instructional/cognitive-behavioral approaches.

Systematic desensitization was developed by Joseph Wolpe (1958). This procedure and its variants—contact desensitization, in vivo desensitization, and group systematic desensitization—have a substantial amount of research supporting their efficacy. The basic assumption of the desensitization approach is that the child's anxiety, fear, or phobic response is learned or conditioned to various eliciting stimuli and, therefore, can be counterconditioned by substituting an activity that is antagonistic to the learned response (Morris & Kratochwill, 1998a). Usually, the antagonistic response that is learned by the child is calmness, which is induced by teaching the child how to relax using a relaxation protocol like the one shown in Box 14.3. Three phases comprise this procedure: (a) development of a fear or anxiety hierarchy that focuses on the specific situations and/or settings that cause the child to be fearful or anxious, (b) teaching the child how to relax through the use of the relaxation protocol like the one in Box 14.3, (c) systematically combining relaxation training with graduated exposure to the anxiety-provoking stimuli.

Although systematic desensitization and its variant procedures have been found to be effective in reducing a variety of children's fears and phobias (e.g., test anxiety, public speaking anxiety, school phobia, nyctophobia, water in a bathtub or swimming pool, loud noises, gaining weight, nondangerous animals, and acrophobia), some of these procedures (e.g., imaginal systematic desensitization) do not appear to be developmentally appropriate for certain age groups (Morris & Kratochwill, 1998a). For example, some writers have suggested that children below 9 years of age should not be exposed to imaginal desensitization since they may not be developmentally capable of visualizing fear-induced scenes as readily as older children (e.g., Morris & Kratochwill, 1983, 1998a). In such cases, it is recommended that in vivo or contact desensitization procedures be used (i.e., methods involving graduated live exposure to the feared stimulus).

A number of contingency management procedures have also been found to be effective in reducing children's fears and related anxieties. These procedures are based on the behavioral psychology laboratory research and writings of B. F. Skinner (e.g., Skinner, 1938). Techniques such as positive reinforcement, shaping, stimulus fading, and extinction are based on the assumption that the child has learned to be fearful or anxious and, therefore, can be taught to respond in a more adaptive manner to the previously feared stimulus/stimuli. For example, positive reinforcement has been used to reduce the frequency and duration of social withdrawal and social isolation in children, as well as to increase social interaction. When combined with shaping, positive reinforcement has also been used to treat school phobia (Morris & Kratochwill, 1983). Stimulus fading is used when the child can perform the desired behavior in some situations but not in others. Here, the child is taught to transfer the success of engaging in nonfearful behaviors from one situation to the next, until she or he is no longer fearful of the particular stimuli in any situation or setting.

BOX **14.3**

Relaxation Protocol

Steps in Relaxation Training

1. Take a deep breath and hold it (for about 10 seconds). Hold it. Okay, let it out.
2. Raise both of your hands about halfway above the couch (or arms of the chair) and breathe normally. Now drop your hands to the couch (or arm).
3. Now hold your arms out and make a tight fist. Really tight. Feel the tension in your hands. I am going to count to three and when I say "three" I want you to drop your hands. One . . . two . . . three.
4. Raise your arms again and bend your fingers back the other way (toward your body). Now drop your hands and relax.
5. Raise your arms. Now drop them and relax.
6. Now raise your arms again, but this time "flap" your hands around. Okay, relax again.
7. Raise your arms again. Now relax.
8. Raise your arms above the couch (chair) and tense your biceps. Breathe normally and keep your hands loose. Relax your hands. (Notice how you have a warm feeling of relaxation.)
9. Now hold your arms out to your side and tense your triceps. Make sure that you breathe normally. Relax your arms.
10. Now arch your shoulders back. Hold it. Make sure your arms are relaxed. Now relax.
11. Hunch your shoulders forward. Hold it and make sure that you breathe normally and keep your arms relaxed. Okay, relax. (Notice the feeling or relief from tensing and relaxing your muscles.)
12. Now turn your head to the right and tense your neck. Relax and bring your head back to its natural position.*
13. Turn your head to the left and tense your neck. Relax and bring your head back again to its natural position.*
14. Now bend your head back slightly toward the chair. Hold it. Okay, now bring your head back slowly to its natural position.*
15. This time bring your head down almost to your chest. Hold it. Now relax and let your head come back to its natural resting position.*
16. Now open your mouth as much as possible. A little wider, okay, relax (mouth should be partly open afterward).
17. Now tense your lips by closing your mouth. Okay, relax.
18. Now put your tongue at the roof of your mouth. Press hard. (Pause.) Relax and allow your tongue to come to a comfortable position in your mouth.
19. Now put your tongue at the bottom of your mouth. Press down hard. Relax and let your tongue come to a comfortable position in your mouth.
20. Now just lie (sit) there and relax. Try not to think of anything.
21. To control self-verbalizations, I want you to go through the motions of singing a high note—not aloud. Okay, start singing to yourself. Hold that note. Okay, relax. (You are becoming more and more relaxed.)

22. Now sing in a medium tone and make your vocal cords tense again. Relax.
23. Now sing in a low tone and make your vocal cords tense again. Relax. (Your vocal apparatus should be relaxed now. Relax your mouth.)
24. Now close your eyes. Squeeze them tight and breathe naturally. Notice the tension. Now relax. Notice how the pain goes away when you relax.
25. Now let your eyes relax and keep your mouth open slightly.
26. Open your eyes as much as possible. Hold it. Now relax your eyes.
27. Now wrinkle your forehead as much as possible. Hold it. Okay, relax.
28. Now take a deep breath and hold it. Relax.
29. Now exhale. Breathe all the air out? All of it. Relax. (Notice the wondrous feeling of breathing again.)
30. Imagine that there are weights pulling on all your muscles making them flaccid and relaxed . . . putting your arms and body down into the couch.
31. Pull your stomach muscles together. Tighter. Okay, relax.
32. Now extend your muscles as if you were a prizefighter. Make your stomach hard. Relax. (You are becoming more and more relaxed.)
33. Now tense your buttocks. Tighter. Hold it. Now relax.
34. Now search the upper part of your body and relax any part that is tense. First the facial muscles. (Pause 3 to 5 seconds.) Then the vocal muscles. (Pause 3 to 5 seconds.) The neck region. (Pause 3 to 5 seconds.) Your shoulders? Relax any part that is tense. (Pause.) Now the arms and fingers. Relax these. Becoming very relaxed.
35. Maintaining this relaxation, raise both your legs (about a 45% angle). Now relax. Notice how this further relaxes you.
36. Now bend your feet back so that your toes point toward your face. Relax your mouth. Bend them hard. Relax.
37. Bend your feet the other way, away from your body. Not far. Notice the tension. Okay, relax.
38. Relax. (Pause.) Now curl your toes together as hard as you can. Tighter. Okay, relax. (Quiet—silence for 30 seconds.)
39. This completes the formal relaxation procedure. Now explore your body from your feet. Make sure that every muscle is relaxed. Say slowly—first your toes, your feet, your legs, buttocks, stomach, neck, eyes, and finally your forehead—you should be very relaxed now.

    (Quiet—silence for 10 seconds.) Just lie (sit) there and feel very relaxed, noticing the warmness of the relaxation. (Pause). I would like you to stay this way for about 1 minute, and then I am going to count to five. When I reach five, I want you to open your eyes feeling very calm and refreshed. (Quiet—silence for about 1 minute.) Okay, when I count to five, I want you to open your eyes feeling very calm and relaxed. One. Feeling very calm; two . . . very calm, very refreshed; three . . . very refreshed; four . . . and five.

*The child or adolescent should not be encouraged to turn or bend his or her neck all the way to either one side or the other or all the way back or forward.

Source: Morris, R. J. & Kratochwill, T. R. (1998a). Fears and phobias. In R. J. Morris and T. R. Kratochwill (Eds.), *The practice of child therapy* (3rd ed., p. 98). Needham Heights, MA: Allyn & Bacon. Reprinted with permission.

Modeling, based on Albert Bandura's (1969) social learning theory, assumes that fears and related anxieties are learned and unlearned through vicarious learning experiences. In this procedure, the child observes the fearless child model (or therapist) encounter, overcome, and successfully interact in the presence of the feared situation. Modeling can be performed live or through symbolic means such as in videotape modeling displays, and it is often used with clearly identifiable fears and phobias (e.g., fears of specific animals; fear of riding on the school bus; fear of entering a swimming pool when the person knows how to swim). Before modeling can take place, however, the therapist needs to be certain that the child meets the following pretreatment criteria established by Bandura (1977): (a) the child can attend to the various aspects of the modeling situation, (b) the child can retain what has been learned in the modeling endeavor, (c) the child can motorically reproduce or match what has been observed, and (d) the child is motivated to perform the observed behavior.

Cognitive behavioral therapy (CBT) has been used increasingly over the past 20 to 25 years in the treatment of children's fears, phobias, and related anxieties (see, e.g., Durham & Allan, 1993; Silverman, Kurtines, Ginsburg, Weems, & Serafini, 1999). This technique assumes that a child's fear or anxiety is due to the learning of deficient cognitions or cognitive processes associated with the feared or anxiety-provoking situation. Treatment is therefore oriented toward teaching the child new self-statements or instructions to practice each time he or she is exposed to the feared stimulus or situation (Kendall & Braswell, 1985; Kendall et al., 1992). Although appearing to encompass a defined procedure, these methods actually include a number of variations in the application of cognition to the treatment of fears and phobias in children. Each method shares, however, the assumptions that (a) cognitive processes contribute substantially to behavior change and (b) individuals can regulate their own behavior. These methods include such procedures as self-instructional training, rational-emotive therapy, and self-control. Each teaches children to recognize the cognitive and physiological indicators of emotional distress and to reappraise the manner in which they process this information. For example, in fearful children, catastrophic and fearful thoughts are replaced with more realistic (and appropriate) ones regarding the feared situation, event, or setting (Morris & Kratochwill, 1998a).

Without question, the most researched method of fear reduction involves systematic desensitization and its variants, followed by modeling and contingency management procedures, with less research published on cognitive behavioral approaches—with each of these fear or anxiety reduction methods having more data-based research associated with them than other child therapy approaches.

Childhood Depression

Definition and Characteristics.   There have been many discussions in the literature regarding the definition of childhood depression (see, e.g., Kaslow & Rehm, 1991; Kendall, Cantwell & Kazdin, 1989; Reynolds, 1990). One of the problems in defining this internalizing disorder is that the term *depression* involves the mixed usage of the word *depression* as both a descriptor of behavior (i.e., a symp-

BOX **14.4**

What Teachers Should Be Looking For in Deciding Whether Children or Adolescents Should Be Referred for a Psychological Evaluation for Depression

The behaviors, thoughts, and feelings associated with childhood depression typically involve some of the following symptoms* within the same 14-day period and represent a change from previous functioning:

- Depressed mood (often expressed as irritability in children) almost daily for the majority of the day
- Decreased interest in previously enjoyable activities
- Significant weight loss (not due to dieting) or gain in 1 month
- Psychomotor agitation or retardation
- Loss of energy on a daily basis
- Feelings of worthlessness or excessive guilt
- Decreased ability to concentrate, indecisive
- Recurrent thoughts of death, suicidal ideation, or suicide attempt

* Symptoms should not be due to physiological effects of substance abuse or a general medical condition

Source: American Psychiatric Association (1994).

tom) and as a cluster of behaviors (i.e., a syndrome or diagnostic classification). Box 14.4 lists the major characteristics or symptoms of this internalizing disorder. The major symptom is also the same for adults—namely, dysphoric mood that is also correlated with the presence of various physical, behavioral, and cognitive symptom clusters. Although depressive symptoms in children and adults are generally similar, the manner in which particular symptoms are manifested may vary in children according to their respective age grouping. For example, as shown in Box 14.5, while preschoolers show behaviors such as anger, food and sleep problems, tantrums, and separation anxiety (Carlson & Kashani, 1988), depressed 6- to 8-year-olds are accident-prone, are attention seeking, and have poor school performance (Edelsonh, Ialongo, Werthamer-Larsson, Crockett, & Kellam, 1992). Nine- to 12-year-olds verbalize feelings of low self-esteem along with feelings of guilt, lethargy, and aggression (Weiss, Weisz, Politano, Carey, Nelson, & Finch, 1992). They are also more likely to have suicidal ideation, hallucinations, and self-destructive behaviors (Kaslow, Morris, & Rehm, 1998). Due to the differences in symptom presentation, it is essential for interventions to be sensitive to developmental differences along with sex differences. Notwithstanding these differences, Stark et al. (1993) report that "[o]ver 90 % of the depressed youths that have participated in our research . . . have reported low self-esteem" (p. 115). They further point out that many depressed youths also report feelings of worthlessness.

BOX **14.5**

Age-Related Symptoms of Depression

Preschool: anger, irritability, sad facial expression, labile mood, somatic complaints, feeding and sleep problems, lethargy, excessive crying, hyper- or hypoactivity, decreased socialization, tantrums, separation anxiety, and anhedonia

6 to 8 years of age: prolonged unhappiness, decreased socialization, sleep problems, irritability, lethargy, poor school performance, accident-proneness, phobias, separation anxiety, and attention-seeking behaviors

9 to 12 years of age: verbalized feelings of decreased self-esteem and helplessness, irritability, depressed mood, sad expression, aggression, lethargy, guilt, poor school performance, phobias, separation anxiety, suicidal ideation, hallucinations, and self-destructive behavior

Source: Kaslow, Morris, and Rehm (1998).

Treatment Methods.   Although interest in the treatment of childhood depression has increased tremendously, the amount of child therapy research published in this area is still relatively limited (see, e.g., Kaslow et al., 1998; Kazdin, 1989; Reinecke, Ryan, & DuBois, 1998; Stark et al., 1993; Wood, Harrington, & Moors, 1996). Of the various psychotherapy approaches discussed in the literature, the ones that have received increasing attention involve cognitive therapy and CBT approaches, problem solving/skills training, and activity-level programs (e.g., Kaslow et al., Rehm, 1977; Kazdin, 1989; Stark et al., 1993).

The cognitive therapy approach follows Aaron Beck's model (e.g., Beck, Rush, Shaw, & Emery, 1979) and examines the distorted cognitions and related attributions that a child may have about his or her current life experiences, as well as the cognitions associated with the child's low level of self-esteem and feelings of helplessness and rejection. The CBT approach is consistent with a number of cognitively based behavior therapy models, such as the self-control model of Rehm (1977) and Ellis's (1962) rational-emotive therapy. Rehm's model assumes that depression results from deficits in such self-control areas as self-evaluation, self-monitoring, self-reinforcement, and the attributions one forms about events in her or his life. Therapy, therefore, focuses on teaching children adaptive skills with regard to the ways in which they self-monitor, self-reinforce, self-evaluate, and attribute the causes of good and bad outcomes. Homework assignments are also given to the child to assist him or her in practicing these newly learned self-control procedures in those settings in which they typically experience depressed feelings or thoughts (e.g., Kaslow & Rehm, 1991; Stark, Reynolds, & Kaslow, 1987).

In rational-emotive therapy, the child therapist assumes that the irrational statements that the child makes about herself or himself contribute to the development of depression. For example, such self-statements as the following could cause the child to feel depressed and engage in depression-like behaviors: "No one is really interested in who I am or what I have to say. Even if someone did become interested, he would soon discover, as I already know, that I am not worth it" (Bernard & Joyce, 1993). The therapist examines with the child the irrational nature of these and other statements that the child formulates about himself or herself whenever certain events occur in his or her life and works with the child in reconfiguring and building a new set of rational statements about the same life events.

The problem-solving/skills-training approach involves the identification of the problematic social skills that a child manifests and teaches him or her to respond in a manner that is more likely to lead on a regular basis to positive reinforcement and feedback from significant others in his or her environment. Modeling, role playing, and social reinforcement are also used in this approach to assist in the education of the children (e.g., Clarke, Hawkins, Murphy, Sheeber, Lewinsohn, & Seeley, 1995; Frame, Matson, Sonis, Fialkov, & Kazdin, 1982; Kaslow et al., 1998).

Programs designed to increase the activity level of children having depression are based on the assumption that reduced rates of environmental reinforcement contribute to them developing the disorder. The purpose, therefore, of this type of treatment is to increase the frequency of pleasurable activities and response-contingent reinforcement experiences that a particular child experiences on a daily basis (Kaslow et al., 1998). It is usually recommended that the behaviors and activities that are reinforced involve those that the children enjoyed in the past or those activities that have been shown to result in positive moods. The main techniques that have been used to increase activity levels include modeling, individual and group reinforcement contingencies, and social reinforcement from the teacher or other significant adults (Kaslow et al., 1998).

As is the case with children's fears, phobias, and related anxieties, particular attention should be given to the child's age and developmental level to determine whether she or he is developmentally ready to participate in the type of therapy being proposed. Many times, the parents of the child will also need to be seen in therapy because the cognitive strategies and/or behaviors that the child manifests may be modeled by the parents; therefore, the parents may need to learn alternative strategies for teaching their child how to deal more effectively with various life events. The parents may also need to be taught how to address more effectively conflict between one or both of them and their child. In addition, the therapist may need to consult with the child's teacher(s) regarding how she or he could best create a positive and rewarding classroom and school environment for the child.

Obsessive-Compulsive Disorder

Definition and Characteristics.   As indicated earlier regarding the definitions of childhood depression and fears, phobias and related anxieties, problems have also been noted in the literature with respect to the definition of OCD in children (Milby et al., 1998). Based on the widely accepted definition used by the American

BOX 14.6

What Teachers Should Be Looking For in Deciding Whether Children or Adolescents Should Be Referred for a Psychological Evaluation for Obsessive-Compulsive Disorder

The behaviors, thoughts, and feelings associated with obsessive-compulsive disorder typically involve obsessions/compulsions causing marked distress and often lasting more than 1 hour a day.

- Interference with the student's normal routine or academic functioning or social activities/relationships
- Gradual decline in schoolwork

Common obsessions

- Repeated thoughts of contamination (e.g., germs)
- Repeated doubts about having performed an action (e.g., having locked a locker, turned in an assignment)
- Need to have things in a particular order (e.g., either on top of or inside the desk) and/or need for symmetry

Common compulsions

- Repeated behaviors (e.g., hand washing, checking that an act was performed, and touching objects)
- Repeated mental acts (e.g., praying, counting, and repeating words silently)
- Requesting/demanding assurances

Psychiatric Association (1994), and as summarized briefly in Box 14.6, *obsessions* are defined as persistent, intrusive, and inappropriate thoughts, images, or impulses causing a great deal of anxiety and discomfort in the person. Individuals having obsessions (or obsessive thoughts) feel that the content of these obsessions are foreign, uncontrollable, and unexpected—although they know that the obsessions are self-generated and not imposed on them by anyone (or by any object or event). Examples of common obsessions include recurring thoughts about being contaminated (through contact with a person or object), doubts about one's actions (leaving the stove on; hurting another individual with one's bicycle or car), having aggressive impulses (hurting/killing a person), or a need for orderliness and symmetry. Those children or adolescents who have obsessions often try to suppress their ideas or impulses or use actions such as checking, counting, or praying to try to offset them (APA, 1994).

While obsessions are repeated thoughts, images, or impulses, *compulsions* are defined as excessive and repetitive behaviors (cleaning, hand washing, or checking) or mental acts (praying or counting) used (unrealistically) in an attempt to decrease the anxiety resulting from an obsession or to prevent an undesired event from taking place. Handwashing/cleaning, checking, and ordering are the most frequently seen compulsive behaviors in children (APA, 1994). Children having compulsions will repeatedly perform stereotyped actions according to certain rules or rituals without being able to explain why they are doing them. Research findings by Swedo, Leonard, and Rapoport (1992) suggest that obsessions alone are extremely uncommon in children while rituals alone are much more common, especially in children between 6 and 8 years of age. In addition, Swedo et al. found that washing behaviors affected 85% of the children they studied, repeating rituals occurred in 51% of the cases, checking behaviors were seen in 46% of the children, ordering in 17%, and aggressive or sexual obsessive images in 4% of the sample.

While it is necessary for adults with OCD to recognize their obsessions and/or compulsions as excessive, this is not a requirement for making this diagnosis in children. This is because many children do not have the cognitive skills to make this "excessive" determination. For children to be diagnosed as having OCD, it is necessary for their obsessions or compulsions to cause them a great deal of distress, interfere with their daily functioning, and be time-consuming (i.e., more than 1 hour per day being devoted to the obsession or compulsion) (APA, 1994). A diagnosis of OCD, however, excludes those children diagnosed as having psychoses, but not those who have mental retardation or who had OCD prior to having a brain injury (Milby et al., 1998).

Treatment Methods.   Treatment for OCD usually consists of a three-stage approach: (a) information gathering, (b) therapist-assisted exposure and response prevention (ERP), and (c) homework assignments. In the information-gathering phase, the therapist works with the child, parents, and teachers to identify and analyze the various settings, events, and circumstances that contribute or produce the obsessional and/or compulsive behaviors. ERP is based on the notion that anxiety usually decreases following sufficient and gradual contact with the feared or anxiety-producing stimulus and learning to cope with anxiety in the presence of the stimulus. Through imagery tasks—such as imagining oneself in the same room with the anxiety-provoking stimulus and imagining coping with the anxiety as well as touching the stimulus—the child or adolescent is exposed to the anxiety-provoking stimulus in a systematic and graduated fashion. He or she is repeatedly exposed to the stimulus in the therapist's presence through imagery training (and/or through in vivo exposure experiences) until anxiety decreases. The child is also asked to engage in response prevention practices, which means that he or she must practice a behavior(s) in the presence of the anxiety-producing stimulus that is incompatible with the performance of the ritualized or compulsive behavior. The child is also given homework assignments that typically involve practicing the coping self-statements at home and the promotion of positive thought patterns regarding coping with the obsessions and/or compulsions (Milby et al., 1998).

In a variation of this latter procedure, Franklin, Kozak, Cashman, Coles, Rheingold, and Foa (1998) used CBT plus in vivo exposure and ritual prevention with children between 10 and 17 years old. They found that this form of treatment was effective in treating the children's OCD. Similarly, de Hann, Hoogduin, Buitelaar, and Keiksers (1998) studied the effects of the same type of procedure but compared it with the use of drug treatment (clomipramine) in children between 8 and 18 years of age. They found significant improvement in the children in each treatment condition, suggesting that CBT with exposure and response prevention is a good alternative to drug treatment.

Summary

In this chapter, we have presented an overview of the assessment, diagnosis, and treatment literature regarding the major internalizing behavior disorders in children: fears, phobias, and related anxieties, childhood depression, and obsessive-compulsive disorder. Clearly, much progress has been made in the past 25 years in identifying effective assessment, diagnostic and treatment procedures that can be used in school and clinic settings. The literature suggests that the child therapist, parents, and teachers need to be sensitized to comorbidity issues since coexisting behavior problems may affect the outcome of child therapy—and may necessitate a change in the treatment plan for a child. Additional research is needed regarding the contribution of such variables as child and/or therapist ethnicity and cultural background on the outcome of treatment, as well as controlled comparison outcome studies involving more than one treatment procedure.

REFERENCES

Achenbach, T. M., & Edelbrock, C. (1983). *Manual for the child behavior checklist and revised child behavior profile.* Burlington: University of Vermont, Department of Psychiatry.

Achenbach. T. M., & Edelbrock, C. (1986). *Manual for the teacher's reports form and teacher version of the child behavior profile.* Burlington: University of Vermont, Department of Psychiatry.

American Psychiatric Association. (1994). *Diagnostic and statistical manual of mental disorders* (4th ed.). Washington. DC: Author.

Angold. A., & Costello, E. J. (1993). Depressive comorbidity in children and adolescents: Empirical, theoretical, and methodological issues. *American Journal of Psychiatry, 150,* 1779–1791.

Bandura, A. (1969). *Principles of behavior modification.* New York: Holt.

Bandura, A. (1977). *Social learning theory.* Englewood Cliffs, NJ: Prentice Hall. New York: Guilford.

Bear, G. C., Minke, K. M., & Thomas, A. (Eds.). (1997). *Children's needs II- Development, problems, and alternatives.* Bethesda, MD: National Association of School Psychologists.

Beck, A. T., Rush, A. G., Shaw, B. F., & Emery, G. (1979). *Cognitive therapy of depression.* New York: Guilford.

Benjamin, R. S., Costello, E. J., & Warren, M. (1990). Anxiety disorders in a pediatric sample. *Journal of Anxiety Disorders, 4,* 293–316.

Bergan, J. R., & Kratochwill, T. R. (1990). *Behavioral consultations and therapy.* New York: Plenum.

Bernard, M. E., & Joyce, M. R. (1993). Rational-emotive therapy with children and adolescents. In T. R. Kratochwill & R. J. Morris (Eds.), *Handbook of psychotherapy with children and adolescents* (pp. 221–246). Needham Heights, MA: Allyn & Bacon.

Bijou, S. W. (1955). A systematic approach to an experimental analysis of young children. *Child Development, 26,* 161–168.

Carlson, G. A., & Kashani, J. H. (1988). Phenomenology of major depression form childhood through adulthood: Analysis of three studies. *American Journal of Psychiatry, 145,* 1222–1225.

Clarke. G. N., Hawkins. W., Murphy, M., Sheeber, L. B., Lewinsohn, P. M., & Seeley J. R. (1995). Targeted prevention of unipolar depressive disorder in an at-risk sample of high school adolescents: A randomized trial of a group cognitive intervention. *Journal of the American Academy of Child and Adolescent Psychiatry, 34,* 312–321.

Cole, D. A., Peeke, L. G., Martin, J. M., Truglio, R., & Serocyznski, A. D. (1998). A longitudinal look at the relation between depression and anxiety, in children and adolescents. *Journal of Consulting and Clinical Psychology, 66,* 451–460.

Coleman, M. C. (1996). *Emotional and behavioral disorders: Theory and practice* (3rd ed.). Needham Heights, MA: Allyn & Bacon.

de Hann, E., Hoogduin, K. A. L., Buitelaar, J. K, & Keiksers, G. P. J. (1998). Behavior therapy versus clomipramine for the treatment of obsessive-compulsive disorder. *Journal of the American Academy of Child and Adolescent Psychiatry, 37,* 1022–1029.

Durham, R. C., & Allan, T. (1993). Psychological treatment of general anxiety disorder: a review of the clinical significance of results in outcome studies since 1980. *British Journal of Psychiatry, 163,* 19–26.

Edelsohn, G., Ialongo, N., Werthamer-Larsson, L., Crockett, I., & Kellam, S. (1992). Self-reported depressive symptoms in first-grade children: Developmentally transient phenomena. *Journal of the American Academy of Child and Adolescent Psychiatry, 31,* 282–290.

Ellis, A. (1962). *Reason and emotion in psychotherapy.* New York: Stuart.

Essau, C. A., Conradt, J., & Peterman, F. (2000). Frequency, comorbidity, and psychosocial impairment of specific phobia in adolescents. *Journal of Clinical Child Psychology, 29,* 221–231.

Frame, C., Matson, J. L., Sonis, W. A., Fialkov, M. J., & Kazdin, A. E. (1982). Behavioral treatment of depression in a prepubertal child. *Journal of Behavioral Therapy and Experimental Psychiatry, 3,* 239–243.

Franklin, M. E., Kozak, M. J., Cashman, L. A., Coles, M. E., Rheingold, A. A., & Foa, E. B. (1998). Cognitive-behavioral treatment of pediatric obsessive-compulsive disorder: An open clinical trial. *Journal of the American Academy, of Child and Adolescent Psychiatry. 37,* 412–419.

Gresham. F. M., & Elliott, S. N. (1990). *Social skills rating system.* Circle Pines, MN: American Guidance Service.

Jones, M. C. (1924). A laboratory, study, of fear: The case of Peter. *Journal of Genetic Psychology 31,* 308–315.

Kanner, L. (1948). *Child psychiatry.* Springfield, IL: Thomas.

Kaslow,. N. J., & Rehm. L. P. (1998). Childhood depression. In R. J. Morris & T. R. Kratochwill (Eds.). *The practice of child therapy* (3rd ed., pp. 48–90). Needham Heights, MA: Allyn & Bacon.

Kaslow, N. J.. & Rehm, L. P. (1991). Childhood depression. In T. R. Kratochwill & R. J. Morris (Eds.), *The practice of child therapy,* (2nd ed.) (pp. 43–75). New York: Pergamon.

Kauffman, J. M. (1981). *Characteristics of children's behavior disorders.* Columbus, OH: Merrill.

Kazdin, A. E. (1989). Childhood depression. In E. J. Mash & R. A. Barkley (Eds.), *Treatment of childhood disorders* (pp. 135–166). New York: Guilford.

Kazdin, A. E., (1994). *Behavior modification in applied settings* (4th ed.). Homewood, IL: Dorsey.

Kazdin, A. E., Siegel, T. C., & Bass, D. (1990). Drawing on clinical practice to inform research on child and adolescent psychotherapy: Survey of practitioners. *Journal of Consulting and Clinical Psychology, 21,* 189–198.

Kendall, P. C., & Braswell, L. (1985). *Cognitive-behavioral therapy for impulsive children:* New York: Guilford.

Kendall, P. C., Cantwell, D. A., & Kazdin, A. E. (1989). Depression in children and adolescents: Assessment issues and recommendations. *Cognitive Therapy and Research, 13,* 109–146.

Kendall, P. C., Chansky, T. E., Kane, M. T., Kim R. S., Kortlander, E., Roman, K. R., Sessa, F. M., & Siqueland, L. (1992). *Anxiety disorders in youth: Cognitive-behavioral interventions.* New York: Allyn & Bacon.

Kendall, P. C., & Chu, B. C. (2000). Retrospective self-reports of therapist flexibility in a manual-based treatment for youths with anxiety disorders. *Journal of Clinical Child Psychology, 29,* 209–220.

Kendall. P. C., & Morris, R. J. (1991). Child therapy: Issues and recommendations. *Journal of Consulting and Clinical Psychology, 59,* 777–784.

King, N. J.,. Hamilton, D. I., & Ollendick, T. H. (1988). *Children's phobias: A behavioral perspective.* New York: Wiley.

King,. N. J., Ollendick, T. H.. & Mattis, S. G. (1994). Panic in children and adolescents: Normative and clinical studies. *Australian Psychologist, 40*, 89–93.

Kratochwill, T. R., Morris, R. J. (Eds.). (1993). *Handbook of psychotherapy with children and adolescents*. Needham Heights, MA: Allyn & Bacon.

Lachar. D. (1993). Symptom checklists and personality inventories. In T. R. Kratochwill & R. J. Morris (Eds.), *Handbook of psychotherapy with children and adolescents* (pp. 38–57). Needham Heights, MA: Allyn & Bacon.

Mace, F. E., Brown, K. B., & West B. J. (1987). Behavioral self-management in education. In C. A. Maher & J. E. Zins (Eds.), *Psychoeducational interventions in the schools* (pp. 160–176). New York: Pergamon.

March, J. S., Leonard, H.L., & Swedo, S. E. (1995). Obsessive-compulsive disorder. In J. S. March, Duke University Medical Center, Department of Psychiatry, Program in Child & Adolescent Anxiety, Disorders (Eds.), *Anxiety disorders in children and adolescents* (pp. 251–275). New York: Guilford.

Messer, S. C., & Beidel, D. C. (1994). Psychosocial correlates of childhood anxiety disorders. *Journal of the American Academy of Childhood Psychiatry, 33*, 975–983.

Milby, J. B., Robinson–, S. L., & Daniel S. (1998). Obsessive compulsive disorders. In R. J. Morris & T. R. Kratochwill (Eds.), *The practice of child therapy* (3rd ed., pp. 5–47). Needham Heights, MA: Allyn & Bacon.

Morris, R. J. (1985). *Behavior modification with exceptional children: Principles and practices*. Glenview, IL: Scott, Foresman.

Morris, R. J., & Kratochwill, T. R. (1983). *Treating children's fears and phobias. A behavioral approach*. New York: Pergamon.

Morris, R. J., & Kratochwill T. R. (1998a). Fears and phobias. In R. J. Morris & T. R. Kratochwill (Eds.), *The practice of child therapy* (3rd ed. pp. 91–131). Needham Heights, MA: Allyn & Bacon.

Morris, R. J., & Kratochwill, T. R. (Eds.). (1998b). *The practice of child therapy* (3rd ed.). Needham Heights, MA: Allyn & Bacon.

Morris, R. J., & Morris, Y. P. (2000). Practice guidelines regarding the conduct of psychotherapy with children and adolescents. In G. Stricker, W. G. Try, & S. A. Shueman (Eds.), *Handbook of quality management in behavioral health* (pp. 237–265). New York: Kluwer Academic/Plenum.

Morris, R. J., & Nicholson, J. (1993). The therapeutic relationship in child and adolescent psychotherapy. In T. R. Kratochwill & R. J. Morris (Eds.), *Handbook of psychotherapy with children and adolescents* (pp. 405–425). Needham Heights, MA: Allyn & Bacon.

Mowrer, O. H. (1960). *Learning theory and behavior.* New York: Wiley.

Nelson, R. O., Hay, L. R., Devany, J., & Koslow-Green, L. (1980). The reactivity and accuracy, of children's self-monitoring: Three experiments. *Child Behavior Therapy, 2*, 1–24.

Orvaschel, H., & Weissman, M. (1986). Epidemiology of anxiety in children. In R. Gittleman (Ed.), *Anxiety disorders of childhood* (pp. 58–72). New York: Guilford.

Pavlov, I. P. (1927). *Conditioned reflexes.* Trans. G. V. Anrep. London: Oxford University, Press.

Rehm, L. P. (1977). A self-control model of depression. *Behavior Therapy, 8*, 787–804.

Reinecke,. M. A., Ryan, N. E., & DuBois, D. L. (1998). Cognitive-behavioral therapy of depression and depressive symptoms during adolescence: A review and meta-analysis. *Journal of the American Academy of Child and Adolescent Psychiatry, 37*, 26–34.

Reynolds, W. M. (1987). *Reynolds's adolescent depression scale.* Odessa, FL: Psychological Assessment Resources.

Reynolds, W. M. (1990). Depressions in children and adolescents: Nature, diagnosis, assessment, and treatment. *School Psychology Review, 19*, 158–173.

Riddle, M. A., Scahill, L., King, R., Hardin, M. T., Towbin, K. E., Ort, S. I., Leckman, J. F., & Cohen, D. J. (1990). Obsessive-compulsive disorder in children and adolescents: Phenomenology and family history. *Journal of the American Academy of Child and Adolescent Psychiatry, 29*, 766–772.

Shapiro, E. S. (1987). *Behavioral assessment in school psychology.* Hillsdale, NJ: Erlbaum.

Shapiro, E. S., & Skinner, C. H. (1993). Childhood behavioral assessment and diagnosis. In T. R. Kratochwill & R. J. Morris (Eds.), *Handbook of psychotherapy with children adolescents* (pp. 75–107). Needham Heights, MA: Allyn & Bacon.

Silverman, W. K., Kurtines, W. M., Ginsburg, G. S., Weems, C. F., Rabian, B. R., & Serafini, L. T (1999). Contingency management, self-control, and education support in the treatment of childhood phobic disorders: A randomized clinical trial. *Journal of Consulting and Clinical Psychology, 67,* 675–687.

Skinner, B. F. (1938). *The behavior of organisms.* New York: Appleton-Century-Crofts.

Skinner, B. F. (1953). *Science and human behavior.* New York: Macmillan.

Stark, K. D., Dempsey, M., & Christopher, J. (1993). Depressive disorders. In R. T. Ammerman, C. G. Last, & M. Hersen (Eds.), *Handbook of prescriptive treatments for children and adolescents* (pp. 115–143). Needham Heights, MA: Allyn & Bacon.

Stark, K. D., Reynolds, W. M., & Kaslow, N. J. (1987). A comparison of the relative efficacy of self-control therapy and a behavioral problem solving therapy for depression in children. *Journal of Abnormal Child Psychology, 15,* 91–113.

Swedo, S. E., Leonard, H. L., & Rapoport, J. L. (1992). Childhood-onset obsessive-compulsive disorder. *Psychiatric Clinics of North America, 5,* 767–775.

Walker, H. M., & McConnell, S. R. (1988). *The Walker-McConnell scale of social competence and school adjustment.* Austin, TX: Pro-Ed.

Watson, J. B., & Rayner, R. (1920). Conditioned emotional reactions. *Journal of Experimental Psychology, 3,* 1–14.

Weiss, B., Weisz, J. R., Politano, M., Carey, M., Nelson, W. M., & Finch, A. J. (1992). Relations among self-reported depressive symptoms in clinic-referred children versus adolescents. *Journal of Abnormal Psychology, 101,* 391–397.

Witt, J. C., Elliott, S. N., & Gresham, F. M (Eds.). (1988). *Handbook of behavior therapy in education.* New York: Plenum.

Wolple, J. (1958). *Reciprocal inhibition therapy.* Stanford, CA: Stanford University Press.

Wood, A., Harrington, R. & Moore, A. (1996). Controlled trial of a brief cognitive-behavioral intervention in adolescent patients with depressive disorders. *Journal of Child Psychology & Psychiatry & Allied Disciplines. 37,* 737–746.

15

Social Skills Assessment and Instruction for Students with Emotional and Behavioral Disorders

FRANK M. GRESHAM
University of California–Riverside

Introduction

The degree to which a child is able to interact successfully with peers, teachers, and parents represents one of the most important developmental accomplishments. The extent to which children and youth are able to establish and maintain satisfactory interpersonal relationships, gain peer acceptance, make meaningful friendships, and terminate negative or pernicious social interactions defines social competence and predicts adequate long-term psychological and social adjustment (Kupersmidt, Coie, & Dodge, 1990; Parker & Asher, 1987).

Social competence deficits are particularly salient for students having emotional and behavioral disorders (E/BD) (Forness & Knitzer, 1992). In fact, two of the five criteria specified in the Individuals with Disabilities Education Act (IDEA) are pivotal in identifying students with emotional disturbance: (a) an inability to build or maintain satisfactory interpersonal relationships with peers and teachers and (b) inappropriate types of behavior or feelings under normal circumstances.

Social competence deficits are particularly critical in the development and maintenance of childhood disorders characterized by an *externalizing* behavior pattern such as oppositional defiant disorder, conduct disorder, and attention deficit hyperactivity disorder (ADHD) (Achenbach, 1985; Hinshaw, 1987). Social competence deficits also are problematic for students having *internalizing* behavior disorders (see Chapter 14 Morris, Shah, & Morris, this text). For example, students exhibiting an antisocial behavior pattern characterized by aggression, hostility, and violation of social norms are highly resistant to intervention, particularly if intervention does not occur early in the child's educational career (Walker,

Colvin, & Ramsey, 1995). Kazdin (1987) suggests that, after about age 8 (grade 3), an antisocial behavior pattern should be viewed as a chronic condition (e.g., diabetes) that cannot be cured but rather managed with appropriate interventions and supports.

Students with ADHD also exhibit significant deficits in social competence and difficulties in interpersonal relationships (Landau & Moore, 1991). Landau and Moore (1991) suggest that these children evoke an extremely negative response from their peer group, which, in turn, leads to high levels of peer rejection. These students are perceived by their peers and teachers as annoying, boisterous, intractable, and irritating—much of which can be attributed to the core ADHD behavioral characteristics of impulsivity, inattention, and overactivity.

It is clear that students with EB/D experience significant deficits in social competence that adversely impacts on the quality and nature of their interpersonal relationships with peers and significant adults. The purpose of this chapter is to present readers with practical information and strategies for the assessment of and intervention with social competence deficits of these students.

Conceptualization of Social Competence

A comprehensive review of theories and definitions of social skills by Merrell and Gimpel (1998) indicates that at least 15 definitions that have been used in the literature. Although many definitions and conceptualizations of social competence have been discussed, the *social validity* definition is a particularly useful way of conceptualizing social competence (Gresham, 1983; Wolf, 1978). A social validity conceptualization defines social skills as socially significant behaviors exhibited in specific situations, which predict important social outcomes for children and youth. *Socially significant* behaviors are those behaviors that treatment consumers (e.g., teachers, parents, and peers) consider desirable and that predict an individual's standing on socially important outcomes. *Socially important* outcomes are outcomes that treatment consumers consider important and/or that are adaptive or functional in particular environments. In short, socially important outcomes make a difference in terms of an individual's functioning or adaptation to environmental demands and age-appropriate societal expectations. Socially important outcomes might include peer acceptance and friendships (Newcomb, Bukowski, & Pattee, 1993), teacher and parental judgments of social competence (Gresham & Elliott, 1990), and school adjustment (Walker, Irvin, Noell, & Singer, 1992).

The social validity definition also distinguishes between the concepts of *social competence* and *social skill* (see, McFall, 1982). In this view, social skills are specific behaviors than an individual exhibits to perform competently on a social task (e.g., starting a conversation or entering an ongoing play group). *Social competence* is an evaluative term based on opinions or judgments of significant others (e.g., teachers, parents, peers), comparisons to explicit criteria (e.g., number of social tasks performed correctly), and/or comparisons to a normative sample. In summary, social skills are behaviors that must be taught, learned, and performed, whereas social competence represents judgments or evaluations by others of these behaviors within and across situations over time.

Taxonomy of Social Skills

A great deal of research has focused on developing a taxonomy or dimensional approach to classifying maladaptive or problem behaviors. Achenbach and colleagues have developed a comprehensive, reliable, and valid classification of externalizing and internalizing behavior patterns that are reflected in teacher, parent, and student rating scales (Achenbach, 1985).

Caldarella and Merrell (1997) provide a taxonomy of social skills based on a synthesis review of 21 investigations using 19 social skills rating scales or inventories. Studies in this synthesis of factor-analytic research included 22,000 students ranging in age from 3 to 18 years, with approximately equal gender representation across studies. Teacher ratings were used in approximately 75% of the studies, with parent and self-report measures being used in about 19% of the studies. Peer sociometrics were used in only 5% of the studies.

Caldarella and Merrell (1997) derived a taxonomy from their review that included five broad dimensions of social skills: (a) peer relations skills, (b) self-management skills, (c) academic skills, (d) compliance skills, and (e) self-management skills. This taxonomy provides useful directions for selecting target social skills for more in-depth assessments and interventions. A number of these social skills domains have been used in social skills intervention programs such as social problem-solving skills curricula (Elias & Clabby, 1992), *Social Skills Intervention Guide* (Elliott & Gresham, 1992), *The Prepare Curriculum* (Goldstein, 1988), and the *ACCEPTS Program* (Walker, McConnell, Holmes, Todis, Walker, & Golden, 1983) (see Chapter 4 by Howell & Kelley, this text).

Classification of Social Skills Deficits

An important aspect of social skills assessment that is relevant for designing interventions is an accurate classification of the specific type(s) of social skills deficits a student may have. Gresham (1981) distinguishes between social skill *acquisition* and *performance* deficits. This distinction is important because it suggests different intervention approaches in remediating social skills deficits and may indicate different settings for carrying out social skills training (e.g., pullout groups vs. contextually based interventions in naturalistic settings). A third type of social skill deficit may be called a *fluency* deficit in which a student may know how to and wants to perform a given social skill but executes an awkward or unpolished performance of the social skill. A social skill fluency deficit is similar to readers who can accurately decode words but render slow, dysfluent oral reading performances.

Social skills *acquisition deficits* refer to the absence of knowledge for executing a particular social skill even under optimal conditions. Social *performance deficits* represent the presence of a social skill in an individual's behavioral repertoire but a failure to perform this skill at an acceptable level in a particular situation or situations. Acquisition deficits can be conceptualized as "can't do" problems, whereas performance deficits are "won't do" or motivational deficits. Fluency deficits may stem from a lack of exposure to competent models of social behavior or from inadequate behavioral rehearsal of newly acquired or infrequently used social skills.

This social skills classification model has been expanded to include the notion of *competing problem behaviors* (Gresham & Elliott, 1990). In this model, two dimensions of behavior, social skills and competing problem behaviors, are combined to classify social skills difficulties. Competing behaviors can include internalizing or overcontrolled behavior patterns (e.g., anxiety, depression, and social withdrawal) or externalizing or undercontrolled behavior patterns (e.g., aggression, impulsivity, and disruption). Box 15.1 presents this social skill classification model.

The two-dimensional social skill deficit classification model shown in Box 15.1 is pivotal in linking assessment results to interventions for social skills deficits. It is inappropriate to teach a social skill to students who already have that skill in their repertoires (i.e., with performance deficits). Similarly, intervention procedures designed to increase the performance of a social skill (e.g., prompting, reinforcement) are not particularly efficient in remediating acquisition deficits. Finally, students having fluency deficits do not require that a skill be taught nor do they require intervention procedures to increase the frequency of behavioral performances. Instead, these students would require more opportunities to respond and rehearsal (repetitions) of the skill for adequate and socially effective behavioral performances. Specific intervention procedures for acquisition, performance, and fluency deficits are presented later in this chapter.

BOX 15.1
Social Skills Classification Model

Competing

Problem Behavior(s)	Performance	Acquisition	Fluency
Present	Performance deficit	Acquisition deficit	Fluency deficit
Absent	Performance deficit	Acquisition deficit	Fluency deficit

Source: Adapted from Gresham (1998a, p. 479).

Considerations in Social Skills Assessment

A comprehensive discussion of social skills assessment methods is beyond the scope of this chapter; however several considerations should be entertained in linking social skills assessment information to intervention strategies. Social skills assessment takes place in five major stages of the assessment/intervention sequence: (a) screening/ selection, (b) classification of social skills deficits, (c) target behavior selection, (d) functional assessment, and (e) evaluation of intervention outcomes. Box 15.2 presents the major goals of social skills assessment, which can be classified within the four stages of a problem-solving model: problem identification, problem analysis, plan implementation, and treatment evaluation (Bergan & Kratochwill, 1990).

Like all behavioral assessment methods, social skills assessment methods can be broadly classified as *indirect* or *direct* (Gresham, 1998b). Indirect behavioral assessment methods assess behavior that is removed in time and place from its actual occurrence. Examples of these methods include interviews, ratings by others, and peer assessment methods. Direct methods assess behavior at the time and place of its actual occurrence, to include naturalistic observations of social behav-

---

B O X 15.2

Goals of Social Skills Assessment

Problem Identification
- Identify social skills strengths.
- Identify social skills acquisition deficits.
- Identify social skills performance deficits.
- Identify social skills fluency deficits.
- Identify competing problem behaviors.

Problem Analysis
- Conduct functional assessment.
- Determine the social validity of specific social skills for treatment consumers.
- Select target behaviors for intervention.

Plan Implementation
- Develop and implement intervention strategies based on assessment information.
- Assess integrity of intervention procedures.

Treatment Evaluation
- Select appropriate outcome measures.
- Evaluate effects of intervention.
- Assess topographical and functional generalization effects.
- Assess maintenance of effects.

Source: In F. M. Gresham (1998) Social skill training with children: Social learning and applied behavioral analytic approaches. In Watson & Gresham (Eds) *Handbook of child behavior therapy: Issues in clinical child psychology* (pp. 479) New York: Plenum

ior (e.g., classroom and playground) and self-monitoring strategies. Three assessment methods will be highlighted in this chapter because of their importance in assessing key aspects of students' social behavior: functional assessment interviews, behavior ratings, and observation of social behavior in naturalistic settings.

Functional Assessment Interviews

A functional assessment interview (FAI) has four primary goals: (a) to identify and define social skill difficulties; (b) to assist in the differentiation of social skill acquisition, performance, and fluency deficits; (c) to identify competing problem behaviors that interfere with acquisition, performance, and/or fluency deficits; and (d) to obtain preliminary information regarding the possible functions of competing problem behaviors. A *functional assessment* of behavior seeks to identify the functions or "causes" of behavior. This information is valuable because once a behavioral function is identified, specific intervention strategies based on behavioral function can be prescribed.

Fundamentally, behavior may serve two functions: (a) to *obtain* something desirable (e.g., social attention, preferred activities, or material objects) and (b) to *avoid, escape,* or *delay* something undesirable (e.g., difficult tasks, social activities, or interruption of preferred activities). These two functions describe the processes of positive and negative reinforcement, respectively. For example, a student's social withdrawal behavior may serve to increase the frequency of adult and/or peer prompts to join an ongoing activity. In this case, social withdrawal behavior would serve a positive reinforcement function that is maintained by adult and peer social attention prompts. Alternatively, social withdrawal may allow a child to terminate aversive social interactions with peers. As such, social withdrawal would serve a negative reinforcement function maintained by escape from aversive social interactions with peers.

Persons conducting FAIs should engage in the following: (a) elicit from the interviewee specific, precise descriptions of social skill deficits and competing problem behaviors; (b) formulate a tentative description of environmental conditions surrounding socially skilled and competing problem behaviors; and (c) evaluate the effects of social skills interventions in terms of measurable behavior change. These behaviors can be described as problem identification, problem analysis, and problem evaluation, respectively (Bergan & Kratochwill, 1990; Gresham, 1998b). For more specific and comprehensive information concerning FAIs, readers should consult texts by Bergan and Kratochwill (1990) and O'Neill and colleagues (O'Neill, Horner, Albin, Sprague, Storey, & Newton, 1997).

Naturalistic Observations of Social Behavior

Systematic behavioral observations represent one of the most important social skills assessment methods. Observational data are very sensitive to intervention effects and should be included in all social skills assessment and intervention activities. Although a variety of elaborate coding systems are available for naturalistic observations of social behavior, recording procedures should be kept as simple as possible. Four factors should be considered in using systematic behavioral observations for social skills assessment: (a) precise definitions of behavior,

(b) dimensions of behavior being assessed (frequency, intensity, duration), (c) number of behaviors assessed, and (d) number of observation sessions.

Operational Definitions of Behavior. The first and most important step in collecting social skills observational data is to have a clear, objective *operational definition* of the social behavior being measured. Operational definitions should be clear, objective, and complete. Walker and Severson (1992) provide a clear example of an operational definition for the social skill of *participation:* "This is coded when the target child is participating in a game or activity (with two or more children) that has a clearly specified and agreed upon set of rules. Examples would be kickball, four-square, dodgeball, soccer, basketball, tetherball, hopscotch, and so forth. Nonexamples would include tag, jump rope, follow the leader, and other unstructured games" (pp. 23–24).

Dimensions of Behavior. Social behavior can be described and measured along the behavioral dimensions of frequency, duration, and quality. Frequency, or how often a social behavior occurs, is often used as an index of social competence. Frequency, however, sometimes can be misleading because how often a person exhibits a social behavior may not predict important social outcomes from them, such as peer acceptance. Clearly, some social skills are defined as problems because they occur at low frequencies (e.g., saying "please," "thank you," or "excuse me").

Some social behaviors may be more appropriately measured using duration recording. Duration reflects how long a particular behavior lasts. Examples of social behaviors that can be measured by this method are durations of social interactions with others, amount of time engaged in cooperative play, or the ratio of positive to negative social interactions measured in durations. An easy way of assessing the duration of social behavior is to start a stopwatch whenever a student meets the definition of the behavior and stop it when the student is not engaged in the behavior. This process continues throughout the observation session. The duration is calculated by dividing the elapsed time on the stopwatch by the total time observed and multiplying by 100, thereby yielding a percentage duration.

Quality of Social Behavior. A particularly important aspect of social behavior is the quality of the behavior. In fact, it could be argued that the most important aspect of what makes a behavior "socially skilled" is its quality and not its frequency or duration. Quality of social behavior, however, must be judged by others. This can be accomplished by exposing judges to videotaped or live samples of social behavior and having them rate its quality. This is similar to what is being measured by behavior ratings scales except that the measurement is direct (i.e., at the time and place of its actual occurrence) rather than indirect (i.e., based on a rater's judgment of a student's typical behavior).

Number of Behaviors to Observe. Some students have social skills deficits and competing problem behaviors limited to one or two behaviors. Others exhibit multiple social skill deficits and competing problem behavior excesses, thereby presenting an unmanageable number of behaviors to assess. An important decision facing assessors is how many behaviors should be observed. This decision is influenced by the nature and severity of the student's social competence difficulties as well as the degree of teacher and/or parent concern with each behavioral excess and deficit.

Some teachers and parents may identify as many as 5 to 10 behaviors they consider problematic. Although some students will display 10 or more problem behaviors and/or social skills deficits, not all of these behaviors are independent. Some behaviors are subsets of a larger class or category of behaviors that have similarities. These larger categories, known as *response classes*, describe a class or category of behaviors that share common features similarities. For example, the response class of *social withdrawal* might include the behaviors of sulking, standing alone on the playground, walking away from peers, and ignoring social bids from peers to join games or activities. Although these behaviors may appear different, they may belong to the same response class, and the operational definition of social withdrawal would include the behaviors listed earlier. In this example, social withdrawal (the response class) could be measured using the duration recording procedures described earlier. Practitioners should determine which behaviors are and are not members of specific response classes for meeting observational purposes and for conceptualizing social skills interventions.

Number of Observation Sessions.   Another consideration in using naturalistic observations is the number of times a student should be observed. The central issue here is the *representativeness* of observational data. That is, are the observations representative of the student's typical behavior in classroom, playground, or other settings? Based on observations of actual behavior, the observer infers that the observed behavior is representative of the student's typical behavior in that setting. Depending on the representativeness of the observation, this inference may or may not be justified.

Observers cannot be present in the classroom or playground every minute of every day. As such, observers must sample the behavior(s) of concern to obtain reasonable estimates of the baseline rates or durations of behavior. Observational data should be collected two to three sessions in the setting of concern (e.g., classroom; playground). These sessions should reflect the setting(s) of most concern to those referring the student for social skills assessment and intervention.

Behavior Rating Scales

Ratings of social behavior by significant others such as teachers and parents represent a useful and efficient method of obtaining information in school and home settings. Behavior ratings can be used prior to functional assessment interviews to guide the direction and topics discussed in the interview. Raters may also have their own idiosyncratic definitions of what constitutes any given social skill or problem behavior and their own notions of the relative frequency of behavior (e.g., "sometimes" vs. "a lot").

Users of behavior ratings scales should consider several factors when administering and interpreting these measures. One, ratings are summaries of observations of the relative frequency of specific behaviors. Two, raters may have their own idiosyncratic definitions of what constitutes a given social skill or problem behavior (e.g., "sometimes" vs. "a lot"). Three, ratings of social behavior are evaluative judgments affected by environmental and a rater's standard for behavior. Four, multiple raters of a child's behavior may agree only moderately and, in some cases, very little (Achenbach, McConaughy, & Howell, 1987). This is based on three factors: (a) many social behaviors are situationally specific, (b) all measures contain some degree of error, and (c) rating scales use rather simple frequency categories (e.g., "very little," "sometimes," and "a lot") for quantifying behaviors that may range widely in their frequency, intensity, duration, or quality.

Although several social skills rating scales are available, the *Social Skills Rating System* (SSRS; Gresham & Elliott, 1990) is the most comprehensive approach to assessing the social behavior of children and adolescents. The SSRS is a broad, multirater assessment of students' social behaviors that can affect teacher–student relations, peer acceptance, and academic performance. The SSRS consists of three separate rating forms for teachers, parents, and students and has three forms: Preschool (ages 3–5 years), Elementary (grades K–6), and Secondary (grades 7–12). The SSRS uses the teacher, parent, and student rating forms to sample three domains of social skills, problem behaviors, and academic competence.

The SSRS was standardized on a national sample of 4,170 children and adolescents in grades 3 through 12 with equal numbers of boys and girls in the standardization sample. Preschool norms (ages 3–5 years) were constructed from a smaller tryout sample of children ($N = 200$). The SSRS manual provides extensive information concerning the psychometric properties of the scales, and research studies published over the past 10 years provide additional support for the validity of the scales.

The SSRS offers several unique features to facilitate more comprehensive assessment and intervention services for children experiencing social behavior problems. The SSRS is the first multirater (teacher–parent–student) scale focusing on social skills in children and adolescents. The SSRS was designed specifically to advance intervention planning through the use of the *Assessment-Intervention Record,* which provides professionals with useful information needed for intervention planning.

Social Skills Intervention Practices

Social skills instruction (SSI) should emphasize the acquisition, performance, generalization, and maintenance of prosocial behaviors and the reduction or elimination of competing problem behaviors. A large number of intervention procedures have been identified for teaching social skills to children and youth with E/BD.

Types of Social Skills Intervention

The school is an ideal setting for teaching social skills because of its accessibility to children, their peers, teachers, and parents. Fundamentally, social skills intervention takes place in school and home settings both informally and formally using either *universal* or *selected* intervention procedures. *Informal* social skills interventions are based on the notion of incidental learning, which takes advantage of naturally occurring behavioral incidents or events to teach appropriate social behavior. Most social skill instruction in home, school, and community settings can be characterized as informal or incidental. Literally thousands of behavioral incidents occur in home, school, and community settings, creating rich opportunities for making each of these behavioral incidents a potentially successful learning experience.

Formal social skill instruction can take place in a classroom setting in which the entire class is exposed to a social skill curriculum or in a small group setting removed from the classroom. Walker et al. (1995) refer to these teaching formats as *universal* or *selected* interventions, respectively. *Universal* interventions are not unlike vaccinations, schoolwide discipline plans, or school rules that are designed to affect all children under the same conditions. Universal interventions are designed to prevent more serious behavior problems from developing later in a student's educational career and, as such, are primary prevention strategies. Few children with E/BD will respond to these universal intervention strategies and will require more intense social skills instruction (Walker et al., 1995).

Selected interventions are typically conducted with students who have been identified as being at risk for behavior problems and are based on an individual assessment of a student's social skills deficits and competing problem behaviors. These interventions are undertaken either to prevent existing behavior problems from developing into more serious behavior problems (secondary prevention) or to halt the progression of an established EB/D into a more serious problem (tertiary prevention).

Objectives of Social Skills Instruction

Social skills instruction (SSI) has four primary objectives: (a) promoting skill acquisition, (b) enhancing skill performance, (c) reducing or elimination of competing problem behaviors, and (d) facilitating generalization and maintenance of social skills. Some students will likely have some combination of acquisition and performance deficits, some of which may be accompanied by competing problem behaviors and others that are not. Any given student may require some combination of acquisition, performance, and behavior reduction strategies. All students will require procedures to facilitate generalization and maintenance of social skills.

Box 15.3 lists specific social skills and behavior reduction strategies for each of the four goals of SSI. Teachers should match appropriate intervention strategies with the particular deficits or competing problem behaviors the student exhibits. A common misconception is that one seeks to facilitate generalization and maintenance *after* implementing procedures for acquisition and performance of social skills. The evidence is clear that the best practice is to incorporate generalization from the beginning of any SSI program (Gresham, 1998a).

BOX **15.3**

Social Skills Training Objectives and Strategies

I. Promoting Skill Acquisition
   A. Modeling
   B. Coaching
   C. Behavioral Rehearsal

II. Enhancing Skill Performance
   A. Manipulation of antecedents
      1. Peer initiation strategies
      2. Proactive classroom management strategies
      3. Peer tutoring
      4. Incidental teaching
   B. Manipulation of consequences
      1. Contingency contracting
      2. Group-oriented contingency systems
      3. School–home notes
      4. Verbal praise
      5. Activity reinforcers
      6. Token/point systems

III. Removing Competing Problem Behaviors
   A. Differential reinforcement
      1. Differential reinforcement of other behavior (DRO)
      2. Differential reinforcement of low rates of behavior (DRL)
      3. Differential reinforcement of incompatible behaviors (DRI)
   B. Overcorrection
      1. Restitution
      2. Positive practice
   C. Time-out
      1. Nonexclusionary (contingent observation)
      2. Exclusionary
   D. Systematic desensitization (for anxiety-based competing behaviors)
   E. Flooding/exposure (for anxiety-based competing behaviors)

IV. Facilitating Generalization and Maintenance
   A. Topographical generalization
      1. Training diversely
      2. Exploiting functional contingencies
      3. Incorporating functional mediators
   B. Functional generalization
      1. Identify strong competing stimuli in specific situations
      2. Identify strong competing problem behaviors in specific situations
      3. Identify functionally equivalent socially skilled behaviors
      4. Increase reliability and efficiency of socially skilled behaviors (build fluency)
      5. Decrease reliability and efficiency of competing problem behaviors

Source: Table 6 in F. M. Gresham (1998) Social skill training with children: Social learning and applied behavioral analytic approaches. In Watson & Gresham (Eds) *Handbook of child behavior therapy: Issues in clinical child psychology* (pp. 488) New York: Plenum

Promoting Skill Acquisition

Procedures designed to promote skill acquisition are applicable when students do not have a particular social skill in their repertoire, when they do not know a particular step in the performance of a behavioral sequence, or when their execution of the skill is awkward or ineffective (i.e., a fluency deficit). It should be noted that a relatively small percentage of students will need social skills intervention based on acquisition deficits; far more students have performance deficits (Gresham, 1998b).

Three procedures represent pathways to remediating social skill acquisition deficits: modeling, coaching, and behavioral rehearsal. Social problem solving is another pathway but is not discussed here because of space limitations and the fact that it incorporates a combination of modeling, coaching, and behavioral rehearsal. More specific information on social problem-solving interventions can be found in Elias and Clabby (1992).

Modeling is the process of learning a behavior by observing another person performing that behavior. Modeling instruction presents the entire sequence of behaviors involved in a particular social skill and teaches how to integrate specific behaviors into a composite behavior pattern. Modeling is one of the most effective and efficient ways of teaching social behavior (Elliott & Gresham, 1992; Schneider, 1992).

Coaching is the use of verbal instruction to teach social skills. Unlike modeling, which emphasizes visual displays of social skills, coaching utilizes a student's receptive language skills. Coaching is accomplished in three fundamental steps: (a) presenting social concepts or rules, (b) providing opportunities for practice or rehearsal, and (c) supplying specific informational feedback on the quality of behavioral performances.

Behavioral rehearsal refers to practicing a newly learned behavior in a structured, protective situation of role playing. In this way, students can enhance their proficiency in using social skills without experiencing adverse consequences. Behavioral rehearsal can be covert, verbal, or overt. Covert rehearsal involves students imagining certain social interactions (e.g., being teased by another student or group of students). Verbal rehearsal involves students verbalizing what specific behaviors they would exhibit in a social situation. Overt rehearsal is the actual role playing of a specific social interaction.

Enhancing Skill Performance

Most social skills interventions will involve procedures that increase the frequency of particular prosocial behaviors in specific social situations because most social skill difficulties are performance rather than acquisition deficits. This suggests that most social skills interventions for most students should take place in naturalistic environments (e.g., classrooms and playgrounds) rather than small pullout groups. Failure to perform certain social skills in specific situations results from two fundamental factors: (a) inappropriately arranged antecedents and/or (b) inappropriately arranged consequences. A number of specific procedures can be classified under the broad rubric of antecedent and consequent strategies.

Interventions based on antecedent control assume that the environment does not set the occasion for the performance of prosocial behavior. That is, cues, prompts, or other events are either not present or not salient for the child to discriminate these stimuli in relation to the performance of prosocial behavior. A cueing and prompting procedure uses verbal and nonverbal cues or prompts to facilitate prosocial behavior. Simple prompts or cues for some children may be all that is needed to signal them to engage in socially appropriate behavior (e.g., "Say thank you;" "Ask Katina to join your group"). Cueing and prompting represent one of the easiest and most efficient social skills intervention strategies (Elliott & Gresham, 1992; Walker et al., 1995).

Interventions based on consequent control can be classified into three broad categories: (a) reinforcement-based strategies, (b) behavioral contracts, and (c) school–home notes. Reinforcement-based strategies assume that the student knows how to perform a social skill but is not doing so because of little or no reinforcement for the behavior. The objective in using these strategies is to increase the frequency of reinforcement for prosocial behavior. Reinforcement strategies include attention, social praise, tokens/points, and activity reinforcers as well as group-oriented contingency systems. More extensive discussions of behavioral contracts, school–home notes, and group-oriented contingency systems can be found in more comprehensive treatments of these subjects (Kelley, 1990; Kohler & Strain, 1990; Stuart, 1971).

Removing or Eliminating Competing Problem Behaviors

The focus of SSI is clearly on developing and refining prosocial behaviors. However, the failure of some students to either acquire or perform certain social skills may be due to the presence of competing problem behaviors. This is particularly true of students having EBDs whose externalizing and/or internalizing behaviors compete with or block the acquisition or performance of prosocial behaviors. For example, aggressive behavior may be performed instead of a prosocial behavior because it may be more efficient and reliable in producing reinforcement. A number of techniques are effective in reducing competing problem behaviors and are presented in Box 15.3. Because of space considerations and the author's interest in delivering positive behavioral interventions, only differential reinforcement techniques are discussed here.

Differential reinforcement is based on the principle of stimulus control in which a behavior is reinforced in the presence of one stimulus and is not reinforced in the presence of other stimuli. After a number of trials of differential reinforcement, a behavior will come under the control of the stimulus associated with reinforcement and thus is said to be under stimulus control. Once a behavior is under stimulus control, the student will be able to *discriminate* situations in which to perform the behavior. Principles of stimulus control can be used to decrease rates of undesirable behavior and increase rates of prosocial behavior. Three types of differential reinforcement are used most frequently: differential reinforcement of other behavior (DRO), differential reinforcement of low rates of behavior (DRL), and differential reinforcement of incompatible behavior (DRI).

DRO refers to the delivery of a reinforcer for any appropriate behavior except the target inappropriate behavior. The effects of DRO are to decrease the frequency of a target behavior and to increase the frequencies of all other behaviors. Two types of DRO are used: interval DRO and momentary DRO. Interval DRO involves the reinforcement of a behavior if the targeted behavior does not occur in a specified time interval. Thus, in an interval DRO-2-minute, the first behavior occurring after a 2-minute interval in which the target behavior (e.g., cursing) did *not* occur is reinforced. If cursing occurs at any time during the 2-minute interval, the timer is reset to the beginning of the interval thereby delaying the time in which reinforcement will be available. In momentary DRO, behavior is *sampled* at the end of a specified time interval. If the target behavior is *not* occurring at the end of the interval, the first behavior occurring after the interval is reinforced. Either DRO schedule can be used to reduce the frequency of problem behaviors. The primary problem with interval DRO schedules is keeping up with the time intervals and resetting the timer. Momentary DRO schedules are more user-friendly than interval DROs and should be more reasonable for practical purposes.

DRL involves the reinforcement of reductions in the frequency of target behaviors in a specified time interval. Two variations of DRL are described: classic DRL and full-session DRL. In classic DRL, the time elapsing between behaviors, or what is known as *interresponse times* (IRTs), is gradually lengthened. For example, if a student frequently interrupts others, interruptions could be reduced in frequency by reinforcing the child for waiting 5 minutes between instances of interruptions. If the child interrupted before 5 minutes elapses (e.g., 2 minutes or 4 minutes), the timer would be reset, and the 5-minute waiting requirement would remain in effect.

In a full-session DRL, reinforcement is provided when the overall frequency of a target behavior is reduced by a specified time session. The difference between a full-session DRL and a classic DRL is that a full-session DRL does not require longer and longer intervals between occurrences of target behavior. Instead, the requirement is that overall frequency of a target behavior in a specified time interval be reduced. For instance, a teacher might set a criterion of five or fewer occurrences of disruptive behavior during a 20-minute reading lesson. If this criterion was met, the student would receive reinforcement. Full-session DRLs, like momentary DROs, are more user-friendly than classic DRLs and are easily adapted within the context of a group contingency system.

In *DRI*, behaviors that are incompatible with the target behavior are reinforced. Whereas DRO and DRL focus on reducing the frequencies of problem behaviors, DRI emphasizes *increasing* the frequencies of prosocial behaviors. DRI reduces the frequency of competing problem behaviors because prosocial behaviors that are incompatible with problem behaviors are increased in frequency. Several examples should make this clear: sharing behavior is incompatible with stingy behavior; complimenting others is incompatible with teasing others; asking others to borrow a toy is incompatible with grabbing a toy; compromising with others is incompatible with fighting.

Facilitating Generalization and Maintenance

Basically, only two processes are essential to all behavioral interventions: discrimination and generalization (Stokes, 1992). Discrimination was discussed in this chapter within the context of stimulus control. A major problem confronting social skills interventions is that it is much easier to get some behaviors to occur in one place for a limited period of time than it is to get those same behaviors to occur in a variety of places for an extended period of time. That is, it is infinitely easier to teach discriminations than it is to teach generalization and maintenance.

Generalization of behavior change is directly related to the notion of resistance to intervention. If social skill deficits occur at low frequencies, competing problem behavior excesses occur at high frequencies, and if both of these deficits and excesses are chronic (i.e., they have lasted a relatively long period of time), then they will tend to show less generalization across different nontraining conditions and less maintenance over time when SSI is withdrawn (Gresham, 1991). In effect, these students quickly discriminate training from nontraining conditions, particularly when training conditions are vastly different from nontraining conditions.

Students with E/BD often show excellent initial behavior change, particularly with their competing problem behavior excesses, but fail to show generalization or maintenance of these behavior changes. One reason for this may be that exclusive attention often is focused on decreasing the momentum of undesirable behavior to the exclusion of facilitating the momentum of desirable behaviors such as social skills. The main reason for the lack of generalization and maintenance is that essential components of behavior change are not actively programmed to occur as part of SSI.

Various generalization programming strategies can be found in Box 15.3 under the headings of topographical and functional generalization. The topographical description of generalization refers to the occurrence of relevant behaviors (e.g., social skills) under different, nontraining conditions (Stokes & Osnes, 1989). These nontraining conditions can be settings or situations (setting generalization), behaviors (response generalization), and/or time (maintenance). A more detailed treatment of topographical generalization is described by Stokes and Osnes (1989).

A functional approach to generalization consists of two types: (a) *stimulus generalization*, which is the occurrence of the same behavior under variations of the original training conditions (the greater the difference between training conditions and subsequent environmental conditions, the less the generalization), and (b) *response generalization*, which is the control of multiple behaviors by the same stimulus.

An extremely important goal of SSI is to determine the *reliability* and *efficiency* of competing problem behaviors relative to socially skilled alternative behaviors. Competing problem behaviors will be performed instead of prosocial behaviors if the competing behaviors are more efficient and reliable than the prosocial behavior. Efficient behaviors are (a) easier to perform in terms of response effort and (b) produce reinforcement more rapidly. Reliable behaviors are those that produce the desired outcomes more frequently than do prosocial behaviors. For example, pushing into the lunch line may be more efficient and reliable than politely asking to cut into line.

To program for functional generalization, teachers should (a) decrease the efficiency and reliability of competing, inappropriate behaviors and (b) increase the efficiency and reliability of prosocial behaviors. The former can be accomplished by many of the procedures listed in Box 15.3 under "Removing Competing Problem Behaviors." The latter can be achieved by spending more time and effort in building fluency of trained social skills using combinations of modeling, coaching, and, most important, behavioral rehearsal with specific performance feedback.

Summary

Social skills are behaviors that lead to judgments of social competence by significant others such as teachers, parents, and peers. Social skills are the tools by which students build, maintain, and improve the quality of their interpersonal relationships. Social skills deficits can be classified as being acquisition, performance, or fluency deficits, which may or may not be accompanied by competing problem behaviors. This classification was described as being essential in determining the most appropriate social skills intervention strategies.

SSI was viewed as having four objectives: (a) promoting skill acquisition, (b) enhancing skill performance, (c) removing or reducing competing problem behaviors, and (d) facilitating generalization and maintenance of prosocial behaviors. Particular emphasis was placed on the notion of functional generalization as it relates to efficiency and reliability of behavior and the resistance of social behavior to intervention for students with EBDs.

REFERENCES

Achenbach, T. (1985). *Assessment and taxonomy of child and adolescent psychopathology.* Beverly Hills, CA: Sage.

Achenbach, T., McConaughy, S., & Howell, C. (1987). Child/adolescent behavioral and emotional problems: Implications of cross-informant correlations for situational specificity. *Psychological Bulletin, 101,* 213–232.

Bergan, J., & Kratochwill, T. (1990). *Behavioral consultation and therapy.* New York: Plenum.

Caldarella, P., & Merrell, K. (1997). Common dimensions of social skills of children and adolescents: A taxonomy of positive behaviors. *School Psychology Review, 26,* 264–278.

Elias, M., & Clabby, J. (1992). *Building social problem skills: Guidelines from a school-based program.* San Francisco: Jossey-Bass.

Elliott, S. N., & Gresham, F. M.. (1992). *Social skills intervention guide.* Circle Pines, MN: American Guidance Service.

Forness, S., & Knitzer, J. (1992). A new proposed definition and terminology to replace "serious emotional disturbance" in Individuals with Disabilities Education Act. *School Psychology Review, 21,* 12–20.

Goldstein, A. (1988). *The Prepare Curriculum.* Champaign, IL: Research Press.

Gresham, F. M.. (1981). Social skills training with handicapped children: A review. *Review of Educational Research, 51,* 139–176.

Gresham, F. M.. (1983). Social validity in the assessment of children's social skills: Establishing standards for social competency. *Journal of Psychoeducational Assessment, 1,* 297–307.

Gresham, F. M.. (1991). Conceptualizing behavior disorders in terms of resistance to intervention. *School Psychology Review, 20,* 23–36.

Gresham, F. M.. (1998a). Social skills training: Should we raze, remodel, or rebuild? *Behavioral Disorders, 24,* 19–25.

Gresham, F. M.. (1998b). Social skills training with children. In T. S. Watson & F. M. Gresham (Eds.), *Handbook of child behavior therapy* (pp. 475–497). New York: Plenum.

Gresham, F. M.., & Elliott, S. N.. (1990). *Social Skills Rating System.* Circle Pines, MN: American Guidance Service.

Hinshaw, S. (1987). On the distinction between attention deficit/hyperactivity and conduct problems/aggression in child psychopathology. *Psychological Bulletin, 101,* 443–463.

Kazdin, A. (1987). Treatment of antisocial behavior in children: Current status and future directions. *Psychological Bulletin, 102,* 187–203.

Kelley, M. L.. (1990). *School–home notes.* New York: Guilford.

Kohler, F., & Strain, P. (1990). Peer-assisted interventions: Early promises, notable achievements, and future aspirations. *Clinical Psychology Review, 10,* 441–452.

Kupersmidt, J., Coie, J., & Dodge, K. (1990). The role of peer relationships in the development of disorder. In S. Asher & J. Coie (Eds.), *Peer rejection in childhood* (pp. 274–308). New York: Cambridge University Press.

Landau, S., & Moore, L. (1991). Social skills deficits with attention deficit hyperactivity disorder. *School Psychology Review, 20,* 235–251.

McFall, R. (1982). A review and reformulation of the concept of social skills. *Behavioral Assessment, 4,* 1–33.

Merrell, K., & Gimpel, G. (1998). *Social skills of children and adolescents: Conceptualization, assessment, and treatment.* Mahwah, NJ: Erlbaum.

Newcomb, A., Bukowski, W., & Pattee, L. (1993). Children's peer relations: A meta-analytic review of popular, rejected, neglected, controversial, and average children. *Psychological Bulletin, 113,* 99–128.

O'Neill, R., Horner, R., Albin, R., Sprague, J., Storey, K., & Newton, J. (1997). *Functional assessment of problem behavior: A practical assessment guide.* Pacific Grove, CA: Brooks/Cole.

Parker, J., & Asher, S. (1987). Peer relations and later personal adjustment: Are low-accepted children at risk? *Psychological Bulletin, 102,* 357–389.

Schneider, B. (1992). Didactic methods for enhancing children's peer relations: A quantitative review. *Clinical Psychology Review, 12,* 363–382.

Stokes, T. (1992). Discrimination and generalization. *Journal of Applied Behavior Analysis, 25,* 429–432.

Stokes, T., & Osnes, P. (1989). An operant pursuit of generalization. *Behavior Therapy, 20,* 337–355.

Stuart, R. (1971). Behavioral contracting with families of delinquents. *Journal of Behavior Therapy and Experimental Psychiatry, 2,* 1–11.

Walker, H., Colvin, G., & Ramsey, E. (1995). *Antisocial behavior in school: Strategies and best practices.* Pacific Grove, CA: Brooks/Cole.

Walker, H., Irvin, L., Noell, J., & Singer, G. (1992). A construct score approach to the assessment of social competence: Rationale, technological considerations, and anticipated outcomes. *Behavior Modification, 16,* 448–474.

Walker, H., McConnell, S., Holmes, D., Todis, B., Walker, J., & Golden, N. (1983). *The Walker Social Skills Curriculum: The ACCEPTS Program (a curriculum for children's effective and peer and teacher skills).* Austin, TX: Pro-Ed.

Walker, H., & Severson, H. (1992). *Systematic screening for behavior disorders.* Longmont, CO: Sopris West.

Wolf, M. (1978). Social validity: The case for subjective measurement or how applied behavior analysis is finding its heart. *Journal of Applied Behavior Analysis, 11,* 203–214.

PART FOUR

Providing Services:
An Integrated Approach

16 An Integrated Approach to Prevention and Management of Aggressive Behavior Problems in Preschool and Elementary Grade Students

Schools and Parents Collaboration

CAROLYN WEBSTER-STRATTON

M. JAMILA REID
University of Washington

Introduction

Teachers across the nation daily face classrooms with increasing numbers of students who exhibit "conduct problems," characterized by high rates of aggression, inattention, hyperactivity, defiance, and noncompliance. Conduct problems are escalating at younger ages (Campbell, 1995; Webster-Stratton & Hammond, 1998), and prevalence rates indicate that 7% to 20% of preschool and early school-age children meet the diagnostic criteria for oppositional defiant disorder (ODD) or conduct disorder (CD). These rates are even higher for low-income families (Offord, Boyle, & Szatmari, 1987). Not only are aggressive children a management problem, but they often need extra assistance with co-occurring academic problems such as learning, reading, and language delays (Bryan, 1991; Gresham, 1986;

Kavale & Forness, 1998) (see Chapter 1 by O'Shaughnessy, Lane, Gresham, & Beebe-Frankenberger, this text).

The need for teachers and parents to manage young aggressive and noncompliant children successfully is particularly urgent because, if left unmanaged, these behaviors are stable over time and appear to be the most important behavioral risk factors for antisocial behavior in adolescence (Offord et al., 1987). Early behavior problems are repeatedly identified as predictor of later drug abuse (Brook, Whiteman, Gordon, & Cohen, 1986; Dishion & Ray, 1991), juvenile delinquency, violence, and school dropout (Kazdin, 1995; Tremblay, Mass, Pagani, & Vitaro, 1996). Unfortunately, the rise in schools' zero-tolerance policies (suspension and expulsion) for antisocial behavior increases the likelihood that such children will leave school early without the assistance they need. Recent projections suggest that approximately 70% of young children with conduct problems do not receive services (Hobbs, 1982; Kazdin & Kendall, 1998), and even fewer receive empirically supported interventions. Interestingly, the majority of youth who receive any help for a mental health problem receive interventions within the school, but such services tend to be brief and often do not result in sustained change.

Causes of Conduct Problems

Theories regarding the causes of child conduct problems include child biological and developmental risk factors (e.g., attention deficit disorders, learning disabilities, and language delays); family factors (e.g., marital conflict, depression, drug abuse, and criminal behavior); ineffective parenting (e.g., harsh discipline, and low parent involvement in school activities); school risk factors (e.g., teacher's use of poor classroom management strategies, classroom level of aggression, large class sizes, and low teacher involvement with parents); and peer and community risk factors (e.g., poverty and gangs). Emerging data suggest that there are no clear-cut causal links between single risk factors and a child's academic and social-emotional problems; most of these factors are intertwined, synergistic, and cumulative (Group, 1992; Hawkins & Weiss, 1985; Reid & Eddy, 1997). For example, a child who is temperamentally hyperactive, impulsive, and inattentive will be more difficult to parent or teach. This child will be more likely to receive harsh discipline than encouragement. This critical discipline style will not promote prosocial behaviors and provides negative models of behavior, thereby further impeding the development of adaptive social-cognitive skills. Family stress, such as that associated with unemployment, marital difficulties, and poverty, often contributes to ineffective parenting, resulting in poor cognitive stimulation and academic support. Upon school entry, behavioral and academic problems are likely to result in frequent discipline from the teacher and peer rejection. This leads to fewer opportunities to practice both academic and social skills and poor parent and child school involvement. Teachers may misunderstand the reasons for lack of parental involvement and respond more critically to the parent, further eroding the bonds between the home and school. Moreover, teachers may lack the knowledge, skills, and resources to assist children with behavior problems and their families. Poor classroom management may result in increasing levels of classroom disruption/ aggression, which can have significant effects on the individual child's risk for continuing aggression. Thus, spiraling risk factors continue the cycle of developing conduct problems over time. A more complete review of etiological factors can be found elsewhere (e.g., Stoff, Breiling, & Masters, 1997).

Implications of Risk Factors for Preventive Intervention

The Earlier the Intervention the Better

The developmental model illustrating cascading risk factors as children transition to school and the longitudinal research on the poor prognosis for "early starter" aggressive children suggest that early intervention is crucial. Evidence indicates that the earlier intervention is offered, the more positive the child's behavioral adjustment and the greater chance of preventing later delinquency (Taylor & Biglan, 1998). In fact, there is some evidence that if children with conduct problems are not treated by age 8, their problems become less responsive to intervention and more likely to become chronic (Bullis & Walker, 1994; Francis, Shaywitz, Stuebing, Shaywitz, & Fletcher, 1991). Developmental research indicates that these "early-starters" can be identified at school entry by the occurrence of aggressive problems across the home and school settings (Campbell, 1995; Group, 1999a). Researchers have demonstrated that violent adolescents could be identified with almost 50% reliability by at least age 6 (Campbell & Ewing, 1990; Group, 1999a; Loeber et al., 1993; Tremblay et al., 1999). The transition to school is a strategic time to begin early intervention since this time can be stressful for parents and children. Key developmental issues for high-risk children at school entry are the control of aggressive behavior, the acquisition and use of prosocial skills, positive relationships with others, and the development of a positive interest in school.

Target Multiple Risk Factors

Significant advances in the conceptualization of the practice of prevention science in mental health (Mrazek & Haggerty, 1994) emphasize that interventions must target multiple risk and protective factors and be tied to theoretical and life course models. Programs should be developmentally based and target reductions in risk factors such as harsh discipline as well as increase in protective factors such as children's social and academic competence. This comprehensive model could be the single most important step in preventing and reducing conduct problems before they "cascade" (Patterson, Reid, & Dishion, 1992) across developmental periods and result in cumulating and intensifying risk factors (Bierman, Miller, & Stab, 1987; Coie, 1990a, 1990b; Dodge, Bates, & Pettit, 1990). In summary, this multi risk factor view of the development of conduct problems indicates that interventions for at-risk children must begin early and address both home and school risk factors.

Effective Intervention Strategies

This chapter will describe empirically supported family and parenting interventions that can be offered by schools to reduce conduct problems and promote social and academic competence. "Empirically supported" interventions will be defined here based on the Chambless and Hollon criteria (1998), a standard that is generally accepted in the scientific community (APA Task Force on Psychological Intervention Guidelines, 1995). This standard relies on interventions being evaluated in randomized control designs, demonstrating changes in observations of behavior (not only in parent or teacher reports), replication by an independent research group, provision of detailed training manuals and intervention materials, and publication in peer-reviewed journals. These criteria promote selection of interventions that are based on evidence about what is proven to work for conduct problem children and their families.

Family-Focused Interventions

Rationale for Parent Training.   Parenting interactions are clearly the most well-researched and proximal causes of conduct problems in children. Research shows that some parents of children who are highly aggressive lack certain fundamental parenting skills (Patterson, 1982). For example, parents of such children may be less positive and more coercive, permissive, erratic, and inconsistent. They are less likely to monitor behavior and more likely to reinforce inappropriate and ignore prosocial behaviors (Chamberlain, Reid, Ray, Capaldi, & Fisher, 1997; Reid & Eddy, 1997). These parental constructs at age 10 predict later antisocial behavior and drug abuse (Patterson, Crosby, & Vuchinich, 1992). Many factors disrupt parenting, including family life stressors (often associated with socioeconomic disadvantage) (Forgatch, 1989; Forgatch, Patterson, & Skinner, 1988; Wahler & Sansbury, 1990; Webster-Stratton, 1990a); maternal insularity and lack of support (Wahler, 1980); parental psychopathology or substance abuse (Kazdin, 1987); and marital discord (Cummings & Davies, 1994; McMahon & Forehand, 1984; Webster-Stratton & Hammond, 1999). Low parent involvement in school also puts children at risk for academic failure and antisocial behavior (Reid & Eddy, 1997).

Parent training programs help counteract the *parent and family risk factors* by teaching positive, nonviolent discipline methods and supportive parenting that promotes children's self-confidence, prosocial behaviors, problem-solving skills, and academic success. Parent interventions help parents respond effectively to normal behavior problems so that these problems do not escalate. Parents learn to provide support for their children's cognitive, social, and emotional growth. Parent training programs can also help parents communicate effectively with teachers and advocate for their child's social and academic development. Group format parent training that also focuses on family issues such as communication and problem-solving skills addresses some of these family risk factors by facilitating parent support, decreasing parents' isolation, and providing strategies to cope with stressful life events.

Empirical Validation for Parent Training Programs.   Extensive research indicates that parent training is the single most effective intervention available for reducing early conduct problems (Kazdin, 1985; Tanaka, 1987; Taylor & Biglan, 1998). In a review of 82 empirically tested psychosocial interventions for conduct problem children and adolescents (Brestan & Eyberg, 1998), the two found to be effective were parent training programs: a program derived directly from Patterson's social learning model (Patterson & Chamberlain, 1988) and a program based on videotape modeling developed by Webster-Stratton (Webster-Stratton, 1996; Webster-Stratton & Hancock, 1998). Of the 10 additional programs judged to be "probably efficacious," three were parent training or family therapy programs. Likewise, a review by Kazdin and Kendall (1998) of interventions for treating antisocial children found that two of four interventions showing the greatest promise emphasized the family.

The successful short-term outcome of parent training has been repeatedly verified by significant changes in parents' and children's behavior and adjustment (Dishion & Andrews, 1995; Eyberg, Boggs, & Algina, 1995; Kazdin & Kendall, 1998; Patterson & Narrett, 1990; Webster-Stratton & Hammond, 1997). Home observations indicate reductions in children's levels of aggression by 20% to 60% (Patterson, Chamberlain, & Reid, 1982; Webster-Stratton & Hammond, 1997). Researchers have found improvements in other outcomes, including school dropout and attendance, disruptive behavior, and criminal activity (Kazdin, Siegel, & Bass, 1992). Generalization of behavior improvements from the clinic setting to the home over reasonable follow-up periods (1–4 years) and to untreated child behaviors have also been demonstrated (Taylor & Bilan, 1998). Studies typically find that approximately two-thirds of children show clinically significant improvements, which means that their behavior falls in the normal range following the family intervention (Webster-Stratton, Hollinsworth, & Kolpacoff, 1989). There is mixed evidence on generalization of improvements from home to school; parent training studies have indicated that improvements in the child's behavior at home are not necessarily associated with improved peer relationships, particularly if teachers are not involved in the intervention. Evidence does indicate that early intervention has longer-lasting effects when parent programs incorporate a cognitive/academic component (Yoshikawa, 1994). Programs are also more likely to generalize when parent training is combined with child and teacher training (Kazdin, Esveldt-Dawson, French, & Unis, 1987; Kazdin et al., 1992; Webster-Stratton & Hammond, 1997; Webster-Stratton & Reid, 1999c).

For older adolescents with conduct disorders, an intensive parent component, as a part of a more comprehensive therapeutic program, is necessary for reducing violence. In addition to parent education programs reviewed later in this chapter (under model programs), research supports the effectiveness of multisystemic therapy (MST) (Henggeler, Melton, & Smith, 1992; Henggeler, Schoenwald, & Pickrel, 1995) and functional family therapy (Alexander & Parsons, 1982; Morris, Alexander, & Waldron, 1990). MST is a comprehensive, family-oriented program that has been effective in reducing a variety of antisocial and delinquent outcomes (Henggeler, Schoenwald, Borduin, & Rowland, 1998). Programs based on this model use individualized wraparound service plans for each child and family, an approach familiar to school psychologists (Eber & Nelson, 1997). See Eber and Nelson (1997) for an example of how schools can assume the lead role in a system of care. Although family therapy is critical for older students with chronic behavior problems, less intensive parent interventions are sufficient for most younger students. Christenson, Rounds, and Franklin (1992) and Sheridan, Kratochwill, and Bergan (1996) present thorough reviews of home–school collaboration strategies found to be effective in preventing and reducing children's academic and social problems.

School-Based Prevention Strategies

Rationale for Parent Training in School Settings.   While parent training historically has not been seen as an essential element of school services, there are several advantages to offering parent training in a school-based preventive model rather than in a mental health setting. First, school-based programs are ideally placed to target multiple risk factors in the child, family, and school and build links between these three areas. Second, school-based programs are more accessible to families and eliminate the stigma associated with services offered in traditional mental health settings as well as some of the practical and social barriers to treatment access (e.g., lack of transportation, insurance, child care, or financial resources). Third, school interventions can be offered before low-level behavior problems have escalated into severe problems that require referral and extensive clinical treatment. Moreover, when intervention is offered in communities, these communities become natural sources of support for parents and teachers (Webster-Stratton, 1997). Lastly, on-site school interventions can provide services to high numbers of high-risk families and children at comparatively low cost.

Empirical Validation of School-Based Prevention.   As indicated by the preceding review, there is extensive knowledge about the development and treatment of conduct disorders using parent training. Work in the area of prevention of conduct problems is also extremely promising. In the past decade several multifaceted, randomized control, longitudinal prevention programs have shown that rates of later delinquency and school adjustment problems can be lowered by early parent–school intervention. Tremblay and colleagues (Tremblay, Pagani, Masse, & Viatro, 1995; Tremblay et al., 1996) found that a combination of parent and child training for high-risk children in kindergarten and first grade reduced delinquency and school adjustment problems at age 12. Similar findings using child and parent training for fourth- and fifth-grade students were reported by Lochman and Wells (Lochman & Wells, 1996). FAST TRACK, a large scale, multicenter, multicomponent program, provided ongoing services to children exhibiting conduct problems from first to fifth grade. The intervention included a classroom management component, social skills training called PATHS, (Kusche & Greenberg, 1994), academic tutoring, parent training (based on Forehand, Rogers, McMahon, Wells, & Griest, 1981), home visits, and friendship enhancement. Outcome at 1 and 3 years showed reductions in conduct problems and special education resource use

(Group 1999a, 1999b). The LIFT project (Reid, Eddy, Fetrow, & Stoolmiller, 1999), another school-based prevention program, provided parent training, classroom social skills training, a behavioral playground program, and a parent–teacher communication program to all students in high-risk schools. Results showed intervention effects on physical aggression, behavior improvements in the classroom, and reductions in maternal aversive behavior at home (Reid et al., 1999). Two randomized prevention trials of Webster-Stratton's parent intervention program (The Incredible Years Training Series) produced positive change in Head Start parents and their 4-year-old children immediately at posttreatment and at 1-year follow-up. Intervention produced positive changes in parenting, parents' school involvement, children's levels of aggression, conduct problems, and social skills (Webster-Stratton, 1998b; Webster-Stratton & Reid, 1999c).

Prevention Programs That Include Teacher Training

To promote student's behavioral and academic success, teachers must be well trained in effective classroom management. Schoolwide approaches that provide consistent classroom discipline plans and individualized plans for children with conduct problems can be highly effective (Cotton & Wikelund, 1990; Gottfredson, Gottfredson, & Hybl, 1993; Knoff & Batsche, 1995). Specific teacher behaviors associated with improved classroom behavior include the use of high levels of praise and social reinforcement (Walker, Colvin, & Ramsey, 1995); proactive strategies such as preparation for transitions and clear, predictable classroom rules (Hawkins, Von Cleve, & Catalano, 1991); short, clear commands, warnings, reminders, and distractions (Abramowitz, O'Leary, & Futtersak, 1988; Acker & O'Leary, 1987); tangible reinforcement for appropriate social behavior (Pfiffner, Rosen, & O'Leary, 1985); team-based rewards (Kellam, Ling, Merisca, Brown, & Ialongon, 1998); mild but consistent response costs (time-out or loss of privileges) for aggressive or disruptive behavior (Pfiffner & O'Leary, 1987); and direct instruction in appropriate social and classroom behavior (Walker, Schwartz, Nippold, Irvin, & Noell, 1994) and problem-solving skills (Shure & Spivack, 1982).

Classroom management training is promising in demonstrating short-term improvements in disruptive and aggressive behavior in the classroom for approximately 78% of disruptive students (Stage & Quiroz, 1997). Programs such as ACHIEVE (Knoff & Batsche, 1995) and BASIS (Gotfredson et al., 1993) that focus on classroom management skills and discipline, social skills training, and home–school collaboration are effective in reducing teacher reports of antisocial behavior and improving academic achievement. However, these studies did not use randomized control designs or measure the programs' effects across settings and over time.

Several studies using randomized control designs have extended this teacher training research. Two large-scale prevention projects, the Seattle Social Development Project (Hawkins, Catalano, Kosterman, Abbott, & Hill, 1999) and the Child Development Project (Battistich et al., 1991), emphasized training teachers in classroom management. Six-year follow-up of the Hawkins study (Hawkins et al., 1999) with children who received school-based intervention in first through fifth grades showed reduced violent delinquent acts, lower drinking age, less sexual activity, and fewer early pregnancies. Child Development Project results show improvements in prosocial and problem-solving skills (Battistich, Schaps, Watson, Solomon, & Schaps, 1989). A follow-up study of these children demonstrated intervention students were less likely to use alcohol and exhibited fewer delinquent behaviors (Battistich, Schaps, Watson, & Solomon, 1996). Webster-Stratton (Webster-Stratton & Reid, 1999b, 1999c) evaluated the combined effects of parent and teacher training in two randomized control studies, as prevention in Head Start and as treatment with a sample of diagnosed 4- to 8-year-old children. The teacher program significantly enhanced the effectiveness of parent and child training in terms of decreasing aggressive behavior in the classroom, promoting academic readiness, and increasing on-task work. Moreover, participating teachers were observed to use fewer inappropriate and harsh discipline strategies and to be more nurturing and positive than nonintervention teachers.

Key Features of Effective Parent Programs

Several excellent literature reviews indicate that cognitive-behavioral family interventions are helpful for prevention and treatment of conduct disorders and promotion of social competence (Brestan & Eyberg, 1998; Taylor & Biglan, 1998). These reviews can help schools evaluate the appropriateness of particular parenting programs for their needs. Based on research, schools are advised to use the following guidelines to select an effective parenting/teacher intervention.

Broad-Based Content.   Program content and process must be relevant and sensitive to individual parent needs and circumstances. A focus on problem solving, communication with teachers, personal family issues, and other risk or protective factors in addition to parenting skills is more effective. Moreover, the combination of child *and* parent training results in better early peer interactions and later reductions in delinquent behavior and drug abuse (Kazdin, Bass, Siegel, & Thomas, 1989; Kazdin, Esveldt, French, & Unis, 1987; Kazdin et al., 1992; Webster-Stratton & Hammond, 1997). Although all these facets of interventions are not required for every family, the ability to integrate them into treatment clearly enhances the effectiveness of parent training, especially when parents are coping with issues such as serious depression, drug abuse, marital discord, or extreme poverty.

Cognitive, Behavioral, and Affective Components.   Programs that emphasize parents' feelings and cognitions and promote self-management as well as teaching behavioral "principles" have higher consumer satisfaction and longer-lasting effects. Programs should include parent–child relationship building through positive parenting practices and child-directed play as well as behavioral strategies such as timeout and loss of privileges (rather than relying on exclusively one focus or the other).

Length Greater than 20 Hours.   Programs that are at least 20 hours (extending to 50 hours) in length have more sustained and significant effects (Kazdin, 1987). Parenting programs offered in schools can be provided across key transition points such as entry to preschool, kindergarten, middle school, and high school. This approach provides a lengthier and more comprehensive approach and also provides parents with periodic "boosts" to keep up their efforts at home and to facilitate relationships with new teachers.

Early Intervention and Developmental Focus.   The earlier intervention begins, the more positive the child's behavioral improvements. This does not mean that programs for parents of antisocial adolescents should be eliminated but that it is far easier to impact behavior problems when children are young. Parenting programs should focus on a particular developmental stage and age. Programs that attempt to address issues for all ages are likely to fail because different parenting strategies are appropriate for children of different ages, and parents may be confused and frustrated by strategies that do not apply their own child's developmental level.

Collaborative Process.   Programs that are collaborative (i.e., parents are given responsibility for identifying their own goals and developing their own solutions with the guidance of the group leader) result in more parental engagement and fewer dropouts and are perceived as more culturally sensitive. When parents are involved in self-management (e.g., determining their priorities for home activities) and a coping or problem-solving model (vs. a mastery model) is used, programs are perceived as more meaningful and relevant to parents' needs and cultural traditions. This will result in greater parental attendance, retention, and behavior change (Webster-Stratton & Herbert, 1994).

Focus on Strengths.   Programs that focus on parents' strengths (as opposed to their deficits), assuming that even highly stressed parents bring knowledge and expertise regarding their child and their needs, result in less dropout, more involvement, and more behavior change.

Building Family and Social Support.   Programs that are offered in group format, encourage partners' involvement, and promote within-group relationships are more cost-effective. They also reduce parents' sense of isolation, increase their sense of support, reduce dropout rates, and result in lasting effects (Webster-Stratton, 1985).

Performance Training Methods.   Training methods need to be responsive to a variety of parental learning styles and should utilize "performance-based" training methods such as videotape modeling, role playing, and home practice assignments. Direct feedback, instruction, and active practice of skills are more effective than "verbal-based" learning methods such as discussion and written handouts.

"Principles" Training.   There is greater behavior improvement and generalization when parents are taught behavioral principles (not just specific strategies). Parents who understand the rationale behind parenting strategies and their long-term results are more motivated to implement them.

Parent–Teacher Partnerships.   Parenting programs that promote skills in school collaboration and help parents and teachers develop consistent home–school behavior plans are more effective than programs offered in isolation from schools and teachers. Programs that include teacher training result in more generalization and consistency of behavior improvements across settings.

Group Leader Clinical Skills.   Leaders who are warm, collaborative, nonhierarchical, nonblaming, and supportive and demonstrate a coping model are more effective than program leaders who are "expert," distanced, and prescriptive. A collaborative approach (i.e., leader acts as a "coach" to provide support and encouragement) will facilitate active parent participation and interaction. The "expert" model frequently fosters passive resistance on the part of parents. It is important that leaders receive appropriate training and ongoing supervision until they are proficient with intervention implementation. Many empirically validated programs have developed certification procedures for assuring that the program is delivered with integrity and a high level of quality.

Sensitivity to Barriers for Low-Income Families.   Programs should be accessible and realistic about the practical constraints of low-income families. This may mean providing child care, transportation, food, flexible meeting times, and community meeting places (Webster-Stratton, 1998a). Weekly support calls from leaders and group "buddy systems" help engage families and result in lower dropout and higher attendance rates, particularly in highly stressed families. Leaders can also help parents make up missed group sessions in a home-visit format.

Model Programs

The following discussion highlights several model parent/family training programs (with an emphasis on programs targeting younger children) that were selected on the basis of their widespread availability, detailed descriptions of training procedures, and empirical validation, including data concerning their long-term effectiveness in reducing conduct problems.

Parenting Programs from the Oregon Social Learning Center.   The most highly influential parent training program was developed by Patterson, Reid, and their colleagues at the Oregon Social Learning Center. Spanning two decades of research with more than 400 families, their work provides an exemplary model for outcome research with conduct-problem children. Although directed toward parents of older children with conduct disorders, their program will be described here because it has provided the foundation for numerous other parent training programs.

The program uses an individual counseling model in a step-by-step approach wherein each newly learned skill forms the foundation for the next new skill. Five behavior management practices form the core content of the program: tracking behavior problems, using social and tangible reinforcement, using time-out and other limit-setting techniques, monitoring child behavior, and problem-solving/negotiation strategies. Parents become increasingly responsible for designing their own programs. The treatment content is described in a manual by Patterson and Chamberlain (1988), elaborated upon by Reid et al. (1999), and has undergone extensive evaluation. An assigned text, *Living with Children* or *Families,* is used with the program.

Adolescent Transition Program. A group-based version of this program called the Adolescent Transition Program, Parent Focus (ATP; Dishion & Kavanagh, in press), was developed for parents of older children with at-risk behaviors (ages 11–15 years). This 12-session, group-based parenting program has been shown to improve both parenting practices and youth behaviors. The program uses videotape examples and discussion.

Helping the Noncompliant Child. Another influential parent training program for noncompliant 3- to 8-year-old children was developed by Hanf (Hanf & Kling, 1973) and modified and evaluated by McMahon and Forehand (1984). As described by Forehand and McMahon (1981) in their book *Helping the Noncompliant Child,* this comprehensive parent training program begins by teaching parents to engage in nondirective play with their children and to identify and reward children's prosocial behaviors through praise and attention. Parents then learn to increase child compliance using direct commands and time-out. Progression to each new skill is contingent on achieving competence in the previous skills. The therapist works with individual parents and children together. Training methods include role playing, modeling, coaching, and a "bug-in-the-ear" device so therapists can provide feedback during parent–child interactions. This intervention is effective in reducing noncompliance and conduct problems with long-lasting effects.

Parent–Child Interaction Therapy. An emphasis on improving parent–child relationships is also found in Parent–Child Interaction Therapy developed by Eyberg (Eyberg et al., 1995). While the importance of behavior management principles is maintained, child-directed play (describe, reflect, imitate, and praise) is a major focus of intervention. Eyberg presents this program as an integration of traditional play therapy and current behavioral thinking about child management. It is felt that nondirective parent–child play improves children's frustration tolerance, reduces the anger level of oppositional children, and offers opportunities for prosocial behavior to occur. Engaging in play also helps parents recognize children's positive qualities. Nondirective play teaches parents to respond in a sensitive and genuine manner, to relate to their child's development, and to stimulate learning.

The Incredible Years Parenting Programs. Another parent training program, The Incredible Years, developed by Webster-Stratton (1984, revised 2001) contains two 12- to 14-week programs (for ages 3–8 and 5–10). Based on the early theoretical work of Patterson (Patterson, 1976a, 1982; Patterson, Reid, Jones, & Conger, 1975) and Hanf (Hanf, 1970; Hanf & Kling, 1973) regarding key parenting and relationship skills and behavioral principles to reduce conduct problems, the program makes extensive use of videotape modeling methods. The content of the BASIC program incorporates Patterson's (1982) nonviolent discipline concepts, Hanf's

(1970) "child-directed play" approaches, and the strategic use of differential-attention, encouragement, praise, and effective commands. It also includes cognitive behavioral approaches such as problem-solving strategies, self-management principles, and self-talk to cope with depressive and self-defeating thoughts. This content has been embedded in a relational framework including parent group support and a collaborative relationship with the group leader. This approach is designed to promote parental self-efficacy and engagement with the program and reduce parental resistance and dropout (Webster-Stratton, 1998a; Webster-Stratton & Hancock, 1998). Parent discussion centers around the videotape vignettes that show parent models in natural situations (unrehearsed) with their children "doing it right" and "doing it wrong." Each parent identifies goals for the program and then applies the "parenting principles" learned in the program to their individualized goals. The group discussion and collaborative format were chosen to ensure that the intervention would be sensitive to individual cultural differences and personal values. A book for parents entitled *The Incredible Years: A Trouble-Shooting Guide for Parents* (Webster-Stratton, 1992), as well as a self-administered version of the videotape program, are also available. This program is effective as a prevention program (12 weeks) and as an intensive intervention (22 weeks) for parents of children with diagnosed ODD/CD.

In addition to the BASIC program (described earlier), Webster-Stratton has developed two other parent videotape training series. The first, The ADVANCE parent program, includes content on problem solving, communication, anger management, and support (Webster-Stratton, 1990b). This 14-week program enhances the effects of BASIC by promoting children's and parent's conflict management skills and self-control techniques (Webster-Stratton, 1994a). The other videotape program, *Supporting Your Child's Education*, helps parents support their children's learning at home and to communicate with teachers more successfully. This 6-week program results in increased parental involvement in school-related activities (Webster-Stratton & Reid, 1999c).

Finally, Webster-Stratton has developed two other videotape-based training programs, one for training children directly in problem-solving, anger management, and social skills (Webster-Stratton, 1990a, Webster-Stratton & Hammond, 1997) and the other for training teachers in positive classroom management strategies and effective methods of communicating and involving parents (Webster-Stratton, 1994b, Webster-Stratton & Reid, 1999a, 1999b).

Summary

As has been demonstrated in this chapter, a parent component is critical to the success of schools' efforts to provide programs for preventing conduct problems and promoting social competence in students. The review herein is not all-inclusive, focusing instead on a few programs that have been shown to be effective using rigorous evaluation standards. Given the powerful potential of these programs, school psychologists involved in preventing and reducing school aggression should be trained in empirically validated interventions (Brestan & Eyberg, 1998) and consider strategies to integrate these effectively into a schoolwide plan. Central to any of these programs' success is the parent–teacher–school counselor partnership model, a supportive network that leads to parents and teachers feeling more supported in their efforts and results in more success than those that target either teachers or parents alone. When schools offer comprehensive intervention programs, they can expect to have reduced levels of conduct problems and school violence, increased academic success, and greater collaboration between home and school. Schools could initiate this process by routinely screening children to determine who could benefit from additional support, such as parent training or social skills programs. Then they could provide parenting programs by training school counselors, psychologists, nurses, or teachers so that they are confident in offering group-based parent programs. Moreover, they could provide a resource room for parents that includes books and videotapes on parenting, social skills, and problem-solving teaching for children. There is great need for schools to find the resources for such programs and to define their role as partners with parents in efforts to prevent conduct problems and promote social competence.

This chapter was supported by a Research Scientist Development Award MH00988-07 from the National Institute of Mental Health. Correspondence concerning this chapter should be sent to Carolyn Webster-Stratton, Parenting Clinic, Box 354801, School of Nursing, University of Washington, Seattle, WA 98195.

REFERENCES

Abramowitz, A. J., O'Leary, S. G., & Futtersak, M. W. (1988). The relative impact of long and short reprimands on children's off-task behavior in the classroom. *Behavior Therapy, 19*, 243–247.

Acker, M. M., & O'Leary, S. G. (1987). Effects of reprimands and praise on appropriate behavior in the classroom. *Journal of Abnormal Child Psychology, 15*(4), 549–557.

Alexander, J. F., & Parsons, B. V. (1982). *Functional family therapy*. Monterey, CA: Brooks/Cole.

American Psychological Association (1995). Template for developing guidelines: Interventions for mental disorders and psychosocial aspects of physical disorders. Washington, DC: Author.

Battistich, V., Schaps, E., Watson, M., & Solomon, D. (1996). Prevention effects of the child development project: Early findings from an ongoing multisite demonstration trial. *Journal of Adolescent Research, 1*, 12–35.

Battistich, V., Schaps, E., Watson, M., Solomon, D., & Schaps, E. (1989). Effects of an elementary school program to enhance prosocial behavior on children's cognitive social problem-solving skills and strategies. *Journal of Applied Developmental Psychology, 10*, 147–169.

Battistich, V., Watson, M., Solomon, D., & Schaps, E. (1991). The child development project: A comprehensive program for the development of prosocial character. In W. M. Kurtines & J. L. Gewirtz (Eds.), *Handbook of moral behavior and development* (Vol. 2, pp. 1–34). Ellsdale, NJ: Erlbaum.

Bierman, K. L., Miller, C. M., & Stabb, S. (1987). Improving the social behavior and peer acceptance of rejected boys: Effects of social skill training with instructions and prohibitions. *Journal of Consulting and Clinical Psychology, 55*, 194–200.

Brestan, E. V., & Eyberg, S. M. (1998). Effective psychosocial treatments of conduct-disordered children and adolescents: 29 years, 82 studies, and 5,272 kids. *Journal of Clinical Child Psychology, 27*(2), 180–189.

Brook, J. S., Whiteman, M., Gordon, A. S., & Cohen, P. (1986). Dynamics of childhood and adolescent personality traits and adolescent drug use. *Developmental Psychology 22*(3), 403–414.

Bryan, T. (1991). Social problems and learning disabilities. In B. L. Wong (Ed.), *Learning about learning disabilities* (pp. 195–226). New York: Academic Press.

Bullis, M., & Walker, H. M. (Eds.). (1994). *Comprehensive school-based systems for troubled youth.* Eugene: University of Oregon, Center on Human Development.

Campbell, S. (1995). Behavior problems in preschool children: A review of recent research. *Journal of Child Psychology and Psychiatric & Allied Disciplines, 36*(1), 113–149.

Campbell, S. B., & Ewing, L. J. (1990). Follow-up of hard-to-manage preschoolers: Adjustment at age 9 and predictors of continuing symptoms. *Journal of Child Psychology and Psychiatry, 31*(6), 871–889.

Chamberlain, P., Reid, J. B., Ray, J., Capaldi, D. M., & Fisher, P. (1997). Parent inadequate discipline (PID). In T. A. Widiger, A. J. Frances, H. A. Pincus, R. Ross, M. B. First, & W. Davis (Eds.), *DSM-IV source book* (Vol. 3, pp. 569–629). Washington, DC: American Psychiatric Association.

Chambless, D. L., & Hollon, S. D. (1998). Defining empirically supported therapies. *Journal of Consulting and Clinical Psychology, 66*(1), 7–18.

Christenson, S. L., Rounds, T., & Franklin, M. J. (1992). Home–school collaboration: Effects, issues, and opportunities. In S. L. Christenson & J. C. Conoley (Eds.), *Home–school collaboration: Enhancing children's academic and social competence* (pp. 19–51). Bethesda, MD: National Association of School Psychologists.

Coie, J. D. (1990a). Adapting intervention to the problems of aggressive and disruptive rejected children. In S. R. Asher & J. D. Coie (Eds.), *Peer rejection in childhood* (pp. 309–337). Cambridge: Cambridge University Press.

Coie, J. D. (1990b). Toward a theory of peer rejection. In S. R. Asher & J. D. Coie (Eds.), *Peer rejection in childhood* (pp. 365–398). Cambridge: Cambridge University Press.

Cotton, K., & Wikelund, K. R. (Eds.). (1990). *School-wide and classroom discipline* Portland, OR: Northwest Regional Education Laboratory.

Cummings, E. M., & Davies, P. (1994). *Children and marital conflict.* New York: Guilford.

Dishion, T. J., & Andrews, D. W. (1995). Preventing escalation in problem behaviors with high-risk young adolescents: Immediate and 1-year outcomes. *Journal of Consulting and Clinical Psychology, 63*(4), 538–548.

Dishion, T. J., & Kavanagh, K. (in press). Adolescent problem behavior: A family-centered intervention and assessment sourcebook. New York: Guilford.

Dishion, T. J., & Ray, J. (1991). *The development and ecology of substance abuse in adolescent boys.* Unpublished manuscript. Eugene: Oregon Social Learning Center.

Dodge, K. A., Bates, J. E., & Pettit, G. S. (1990). Mechanisms in the cycle of violence. *Science, 250,* 1678–1683.

Eber, L., & Nelson, M. C. (1997). School-based wraparound planning: Integrating services for students with emotional and behavioral needs. *American Journal of Orthopsychiatry, 67,* 385–395.

Eyberg, S. M., Boggs, S., & Algina, J. (1995). Parent–child interaction therapy: A psychosocial model for the treatment of young children with conduct problem behavior and their families. *Psychopharmacology Bulletin, 31,* 83–91.

Forehand, R., Rogers, T., McMahon, R. J., Wells, K. C., & Griest, D. L. (1981). Teaching parents to modify child behavior problems: an examination of some follow-up data. *Journal of Pediatric Psychology, 6*(3), 313–322.

Forehand, R. L., & McMahon, R. J. (1981). *Helping the noncompliant child: A clinician's guide to parent training.* New York: Guilford.

Forgatch, M. (1989). Patterns and outcome in family problem solving: The disrupting effect of negative emotion. *Journal of Marriage and the Family, 5*(1), 115–124.

Forgatch, M., Patterson, G., & Skinner, M. (1988). A mediational model for the effect of divorce in antisocial behavior in boys. In E. M. Hetherington & J. D. Arasteh (Eds.), *The impact of divorce, single parenting and stepparenting on children* (pp. 135–154). Hillsdale, NJ: Erlbaum.

Francis, D. J., Shaywitz, S. E., Stuebing, K. K., Shaywitz, B. A., & Fletcher, J. M. (1991). Analysis of change: Modeling individual growth. *Journal of Consulting and Clinical Psychology, 59,* 27–37.

Gottfredson, D. C., Gottfredson, G. D., & Hybl, L. G. (1993). Managing adolescent behavior: A multiyear, multischool study. *American Education Research Journal, 30,* 179–215.

Gresham, F. M. (1986). Conceptual issues in the assessment of social competence in children. In P. Strain, M. Guralink, & H. Walker (Eds.), *Children's social behavior: Development, assessment, and modification* (pp. 143–186). New York: Academic Press.

Group, Conduct Problems Prevention Research. (1992). A developmental and clinical model for the prevention of conduct disorder: The FAST Track Program. Special Issue: Developmental approaches to prevention and intervention. *Development and Psychopathology. 4*(4), 509–527.

Group, C. P. P. R. (1999, August). *Results of Fast Track Prevention Project: Grade 3 outcomes.* Paper presented at the American Psychological Association, San Francisco.

Group, C. P. P. R. (1999a). Initial impact of the Fast Track prevention trial for conduct problems: I. The high-risk sample. *Journal of Consulting and Clinical Psychology. 67*, 631–647.

Group, C. P. P. R. (1999b). Initial impact of the Fast Track prevention trial for conduct problems: II. Classroom effects. *Journal of Consulting and Clinical Psychology. 67*, 631–647.

Hanf, C. (1970). *Shaping mothers to shape their children's behavior:* Unpublished manuscript. Portland: University of Oregon Medical School.

Hanf, E., & Kling, J. (1973). *Facilitating parent–child interactions: A two-stage training model.* Portland: University of Oregon Medical School.

Hawkins, J. D., Catalano, R. F., Kosterman, R., Abbott, R., & Hill, K. G. (1999). Preventing adolescent health-risk behaviors by strengthening protection during childhood. *Archives of Pediatrics and Adolescent Medicine, 153*, 226–234.

Hawkins, J. D., Von Cleve, E., & Catalano, R. F. (1991). Reducing early childhood aggression: Results of a primary prevention program. *Journal of the American Academy of Child and Adolescent Psychiatry, 30*(2), 208–217.

Hawkins, J. D., & Weiss, J. G. (1985). The social developmental model: An integrated approach to delinquency prevention. *Journal of Primary Prevention, 6*, 73–95.

Henggeler, S. W., Melton, G. B., & Smith, L. A. (1992). Family preservation using multisystemic therapy: An effective alternative to incarcerating serious juvenile offenders. *Journal of Consulting and Clinical Psychology, 60*, 953–961.

Henggeler, S. W., Schoenwald, S. K., Borduin, C. M., & Rowland, M. D. (1998). *Multsystemic treatment of antisocial behavior in children and adolescents.* New York: Guilford.

Henggeler, S. W., Schoenwald, S. K., & Pickrel, S. A. G. (1995). Multisystemic therapy: Bridging the gap between university- and community-based treatment. *Journal of Consulting and Clinical Psychology, 63*, 709–717.

Hobbs, N. (1982). *The troubled and troubling child.* San Francisco: Jossey-Bass.

Kavale, K. A., & Forness, S. R. (1998). Covariance in learning disability and behavior disorder: An examination of classification and placement issues. In T. E. Scruggs & M. A. Mastropieri (Eds.), *Advances in learning and behavioral disabilities* (pp. 1–42). Greenwich, CT: JAI Press.

Kazdin, A. (1985). *Treatment of antisocial behavior in children and adolescents.* Homewood, IL: Dorsey.

Kazdin, A. E. (1987). Treatment of antisocial behavior in children: Current status and future directions. *Psychological Bulletin, 102*(2), 187–203.

Kazdin, A. E. (1995). *Conduct disorders in childhood and adolescence.* Thousand Oaks, CA: Sage.

Kazdin, A. E., Bass, D., Siegel, T., & Thomas, C. (1989). Cognitive-behavioral therapy and relationship therapy in the treatment of children referred for antisocial behavior. *Journal of Consulting, and Clinical Psychology, 57*(4), 522–535.

Kazdin, A. E., Esveldt, D. K., French, N. H., & Unis, A. S. (1987). Problem-solving skills training and relationship therapy in the treatment of antisocial child behavior. *Journal of Consulting and Clinical Psychology, 55*(1), 76–85.

Kazdin, A. E., Esveldt-Dawson, K., French, N. H., & Unis, A. S. (1987). Problem-solving skills training and relationship therapy in the treatment of antisocial child behavior. *Journal of Consulting and Clinical Psychology, 55*, 76–85.

Kazdin, A. E., & Kendall, P. C. (1998). Current progress and future plans for developing effective treatments: Comments and perspectives. *Journal of Clinical Child Psychology, 27*(2), 217–226.

Kazdin, A. E., Siegel, J. C., & Bass, D. (1992). Cognitive problem-solving skills training and parent management training in the treatment of antisocial behavior in children. *Journal of Consultation, and Clinical Psychology, 60*, 733–747.

Kellam, S. G., Ling, X., Merisca, R., Brown, C. H., & Ialongon, N. (1998). The effect of the level of aggression in the first grade classroom on the course and malleability of aggressive behavior into middle school. *Development and Psychopathology, 10*, 165–185.

Knoff, H. M., & Batsche, G. M. (1995). Project ACHIEVE: Analyzing a school reform process for at-risk and underachieving students. *School Psychology Review, 24*, 579–603.

Kusche, C. A., & Greenberg, M. T. (1994). *The PATHS Curriculum.* Seattle, WA: Developmental Research and Programs.

Lochman, J. E., & Wells, K. (1996). A social-cognitive intervention with aggressive children: Prevention effects and contextual implementation issues. In R. D. Peters & R. J. McMahon (Eds.), *Prevention and early intervention: Childhood disorders, substance use, and delinquency* (pp. 111–143). Newbury Park, CA: Sage.

Loeber, R., Wung, P., Keenan, K., Giroux, B., Stouthamer-Loeber, M., Van Kammen, W. B., & Maughan, B. (1993). Developmental pathways in disruptive child behavior. *Development phsychopathology, 5,* 103–133.

McMahon, R. J., & Forehand, R. (1984). Parent training for the noncompliant child: Treatment outcome, generalization, and adjunctive therapy procedures. In R. F. Dangel & R. A. Polster (Eds.), *Parent training: Foundations of research and practice* (pp. 298–328). New York: Guilford.

Morris, S. B., Alexander, J. F., & Waldron, H. (1990). Functional family therapy: Issues in clinical practice. In I. R. H. Fallon (Ed.), *Handbook of behavior therapy.* New York: Guilford.

Mrazek, P. J., & Haggerty, R. J. (1994). Illustrative preventive intervention research programs. In P. J. Mrazek & R. J. Haggerty (Eds.), *Reducing risks for mental disorders. Frontiers for preventive intervention* research (pp. 215–313). Washington, DC: National Academy Press.

Offord, D. R., Boyle, M. H., & Szatmafi, P. (1987). Ontario Child Health Study 11: Six month prevalence of disorder and rates of service utilization. *Archives of General Psychiatry, 44,* 832–836.

Patterson, G., Reid, J., & Dishion, T. (1992). *Antisocial boys: A social interactional approach* (Vol. 4). Eugene, OR: Castalia.

Patterson, G. R. (1976). The aggressive child: Victim and architect of a coercive system. In E. J. Mash, L. A. Hamerlynck, & L. C. Handy (Eds.), *Behavior modification and families* (pp. 267–316). New York: Brunner/Mazel.

Patterson, G. R. (1982). *Coercive family process.* Eugene, OR: Castalia.

Patterson, G. R., & Chamberlain, P. (1988). Treatment process: A problem at three levels. In L. C. Wynne (Ed.), *The state of art in family therapy research: Controversies and recommendations* (pp. 189–223). New York: Family Process Press.

Patterson, G. R., Chamberlain, P., & Reid, J. B. (1982). A comparative evaluation of a parent training program. *Behavior Therapy, 13,* 638–650.

Patterson, G. R., Crosby, L., & Vuchinich, S. (1992). Predicting risk for early police arrest. *Journal of Quantitative Criminology, 8*(4), 335–355.

Patterson, G. R., & Narrett, C. M. (1990). The development of a reliable and valid treatment program for aggressive young children. *International Journal of Mental Health, 19*(3), 19–26.

Patterson, G. R., Reid, J. B., Jones, R. R., & Conger, R. W. (1975). *A social learning approach to family intervention* (Vol. 1). Eugene, OR: Castalia.

Pfiffner, L. J., & O'Leary, S. G. (1987). The efficacy of all-positive management as a function of the prior use of negative consequences. *Journal of Applied Behavior Analysis, 20*(3), 265–271.

Pfiffner, L. J., Rosen, L. A., & O'Leary, S. G. (1985). The efficacy of an all-positive approach to classroom management. *Journal of Applied Behavior Analysis, 18,* 257–263.

Reid, J. B., & Eddy, J. M. (1997). The prevention of antisocial behavior: Some considerations in the search for effective interventions. In D. M. Stoff, J. Breiling, & J. D. Maser (Eds.), *The handbook of antisocial behavior* (pp. 343–356). New York: Wiley.

Reid, J. B., Eddy, J. M., Fetrow, R. A., & Stoolmiller, M. (1999). Description and immediate impacts of a preventive intervention for conduct problems. *American Journal of Community Psychology, 27*(4), 483–517.

Sheridan, S. M., Kratochwill, T. R., & Bergan, J. R. (1996). *Conjoint behavioral consultation: A procedural manual.* New York: Plenum.

Shure, M. B., & Spivack, G. (1982). Interpersonal problem-solving in young children: A cognitive approach to prevention. *American Journal of Community Psychology. 10*(3), 341–356.

Stage, S. A., & Quiroz, D. R. (1997). A meta-analysis of interventions to decrease disruptive classroom behavior in public education settings. *School Psychology Review, 26,* 333–368.

Stoff, D. M., Breiling, J., & Masters, J. D. (1997). *The handbook of antisocial behavior.* New York: Wiley.

Tanaka, J. S. (1987). How big is big enough? Sample size and goodness of fit in structural equation models with latent variables. *Child Development, 58,* 134–146.

Taylor, T. K., & Biglan, A. (1998). Behavioral family interventions for improving childrearing: A review for clinicians and policy makers. *Clinical Child and Family Psychology Review, 1*(1), 41–60.

Tremblay, R. E., Japel, C., Perusse, D., McDuff, P., Boivin, M., Zoccolillo, M., & Montplaisir, J. (1999). The search for the age of "onset" of physical aggression: Rousseau and Bandura revisted. *Criminal Behavior and Mental Health, 9*(1), 8–23.

Tremblay, R. E., Mass, L. C., Pagani, L., & Vitaro, F. (1996). From childhood physical aggression to adolescent maladjustment: The Montreal Prevention Experiment. In R. D. Peters & R. J. MacMahon (Eds.), *Preventing childhood disorders, substance abuse and delinquency* (pp. 268–298). Thousand Oaks, CA: Sage.

Tremblay, R. E., Pagani, K. L., Masse, L. C., & Vitaro, F. (1995). A biomodal preventive intervention for disruptive kindergarten boys: Its impact through mid-adolescence. Special section: Prediction and prevention of child and adolescent antisocial behavior. *Journal of Consulting and Clinical Psychology, 63,* 560–568.

Tremblay, R. E., Vitaro, F., Bertrand, L., LeBlanc, M., Beauchesne, H., Boileau, H., & David, L. (1996). Parent and child training to prevent early onset of delinquency: The Montreal longitudinal-experimental study. In J. McCord & R. E. Tremblay (Eds.), *Preventing antisocial behavior: Interventions from birth through adolescence* (pp. 117–138). New York: Guilford.

Wahler, R. G. (1980). The insular mother: Her problems in parent–child treatment. *Journal of Applied Behavior Analysis, 13*(2), 207–219.

Wahler, R. G., & Sansbury, L. E. (1990). The monitoring skills of troubled mothers: Their problems in defining child deviance. *Journal of Abnormal Child Psychology, 18(5),* 577–589.

Walker, H. M., Colvin, G., & Ramsey, E. (1995). *Antisocial behavior in school: Strategies and best practices.* Pacific Grove, CA: Brooks/Cole.

Walker, H. M., Schwartz, 1. E., Nippold, M. A., Irvin, L. K., & Noell, J. W. (1994). Social skills in school-age children and youth: Issues and best practices in assessment and intervention. *Topics in Language Disorders, 14*(3), 70–82.

Webster-Stratton, C. (Ed.). (1984, revised 2001). *The Incredible Years parent training manual: BASIC program.* 1411 8th Avenue West, Seattle, WA 98119.

Webster-Stratton, C. (1985). The effects of father involvement in parent training for conduct problem children. *Journal of Child Psychology and Psychiatry, 26*(5), 801–810.

Webster-Stratton, C. (1990a). *Dina Dinosaur's Social Skills and Problem-Solving Curriculum.* 1411 8th Avenue West, Seattle, WA.

Webster-Stratton, C. (1990b). *The Incredible Years parent training program manual: Effective communication, anger management and problem-solving (ADVANCE).* 1411 8th Avenue West, Seattle, WA 98119.

Webster-Stratton, C. (1990c). Stress: A potential disruptor of parent perceptions and family interactions. *Journal of Clinical Child Psychology, 19,* 302–312.

Webster-Stratton, C. (1992). *The Incredible Years: A trouble-shooting guide for parents of children ages 3–8 years.* Toronto: Umbrella.

Webster-Stratton, C. (1994a). Advancing videotape parent training: A comparison study. *Journal of Consulting and Clinical Psychology, 62*(3), 583–593.

Webster-Stratton, C. (1994b). *The Incredible Years teacher training series.* 1411 8th Avenue West, Seattle, WA 98119.

Webster-Stratton, C. (1996). Videotape modeling intervention programs for families of young children with oppositional defiant disorder or conduct disorder. In P. S. Jensen & E. D. Hibbs (Eds.), *Psychosocial treatments for child and adolescent disorders: Empirically based approaches* pp. 435–475. Washington, DC: American Psychological Association.

Webster-Stratton, C. (1997, March/April). From parent training to community building. *Families in society. Journal of Contemporary Human Services,* 156–171.

Webster-Stratton, C. (1998a). Parent training with low-income clients: Promoting parental engagement through a collaborative approach. In J. R. Lutzker (Ed.), *Handbook of child abuse research and treatment* (pp. 183–210). New York: Plenum.

Webster-Stratton, C. (1998b). Preventing conduct problems in Head Start children: Strengthening parent competencies. *Journal of Consulting and Clinical Psychology, 66*(5), 715–730.

Webster-Stratton, C., & Hammond, M. (1997). Treating children with early-onset conduct problems: A comparison of child and parent training interventions. *Journal of Consulting and Clinical Psychology, 65*(1), 93–109.

Webster-Stratton, C., & Hammond, M. (1998). Conduct problems and level of social competence in Head Start children: Prevalence, pervasiveness and associated risk factors. *Clinical Child Psychology and Family Psychology Review, 1*(2), 101–124.

Webster-Stratton, C., & Hammond, M. (1999). Marital conflict management skills, parenting style, and early-onset conduct problems: Processes and pathways. *Journal of Child Psychology & and Psychiatry, 40,* 917–927.

Webster-Stratton, C., & Hancock, L. (1998). Parent training: Content, methods and processes. In E. Schaefer (Ed.), *Handbook of parent training,* (2nd ed., pp. 98–152). New York: Wiley.

Webster-Stratton, C., & Herbert, M. (1994). *Troubled families—Problem children: Working with parents: A collaborative process.* Chichester: Wiley.

Webster-Stratton, C., Hollinsworth, T., & Kolpacoff, M. (1989). The long-term effectiveness and clinical significance of three cost-effective training programs for families with conduct-problem children. *Journal of Consulting and Clinical Psychology, 57*(4), 550–553.

Webster-Stratton, C., & Reid, M. J. (1999a, December). *Effects of parent and teacher training in Head Start.* Paper presented at the Advances in Substance Abuse Prevention Research, Washington, DC.

Webster-Stratton, C., & Reid, M. J. (1999b, June). *Effects of teacher training in Head Start classrooms: Results of a randomized controlled evaluation.* Paper presented at the Society for Prevention Research, New Orleans.

Webster-Stratton, C., & Reid, M. J. (1999c, November). *Treating children with early-onset conduct problems: The importance of teacher training.* Paper presented at the Association for the Advancement of Behavior Therapy, Toronto, Canada.

Yoshikawa, H. (1994). Prevention as cumulative protection: Effects of early family support and education on chronic delinquency and its risks. *Psychological Bulletin, 115,* 28–54.

17 Paraprofessionals as Members of the Team

Supporting Students with Behavioral Difficulties

MARY BETH DOYLE

Vermont State Department of Education

Introduction

Currently the professional literature is being inundated with articles and training materials that focus on the roles and responsibilities of paraprofessionals (Doyle, 1997; Pickett, Faison, & Formanek, 1993; Pickett & Gerlach, 1997). Some of these materials focus specifically on training paraprofessionals who work on educational teams to support students who experience behavioral challenges (Backus, Keogh, CichoskiKelly, Giangreco, & Tucker, 2000; Hewitt & Langenfeld, 1999). Interestingly, this increase in written materials parallels (a) the increasing numbers of students with disabilities who are receiving part or all of their educational services in general education classrooms (Blalock, 1991; Simpson & Myles, 1990; Walther-Thomas, Korinek, McLaughlin, & Williams, 2000) and (b) the mandates of the Individuals with Disabilities Education Act Amendments of 1997 (IDEA) (20 U.S.C. 1400 et seq.), which requires students to receive educational services in the least restrictive environment. Often, paraprofessionals are used to support the education of students with disabilities in these general education settings. In using paraprofessionals to provide support, IDEA clearly states that state education agencies must "appropriately and adequately prepare, train and supervise" them (20 U.S.C. 1412, 612[5]). Such legal requirements account, at least in part, for the swell in the professional literature in the area of paraprofessionals. Additional reasons for this focus on training materials may include (a) the professional acknowledgment of the active involvement of paraprofessionals in supporting the participation of students with disabilities in general education settings and (b) the recognition that in order to support the educational process, training is necessary.

Collision between Theory and Practice

In classrooms in which individual students demonstrate unusual or disturbing behaviors it is often necessary for team members (e.g., classroom teacher, special educator, paraprofessional, and behavior specialist) to design specific behavioral support plans. The plans are meant to support the student(s) in learning and maintaining appropriate behaviors. Each member of the student educational team has certain responsibilities in the design, implementation, and evaluation of the behavior plan. Clearly there should be differences in the responsibilities assumed by certified (e.g., classroom teacher, special educator, and psychologist) versus noncertified personnel (e.g., paraprofessional and classroom volunteer).

A key difference in the responsibilities of team members is that ultimately the certified personnel are responsible for all aspects of each student's educational program, regardless of who (i.e., noncertified personnel) assists with the implementation of the program. To support individual students in a consistent manner, responsibilities should be specified. Most simply stated, in *all* situations, it is the responsibility of the certified educational team members (e.g., classroom teacher, special educator, behavior support specialist, or school psychologist) to design, implement and evaluate educational and behavioral support plans that reflect the underlying policies of the school and classroom, while meeting the individualized needs of students who have disabilities. The certified personnel are also responsible for providing ongoing training, monitoring, and feedback to anyone (e.g., paraprofessionals and classroom volunteers) who will be assisting the team with the implementation of the educational and behavioral support plans for the individual student. These responsibilities may include implementing specified positive behavioral support strategies, collecting data, and reporting data. Clearly, in all situations, the paraprofessional's responsibilities should be more limited than those of certified personnel.

While the professional data-based and descriptive literature concerning the use and impact of paraprofessionals is limited in depth and breadth, there is helpful information to consider. First, however, it is important to acknowledge aspects of the educational context (i.e., public school classrooms and structures) within which the paraprofessionals function. Such consideration provides a contextual reference point from which to better understand the challenges associated with the evolving nature of the roles and responsibilities of paraprofessionals.

The cultural context of schools has evolved significantly over the past century, while the daily structures have changed very little. The contextual changes range from increased racial and ethnic diversity, to the very invention and use of the personal computer. Students who were at one time considered to be "uneducable" (e.g., students with severe disabilities and children of migrant workers) are now included as full members of elementary, middle school, and high school communities. Interestingly enough, as our schools have evolved culturally (e.g., increased diversity) and pedagogically (e.g., integration of technology), they have not changed in the most common daily structures (e.g., use of adults and daily scheduling). Most students still attend school for approximately 6 hours per day and 175 days per year, and there is typically one adult (i.e., classroom teacher) who maintains primary responsibility for a large group of students.

The significance of acknowledging this stagnation in the midst of so many dramatic changes is seen most clearly when examining the frequent collisions between what most teachers are expected to do (i.e., theory) each day with the demands of their cultural context (i.e., practice). For example, as is highlighted in the professional literature, there is often a discrepancy between the theoretical expectations for the most appropriate use of paraprofessionals and the actual practice. This discrepancy is not because teachers deliberately set out to create such disequilibrium; rather, the complexities associated with the demands of everyday teaching are extraordinary. The skillful incorporation of a paraprofessional into the physical and pedogogical fabric of the classroom is, at the very least, difficult. Compounding this reality is the fact that it is highly unusual for teachers to receive any instruction during their preservice education related to how to work with paraprofessionals. As Salzeberg and Morgan (1995) state, "teachers are not generally prepared for this role (supervising paraprofessionals)" (p. 49).

Now take a moment to enter the education of students who experience behavioral challenges into the core of general education. Often paraprofessionals are hired and assigned to provide one-to-one support to the individual student (Giangreco, Broer, & Edelman, 1999; Werts, Wolery, Snyder, & Caldwell, 1996; Wolery, Werts, Caldwell, Snyder, & Liskowski, 1995; Wolery et al., 1994). The practice of assigning this type of support to an individual student is often made without consideration of the entire classroom community. This practice represents one example of the clash between theory and practice. Theoretically, both the law (i.e., IDEA) and professional literature (Doyle, 1997; French, 1998; Giangreco et al., 1999; Pickett & Gerlach, 1997) support the use of paraprofessionals in five major categories:

1. Implementation of instruction that is designed and ultimately evaluated by licensed personnel
2. Implementation of elements of individualized behavioral support plans that are designed and ultimately evaluated by licensed personnel
3. Provision of general supervision of students during noninstructional time such as recess
4. Preparation of teacher-designed instructional materials and adaptations
5. Completion of clerical tasks

However, it is common practice in many situations for paraprofessionals to become the primary responsible team member (i.e., the "teacher") for the individual student with behavioral challenges (Doyle, 1995; French & Chopra, 1999; Marks, Schrader, & Levine, 1999; Wadsworth & Knight, 1996).

In a study conducted by Marks and colleagues (1999), paraprofessionals assumed significant responsibility for the educational programs of the students they support, regardless of the paraprofessional's limited pedagogical expertise. They found that while paraprofessionals generally believed that it actually was the classroom teacher's responsibility to manage the academic and social curriculum for all students, that rarely happened for students with disabilities. The following quotations (Marks et al., 1999) exemplify this situation:

> "What happens is that they [teachers] leave it up to the aide to do a lot of the work" (p. 320).

> "It just got to the point that it was easier for me [the paraprofessional] to do it [take responsibility for the curriculum] than to keep asking people" (p. 320).

Clearly there is an emerging pattern within the field whereby the least trained personnel are taking significant responsibility for students who have complex learning and behavioral challenges (Giangreco et al., 1999). Harper (1994) points out a significant concern with such a model: "Without appropriate understanding of the theoretical and methodological rationale for sound educational practice, paraprofessionals often perform reductionist activities disconnected from individual needs and knowledge that each child brings to the classroom" (p. 68). As early as 1993, Martella and his colleagues estimated that paraprofessionals "deliver approximately 80% of instruction that students with severe disabilities receive" (Martella, Marchand-Martella, Miller, Macfarlane, & Young, 1993, p. 34). Complicating this situation, as already noted, the results of a literature review conducted by Salzberg and Morgan (1995) indicate that teachers typically do not receive significant training in their preservice training in how to train and supervise paraprofessionals.

Paraprofessionals as Facilitators of Social Support

Another specific area identified in the professional literature in which paraprofessional support is often targeted is in the facilitation of social supports for students who experience behavioral difficulties. Again, theoretical understanding based on early research and actual practice appear to be in conflict. Professional literature indicates that while one of the roles of many paraprofessionals is to facilitate relationships between students with and without disabilities, outcome data indicate many negative effects are associated with this practice. Giangreco, Edelman, Luiselli, and MacFarland (1997) first describe the "hovering" effect of paraprofessionals as they become a type of force field interfering with nondisabled peers initiating interactions with the student(s) with disabilities. This same phenomenon is noted throughout the professional literature (Giangreco et al., 1999; Guralnick, 1990; Shulka, Kennedy, & Cushing, 1999). Furthermore, research (Egel, Richman, & Koegel, 1981; Shulka et al., 1999; Werts, Caldwell, & Wolery, 1996) suggests that direct support and interactions with nondisabled peers, as compared to interactions with paraprofessionals, is more likely to improve social competence of students with disabilities.

Where does the current literature leave us? Are we to conclude that there is no place for paraprofessionals in public school classrooms? No. Paraprofessionals do serve vital functions within the public school community. However, I would suggest that with the best of intentions, all too often the identification of paraprofessionals as the "key" to the successful education and inclusion of students with disabilities (in this situation students with behavioral challenges) is far too simplistic. It is important that we consider the educational context as a whole, engage in systematic decision making regarding the use of supports and accommodations, and then, if a paraprofessional is involved in the education of children and youth, he or she should receive ongoing training and monitoring. Ultimately, as educators we must examine the outcome data from the student and ask the following difficult questions:

> How is this student's educational experience enhanced because of the paraprofessional?
>
> How is this student's participation in common daily routines and activities better because of the paraprofessional?
>
> How can peers and natural supports step in to take responsibility to welcome and include the student?

The certified personnel (e.g., classroom teacher, special educator, other teacher, or behavioral consultant) should maintain instructional responsibility for all students, including the student(s) with behavioral challenges. The bottom line is that the paraprofessional is present to assist.

The purpose of this chapter is to provide certified staff members, specifically teachers, with information and strategies that can be used to involve paraprofessionals in an appropriate manner in supporting students who experience behavioral difficulties. The focus is twofold. First, ways to establish a sense of connection among the adult members of the classroom community (i.e., the classroom teacher and paraprofessional) will be provided. This section includes ways to create a sense of welcome, a shared vision, and respect among adults and children. Necessary structural supports such as strategies for communication, daily scheduling and role clarification, will also be presented. The next part of the chapter will focus on specific knowledge and skills that can provide a helpful base for paraprofessionals in their daily work in classrooms. This includes general approaches to behavioral supports, specific strategies, working with small groups and individual students, and confidentiality. Note that throughout this chapter the term *classroom teacher* and *certified personnel* will be used interchangeably to refer to any *certified* personnel (e.g., general education teachers, special education teachers, and behavior specialists) involved in supporting students with and without disabilities. These terms are meant to distinguish certified personnel from noncertified personnel such as paraprofessionals.

Create a Sense of Connection

A Deliberate Sense of Welcome for the Paraprofessional

While it may seem overly simplistic, perhaps the most important thing that a classroom teacher can do for the paraprofessional who will be working in her classroom is to *welcome* her (Doyle & Lee, 1997). As the classroom leader, this can be done by providing the paraprofessional a space of her own and place to put her belongings, such as a desk or table. Show her around the school building and classroom. Show her where frequently used classroom materials are kept. Introduce her to other members of the school community, including other paraprofessionals, teachers, secretary staff, and maintenance personnel. Remember her on special occasions such as her birthday and holidays. Say "please" and "thank you" often. These simple acts of welcome and kindness will contribute to the underlying positive atmosphere that will permeate the classroom.

The importance of creating a sense of welcome extends far beyond the positive relationship that is established between the classroom teacher and the paraprofessional. It is likely to affect the classroom climate. A positive and supportive classroom climate, void of unnecessary tension, is helpful for all students, especially for those students who experience behavioral difficulties.

A Shared Vision with the Paraprofessional

After the paraprofessional is welcomed into the instructional space of the school and classroom, it is important to invite her to contribute to the creation of the vision for the classroom community. A shared understanding is the collaborative vision of *how* the classroom community will be, as well as the structures that will need to be in place in order for the classroom teacher and paraprofessional to guide the classroom community (i.e., the students) in a particular direction. Creating a shared understanding of the underlying principles of how the classroom will operate is an important step in ensuring that the classroom teacher and the paraprofessional will work well together (Giangreco et al., 1999). Some of the guiding questions for discussion between the classroom teacher and the paraprofessional are as follows:

How do we want members of our classroom community to feel as learners?

What do we need to do in order to support the students in feeling those ways?

For example, an answer to the first question is "We would like all students to feel safe and welcomed." Then several simple structures could contribute to an increased sense of safety and welcome for all students, specifically those students with behavioral challenges—for example, all students' names are listed in the teacher's attendance book in alphabetical order, all students arrive and leave through the same door and at the same time, each student is greeted by name, and all students maintain similar types of classroom responsibilities (e.g., messenger and line leader). Additionally, the classroom teacher explicitly teaches a social curriculum in which students learn the skills necessary to contribute to a positive classroom community. These ordinary routines and structures help create a sense of welcome, belonging, and safety.

Several specific areas are important to discuss in relationship to developing a shared vision for the classroom community. These include typical daily routines, behavioral expectations for students (see Chapter 10 by Colvin, this text), expected course of the curriculum (e.g., unit topics) (see Chapter 2 by Daly, Duhon, & Witt, this text), communication with families, positive ways to interact with students, and ways to respond to students in a variety of behavioral states (e.g., excited, angry, and upset). Prior to facilitating a discussion with the paraprofessional, the classroom teacher should think about how she thinks and feels in relationship to each of these areas. Such reflection will bring a sense of clarity to the conversation with the paraprofessional.

After the important areas are discussed and appropriate practices are agreed on, the classroom teacher and paraprofessional need to explicitly identify what they need to do and how they will work together to help the whole community move in the direction toward their shared vision. Specifically, a focus is on how the adults will work together (i.e., clarify specific roles and responsibilities). Proactive strategies for communication and clarification of specific roles and responsibilities related to supporting students who experience behavioral challenges are key elements in this discussion.

The results of these discussions become the basis for the shared vision for the classroom community. As the classroom teacher and paraprofessional work together, the vision will evolve, becoming richer as they have more shared experiences. It is important that they continue the dialogue, focusing the decisions of everyday teaching and learning around the original questions: How do we want members of our classroom community to feel as learners? And, if we choose to respond to a situation in that manner, will all of the members of our community be closer to our vision? Decisions of daily behaviors and activities must reflect movement toward the vision so that the atmosphere being created is respectful, positive, and in alignment with the shared vision. Students are more likely to do well in such an environment.

An Attitude of Respect

The atmosphere that the adults in the classroom create is a significant proactive step that can be taken in supporting each other and all students in maintaining positive and acceptable behaviors. Demonstrating an attitude of unconditional respect communicates to both the adult and youth members of the classroom community that no matter what situation may arise, together they can solve it in ways that honor and respect each person. The teacher should facilitate a specific discussion on the topic of respect. This attitude can become the basis for building a positive and strong relationship with all of the students, regardless of their behavioral support needs.

Generate explicit examples of respect with the paraprofessional that include addressing each adult and student by name, saying "please" and "thank you" frequently; praising students for specific acts of kindness; using students' names as examples during instruction; and never raising your voice in the presence of students. Tell the paraprofessional that each member of the classroom community—students, teacher, and paraprofessional—needs to experience many more positive interactions than negative during any given day. It is the feelings associated with positive regard that encourage community members to continue to strive to meet the behavioral expectations established by the classroom community. This is especially true for students who experience behavioral difficulties because historically they are less likely to receive consistent positive feedback. These students in particular need to hear time and again that they are inherently good and have positive things to contribute to the classroom community. It must become a priority to "catch these students being good." A simple yet effective strategy that the teacher can share with the paraprofessional is to set a goal with the paraprofessional to engage in a certain number of positive interactions or to initiate a certain number of positive statements to the student who experiences behavioral difficulties. Be explicit: "Today let's each try to offer 10 positive statements or interactions (e.g., hand on shoulder or thumbs-up gesture) to Sara and no more than two corrective statements." Design a system to track these statements. For example, each of you could put 10 pennies into a pocket. During the school day, each time you make a negative or corrective statement, you must remove a penny. By the end of the day you can tally up your successes. Hopefully, you've both met your goal for Sara!

Communication among Team Members

Effective communication is the cornerstone to effective teamwork. The classroom teacher and the paraprofessional will need to sustain two levels of communication in order for the classroom to operate smoothly. First, the classroom teacher needs to inform the paraprofessional about the curricular focus on an ongoing basis. This might include instructional unit themes, reading and math content, and so forth. While the paraprofessional is not responsible for planning the curriculum, this awareness helps provide a context for working together. There are many strategies to support this type of communication: a brief weekly meeting to review the topics and projects at hand, informal chats during the workday, writing notes in the plan book, giving the paraprofessional access to the teacher's plan book. The teacher and paraprofessional need to choose the strategy that is most effective for them.

The second level of communication is related to specific student needs in relationship to the curriculum. For example, for the student in the class who has behavioral challenges, it is important for the paraprofessional to receive information on how the student will participate in each specific lesson, as well as the specific roles and responsibilities of the paraprofessional in facilitating that participation. The paraprofessional needs to understand and be prepared to implement the specific instructional and behavioral support strategies that are planned for each lesson. The teacher needs to be prepared to tell and show the paraprofessional how she can support students with and without disabilities in meeting their individual educational goals (academic, social, and behavioral). This communication is critical as it ensures (a) the student's individualized needs are being incorporated into the instruction and (b) the paraprofessional does not become the primary "teacher" for the student with behavioral challenges.

Finally, establish ways to communicate about unexpected situations. When supporting a student with behavioral challenges, it would not be unusual for the student to exhibit a behavior that is inappropriate at a time when only a paraprofessional is present, not a certified person. In these situations, it is the paraprofessional's responsibility to make the best decision that she can, based on the training that she has received from the certified personnel. This needs to be followed by documenting the situation so that the classroom teacher is informed of the situation and will be able to provide support to the paraprofessional. Box 17.1 provides one way to accomplish this communicative function.

BOX 17.1

Communicating Unexpected Events

Student: _____   Date: _____

Staff Name: _____   Class: _____

Directions: Complete this form when an unexpected situation arises. Give it to the classroom teacher and schedule a follow-up meeting to discuss the situation in a timely manner.

1. Describe the situation. What did you see and hear?

2. Who was present? How did they contribute (what did you see or hear) to the situation?

3. What did you try to do to solve the problem?

4. Were your actions effective?   _____ Yes   _____ No
   What did you hear or see that would suggest that your actions were effective?

5. Has this ever happened before?   _____ Yes   _____ No
   If so, when and under what circumstances?

6. Do you have any suggestions for the future?

When communication between the classroom teacher and the paraprofessional is strong, the paraprofessional can act in a clear and confident manner about both what she is supposed to do and how it is to be done. This certainty can lead to correct assumptions and the avoidance of unnecessary mistakes.

Daily Scheduling

Another simple yet critical task for the classroom teacher and paraprofessional to do early in the school year is related to daily scheduling. Clarity around daily responsibilities increases the likelihood that the daily routines will be predictable and smooth. This is especially important for students who experience behavioral difficulties. If both adults are clear about the daily schedule, they are better prepared to assist students with transitions between activities and changes in the daily routine. The classroom teacher should examine the daily schedule, assign responsibilities to the paraprofessional (in writing), and then discuss them with the paraprofessional. Using a scheduling format such as the one found on Box 17.2, the teacher fills in the first two columns with the times and daily activities/classes. Then she indicates via a "T" in columns 3 and 4, which activities or tasks *must* be completed by a certified person versus those that *can* be done by a noncertified person. For example, in most school districts, certified personnel are responsible for the design and presentation of initial instruction. However, in many school districts, noncertified personnel can provide tutoring support based on teacher-made plans. This clarification is critical for both the classroom teacher and the paraprofessional. After the teacher has clarified which tasks can and cannot be completed by a paraprofessional, activities are then assigned to the appropriate person(s). This simple act of scheduling can have a positive impact on the class environment as a whole, as well as increasing the predictability for students who experience behavior challenges. Box 17.2 is one tool for facilitating this outcome.

Role Clarification

Generally speaking, paraprofessionals report that they are unclear about their roles and responsibilities (Doyle, 1995; Giangreco et al., 1997). Actually, it is not uncommon for the classroom teacher to be uncertain about the paraprofessional's responsibilities as well! The lack of clarity is because often they never even discuss the topic with each other. Role clarity is especially important when supporting students who experience behavior difficulties and have a number of certified and noncertified people on their educational teams.

In research conducted on the topic by Doyle (1995), general educators, special educators, and the paraprofessionals with whom they worked were individually asked about the responsibilities of the paraprofessional. It became quite clear that the communication among team members teaching in an inclusive setting was

B O X **17.2**

Daily Schedule

Time	Activity	Classroom Teacher	Paraprofessional	Notes
7:45	Check mailbox	T		
	Check e-mail	T	T	
8:00	Greet children	T		See list in my my plan book
	Set up free-choice areas		T	
8:20	Attendance		T	
	Lunch count		T	
8:40	Morning circle	T		

minimal, typically leaving the paraprofessionals to "figure out" the curriculum for the student with disabilities. A general educator said, "She [the paraprofessional] knows what needs to be done. I don't do any of that [teaching the student with disabilities]" (p. 172). A paraprofessional said, "When it comes to the hard core curriculum decisions . . . you [the paraprofessional] make them" (p. 195). Finally, another paraprofessional reported, "I basically figure things out by myself. The special educator gives me a matrix at the beginning of the year. Then it's my responsibility to prepare for and teach the student every day. No one really talks to me about what to do or how to do it" (p. 196). It is unnecessary and inappropriate for paraprofessionals to be left in the position of having to plan the curriculum and instruction for students with disabilities. The certified teachers (i.e., the special educators and general educators) are responsible to ensure that there is ongoing conversation, planning, and training around issues of roles and responsibilities. Without these conversations, too often paraprofessionals are left in the driver's seat, maintaining the majority of the responsibilities for students who are difficult to teach, yet the paraprofessionals have the least amount of training.

Box 17.3 highlights several specific areas for the educational team to consider. A clear, direct way to avoid misunderstandings about roles and responsibilities is to have specific conversations followed up with written documentation specifying the roles and responsibilities.

BOX **17.3**

Roles and Responsibilities

	Teacher		Training Priority	
			Yes	No
Curriculum	Plans daily and weekly schedule. Plans all lessons/activities. Plans room arrangement and learning centers.	Implements plans as specified by the teacher. Assists with room arrangement. Assists with creating materials.		
Assessment	Assesses individual children. Administers assessments to entire class.	Assists with monitoring and scoring objective assessments.		
Setting objectives	Determines appropriate objectives for all children.	Implements teacher-designed lessons to meet child's instructional objectives.		
Teaching	Teaches lessons for the entire class, small groups, and individual children.	Assists and monitors small groups and individual students with designated lessons.		
Behavior management	Plans behavior management strategies for entire class and individual students.	Implements behavioral management strategies as designed by teacher; reports progress.		
Working with parents	Maintains communication with parents.	May attend parent conferences when appropriate.		
Individual educational planning	Develops and implements IEP. Revises instructional program based on data. Designs instructional materials. Attends inservice meetings and professional development trainings	Carries out portions of the IEP as designated by the teacher. Monitors student progress and relates findings to the teacher. Constructs teacher designed materials. May attend professional development activities.		

Specific Knowledge and Skills

General Approaches to Encouraging Positive Behavioral Supports

It is important to be clear that it is the responsibility of certified staff to design, implement, and evaluate specific strategies for supporting individual students who experience behavior challenges. While paraprofessionals often assist with the implementation of individual behavioral support plans and data collection, the ultimate responsibility always lies with the certified staff.

Given the clear understanding that certified personnel are ultimately responsible for designing student programs, as well as training, supervising, and monitoring the implementation of those programs, it is helpful for paraprofessionals to know and understand basic principles associated with positive behavioral supports. If they know and understand these basic principles associated with positive behavioral approaches, then they are more likely to act in ways that encourage all students to demonstrate positive and acceptable behaviors. These basic principles include (a) examining the adults' roles in the student's behavior and (b) identifying the communicative function that the behavior is serving (Ayers & Hedeen, 1996; Knoster, 1999). Each principle will be discussed in ways that the teacher can share with the paraprofessional.

As adults, we maintain a responsibility to act in ways that support and encourage students to behave appropriately. What we do and say, along with how we do things and how we say things, leave lasting impressions on children. If we want to encourage students to act in prosocial ways, then we must do so, especially when difficult situations arise. It is important to communicate clearly to the paraprofessional that to maximize the likelihood that the students will behave in a socially appropriate manner, the adults must do so *all* of the time. As previously discussed, the teacher needs to set high expectations for creating an environment that supports and encourages respect, responsibility, and positive regard for all students. To accomplish this, adult members of the communities most always choose dignity over humiliation. Tell the paraprofessional this means that behaviors associated with punishment and control (e.g., yelling, lecturing, sarcasm, and physical violence) are always unacceptable.

The second principle that paraprofessionals need to know and understand is that all behavior (Ayers & Hedeen, 1996; Knoster, 1999) serves the communicative function. For example, when a student is jumping up and down with a smile on her face, it is logical to deduce that the student is communicating that she is happy or excited about something. However, given the same behavior of jumping but combined with a frown or scowl, one would deduce that the student is upset, angry, or frustrated about something. In most situations, the communicative intent is fairly simple to understand. A helpful classroom practice in response to students exhibiting unusual behaviors is for the classroom teacher and paraprofessional to help students become aware of the power of spoken language by encouraging the students to "use their words." For example one could say, "You look happy because you are jumping up and down and you have a smile on your face. Is that correct?" or "When you jump up and down and frown at the same time, how do you feel?" This type of mirroring for students helps them see that all behavior communicates something.

When a student engages in an unusual, disruptive or disturbing behavior that appears to be beyond typical behaviors of students within the classroom, it is helpful to document the events quickly so that the team can examine the information and attempt to understand the communicative intent of the specific incident. Whoever is present when the situation arises is the person who should document the incident, regardless of certification. Box 17.4 offers one strategy to support both certified and noncertified personnel in documenting the incident.

Both certified and noncertified members of the team will discuss the situation together using the principles of positive behavior supports. The related focus questions are as follows:

> *Principle 1:* What could I (the adult) have done differently to avoid the situation?
>
> *Principle 2:* What was this student trying to communicate to us?

While both certified and noncertified personnel engage in the discussion, it remains the ultimate responsibility of a certified person (e.g., classroom teacher or special education teacher) to design the written behavior plan and to train those who will be responsible to implement the plan.

Specific Strategies

Typically the classroom teacher utilizes a variety of direct and indirect cues to support students in maintaining appropriate behaviors. The paraprofessional needs to be taught what those cues are, as well as when and how to use them. Box 17.5 highlights several nonintrusive strategies that are supportive of many students. The strategies are presented in a hierarchy from least intrusive to most intrusive. Referring to the Box 17.5, one can see that it is less intrusive for the paraprofessional to stand temporarily in close proximity to a student than to offer a student a choice that involves an incompatible consequence. The classroom teacher and paraprofessional should discuss where to begin in the hierarchy on a student-by-student basis.

It is important to note that certified personnel need to make the judgment call about which cues are appropriate for individual students under specific circumstances. If the paraprofessional makes an error in judgment, again it is the certified person present who is obligated to give feedback to the paraprofessional. Be kind but direct. Tell the paraprofessional what the error was and why it was an error. Then follow up with a check for understanding by asking, "Do you understand why this was wrong in this situation? Can you tell me back what you heard me say?" "What else could you have done?" On the other hand, the certified person should also provide clear and direct positive feedback when the paraprofessional has made the right decision. Remember, just as students need to hear a greater proportion of positive statements to corrective statements, so do adults.

BOX 17.4

Determining Communicative Intent

Use this form to assist the team in understanding the communicative intent of the student's behavior.

Student: _____   Date: _____

Subject: _____

Instructional context:

____ Lecture   ____ Cooperative group   ____ Small group

____ Independent work   ____ Other—specify: _____

Behavior: Describe what the student is doing. How is the student acting? What do you see and hear?

Cause: What do you think might be causing the student to be acting in this manner?

____ Demand or request   ____ Change in activity or location

____ Task difficulty   ____ Interruption

____ Lonely; no attention   ____ Do not know

____ Other—specify

Function: What might the student be trying to communicate?

____ Wants attention   ____ Needs help

____ Wants to be involved   ____ Frustration

____ Anger   ____ Pain or discomfort

____ Other—specify   ____ Do not know

How was the situation handled by the students and staff?

At this point, do you have any suggestions?

Source: Adapted from York, J., Doyle, M. B., & Kronberg, R. (1995). *Creating Inclusive School Communities: Module 3b Curriculum as Everything Students Need to Learn in School: Individualizing Learning Outcomes* (p. 3b/13). Baltimore, MD: Brookes.

BOX 17.5

Nonintrusive Behavior Support Strategies

Strategy	Example
State the expectations	Remember to tell the students what to do and how you want them to do it.
Proximity	Stand closer to the student who is engaged in inappropriate behavior. Do not look at the student; rather, keep your focus on the teaching at hand.
Gentle touch	Touch the student's shoulder while maintaining focus on the instruction at hand.
Nonverbal cues	Smile, nod, or give a thumbs-up sign to reinforce inappropriate or appropriate behaviors.
Indirect verbal cues	"I like the way Sue is raising her hand."
Direct verbal cues	In a quiet and private manner tell the student exactly how you want him or her to behave. End the statement with a "thank you." Step away from the student. During the interaction act calm and dispassionate, regardless of how you actually feel.
Offer a choice	If the behavior continues, offer the student a choice in which the consequences are incompatible with continuing the behavior—for example, "Put your pencil either on your desk or on my desk."

Working with Small Groups and Individual Students

There will also be times when the paraprofessional is implementing teacher-designed instruction without the immediate supervision of a certified person. During these times the paraprofessional should maintain all of the prosocial principles of positive approaches to behavior. During the instructional time, the paraprofessional can take several actions that will increase the likelihood that the student(s) will remain engaged in the instruction with minimal behavioral outbursts. These include the following:

1. Be prepared with all of the necessary teaching materials as they are listed on the teacher-developed lesson plan prior to bringing students to the instructional space.
2. Welcome the student(s) into the instruction in a positive manner (e.g., "Hi, Jose—I'm glad to see you today").
3. Avoid too many yes/no questions during the instruction. Instead, give the student(s) choices, as choices offer a sense of control.

4. Avoid repeated verbal cues. Too often when cues are repeated, they sound like nagging. The student probably heard you the first time and is choosing not to respond. If this is a persistent problem, the paraprofessional needs to request assistance from the teacher. Perhaps together you can determine the communicative intent of the student's behavior.
5. If a student exhibits inappropriate behavior, focus on the behavior at hand. Avoid threats, bribes, lectures, and power struggles.
6. Be consistent in your approach to teaching positive behavioral approaches. Students with behavioral challenges depend on consistency.
7. Implement individual student behavior support plans in a consistent manner as they have been written.
8. Ask for help and feedback on a regular basis.

Finally, it can be helpful for paraprofessionals to have a firm understanding of "planned ignoring." While it is the decision of the certified personnel under which circumstances and with which students planned ignoring will be used, it is implemented frequently in classrooms; therefore, it is helpful for paraprofessionals to have a formal understanding of it. *Planned ignoring* refers to the complete inattention or lack of acknowledgment of a target behavior. When planned ignoring is called for, the paraprofessional needs to do the following:

1. Offer no attention—positive or negative. Do not look, speak to, or touch the student.
2. Act as if the behavior is not happening at all. Act as if the behavior is having no effect (positive or negative) on the situation.
3. Generously praise those students who are behaving appropriately. However, do not compare their behavior to the behavior that is being ignored. For example, it would be appropriate to say, "Sara, thank you for raising your hand. What would you like to say?" It would be inappropriate to say, "Jane, look at Sara raising her hand. If you raise your hand like Sara, I will call on you, too."
4. After the inappropriate behavior has stopped, catch the student "doing the right thing" and then praise the student.
5. Do not discuss the target behavior with the student.
6. Be very consistent!
7. Record the information and give it to the teacher.

Teaching a paraprofessional how and when to ignore a student's behavior is very important. They need to know that generally speaking, if (a) the paraprofessional can teach, (b) the student(s) can learn, and (c) the behavior is likely to remain the same in intensity, then the paraprofessional should ignore the behavior (Knoster, 1999). Planned ignoring is a difficult skill to learn. Certified personnel should teach the paraprofessional what it is and how to ignore before the paraprofessional is in a situation where he or she is likely to need it.

Confidentiality

All paraprofessionals must maintain student confidentiality. When working with paraprofessionals, it is helpful to explain the specifics about confidentiality through a series of examples and nonexamples or perhaps do's and don'ts. It is important that paraprofessionals demonstrate the rule of thumb that only those people who are formally involved with a student's education may have specific information about that student or situations involving the student. The classroom teacher should explain to the paraprofessional that the school district takes issues relating to a breech in student confidentiality very seriously. Review the written school policies about confidentiality with the paraprofessional. Tell her that if there are times when she is unclear about a potential violation of confidentiality, she should ask the supervising teacher or school principal.

Conducting a Cycle of Supportive Supervision

It is the responsibility of certified personnel to establish a system of training and supervision of paraprofessionals. Clearly, the assessment must match the specifics of the training that the paraprofessional has received. To design an individualized supervision plan, the certified teacher (i.e., special educator or general educator) should list the desired outcomes that the paraprofessional will need to demonstrate within a certain time frame. Next, generate a list of training or "input" opportunities that are meant to ensure that the paraprofessional is actually taught the skills prior to being assessed. Finally, list the assessment tools or the ways in which the paraprofessional will show competence in each identified area. For example, if the paraprofessional is to demonstrate the ability to ignore a student's behavior, then the certified personnel needs to teach her how to do that through a series of discussions and actual examples. Then the paraprofessional needs to have several opportunities to practice that skill and to receive specific feedback. Finally, when it is time to conduct a formal evaluation of the paraprofessional's progress, the supervisor will again observe her ability to ignore specific behaviors. While many supervision tools are available for use, the key is that the supervision is in alignment with the training provided to the paraprofessionals.

Conclusion

Classrooms are complex social systems with students who have a variety of needs, interests, and abilities. Often the range of individual differences represented within classrooms necessitates the addition of a paraprofessional to assist the classroom teacher in meeting students' needs. Historically, the roles and responsibilities of paraprofessionals have been somewhat arbitrary. However, more recently the professional literature has focused on providing training materials for paraprofessionals and the teachers with whom they work. As paraprofessionals are more visible in schools and are receiving training, it is important that certified personnel maintain their responsibilities in designing, implementing, and evaluating instruction.

REFERENCES

Ayers, B. J., & Hedeen, D. L. (1996). "Been there, done that, didn't work": Alternative solutions for behavior problems. *Educational Leadership, 53*(5), 48–50.

Backus, L., Keogh, W., CichoskiKelly, E., Giangreco, M. F., & Tucker, P. (2000). *Supporting students with challenging behaviors in general education settings: Paraeducator training curriculum.* Burlington: University of Vermont, Center on Disability and Community Inclusion.

Blalock, G. (1991). Paraprofessionals: Critical team members in our special education programs. *Intervention in School and Clinic, 26*(4), 200–214.

Doyle, M. B. (1995). *A qualitative inquiry into the roles and responsibilities of paraeducators who support students with severe disabilities in inclusive classrooms.* Unpublished dissertation. Minneapolis: University of Minnesota.

Doyle, M. B. (1997). *The paraprofessionals guide to the inclusive classroom: Working as a team.* Baltimore, MD: Brookes.

Doyle, M. B., & Lee, P. (1997). Creating partnerships with paraprofessionals. In M. F. Giangreco (Ed.), *Quick-guides to inclusion: Ideas for educating students with disabilities.* Baltimore, MD: Brookes.

Egel, A. L., Richman, G., & Koegel, R. L. (1981). Normal peer models and autistic children's learning. *Journal of Applied Behavior Analysis, 14,* 3–13.

French, N. (1998). Working together: Resource teachers and paraeducators. *Remedial and Special Education, 19,* 357–368.

French, N., & Chopra, R. (1999). Parent perspectives on the roles of paraprofessionals. *Journal of the Association of Persons with Severe Handicaps, 24,* 258–271.

Giangreco, M. F., Broer, S., & Edelman, S. (1999). The tip of the iceberg: Determining whether paraprofessional support is needed for students with disabilities in general education settings. *Journal of the Association of Persons with Severe Handicaps, 24*(4), 281–291.

Giangreco, M. F., CichoskiKelly, E., Backus, L., Edelman, S., Tucker, P., Broer, S., & CichoskiKelly, C. (1999, March). Developing a shared understanding: Paraeducator supports for students with disabilities in general education. *TASH Newsletter,* 21–23.

Giangreco, M. F., Edelman, S. W., Luiselli, T. E., & MacFarland, S. Z. (1997). Helping or hovering? Effects of instructional assistant proxim-

ity on students with disabilities. *Exceptional Children, 64*(1), 7–18.

Gurnalnick, M. J. (1990). Major accomplishments and future directions in early childhood mainstreaming. *Topics in Early Childhood Special Education, 10*(2), 1–17.

Harper, V. (1994). Multicultural perspectives in the classroom: Professional preparation for educational paraprofessionals. *Action in Teacher Education, 16*(3), 66–78.

Hewitt, A., & Langenfeld, K. (1999). *Positive behavior strategies for paraprofessionals.* Minneapolis: University of Minnesota Institute on Community Integration.

Individuals with Disabilities Education Act Amendments of 1997. Pub. L. No. 105-17, Section 20, 111 Stat. 37 (1997). Washington, DC: U.S. Government Printing Office.

Knoster, T. (1999, November). *Conducting functional assessments and designing ISP's for students at school.* Paper presented at the Association for Persons with Severe Handicaps, Chicago.

Marks, S. U., Schrader, C., & Levine, M. (1999). Paraeducator experiences in inclusive settings: Helping, hovering, or holding their own. *Exceptional Children, 65,* 315–328.

Martella, R. C., Marchand-Martella, N. E., Miller, T. L., Young, K. R., & Macfarlane, C. A. (1995). Teaching instructional aides and peer tutors to decrease problem behaviors in the classroom. *Teaching Exceptional Children 27*(2), 53–56.

Pickett, A. L., Faison, K., & Formanek, J. (1993). *A core curriculum and training program to prepare paraeducators to work in inclusive classrooms serving school-age students with disabilities.* New York: National Resource Center for Paraprofessionals in Education and Related Services, Center for Advanced Study in Education, City University of New York.

Pickett, A. L., & Gerlach, K. (1997). *Supervising paraducators in school settings: A team approach.* Austin, TX: Pro-Ed.

Salzberg, C. L., & Morgan, J. (1995). Preparing teachers to work with paraeducators. *Teacher Education and Special Education, 18,* 49–55.

Shulka, S., Kennedy, C. H., & Cushing, L. S. (1999). Intermediate school students with disabilities: Supporting their social participation in general education classrooms. *Journal of Positive Behavior Interventions, 1*(3), 130–140.

Simpson, R. L., & Myles, B. S. (1990). The general education collaboration model: A model for successful mainstreaming. *Focus on Exceptional Children, 23*(4), 1–10.

Wadsworth, D. E., & Knight, D. (1996). Paraprofessionals: The bridge to successful inclusion. *Intervention in School and Clinic, 31*(3), 166–171.

Walther-Thomas, C., Korinek, L., McLaughlin, V. V. & Williams, B. T. (2000). *Collaboration for inclusive education: Developing successful programs.* Needham Heights, MA: Allyn & Bacon.

Werts, M., Wolery, M., Snyder, E., & Caldwell, N. (1996). Teacher's perceptions of the supports critical to the success of inclusion programs. *Journal of the Association for Persons with Severe Handicaps, 21*, 9–21.

Werts, M. G., Caldwell, N. K., & Wolery, M. (1996). The effects of fluent peer models on the observational learning of response chains by students with peer models. *Journal of Applied Behavior Analysis, 29*, 53–66.

Wolery, M., Werts, M., Martin, C., Schroeder,. C. Huffman, K., Venn, M., Holocombe, A., Brookfield, J., & Fleming, L. (1994). Employment of educators in preschool mainstreaming: A survey of general early educators. *Journal of Early Intervention, 18*, 64–77.

Wolery, M., Werts, M., Caldwell, N., Snyder, E., & Liskowski, L. (1995). Experienced teachers' perceptions of resources and supports for inclusion. *Education and Training in Mental Retardation and Developmental Disabilities, 30*(1), 15–26.

York, J., Doyle, M. B. & Kronberg, R. (1995). *Creating inclusive school communities: Module 3b Curriculum as everything students need to learn in school: Individualizing learning outcomes* (p. 3b/13). Baltimore, MD: Brookes.

18 Transition from School to Community:

Navigating Rough Waters

HEWITT B. CLARK
University of South Florida

MARLO TROI BELKIN
Palm Beach Public School District

LETTI D. OBRADOVICH
Palm Beach Public School District

RICHARD E. CASEY
Florida SEDNET (Multiagency Network for Students with Severe Emotional Disturbance)

ROBERT GAGNON
Opportunity Charter High School

PETER CAPRONI
Robert Morgan Vocational Technical School

NICOLE DESCHENES
University of South Florida

The Challenge to Overcoming Poor Transition Outcomes

Each year thousands of students with emotional or behavioral disorders (E/BD) leave secondary school without adequate preparation for postsecondary education programs, independent living, or for livable wage, career track employment. Their high school experience is often marked by high absenteeism rates, frequent discipline problems, juvenile crime, social isolation, substance abuse (Greenbaum, Prange, Frieman, & Silver, 1991), and failing one or more courses (Davis & Vander Stoep, 1996; Marder & D'Amico, 1992; Wagner, 1993). Sixty-eight percent of students with these disabilities come from households in which the leader of the household did not graduate from high school (Silver, Duchnowski, Kutash, et al., 1992; Wagner, D'Amico, Marder, Newman, & Blackorby, 1992). Studies have shown that students with E/BD drop out of school at a rate that is about three times higher than their nondisabled peers (Marder & D'Amico, 1992) and that they, after exiting secondary school through dropout or graduation, experience about one-third poorer outcomes in securing jobs, about two-thirds poorer outcomes in living on their own, and about two-thirds poorer outcomes in accessing postsecondary education (Marder & D'Amico, 1992; Silver, Unger, & Friedman, 1993), and they have about three times as high of rates of arrests and incarcerations (Marder & D'Amico, 1992; Prange, 1993; Prange, Greenbaum, & Friedman, 1993). They also are significantly more likely to be unemployed, underemployed, or employed part-time than their nondisabled peers and many of their peers with other types of learning, physical, or sensory disabilities (Blackbory & Wagner, 1996; Vander Stoep, Davis, & Collins, 2000).

The middle and secondary schools have not focused on teaching and providing the community-relevant skills and experiences needed to facilitate successful transitions from school to adult life for youth and young adults with E/BD (Patton, Cronin, & Jairrels, 1997). The transition period for these youth and young adults is complicated further by the lack of coordinated services among children's mental health, child welfare, educational, adult mental health, substance abuse treatment, and rehabilitation sectors (Clark, Unger, & Stewart, 1993; Knitzer, Steinberg, & Fleisch, 1990; Koroloff, 1990; Modrcin & Rutland, 1989; Stroul & Friedman, 1986). To improve the likelihood of these individuals becoming contributing members of society, systems and methods that will effectively prepare them for transition to the community need to be explored (Benz & Lindstrom, 1997; Clark & Davis, 2000).

Transition to Independence Process (TIP) System

The Transition to Independence Process (TIP) system prepares and supports youth and young adults in their movement into adult roles through an individualized process that (a) teaches community-relevant skills; (b) encourages completion of secondary education; (c) provides exposure to community life experiences; (d) promotes movements into postschool employment, educational opportunities, living situation, and community life; (e) transcends the age barriers typical of child versus adult services; and (f) respects the self-determination of young persons (Clark, Deschenes, & Jones, 2000; Clark & Foster-Johnson, 1996).

The TIP system promotes independence. However, the concept of "interdependence" is central to implementing the TIP system. This concept nests the focus of independent functioning (e.g., budgeting money and maintaining a job) within the framework of young people learning that there is a healthy, reciprocal role of giving support to others and receiving support (i.e., social support network for emotional, spiritual, and physical support).

TIP System Guidelines

We recommend six guidelines that appear to drive the development and operation of quality transition systems. These guidelines are based on studies regarding best practices of transition programs for these youth and young adults (Clark & Foster-Johnson, 1996; Clark & Stewart, 1992; Clark et al., 1993); programs preparing youth for transition (Modrcin & Rutland, 1989); policy issues related to transition (Koroloff, 1990); and transition outcomes (Davis & Vander Stoep, 1996; Silver et al., 1993; Vander Stoep, Taub, & Holcomb, 1994). The following TIP system guidelines embody the underlying transition values and best practices and put them into a framework for the establishment and operation of the system.

1. *Person-centered planning is driven by young person's interests, strengths, and cultural and familial values.* Improved community outcomes for young people in transition stem from an informal and flexible planning process driven by the young person's interests, strengths, and cultural and familial values that allow for the formulation of the individual's goals. The TIP system uses a person-centered planning approach driven by a strength-based assessment of the young person and his or her environmental situation.

2. *Services and support must be individually tailored and encompass all transition domains.* The TIP system is comprehensive in scope, encompassing three major setting-based domains—employment, education, and living situation—as well as one community life adjustment domain that involves the individual skills and activities that are relevant across all of the setting domains for successful community functioning. The TIP system provides a comprehensive array of community-based service and support options within each of these domains in order to accommodate the strengths, needs, and life circumstances of each young person. For example, in the employment domain, it is helpful whether a system has access to a range of work opportunities with varying levels of support available, including practicum and paid work experience, transitional employment, supported employment, and competitive employment. Similarly, in the domain of community life adjustment, coping skills such as anger management may need to be taught to some young people so that they will be able to function safely and effectively in school, home, and work settings.

3. *Services and supports need to be coordinated to provide continuity from the young person's perspective.* Although the administrators of a transition system may think that their system and its components provide continuity, this attribute of the system must be judged from the "eye of the beholder"—that is, the young person. *Continuity* refers to the extent to which the relevant supports and services are provided to a young person in a coordinated fashion. All too often there is no continuity across services. For example, Judy's school guidance counselor is pushing for her to be placed in special education; her mental health psychiatrist has just increased her medication for ADHD despite the fact that it leaves her nauseated throughout the day; her foster care caseworker is seeking to have Judy removed from her foster home of 4 years to be placed in a residential school facility because she does not seem to be doing well in the foster home; and her teacher is advocating that Judy be given an opportunity to do some person-centered planning. Changes in one domain are bound to affect other aspects of Judy's life; thus, it is important that decisions are made with knowledge of the broader context of her life.

To ensure access to required community resources and the creation of opportunities across all of the transition domains, collaborative linkages must be established at the young person's level and at the system level. At the young person's level, the TIP system needs to assume responsibility to link the young person and his or her family to the resources, services, and supports that are appropriate to the individual's changing needs. This type of planning and service coordination is typically achieved through a transition facilitator (also referred to as *transition specialist, life coach,* or *service coordinator* in different programs and systems).

At the system level, linkages are required with a broad array of child and adult servicing systems. Outreach to develop networks of individuals and organizations to assist in working with a young person is also the responsibility of a TIP system. These efforts must include reaching out to ethnic communities so that culturally relevant supports are available to individuals requiring them.

4. *A safety net of support is provided by the young person's team.* VanDenBerg and Grealish (1996) have defined unconditional commitment as never denying services because of extreme severity of disability, changing services as the needs of the child and family change, and never rejecting the child or family from services. Although the transition team recognizes that the young people, 18 years or older, may refuse services, the team members must remain creative and determined to "stick with" young persons to the extent possible, adjusting services and supports to meet their changing needs.

Unconditional commitment is a powerful expression of the TIP staff's hopefulness and a positive affirmation of the young person's worth and merit (Deschenes & Clark, 1998). This feature is evidenced by staff encouraging young people, speaking respectfully to them, respecting their choices, involving them and their parents as partners, and sharing a sense of humor with all involved. Young people should be allowed to explore their work and social identities with guidance, support, and acceptance.

5. *Achieving greater independence requires the enhancement of the young person's competencies.* Competence in a variety of skills is necessary for successful entry into the workplace and independent community living. In a TIP system, skill development means teaching skills that equip youth with the competencies to meet the demands they will encounter upon leaving school and residential settings. Skill development should occur in educational, work, and living settings within the young person's community. The identification and development of skills are aided by functional assessment, instructional efforts, and curriculum activities focusing on teaching and practicing of these necessary skills (e.g., budgeting of personal earnings, completion of job applications, anger management, and vocational skills) in a context that is functional, meaningful, and relevant to the young person and his or her life and goals in the community (Bullis, Nishoka-Evans, Fredericks, & Davis, 1993; Foster-Johnson, Ferro, & Dunlap, 1992; Horner, Sprague, & Flannery, 1993; Unger, 1994).

6. *The TIP system must be outcome driven.* The five previously discussed guidelines involve processes that can assist youth and young adults in achieving successful outcomes across the transition domains. For each transition goal established by the young person and his or her planning team, written measurable objectives should be established so that progress on individualized goals and successes can be tracked over time.

The TIP system effectiveness should also be assessed. The effectiveness of the system can be assessed through key outcome indicators that are based on the young adult's outcomes in the four transition domains. For example, aggregation of data regarding individuals' employment goals allows for determination of the percentage of youth and young adults who (a) are employed part-time and full-time, (b) are earning a particular wage per hour, (c) have employer-paid benefits, and (d) are in a job that is on a career track that the young person wants to pursue. These types of key outcome indicators, if tracked over an extended period of time, can provide stakeholders and policymakers with valuable information on the effectiveness of the TIP system and permit them to make modifications in their service system to further improve outcomes for young people.

Applications of TIP Guidelines

The TIP guidelines provide a framework for the development, expansion, and operation of a TIP system based on research and studies of the best practices of transition programs for youth and young adults with emotional and behavioral difficulties. As discussed, the transition system must be value driven, with policies and procedures that provide a framework that supports the practices and efforts of the TIP personnel in facilitating the individual goals of their young people (Clark et al., 1993, 2000).

The remainder of this chapter is devoted to a description of the application of the TIP guidelines to three secondary education programs. Each of these three programs is evolving through the tailoring of the TIP guidelines to the unique aspects of the individual program's priorities, targeted students, resources, and community strengths.

School-to-Community Transition at Indian Ridge School

The mission of Indian Ridge School is to provide individually tailored educational and therapeutic services to students who are classified as severely emotionally disturbed (SED)[1] and their parents so that students can establish improved self-control, learn new prosocial skills, and derive maximum academic benefits from their schooling, therefore facilitating their return to home schools or, for older students, transition into community employment or postsecondary educational settings.

Students Served

Indian Ridge School has an enrollment of about 130 students with SED across the elementary, middle, and secondary level grades. The student population is 71%

---

[1]The terms *emotionally* or *behaviorally disturbed* (EBD) and *severely emotionally disturbed* (SED) are somewhat interchangeable but are used in classifications in different systems and states.

male and 21% female, with 47% of students identified as Caucasian, 43% as African American, and 10% as coming from some other racial background. The majority of these students are of low socioeconomic status, with 91% of the students receiving free and reduced breakfast and lunch. Most students are mainstreamed back to their home schools within 2 to 3 years, placed in employment or alternative educational settings of their choice, or graduate from this school.

School Facilities and Personnel Resource

This school has the advantage of being geographically located in a neighborhood that is largely middle-income, single-family homes and multifamily dwellings, with reasonable access to area businesses. Even though the facility was once a private psychiatric hospital, it is an attractive single-level structure with a fully equipped commercial kitchen. The school staff is highly specialized to accommodate the educational, emotional, behavioral, physical, and safety issues of these students. Eighty-five percent of the instructional, therapeutic/behavioral specialists, and administrative staff have earned graduate-level degrees.

Community Orientation Permeates Elementary, Middle, and Secondary Programs

Indian Ridge school provides educational opportunities for elementary, middle, and secondary grade levels. The community orientation permeates all subjects and practicum experiences, across the curriculum. This section will explain the variety of campus-based and community-based vocational experiences in place to assist students in (a) linking their academic studies to community-relevant goals, (b) exploring areas of possible career interest, and (c) learning employability skills that are applicable to all work settings. Although the elementary students are fully integrated into the community orientation through their classes, community field trips, and on-campus practica, it is in the middle and secondary grade levels where the emphasis on community-relevant skills is addressed as a means of orienting and preparing these youth for transition to adult roles. This occurs through community skills training and exposure to community and work environments.

Campus-Based Vocational Program

The campus-based vocational program provides a variety of on-site program components developed to better prepare this at-risk population for productive citizenship. A career lab exists to enhance students understanding of various careers and help students discover individual interest and abilities. The lab is equipped to assist students in gaining a greater understanding of the world of work. Lessons that incorporate decision-making skills and promote career exploration are used to prepare middle and secondary students for the transition from school to work or into career-oriented education.

The other major component of the campus-based vocational program consists of numerous practicum experiences. The culinary practicum (Ridge Kids

Café) focuses on all aspects of the food industry, including food preparation, nutrition and health, designing meals, planning and purchasing food, budgeting, and record keeping. The full-size commercial kitchen allows students, under the direction of the chef, to cater events throughout the county for various organizations.

The horticulture program (Ridge Kids Gardens) is another vocational practicum at Indian Ridge. It is supervised by a teacher knowledgeable in, and passionate about, landscaping and gardening. The program emphasizes hands-on teaching opportunities, and the designation of garden areas to groups of students imparts a sense of ownership that seems to motivate them and keep their interest. Classes have also planted a butterfly garden to attract these insects, providing other study activities for students in other classes (e.g., science). Through the horticultural practicum, students are exposed to activities involving a variety of plants (i.e., flowers, vegetables, and trees), pickling processes, marketing of fruits and vegetables, environmental science, and the integration of math, reading, and science into aspects of landscaping and gardening.

Industrial arts is the newest addition at Indian Ridge School, providing hands-on experiences in woodworking and plastics. Students have an opportunity to choose their projects, providing a sense of creativity and ownership, while learning various employability and vocational skills. The course gives students a chance to implement essential skills of the various trades. As the program grows, opportunities to create and sell products will also be included.

Other vocational practica will be added as interest, resources, space, and instructional expertise allow (e.g., computer software training and programming). Paralleling the vocational practicum class offerings, Indian Ridge works with the Center for Creative Education with a program called Learning through Education and Arts Partnerships (Project L. E. A. P.). This partnership brings local visual and performing artists into the classroom to work with teachers providing an interactive and exciting way to learn. Select teachers and artists plan and teach lessons together to enhance the already exciting programs. The team effort continues to provide students with a positive outlook on school and their ability to succeed.

Middle and Secondary School Programs: Other Major Components

While the school-to-community philosophy begins in the elementary school, it is, nevertheless, at the middle school population where dropout prevention efforts need to be directed to ensure that these students will be inspired enough to continue onto secondary school.

Person-Centered Planning. The entire middle school team is involved in the development of personal planning portfolios, which follow the student through secondary school. Students use their portfolios to record their evolving life and career goals, the results of their interest inventories, their experiences from their community field trips and practica, and record the information gathered during interviews they conduct with community members. The goal of the school-to-community transition process at the secondary level is to assure each student has the opportunity to gain meaningful work that provides maximum compensation in terms of income, job satisfaction, and personal growth. Students are encouraged and guided in exploring their interests and goals and in assuming an active role in their future's planning processes.

Academic Component.   Academics become particularly relevant through the use of *The Real Game Series* curriculum (1996). This program provides teachers with an exciting supplemental curriculum to enhance the teaching of geography, math, science, and language arts by making the lessons more relevant, motivating, and enjoyable for students. Since many of the secondary students are working toward regular high school diplomas, it is essential that the state requirements be met in the course work. Throughout the curriculum, opportunities are provided for students to explore areas of interest in connection with the topics and concepts that are being presented in their classes. Teachers have developed activities that promote an active learning environment, creating visible connections to the world outside the school walls. In conjunction with some academic classes, students participate in a variety of activities that encourage productive citizenship (e.g., raising money for victims of natural disasters and war; collecting food to be shared with others during holidays).

Psychosocial Component.   The therapeutic intervention component is an integrated part of the elementary, middle, and secondary programs and is designed to treat and support students' emotional and behavioral development in the context of home, school, and community. All students are provided with individual, group, and/or family therapy to address issues such as improving peer and family relationships, applying social problem solving methods, developing improved self-awareness and self-confidence, and acquiring improved anger management skills and self-management competencies. Throughout the student-centered planning process, the therapeutic team assumes numerous responsibilities in providing the planning team the information necessary to create an individualized transition plan.

Campus-Based Vocational Program.   The vocational program, as described in a previous section, provides middle and secondary school students exposure to a broad array of practicum experiences designed to enhance academic relevance and teach prevocational job readiness skills. Middle school students also participate in such things as prevocational field trips with concomitant classroom activities, exposing them to a variety of career cluster areas. The teachers and therapists assist the students in gaining prevocational and community readiness skills through the use of person-centered planning, prevocational instructional materials, creative activities, therapeutic games, and computer software activities (e.g., career exploration and simulations).

Unique to the high school vocational program is a course on employability skills and entrepreneurship. The course covers a wide spectrum of issues, including but not limited to résumé writing, job interviewing, career exploration, educational options for pursuing careers, and school and workplace teamwork. The highlight of this course, however, is the component on entrepreneurship. Some classes have participated in creating a business plan related to one of the vocational practicum areas and in a few cases actually implemented the plan. For example, a class developed a business plan for catering of special events for the school district or other community organizations or businesses. Several of the vocational programs now work together to cater some special events, which provides students with education and experience in such areas as advertising, marketing, collaborative planning with community representatives, menu and event planning, cooking, accounting, inventory control, and hosting of events. Students gain a feeling of accomplishment as they develop skills such as meeting deadlines, team cooperation, interpersonal skills, decision making, achieving consensus, and coordinating activities. Money earned from the sale of the products is reinvested into the business, and, based on amount of profit, the "entrepreneurs" and their "associates" choose how they will use the profits to celebrate their success.

Community Employment Training and Experience.   Community-based employment training and experience is a component of the secondary program that relies on partnerships with the business community to provide exposure and work experience. Students are placed in work sites for up to a half a day on 3 to 5 days a week in a paid and/or credit practicum experience in a community business, with individualized supports as necessary to assist the student in learning the job requirements, social expectations, and self-management of one's own emotional and behavioral reactions.

Opportunities for employment are made available for all interested and job ready students. Focusing on the interests and abilities of the student, job matching is done to find meaningful employment for the student to explore. Meaningful work options include competitive employment, with or without support services, supervised work crews in the community or business settings, and sheltered workshops. Depending on the needs of the student, support services may be time limited or ongoing and may include help with job procurement, initial adjustments and interpersonal relations on the job site. Follow-up services may be necessary to ensure that the student is able to maintain the job or find a new one, if needed.

The transition specialist coordinates job development and job placement activities for student practica and postsecondary school employment. These efforts are facilitated in part by some of the benefits that employers can reap from such partnerships (e.g., lower turnover, dependable employees, reduced training costs, guaranteed job performance, and tax credits). Another important part of career-oriented employment is postsecondary education. The Indian Ridge personnel have forged partnerships with community colleges and technical centers throughout the county to assist interested students in accessing technical training. The secondary school program encourages students to explore their role within the community. Activities that foster independence and self-sufficiency, as well as healthy relationships and recreational activities are all incorporated within the program. Together staff and students work toward creating an atmosphere that encourages independence while fostering a sense of unity and hope.

Developing Academic, Social, and Employability Skills for Students through the Lake Learning Center

The Lake Learning Center has developed and implemented a school- and community-based work experience program that teaches functional academic, social, and employability skills that prepares students with EBD and involvement with juvenile justice system for success in the classroom, community, and work settings.[2]

Students Served by the Learning Center

The Learning Center's educational enterprise program serves 30 secondary special education students with EBD. The students targeted for the program have a history of disruptive and/or aggressive behavior, repeated school failure, poor academic, social and employability skills, and/or involvement with the juvenile justice system. Before placement at the Learning Center, the students' disruptive behavior resulted in numerous suspensions from previous schools.

Learning Center Educational Enterprise Program

The curriculum integrates academic, social, and vocational activities through school- and community-based work experience. Various educational enterprises have been developed to provide students the opportunity to learn and apply community skills. Each of the educational enterprises produces and sells products and/or provides services in the community (e.g., construction and installation of storage sheds). The profits from these activities are paid to the student workers contingent upon appropriate classroom and work behavior. This helps the students learn that pay is related to effort, teamwork, and productivity.

Experience at the Learning Center has shown that students are more receptive to learning academic, social, and employability skills if they can see the relevance of applying the skills to real-life situations. For example, in building picnic tables, students learn to plan, measure, quantify, read and follow directions, and work together cooperatively. Students quickly realize the importance of math skills when they are able to apply those skills to activities such as measuring and cutting lumber or figuring out the amount of concrete to mix for pouring a sidewalk. They also learn the importance of working together to finish the products that they produce and sell. These work experience activities are designed to provide students with the opportunity to see the connection between academic competencies and real-life experiences (Norton, King-Fitch, & Harrington, 1986).

The teaching of the academic, social, and vocational skills takes place in the classroom, on school grounds, and in the community. Students learn basic carpentry and construction skills through the building of various projects on campus and in the community. In addition to the building of storage sheds and picnic tables, activ-

[2]Robert Gagnon and Richard Casey were the developers of the program that was implemented at the Learning Center.

ities include construction of saddle stands, outdoor furniture, patio decks, and playground equipment for sale to the general public. Students also learn masonry skills such as pouring of concrete for sidewalks and driveways and the laying of block. The school grounds and local city parks are utilized for teaching students horticulture and lawn maintenance. In addition, students work with the educational staff to acquire building maintenance skills such as painting and custodial skills.

Performance Incentive System

A performance incentive system has been integrated into the Learning Center curriculum to maximize students' learning and application of more appropriate classroom and work-related skills. The criterion for advancement in the system is based on student social and academic behavior in the classroom and work experience program. Each phase of the performance system has criteria for advancement to the next phase. Advancement is based on improved competencies and performance indicated by a specified percentage of daily incentive points being earned for a designated number of weeks.

An interval reinforcement system is used to award points to students. Throughout the school day, students earn points on an average of every 20 minutes (varies from 10 to 30 minutes) for exhibiting appropriate social, academic, and employability skills in the classroom and at the work site. At the end of the day, a daily percentage of points is calculated by dividing the number of points earned by the number of 20-minute intervals for that school day. As students progress through the system, they earn access to phases that (a) allow them greater choice in their program activities; (b) challenge them with more responsibility; (c) focus more time in the vocational components of the program which offer money-making possibilities; (d) teach appropriate classroom, academic, and employability skills that can enable the students to access more vocational training and experience; and (e) set the occasion for greater community integration.

Orientation Phase. All students enter the program at the orientation phase. This allows students to get to know one another and to become familiar with their new school setting, personnel, schedule, rules, and expectations of the program. Similarly, it gives the academic and vocational staff the opportunity to begin to develop positive relationships with the students. In addition, students are taught safety procedures that are required in the vocational settings. The orientation phase is designed for students to progress through quickly and is typically completed in 2 weeks. It enables students to achieve an immediate measure of success by providing students with a rich schedule of reinforcement (e.g., social praise, recognition, and points exchanged for a large array of items and activities).

Apprentice Phase. The apprentice phase fosters the learning of academic, social, and employability skills through academic and vocational classes and through participation in school-based work experience activities (e.g., masonry, painting, and lawn and building maintenance). Concurrent with this phase and subsequent phases, students are also periodically participating in a future-planning process to

identify their dreams, interests, strengths, and goals in the domains of employment, education, and independent living. They also receive training on skills
specifically related to their goals (e.g., interviewing for jobs in Learning Center's
educational enterprise).

Shareholder Phase.   In this third phase of the program, students become shareholders in the educational enterprise, which enables them to receive a paycheck
every 2 weeks. During this phase, they begin to experience and learn the relationship between work performance and a paycheck, which is contingent on appropriate individual and cooperative work-related behaviors. They may earn one
share per day based on their social and academic performance at school and in the
work experience program contingent on earning a specified number of daily
behavior points.

The value of a student's daily share in the shareholder and senior shareholder
phases is determined by daily performance in the work experience program. Each
day the students participate in five work experience intervals that are rated every 20
minutes for exhibiting appropriate employability skills (i.e., following directions,
using appropriate language, demonstrating appropriate interactions, staying on
task, being dependable/trustworthy, and working independently or cooperatively).
At the end of the work experience day, the teachers calculate the percentage of intervals earned for that day. Thus, students can earn anywhere from 0% to 100% of their
daily share based on work performance. For example, if a student does not follow
directions during cleanup he or she would not earn the interval that would represent
the last 20 minutes of the work experience day. This would result in the student earning four of five intervals. When calculating the students' share, he or she would have
earned 80% of a share for that day. The value of a weekly shares range from $1.00 to
$4.00, depending on the productivity of the students in building products.

Students in the shareholder phase participate in the community service component of the educational enterprise where they leave campus for part of the
school day as members of a small supervised work enclave. They work on community projects such as landscaping, land clearing, deck construction, decorative
concrete staining, and park maintenance. These activities give them the opportunity
to apply social and employability skills in various community settings through
interacting with business and community members.

Students learn that appropriate social skills and good work performance are
critical to maintaining money-making contracts in the community. The loss of contracts, due to inappropriate behavior or poor workmanship, will result in the loss
of wages. When business contracts are lost, the share value for the corporation is
lowered, resulting in lower student pay. Thus, students may experience the natural
consequences of their behavior.

Senior Shareholders Phase.   When students move into the fourth phase of the
program, they become senior shareholders in the educational enterprise. They
may earn two shares per day during their work experience, which is primarily
based on construction-related contracts that are built on or off campus.

The vocational focus of this phase is on the acquisition of specific vocational skills. Students learn to operate a variety of power tools and equipment used for construction. Money-producing projects are built using a zone construction process, with a student or team of students completing each component of the building as it progresses through construction and assembly. This procedure teaches students to (a) work as a team, (b) cooperate with one another so activities are coordinated, (c) stay on task to keep productivity maximized, and (d) work accurately so that errors are minimized (which cost time and materials). They learn that the more they produce, with the least wasted time and materials, the greater the monetary reward.

Graduate Phase. During the graduate phase, students have the option to be mainstreamed back to a typical public secondary school setting or remain enrolled at the Learning Center and enter the work/study component of the program. Students who choose to be mainstreamed back to their home school will be enrolled in special education or general education courses based on their respective individualized education program. Based on each student's individual educational needs, he or she will be served in general education courses with special education teacher consultation or in part-time or full-time special education classes.

Students who choose to remain at the Learning Center enter the work/study program component. This experience gives students the opportunity to participate in paid employment for part of the school day and continue to take academic courses that are required for graduation. A student services coordinator assists a student in (a) future planning to determine his or her interests, strengths, and work preferences; (b) identifying possible job sites; (c) learning interview skills; and (d) developing individualized performance contracts between the employer and the student. The coordinator monitors student progress on a weekly basis with the student and his or her employer. If a problem arises with the student's job performance, the coordinator will work with the student and the employer to implement intervention strategies to correct the situation.

Summary and Preliminary Findings

During the second year of the program (1998–99), 26% (8 of 30) of the E/BD students were mainstreamed back to their home schools on a full-time basis. In addition, approximately 50% of the secondary students were employed in the community on a part-time basis. These students were making minimum wage pay. The average daily attendance of the students at the Learning Center was 84%, and none of the students with E/BD were suspended from school during the 1998–99 school year.

The Learning Center offers students with E/BD an alternative to the traditional special education curriculum through the integration of the academic, social skills, and vocational curricula. The likelihood of the students experiencing success in educational, vocational, and community settings is maximized by an instructional process that focuses on actively engaging the students in community relevant academic, vocational, and work experience activities.

Specifically, the student-run educational enterprise is a key component to the success of the Learning Center program. It gives students the opportunity to participate in work experience activities, learn employability and entrepreneurial skills, and begin to see the relationship between their performance, the intrinsic rewards of creating products, and the extrinsic rewards associated with earning a paycheck. Upon completion of the program, students have a greater chance of becoming productive members of the community and workforce.

Steps to Success at a Public School Vocational Technical Institute

Steps to Success is designed to provide the educational, psychosocial, vocational training, and critical follow-along services and supports that students with SED need on an individualized basis to achieve successful transition from secondary school into career-type employment, postsecondary education, independent living, and community life. This secondary education program is operated within the Robert Morgan Vocational Technical Institute (Miami-Dade County Public School District) and in partnership with community social services, vocational services, private industry, secondary students with SED, and their families.

Students Served

The Steps to Success program serves 20 students with SED and histories of academic, attendance, and social difficulties in school, psychological adjustment problems, and/or family difficulties due to such issues as poverty, substance abuse, mental or physical abuse, and transient situations. It is estimated that approximately 70% of the students live in poverty, based on the number who qualify for free or reduced-price lunches. They represent a remarkable mix of cultural and linguistic diversity, reflecting the population of the greater Miami area.

Overview of Steps to Success

The following Steps to Success program description demonstrates how TIP guidelines are being applied to the needs of these students within their technical/vocational school and community (Clark & Foster-Johnson, 1996). The personnel at this secondary education institution have developed active partnerships with a variety of groups and organizations, including the Palace at Kendall Nursing and Rehabilitation Center, Fellowship House of South Miami, the Florida Department of Vocational Rehabilitation, the Florida Department of Developmental Services, Switchboard of Miami, the University of Miami Mobile Pediatric Clinic, other businesses throughout the community, as well as internship/practicum arrangements with several university graduate programs. The Department of Child and Family

Studies within the Florida Mental Health Institute at the University of South Florida provides technical assistance on program development and is beginning to conduct process and outcome evaluations to facilitate stakeholders' abilities to continue to improve the quality and effectiveness of this evolving program. The Steps to Success approach integrates five major program components.

Clinical Component.   Individually tailored clinical services are provided through individual, group, family, and art therapy. Recently, services have also been expanded to provide groups focused specifically on stress management and transition issues for senior students.

Vocational Component.   Vocational training and experience are provided through placements in a variety of school-based programs on campus and in the community. Based on a student's interests, he or she may be placed in one or more of the following types of settings simultaneously or sequentially: (a) one of three campus-based vocational training programs with individualized supervision from the SED staff; (b) one of 20 regular vocational or technical tracks available on campus; (c) school-based on-the-job training experiences (i.e., office aide or paid classroom aide); (d) community-based on-the-job training experiences at a large nursing home facility with mentoring provided by regular supervisors and coworkers and oversight provided by one of the teachers and an aide; and (e) part-time employment in community businesses with, or without, supports as needed. Placements in these programs and practica may involve up to half of each school day.

Educational Component.   The educational classes at Steps to Success emphasize workplace-relevant academic skills, as well as independent and community living skills. In addition, community education counselors from Switchboard of Miami provide groups focusing on employment issues, relationship issues, and social problem-solving strategies.

School-To-Career Transition Component.   This component of Steps to Success encompasses career exploration and individualized futures planning conducted by a team composed of the student, his or her parents, and the relevant program personnel (e.g., teacher, job coach, transition facilitator, and/or psychologist). Although an emphasis is placed on planning in the domains of employment and education to facilitate a career orientation, the planning also addresses the domains of living situation and community life adjustment.

Community Outreach Component.   The community outreach component of Steps to Success has provided distinct normalizing social experiences outside of school hours. A "peer social group," organized by one of our parents, provides parent-supervised activities on weekends that have included professional basketball and baseball games, fishing excursions, and many other age-appropriate developmental opportunities.

Student Outcomes and Program Direction

Steps to Success at Robert Morgan Vocational Technical Institute was started as a combined school-based educational program (currently serving 20 students) and a half-day community-based on-the-job training/transitional program now serving up to 50% of these students. Over the three school years from 1996–97 to 1998–99, this program expanded to today's capacity and has had 15 students graduate or drop out. (Thirteen of these 15 exiters participated in both the academic and the on-the-job training program).

Of these 15 student exiters, only 13% dropped out, 87 % are employed and/or enrolled in postsecondary education programs, about 47% are living independently, and only 7% have been arrested over this three-year follow-up period. These results represent dramatic achievement for our 15 Steps to Success exiters in that these figures closely parallel those of outcomes for the national general population of high school exiters, in contrast to the national outcome figures of exiters with EB/D (Marder & D'Amico, 1992; Prange 1993; Prange, et al. 1993).

Summary

The preliminary findings from these three evolving transition programs and those from elsewhere (Cheney, Martin, & Rodriguez, 2000) are encouraging regarding the validity of the TIP guidelines and the efficacy of the TIP system. However, additional research will be required to guide us in refining the TIP system to be as effective as possible in facilitating these young people to navigate rough waters into productive and satisfying adult roles. If you would like to read more information regarding these types of programs, please refer to the Clark and Davis (2000) book, a book by Benz and Lindstrom (1997), and/or the TIP system Web site at http://www.fmhi.usf.edu/cfs/policy/tip.

Author Note

Correspondence regarding this chapter should be sent to Hewitt B. "Rusty" Clark, Ph.D., Professor and Director, Transition to Independence Process: TIP System Development and Evaluation, Department of Child and Family Studies, Florida Mental Health Institute, University of South Florida, Tampa, FL 33612; e-mail, clark@fmhi.usf.edu. The authors would like to acknowledge Susan Osman and Ray Klein for their role, in concert with Peter Caproni, in creating Steps to Success; Debbie Horvitz and the staff of the Palace Kendall Nursing and Rehabilitation Center and Cindy Schwartz of Fellowship House of South Miami for their continuing contributions to the quality of this program; Hank Sterner, project manager of the multiagency network of Miami-Dade County for his ability to link us continuously to unique opportunities and resources; and a long list of personnel at the Miami-Dade County Public Schools who have supported Steps to Success. We also wish to acknowledge the assistance of Sherle Stevenson, Pat Chapin, and Debra Neeson, who were codevelopers of the Indian Ridge School program; Sara Kuppin, Alyssa Voss, and Mary Irwin for their editorial and clerical help in creating a quality product; Terri Eggers for her initiation of the arrangements to create the collaborations on which all of this fine programmatic work is being accomplished; and Michele Polland for her continuing guidance in this university/state department/school district/private provider partnership.

The preparation of this invited chapter was funded, in part, by the Florida Department of Education under a grant (#291–26290–90654) awarded to the University of South Florida. The views expressed in this chapter are not necessarily those of the Florida Department of Education.

REFERENCES

Benz, M., & Lindstrom, L. E. (1997). *Building school-to-work programs: Strategies for youth with special needs.* Austin, TX: Pro-Ed.

Blackorby, J., & Wagner, M. (1996). Longitudinal postschool outcomes of youth with disabilities: Findings from the National Longitudinal Transition Study. *Exceptional Children, 62*(5), 399–413.

Bullis, M., Nishoka-Evans, V., Fredericks, H., & Davis, C. (1993). Identifying and assessing the job-related social skills of adolescents and young adults with emotional and behavioral disorders. In R. Ilback & M. Nelson (Eds.), *Emerging school-based approaches for children with emotional and behavioral problems: Research and practice in service integration* (pp. 77–96). New York: Haworth.

Cheney, D., Martin, J., & Rodriguez, E. (2000). Secondary and postsecondary education: New strategies for positive outcomes. In H. B. Clark & M. Davis (Eds.), *Transition of youth and young adults with emotional or behavioral difficulties into adulthood: Handbook for practitioners, educators, parents, and administrators.* Baltimore, MD: Brookes.

Clark, H. B. & Davis, M. (Eds.). (2000). *Transition of youth and young adults with emotional or behavioral difficulties into adulthood: Handbook for practitioners, educators, parents, and administrators.* Baltimore, MD: Brookes.

Clark, H. B., Deschenes, N., & Jones, J. (2000). Transition: A framework for the development and operation of a transition system. In H. B. Clark & M. Davis, (Eds.), *Transition of youth and young adults with emotional or behavioral difficulties into adulthood: Handbook for practitioners, educators, parents, and administrators.* Baltimore, MD: Brookes.

Clark, H. B., & Foster-Johnson, L. (1996). Serving youth in transition to adulthood. In B. Stroul (Ed.), *Children's mental health: Creating systems of care in a changing society.* Baltimore, MD: Brookes.

Clark, H. B., & Stewart, E. (1992). Transition into employment, education, and independent living: A survey of programs serving youth and young adults with emotional/behavioral disorders. In K. Kutash, C. Liberton, A. Algarin, & R. Friedman (Eds.), *Fifth Annual Research Conference Proceedings: A system of care for children's mental health: Expanding the research base,* (Vol. 5, pp. 189–198).

Clark, H., Unger, K., & Stewart, E. (1993). Transition of youth and young adults with emotional/behavioral disorders into employment, education, and independent living. *Community Alternatives: International Journal of Family Care, 5,* 20–46.

Davis, M., & Vander Stoep, A. (1996). *The transition to adulthood among adolescents who have emotional disturbance.* Report prepared for the National

Resource Center on Homelessness and Mental Illness Policy Research Associates, Delmar, NY.

Denbo, R. (1992). *Troubled lifestyles: High risk youth in Florida*. Washington, DC: Office of Educational Research and Improvement.

Deschenes, N., & Clark, H. B. (1998). Seven best practices in transition programs for youth. *Reaching Today's Youth, 2*(4), 44–48.

Foster-Johnson, L., Ferro, J., & Dunlap, G. (1992). *Does curriculum affect student behavior?* Paper presented at the 37th Annual Conference of the Florida Educational Research Association, Winter Park, FL.

Greenbaum, P., Prange, M., Friedman, R., & Silver, S. (1991). Substance abuse prevalence and comorbidity with other psychiatric disorders among adolescents with severe emotional disturbances. *Journal of the American Academy of Child and Adolescent Psychiatry, 30*, 575–583.

Horner, R., Sprague, J., & Flannery, K. (1993). Building functional curricula for students with severe intellectual disabilities. In R. Van Houten & S. Axelrod (Eds.), *Behavior analysis and treatment* (pp. 47–71). New York: Plenum.

Knitzer, J., Steinberg, Z., & Fleisch, B. (1990). *At the school door: An examination of programs and policies for children with behavioral and emotional problems*. New York: Bank Street College of Education.

Koroloff, N. (1990). Moving out: Transition policies for adults with serious emotional disabilities. *Journal of Mental Health Administration, 17*, 78–86.

Marder, C., & D'Amico, R. (1992). *How well are youth with disabilities really doing? A comparison of youth with disabilities and youth in general*. Menlo Park, CA: SRI International.

Modrcin, M., & Rutland, A. (1989). Youth in transition: A summary of service components. *Psychosocial Rehabilitation Journal, 12*, 3–15.

Norton, R. E., King-Fitch, C. C. & Harrington, L. G. (1986). *Improving the basic skills of vocational-technical students: An administrator's guide*. Columbus, OH: National Center for Research in Vocational Education, Ohio State University. (ERIC Document Reproduction Service No. ED 266 264.)

Patton, J., Cronin, M., & Jairrels, V. (1997). Curricular implications of transition: life skills instruction as an integral part of transition education. *Remedial and Special Education, 18*, 294–306.

Prange, M. (1993, March). *A longitudinal perspective of youth with conduct disorder problems*. Presentation at the Rehabilitation of Children, Youth & Adults with Psychiatric Disabilities Conference, Tampa, FL.

Prange, M., Greenbaum, P., & Friedman, R. (1993, August). *Predicting correctional placements among adolescents with serious emotional disturbances*. Paper presented at the American Psychological Association Convention.

The Real Game Series. (1996). St. Joseph, New Brunswick: Robinson & Blackmore.

Silver, S., Unger, K., Friedman, R. (1993). *Transition to young adulthood among youth with emotional disturbance*. Unpublished manuscript, University of South Florida, Florida Mental Health Institute.

Silver, S., Duchnowski, A., Kutash, K., et al., (1992). A comparison of children with serious emotional disturbance served in residential and school settings. *Journal of Child and Family Studies, 1*, 43–59.

Stroul, B., & Friedman, R. (1986). *A system of care for severely emotionally disturbed children and youth*. Washington, DC: U.S. Government Printing Office.

Unger, K. (1994). Access to educational programs and its effect on employability. *Psychosocial Rehabilitation Journal, 17*, 117–126.

VanDenBerg, J., & Grealish, M. (1996). Individualized services and supports through the wraparound process: Philosophy and procedures. *Journal of Child & Family Studies, 5*, 7–12.

Vander Stoep, A., Davis, M., & Collins, D. (2000). Transition: A time of developmental and institutional clashes. In H. B. Clark & M. Davis (Eds.), *Transition of youth and young adults with emotional or behavioral difficulties into adulthood: Handbook for practitioners, educators, parents, and administrators*. Baltimore, MD: Brookes.

Vander Stoep, A., Taub, J., & Holocomb, L. (1994). Follow-up of adolescents with severe psychiatric impairment into adulthood. In C., Liberton, K., Kutash, & R., Friedman (Eds.), *6th Annual Conference Proceedings: A system of care for children's mental health: Expanding the research base*, Vol. 6, 373–379.

Wagner, M. (1993). *Dropouts with disabilities: What do we know? What can we do?* Menlo Park, CA: SRI International.

Wagner, M., D'Amico, R., Marder, C., Newman, L., & Blackorby, J. (1992). *What happens next? Trends in postschool outcomes of youth with disabilities*. Menlo Park, CA: SRI International.

Future Directions

19 Identifying, Assessing, and Intervening With Children With or At Risk for Behavior Disorders

A Look to the Future

KATHLEEN L. LANE
Peabody College of Vanderbilt University

FRANK M. GRESHAM
University of California–Riverside

TAM E. O'SHAUGHNESSY
Georgia State University

Introduction

The field of emotional and behavioral disorders has made substantial growth in the areas of identification and assessment over the last 20 years. With the introduction of psychometrically sound instruments such as the Social Skills Rating System (SSRS; Gresham & Elliott, 1990) and Walker-McConnell Scale of Social Competence and School Adjustment (SSCSA; Walker & McConnell, 1993), the research and teaching communities are able to accurately describe the social, behavioral, and academic profiles of students with externalizing and behavioral profiles (Gresham, Lane, MacMillan, & Bocian, 1999). Furthermore, effective, efficient procedures such as the Student Risk Screening Scale (SRSS; Drummond, 1993), the Early Screening Project (Walker, Severson, & Feil, 1994), and Systematic Screening for Behavior Disorders (Walker & Severson, 1990) have been designed to identify students at heightened risk for developing behavior disorders (see Chapter 3 by Severson and

Walker, this text). However, as the research and teaching communities look to the future, several challenges lie ahead.

Specifically, we will discuss three key challenges that we feel require immediate attention. First, now that screening procedures are available, there is a need to move forward with implementation of these procedures in the school setting. Second, the causal relationships between academic underachievement and externalizing behavior patterns need to be explored in an effort to identify school-based intervention aimed at (a) preventing the development of learning and behavior patterns and (b) remediating the deleterious effects of existing problems. Finally, researchers need to examine the curriculum and instruction currently taking place in classrooms serving students with emotional disturbances.

Screening Procedures

As previously mentioned, the last two decades have been very productive in the study of young children's learning difficulties and emotional and behavioral problems. We now possess substantial knowledge about how to identify the factors most often associated with learning and behavior problems. For example, valid and reliable indicators of skills highly associated with early literacy success and behaviors strongly related to adaptive functioning are now available. These research-based procedures give educators meaningful information with which to answer basic questions such as, Which children are at greatest risk of early learning and/or behavioral difficulty? What is the magnitude of the problem? Which children need the most intensive intervention?

Because of the progressive nature of many learning and emotional/behavioral difficulties, it is more effective to provide early identification and intervention than it is to provide remediation after a child has experienced failure or rejection (e.g., Forness, Kavale, MacMillan, Asarnow, & Duncan, 1996; Torgesen & Wagner, 1998). While older children and teenagers can develop literacy skills and prosocial behaviors with intensive and costly intervention, the best time for learning these skills is during preschool and the primary grades.

As a field, we have learned a great deal about the risk factors that predict future learning and behavioral problems, and we have the tools to accurately identify children placed at risk in order to provide them with early intervention. Now that reliable, valid, and cost-effective early screening tools are available, we need to move forward with implementing these procedures in more schools.

Some professionals have questioned why procedures such as the SRSS, ESP, and SSBD are not routinely utilized in public schools. We suggest two concerns that may be preventing prevention (Kauffman, 1999). First, it may be that schools are concerned as to how to address the educational needs of the students identified by early detection procedures. Administrators and teachers alike recognize that if students are nominated as being "at risk," academically or behaviorally, they will need to provide services to address the identified areas of concerns.

However, given the schools' reactive practices to managing student behavior, the lack of definitional clarity surrounding behavioral disorders in general, and the scarcity of treatment outcome studies pertaining to school-based interventions with children at risk for emotional and behavioral disorders (Lane, 1999), the public school system is clearly at a loss as to how to serve students identified as at risk. Second, it is quite possible that schools are reluctant to identify students at risk for E/BD for fear of actually needing to serve students under the emotional disturbed (ED) category. In addition to the fact that the ED label is less than endearing to parents, assigning such a label to students subsequently limits the range of permissible disciplinary actions that administration can use to manage disruptive behavior. Specifically, before any special education students can be suspended or expelled, a meeting must be held to determine whether the infraction was related to the student's disability. The student can only be suspended or expelled from school if the infraction is found to be *unrelated* to the student's disability. More than a few school site administrators have mentioned this later concern to the first author.

Academic Underachievment and Externalizing Behavior

Three hypothetical models have been proposed to describe the relationship between academic underachievement and externalizing behavior patterns (Hinshaw, 1992a, 1992b). The first model suggests that academic underachievement leads to externalizing behavior. Students who lack the ability or desire to participate in the requisite tasks may act out to escape the task's demand. The second model proposes that externalizing behavior problems lead to academic underachievement. In this case, it may be that students who engage in disruptive classroom behaviors miss out on essential instructional activities. Over time, this lack of participation in instructional activities results in academic underachievement. The final model indicates that there may be a transactional relationship between these two domains. Accordingly, these models have direct implication for intervention. If the first model is true, intervention efforts should be aimed at improving academic achievement. If the second model is correct, intervention should target eliminating or reducing problem behaviors. If the transaction model is accurate, then intervention would need to address both domains.

Although the relationship between academic underachievement has been explored for more than 25 years (Berger, Yule, & Rutter, 1975; Hinshaw 1992a, 1992b; Richards, Symons, Greene, & Szuszkrewiz, 1995; Rutter & Yule, 1970), alarmingly few treatment-outcome studies have been conducted to explore the efficacy of these hypothetical causal models (Ayllon, Layman, & Kandel, 1975; Ayllon & Roberts, 1974; Coie & Krehbiel, 1984; Lane, 1999; Lane, O'Shaughnessy, Lambros, Gresham, & Beebe-Frankenberger, in press). Given the host of short- and long-term negative consequences (e.g., academic failure, school dropout, peer rejection, and delinquency) confronting students with behavior disorders (see Chapter 1 by O'Shaughnessy, Lane, Gresham, & Beebe-Frankenberger; Chapter 3 by Severson & Walker; and Chapter 11 by Walker & Severson, this text), it is unfortunate that so few school-based investigations exploring these models have been conducted.

Nonetheless, although few in number, treatment outcome studies conducted to date provide preliminary evidence to support the first causal model: academic underachievement leads to externalizing behaviors (Ayllon et al., 1975; Ayllon & Roberts, 1974; Coie & Krehbiel, 1984; Lane et al., in press). However, these findings must be interpreted with caution given that interventions have not been conducted systematically across students of varying ages. Clearly, additional treatment outcome research is warranted.

Researchers focused on intervention efforts have offered important information regarding levels of intervention (Walker, Colvin, & Ramsey, 1995) and a development approach to providing services (Bullis & Walker, 1994). For example, it is important to consider the notion of "levels of intervention." Primary interventions, which are schoolwide prevention programs involving all students in a given school, focus on removing conditions that place students at a heightened risk for developing learning and/or behavior problems (Walker et al., 1995). Specific examples include early literacy programs, schoolwide social skills curriculum, and schoolwide discipline plans. It is estimated that approximately 80% of the student population will respond to primary intervention efforts. However, approximately 20% of the student population will require more intensive intervention efforts such as secondary or tertiary interventions. Secondary interventions are classwide or small-group interventions aimed at remediating acquisition or performance deficits (Elliott & Gresham, 1991) demonstrated by a small group of students. Examples include reading groups, social skills groups, and group contingency plans. Some students, approximately 5% to 7% of the original student population, require even more intensive, ideographic or tertiary interventions to address acquisition or performance deficits. These interventions include one-to-one reading interventions and functional assessment-based interventions (Lane, Umbreit, & Beebe-Frankenberger, 1999).

Bullis and Walker (1994) have introduced a developmental continuum of services for antisocial behavior. According to this model, as children increase in age, the focus of intervention efforts shifts from prevention (preschool–3rd grade), to remediation (4th–6th grade), to amelioration (7th–8th grade) and, finally, to accommodation (9th–12th grade) with each phase consisting of different types of services and supports.

One major challenge confronted by the field of behavior disorders is the need to explore the causal relationships between academic underachievement and externalizing behavior patterns in light of the level of interventions required for academic and sociobehavioral changes with the various developmental phases proposed by Bullis and Walker (1994) (Lane, 2001). In other words, just how intensive (primary, secondary, or tertiary) must intervention efforts be to produce lasting behavior changes as children progress through their educational careers (preschool, to early elementary, upper elementary, middle school, and high school)? Additionally, it may be that different causal models may hold true for different phases along the developmental continuum of services. For example, it may be that the first causal model is true during the "prevention" window of opportunity (Kazdin, 1987) and that universal and secondary intervention efforts may be of sufficient magnitude to produce lasting academic and sociobehavioral changes. However, it may be that as the children increase in age and their maladaptive behaviors become more resistant to intervention, secondary interventions may simply lack the strength necessary to produce the desired changes. In this instance, it may be that the transactional model is supported and that tertiary interventions in both the academic and behavioral domains will be necessary to accommodate the children's antisocial behaviors.

Yet another question left unanswered in the area of intervention is the necessity of a parent component. Although best practices clearly indicates that parental involvement is preferred, to what extent can schools, in isolation from parent support, prevent the development of emotional and behavioral problems? The proximal and distal stressors (e.g., poverty, alcohol abuse, and poor parenting skills) that place families at risk for producing children with antisocial behavior patterns (Reid & Patterson, 1991) are the same stressors that negatively influence parents' desire or ability to participate in school-based interventions. Therefore, given that parents are not always willing or able to participate in intervention efforts coupled with the fact that schools cannot mandate parental involvement, schools have a *duty* to identify the extent to which schools, in isolation from parent support, can successfully prevent the development of antisocial behavior (Lane et al., in press). Furthermore, because not all children respond uniformly to various interventions, it is also important to identify the characteristics, including risk and protective factors, of those students who do and do not respond to interventions with and without a parent component.

Curriculum and Instruction

Research conducted by Richard Shores and Joseph Wehby on the nature of the teacher–student interactions within the emotional and behavioral disorder (E/BD) classrooms has brought to the forefront concerns regarding the nature of the curriculum within such classrooms (see Shores, Jack, Gunter, Ellis, DeBriere, & Wehby, 1993; Wehby, Symons, & Shores, 1995). In fact, the term *curriculum of noninstruction* has been invoked to describe the curriculum taking place in E/BD classrooms (Wehby et al., 1995). Unfortunately, this descriptor is well earned. Even the textbooks used to prepare teachers to serve the E/BD population have noticeably little content in the area of academic instruction. With the exception of Wallace and Kauffman's (1986) textbook *Teaching Students with Learning and Behavior Problems*, most methods books have little more than one chapter devoted to academic content areas. (This void was actually one of the major motives behind the development of this book). In actuality, the clear majority of the emphasis in most E/BD preparation programs is on sociobehavioral issues such as anger management, social skills training, conflict resolution, and behavior management. While the latter issues are clearly needed, public law *mandates* access to the core curriculum.

Teaching the core curriculum is not an option; it is a legal requirement. To not teach the requisite content areas (reading, language arts, mathematics, social studies, and science) is not only illegal, but socially irresponsible. In a sense, to omit instruction in the core curriculum actually serves to further handicap children with E/BD (Lane, 2001). If instructional goals and objectives, which typically address affective and sociobehavioral domains, are attained, and the students have not simultaneously been provided access to the core curriculum, how are student's with E/BD, who are frequently taught in self-contained settings, supposed then to be successfully transitioned back into the general education setting? At best, these children will have deficits in both academic skills and content knowledge. Yet treatment outcomes investigations exploring the utility of academic interventions are noticeably absent from the E/BD literature.

In 1992, Ruhl and Berlinghoff conducted a review of the literature pertaining to academic skill improvement for students with behavior disorders. Of the 15 empirical studies located, only 7 were conducted at the elementary level, a time when children are more amenable to treatment (Kazdin, 1993; Walker et al., 1995), and only 4 included a reading component. More recently, Coleman and Vaughn (2000), in a review of reading interventions conducted with elementary aged children with emotional and behavioral disorders from 1975 to present, located only eight studies. This scarcity of intervention research and the corresponding limited knowledge base is particularly troublesome given the trend toward inclusive programming, the importance of early literacy skills, and the need to provide all students, including those with E/BD, access to the core curriculum (see Chapter 6 by Bos, Coleman, & Vaughn, this text; Coleman & Vaughn, 2000; Chapter 1 by O'Shaughnessy et al., this text).

Summary

Although by no means an exhaustive list, the issues described here are some of the key challenges yet to be addressed in the field of behavior disorders. Proactive approaches for detecting children with or at risk for E/BD are available and need to implemented on a consistent basis within the school settings. The hypothetical causal models exploring the relationship between academic underachievement and externalizing behavior patterns need to be empirically validated or eliminated. In addition, the curriculum and instruction taking place in classrooms serving students with E/BD warrants further investigation.

REFERENCES

Ayllon, T., Layman, D., & Kandel, H. (1975). A behavioral-educational alternative to drug control of hyperactive children. *Journal of Applied Behavior analysis, 8,* 137–146.

Ayllon, T., & Roberts, M. (1974). Eliminating discipline problems by strengthening academic performance. *Journal of Applied Behavior Analysis, 7,* 71–76.

Berger, M., Yule, W., & Rutter, M. (1975). Attainment and adjustment in two geographical areas: II. The prevalence of specific reading retardation. *British Journal of Psychiatry, 126,* 510–519.

Bullis, M., & Walker, H. M. (1994). *Comprehensive school-based systems for troubled youth.* Eugene: University of Oregon, Center on Human Development.

Coie, J. D., & Krehbiel, G. (1984). Effects of academic tutoring on the social status of low-achieving, socially rejected children. *Child Development, 55*(4), 1465–1478.

Coleman, M. C., & Vaughn, S. (2000). Reading interventions for students with E/BD. *Behavior Disorders, 25,* 93–104.

Drummond, T. (1993). *The Student Risk Screening Scale (SRSS).* Grants Pass, OR: Josephine County Mental Health Program.

Elliott, S., & Gresham, F. (1991). *Social skills intervention guide: Practical strategies for social skills training.* Circle Pines, MN: American Guidance Service.

Forness, S. R., Kavale, K. A., MacMillan, D. L., Asarnow, J. R., & Duncan, B. B. (1996). Early detection and prevention of emotional or behavioral disorders: Developmental aspects of systems of care. *Behavioral Disorders, 21,* 226–240.

Gresham, F. M., & Elliott, S. N. (1990). *Social Skills Rating System.* Circle Pines, MN: American Guidance Service.

Gresham, F. M., Lane, K. L., MacMillan, D. L., & Bocian, K. M. (1999). Social and academic profiles of externalizing and internalizing groups: Risk factors for emotional and behavioral disorders. *Behavior Disorders, 24,* 231–241.

Hinshaw, S. P. (1992a). Academic underachievement, attention deficits, and aggression: Comorbidity and implications for intervention. *Journal of Consulting and Clinical Psychology, 20,* 893–903.

Hinshaw, S. P. (1992b). Externalizing behavior problems and academic underachievement in childhood and adolescence: Causal relationships and underlying mechanisms. *Psychological Bulletin, 111*(1), 127–155.

Kauffman, J. M. (1999). How we prevent the prevention of emotional and behavioral disorders. *Exceptional Children, 65,* 448–468.

Kazdin, A. (1987). Treatment of antisocial behavior in children: Current status and future directions. *Psychological Bulletin, 102,* 187–203.

Kazdin, A. (1993). Treatment of conduct disorder: Progress and directions in psychotherapy research. *Development and Psychopathology, 5,* 1–2, 277–310.

Lane, K. L. (1999). Young students at risk for antisocial behavior: The utility of academic and social skills interventions. *Journal of Emotional and Behavioral Disorders, 7,* 211–223.

Lane, K. L. (2001). *Educating students with or at risk for emotional and behavioral disorders: A call for a balanced curriculum.* Unpublished manuscript.

Lane, K. L., O'Shaughnessy, T. E., Lambros, K. M., Gresham, F. M., & Beebe-Frankenberger, M. E. (in press). The efficacy of phonological awareness training with students who have externalizing and hyperactive-inattentive behavior problems. *Journal of Emotional and Behavioral Disorders.*

Lane, K. L., Umbreit, J., & Beebe-Frankenberger, M. (1999). Functional assessment research on students with or at risk for E/BD: 1990 to the present. *Journal of Positive Behavior Interventions, 2,* 101–111.

Reid, J., & Patterson G. R. (1991). Early prevention and intervention with conduct problems: A social interactional model for the integration of research and practice. In G. Stoner, M. Shinn, & H. M. Walker (Eds.), *Interventions for achievement and behavior problems* (pp. 715–740). Silver Spring, MD: National Association of School Psychologists.

Richards, C. M., Symons, D. K., Greene, C. A., & Szuszkrewiz, T. A. (1995). The bi-directional relationship between achievement and externalizing behavior problems of students with learning disabilities. *Journal of Learning Disabilities, 28*(1), 8–17.

Ruhl, K. L., & Berlinghoff, D. H. (1992) Research on improving behavioral disordered students' academic performance: A review of literature. *Behavior Disorders, 17*(3), 178–190.

Rutter, M., & Yule, W. (1970). Reading retardation and antisocial behavior—The nature of the association. In M. Rutter, J. Tizard, & K. Whitmore (Eds.), *Education, health and behaviour* (pp. 240–255). London: Longman.

Shores, R. E., Jack, S. L., Gunter, P. L., Ellis, D., DeBriere, T. J., & Wehby, J. H. (1993). Classroom interactions of children with behavior disorders. *Journal of Emotional and Behavioral Disorders, 1,* 27–39.

Torgesen, J. K., & Wagner, R. K. (1998). Alternative diagnostic approaches for specific developmental reading disabilities. *Learning Disabilities Research & Practice, 13,* 220–232.

Walker, H. M., Colvin, G., & Ramsey, E. (1995). *Antisocial behavior in school: Strategies and best practices.* Pacific Grove, CA: Brooks/Cole.

Walker, H. M., & McConnell, S. (1993). *The Walker-McConnell Scale of Social Competence and School Adjustment.* Eugene: Center on Human Development, College Education, University of Oregon.

Walker, H. M., & Severson, H. H. (1990). *Systematic Screening for Behavior Disorders (SSBD): User's guide and technical manual.* Longmont, CO: Sopris West.

Walker, H. M., Severson, H. H.,& Feil, E. G. (1994). *The Early Screening Project: A proven child-find process.* Longmont, CO: Sopris West.

Wallace, G., & Kauffman, J. M. (1986). *Teaching students with learning and behavior problems* (3rd ed.). Columbus, OH: Merrill.

Wehby, J. H., Symons, F., & Shores, R. E. (1995). A descriptive analysis of aggressive behavior in classrooms for children with emotional and behavioral disorders. *Behavioral Disorders, 20,* 87–105.

AUTHOR INDEX

SUBJECT INDEX